American Indian Rock Art

Volume 44

"Dos Anthros" from Alamo Mountain, Texas • Jeff LaFave

With Contributions By

Peter Anick
Margaret Berrier
Dorothy Bohntinsky
Peter Boyle
Kevin Conti
Elisa Correa
Angelo Eugenio Fossati
Jon Harman
Sheila Harman
Janine Hernbrode
Judy F. Hilbish
William D. Hyder
David A. Kaiser
James D. Keyser
Jeff LaFave
Daniel Leen
Lawrence Loendorf
Carolynne Merrell
David L. Minick
Eric W. Ritter
Jennifer Rovanpera
Devin Snyder

American Indian Rock Art
Volume 44

Edited by David A. Kaiser and James D. Keyser

American Rock Art Research Association

San Jose, California

2018

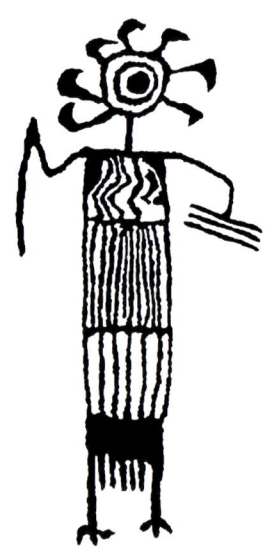

Compilation Copyright © 2018
American Rock Art Research Association

c/o Jack Wedgwood
1884 The Alameda
San Jose, California 95126-1733

This volume is published as a compilation of papers submitted by independent researchers. All rights to the content of individual papers remain with their respective authors.

ISBN 978-0-9888730-5-6

The American Rock Art Research Association is a 501(c)(3) non-profit organization.

Printed and bound in the United States of America.

Editors: *David A. Kaiser and James D. Keyser*
Copy Editing, Layout, and Design: *Ken Hedges and Anne McConnell*
Cover Layout: *Mike Taylor*
Title Page Photograph: *The "Golden Disc" site, Arizona, by Jeff LaFave (see page 1)*
Flyleaf Photograph: *"Dos Anthros" from Alamo Mountain, Texas, by Jeff LaFave (see page 1)*
Preface Facing Page Photograph: *Côa Valley, Portugal, by Jeff LaFave (see page 1)*

About the cover:

This pictograph, from the Big Eddy site along the Columbia River is a rare example of a zoomorph done in the Yakima Polychrome style. Dating to sometime in the last 800 years, the elk has stylized antlers that form a modified rayed arc motif above it, showing the relationship of this style to the much more broadly based and older Central Columbia Plateau style.

Cover Photograph and Design by Mike Taylor

Printed by Jostens Commercial Printing
Visalia, California

Table of Contents

Preface vii

Views and Points of View: Examining the Global Tradition of Rock Art from a Landscape
and Environmental Perspective
  Jeff LaFave 1

Looking at an Old Dog with New Tricks: Review and Documentation of Jaguar Cave, a
Unique Painted Shelter in West Texas
  Margaret Berrier 11

The Quilcene Petroglyph: A Contact Era Site on the Southern Northwest Coast
  Daniel Leen 23

Seeing is Finding: The Value of DStretch for Recording Columbia River Rock Art
at Spedis Creek and Harris Canyon
  David L. Minick and James D. Keyser 29

A Tale of Two Sites: Comparing Two Columbia Plateau Pictograph Sites
  David A. Kaiser and James D. Keyser 45

Exploring the Use of an Idaho Cave by an Antelope Charmer
  Carolynne Merrell 59

Investigating the Co-occurrence of Petroglyphs and Pictographs on the
Volcanic Tablelands of Northeastern California
  Eric W. Ritter, Jon Harman, Jennifer Rovanpera, Devin Snyder, Elisa Correa, and Sheila Harman 69

Dating Western Message Petroglyphs with Aztec and Maya Glyphs
  Judy F. Hilbish 89

Becoming Human: Rock Art Depictions of Transformation in Landscapes
of Emergence
  Janine Hernbrode and Peter Boyle 97

Ritual and Rock Art in Basketmaker Ceremonies from Butler Wash to Atlatl Rock
  William D. Hyder and Dorothy Bohntinsky 111

Pipe Spring: Fremont-Anasazi Interaction in Southeastern Utah
  Kevin Conti, James D. Keyser, David A. Kaiser, and David L. Minick 123

Finding Faded Fremont: Shorthand Anthropomorphs and Fugitive Pigment at
Pipe Spring, Utah
  James D. Keyser, Kevin Conti, and David A. Kaiser 145

Tobacco-related Rock Art and Vertical Series Rock Art in Montana and Wyoming
  Lawrence Loendorf and David A. Kaiser 159

Another Look at the Rock Art of Southeastern New England
  Peter Anick 169

Rock Art in "The Land of Fire" (Azerbaijan): Discovering the Gobustan Rock Art
Cultural Landscape (UNESCO World Heritage List)
  Angelo Eugenio Fossati 193

Côa Valley, Portugal • Jeff LaFave

Preface

The annual conference of the American Rock Art Research Association returned to Oregon in 2017, after a gap of many years. From June 2 to 5, members gathered in Redmond, Oregon, for the traditional mix of papers, posters, field trips, vendors, auctions, and gathering with friends, old and new. The conference location in central Oregon allowed a wide range of field trip opportunities around the state, taking in several different rock art styles and traditions.

Regional rock art is usually well represented when ARARA comes to town. That was true again this year, with several papers focusing on the Northwest, including papers and a couple of posters covering art in Oregon and Washington. The rock art of Idaho was also discussed in multiple presentations. But that isn't to say that other areas were not covered as well. The Southwest had its usual strong contingent, with papers covering numerous states and traditions, including Fremont, Basketmaker, and Hohokam art.

Additional regions of the country were also discussed, including the Great Plains and even as far as New England. International papers covered a wide variety of locations, including South Africa, Brazil, and multiple areas of Mexico. Our plenary speaker even covered the rock art of Azerbaijan.

Other papers looked at plasma oxidation techniques, fire damage to rock art, and site acoustics, and two papers discussed Western Message Petroglyphs. The variety and quality of the presentations remained impressive.

In addition to the presentations at the ARARA conference, speakers also sought to spark interest and bring information to the general public in two public lectures in nearby Bend. The first, by Robert David, discussed the Klamath *Rock Art of Petroglyph Point* in northern California at the monthly meeting of the Archaeological Society of Central Oregon. The following night Angelo Fossati delivered a talk about the *Rock Art of the Ice Man*, discussing art contemporaneous with the Copper Age mummy discovered in the Italian Alps.

Many members also had the opportunity to take part in a salmon bake on the Warm Springs Indian Reservation. But those who weren't able to participate were still treated to sights and sounds of traditional dancers, drummers, and singers from the Confederated Tribes of Warm Springs at our Sunday banquet.

Later in the evening numerous well-deserved awards were presented. Don Hann was awarded the Frank and A.J. Bock Award for Extraordinary Achievement for his long history of research and publications on the rock art of Eastern Oregon. He has sought to educate the public on rock art sites and worked towards their protection. Margaret (Marglyph) Berrier received the Castleton Award for Excellence in Rock Art Research for her work using multiple techniques, including DStretch and 3D modeling, to improve the documentation of complex panels at Jaguar Cave in West Texas, the results of which are published in this volume.

Two Conservation and Preservation awards were given this year. The first was presented to the Picture Canyon Core Group of Flagstaff, Arizona. Robert Mark and Evelyn Billo accepted this award on behalf of the volunteer group which has worked to conserve this resource for over 30 years. Their efforts helped lead to the land being purchased by the city of Flagstaff for its protection. The second Conservation award was given to Washington State Park Ranger Andy Kallinen for his long-time efforts to protect the rock art at Columbia Hills State Park (formerly Horsethief Lake). He has worked to balance the various needs of tribes, researchers, and members of the public in order to grant access while protecting this rock art complex along the Columbia River, noted for the famous image of "She Who Watches."

The Oliver Rock Art Photography Award was presented to Jeff LaFave for his fantastic photos of rock art from around the world, with an emphasis of the site as part of a greater landscape. You can see a selection of his photos at the front of this volume.

Tony Farque, archaeologist with the Sweet Home Ranger District in the Willamette National Forest, was given the Keeper of the Gate Award. Tony has worked for over 20 years to protect Cascadia Cave, the largest rock art site in Oregon's Willamette Valley. The petroglyphs are on private land, but Tony has arranged access to the site to lead numerous educational tours, as well as monitor and research the site on his own time. His passion for the importance and protection of the site is inspirational.

A Special Commendation award was presented to Val Anderson for her role in helping with the 2017 conference. As a resident of central Oregon and an engaged site steward, she helped organize this year's field trips and fostered the support of the Archaeological Society of Central Oregon to help everything go smoothly. Finally, Donna Gillette received the Klaus Wellman Memorial Award for Distinguished Service. A legend in ARARA, Donna was presented with the award for her more than 20 years of organizing ARARA annual conferences. She also has been a long-time board member, worked with the Education Committee, and promoted ARARA at the Society for American Archaeology conferences. Donna has helped make ARARA what it is today.

As if this wasn't enough for one night, the banquet concluded with the opportunity to listen to archaeologist and Klamath tribal member Robert David discuss *The Landscape of Klamath Basin Rock Art*. The evening ran long, as people were very engaged by the unique perspective of his talk and had numerous questions.

Of the 32 papers and 3 posters presented at the conference, 14 are published in this volume. It is a mix that covers much of the U.S. and even as far as Azerbaijan, via Angelo Fossati's plenary speech about rock art in The Land of Fire. Papers discussing the Pacific Northwest include a Northwest Coast style petroglyph found in Washington by Daniel Leen as well as two papers on painted images found in the Columbia River Gorge and along the Deschutes River by David Minick, David Kaiser, and James Keyser. Carolynne Merrell also discusses images at an Idaho cave, which were possibly made as part of antelope-charming rituals. Moving south, Eric Ritter, Jon Harman, Jennifer Rovanpera, Devin Snyder, Elisa Correa, and Sheila Harman investigate rock art on the Volcanic Tablelands of northeast California.

In the Southwest, William Hyder and Dorothy Bohntinsky take a multidisciplinary look at ritual and rock art in Basketmaker Ceremonies, while Janine Hernbrode and Peter Boyle discuss transformations in Hohokam rock art. Another pair of articles, by Kevin Conti, James Keyser, David Kaiser, and David Minick look at faded Fremont images and Fremont-Anasazi interaction in southeastern Utah. Margaret Berrier, this year's Castleton Award winner, presents her documentation of Jaguar Cave in West Texas. Judy Hilbish discusses dating Western Message Petroglyphs, while on the Plains we have Lawrence Loendorf and David Kaiser looking at possible connections between tobacco and Vertical Series rock art. Further afield, Peter Anick surveys the petroglyphs of southeastern New England.

Volume 44 of *American Indian Rock Art* presents another full and diverse collection of papers, maintaining AIRA's place as one of the premiere peer-reviewed rock art journals. Many thanks you to all who helped in its preparation, including our numerous authors and reviewers. Reviewers included Mavis Greer, Bill Hyder, Jenny Huang, Rick McClure, Dave Whitley, Don Hann, Ken Hedges, Todd Bostwick, Robert David, Bill Layman, Janet Lever-Wood, Larry Loendorf, Linea Sundstrom, and Jon Harman. Michael Taylor created the great cover design featuring a polychrome elk pictograph from the Columbia Gorge. Finally, we would also like to acknowledge Ken Hedges and Anne McConnell for their hard work on layout and design and being a final set of eyes before this volume went to print.

—David Kaiser & James Keyser

"Wedding Rocks," Cape Alava, Washington

Views and Points of View:
Examining the Global Tradition of Rock Art from a Landscape and Environmental Perspective

A Portfolio of Photographs by Jeff LaFave
Winner of the 2017 Oliver Rock Art Photography Award

Jeff LaFave was the recipient of ARARA's Oliver Rock Art Photography Award at the 2017 conference in Redmond. Published here is a selection of his winning images, as well as a portion of his written entry. The "criteria and guidelines" for the award focus on the "two critical masters" of "art" and "science." The "art" criteria requires photography which "must illuminate and educate people that have not had the opportunity to see a site first hand…capturing the experience of the site…including evoking a sense of place and the feelings and emotions…one experiences." The "science" criteria requires "objectively evaluating and measuring the subject so that the judgments drawn… from photographs are valid and useful." Entries must also include "a description of the techniques involved" and a "discussion of the ethics of…enhancements or manipulations used" and "how they contribute to the science of rock art research." Finally, the entry must also "summarize the applicant's…work in rock art" including a curriculum vitae.

I have spent most of my "free time" for the last 25 years observing, studying, photographing, documenting and recording, and reading and thinking about rock art, including writing articles and giving talks. During that time, I have photographed rock art on all six continents where it occurs. This application grows out of that background, including a particular interest in rock art photography.

The whole point of photographing rock art in its landscape setting is to show it in its larger-scale context. While images of just the panel or specific elements can be very useful and should be included in any recording, only images of rock art in its landscape/environmental context give a true understanding of the site as it is experienced by the visitor. It is my belief that showing rock art in its landscape context is the best way to "illuminate and educate people that have not had the opportunity to see rock art" first-hand. For me, there is no better way to evoke "a sense of place and the feelings and emotions one experiences at a rock art site" than to show the overall context of the site.

A goal of my photography is to give people who have not been at sites in remote areas a sense of what it feels like to be at those sites. While looking directly at the panel itself can be a big part of that, looking around, looking out from the site, and getting a sense of how the art fits into the landscape is critical to understanding the true context of rock art. Is the site in a forest? Can you see mountains from the site? Is the site near water? What is the geology like? Have bird nests or some other environmental incursion impacted the panel? Context is key! This type of photography is the best way to allow people who are not aware of rock art or who do not visit sites around the globe to appreciate and understand how it relates to its environmental context.

The photographs I have submitted also illustrate the concept that rock art is a global tradition. People around the world have a history of "marking country" by creating images as part of their human experience. When I first became interested in rock art, I naively thought it was something that only existed in the Southwestern United States and French caves. Discovering that rock art was effectively "everywhere" and that it is part of shared human experience was a transcendent event for me and hopefully can be for others. I hope that viewing images that show rock art around the world, in its landscape context, aids that goal. The realization that rock art is a global tradition also underscores the importance of rock art as something deserving of protection, including the need for education and efforts to promote conservation.

Another reason why landscape and environmental context are important is because they are often good predictors for site locations. For example, rock art appears in many similar landscape/geological

Gwion duo, Kimberley, Australia

contexts around the world: paintings often exist in shelters in sandstone outcrops and basalt formations were routinely marked with petroglyphs. Looking at such contexts helps analyze similarities and differences in global rock art traditions, especially in terms of preferred site selection criteria. Hopefully, my photography gives a glimpse into that aspect of world rock art.

Landscape and environmental context photos also best show sites in their true "scientific" context and are crucial as a component to accurate recording and documentation. To document rock art by merely showing the panels and not their context can undermine science since that approach shows the panels in a myopic way. Indeed, rock art is almost always part of an overall archeological site context and such photographs may also reveal other related archaeological features. Furthermore, the view from the site showing a possible "cultural landscape" may be part of what was important to the makers and users of the site. The importance of cultural landscape and/or viewsheds has taken on prominence in recent years both for archaeology in general, and rock art in particular (e.g., Bruno and Thomas 2008; Chippindale and Nash 2004; Robinson 2010, 2011).

Considering landscape context should be a part of site preservation efforts. For instance, in some areas of the U.S. (and elsewhere in the world), development has occurred which did not technically destroy a panel, but negatively impacted the viewshed or other aspects of the cultural landscape. Examples include a site in Southern Arizona with a freeway literally built encircling the rock art, and Dinetah where panels are still intact but gas wells have been placed within sight and sound of rock art panels. Even though these Dinetah panels were not themselves destroyed, their proximity to the wells creates significant noise, smell, and vibration issues. Eventually these impacts can actually damage the art itself, but it is often more important that they impact native peoples' use of these sites. Hopefully, photography of the site context will help acknowledge that a rock art site is usually part of a larger landscape, and in this way, help make the case that site preservation should include more than just a panel.

The "Cornstalk Man" site, Alamo Mountain, Texas

Photos depicting rock art in its environmental context can also be valuable from both a scientific and aesthetic perspective. For instance, images depicting a geologic/environmental context help illustrate how rock art sites often appear in a particular geologic setting. Also, rock art sometimes gets buried over time by sand or dirt and investigators may need to consider that portions of rock art panels are no longer visible, given that geology is an ongoing process. Thus, photographic documentation including geological factors can be important to illustrate issues of site visibility, to show that significant time has passed since the site was made, or to assess whether site documentation requires excavation. Similarly, sites may be impacted by environmental factors such as bird or insect nests, erosion, proximate

The "Wedding Blanket" site, Arizona

vegetation, or other factors which could impact preservation and/or site management considerations. At some sites, environmental/physical concerns including rock surface characteristics (e.g., fragility and spalling) can be an issue. Photography which documents these various environmental and physical factors (as opposed to just the panel) is important for accurate recording and for site management considerations.

My guiding principle regarding rock art photography is to strive for photographs that depict what it was like when I visited the site. My mantra is realism. I am not a fan of over-saturated colors (e.g., HDR or tone mapping) or using Photoshop to "fix" the sky or some other portion of a photo by replacing what was there with clouds or something else from another day or location. I try to focus on obtaining good color by seeking out good light, as opposed to a computer gimmick, even though that often requires me to be at a site pre-dawn, at dusk, or during inclement weather.

Is there another side to this issue? Yes. There is no 100% purity in modern digital photography in terms of processing and enhancement of images. Even before digital photography, master photographers were going to great lengths to process images in the darkroom, including inventing elaborate "dodging" and "burning" techniques. Indeed, I am often reminded of the Ansel Adams quote, "...the negative is like the composer's score...the print is the performance" (Sheff and Sheff 1983:73). I am confident Adams would be a master at Photoshop if he were alive today and I would love to see his genius extended to digital enhancements. Adams himself looked into the future: "Electronic photography will soon be superior to anything we have now" (Sheff and Sheff 1983:86). Indeed, digital photography just gives the photographer more tools for the "performance" of optimizing the image. However, it is my hope that photographers do not go too far with these powerful new tools and keep rock art photographs realistic.

Despite my mantra, I would not claim my photos appear "out of the camera" exactly as I present them to others. That is not reality with modern digital cameras and unsharpened RAW files. RAW files are not "viewer ready" out of camera as they are not subject to the pre-determined algorithms and in-camera processing of most cameras and JPEG files. Anyone who shoots JPEGs is getting files that have been automatically processed by the manufacturers' algorithms. Anyone (like me) who shoots RAW files does some processing in terms of sharpening and taking creative control of the settings that are preset in most cameras which generate JPEGs.

I do make what I consider typical/basic enhancements of my RAW digital files to make them usable. For instance, I sharpen, sometimes adjust color balance, sometimes adjust contrast, sometimes crop, etc. However, to me, the guide is realism and that is the key difference with my view compared to those who engage

Sunset at Red Rock Canyon, California

in "computer gimmick" photography. I try to adjust my RAW files to make them look like what I saw at the site as opposed to altering or over saturating my photos to look like something different than what I witnessed. For example, when Galen Rowell got amazing sunset colors in his famous Evolution Basin photograph, he did so by being there at the right time and not by using Photoshop to alter the colors in post processing. I am not saying people who do so are acting improperly, as long as what they do is disclosed, but for me, that is not what photography is about.

While I personally do not like or use HDR in its commonly known forms, I do sometimes combine two images to obtain a dynamic range that was not possible in the field with a single shot. Master photographers such as Ansel Adams (or Rick Bury in the rock art world) have been doing this for decades, even before digital. I don't think this is "unethical" in any way, especially because it is the only way to overcome the dynamic range limitations of the camera, and create a photograph that shows what I could see when at the site. I do feel it is important to disclose the process, and the "Wedding Rocks" and "Comanche" photos presented here are composite images from two exposures.

I wish to thank ARARA for the opportunity to submit this portfolio for the 2017 Oliver Award. I am honored that the awards committee has recognized these photographs not only for their beauty, but also for the lessons they may teach about the importance of documenting rock art in its total context.

Acknowledgments. Courtney Smith, Don Christensen, David Lee, Rick Bury, Steve Freers, Ken Hedges, Mike Donaldson, Leigh Marymor, Margaret Berrier, and Greg Dziewit.

References Cited

Bruno, David, and Julian Thomas
   2008 *Handbook of Landscape Archaeology*. Left Coast Press, Walnut Creek, California.

Chippindale, Christopher, and George Nash
   2004 *The Figured Landscapes of Rock-Art: Looking at Pictures in Place*. Cambridge University Press, Cambridge, United Kingdom.

Robinson, David W.
   2010 Land Use, Land Ideology: An Integrated Geographic Information Systems Analysis of Rock Art within South-Central California. *American Antiquity* 75(4):792–818.
   2011 Rock Art Landscapes of Inland and Interior South-Central California. *California Archaeology* 3(1):31–52.

Sheff, David, and Victoria Sheff
   1983 Playboy Interview: Ansel Adams. *Playboy* 30(5):67–87, 222–226 (May 1983).

Comanche "cultural contact" panel, New Mexico

Chattisgarh Province, India

Walcott Inlet Wanjina site, Kimberley, Australia

Stingrays from Piedras Pintas, Baja California Sur, Mexico

Game Pass, Drakensberg, South Africa

The "Deighton Lady," Cape York Peninsula, Australia

Elegant cows at the "Lost Site," Ennedi Plateau, Chad

The "Jabberwocky" site, Arizona

Virgin River anthropomorphs with fall colors, Utah

The "Great God of Sefar" site, Tassili n'Ajjer Plateau, Algeria

Looking at an Old Dog with New Tricks: Review and Documentation of Jaguar Cave, a Unique Painted Shelter in West Texas

Margaret Berrier
Winner of the 2017 Castleton Award for Excellence in Rock Art Research

Thousands of petroglyphs are found on the heavily patinated surfaces of the Cox sandstone in far west Texas but pictographs are rare. Jaguar Cave, the largest rockshelter at the Diablo Dam site (41HZ375), is a painted site that has been documented several times in the past. Using more recent technology (DStretch and 3-D modeling) along with careful observation, I created tracings to clarify the images and their relationships with one another. All three techniques were necessary to document the shelter completely.

Jaguar Cave has been known by locals and researchers for at least 80 years and yet no one has completely documented the paintings on its ceiling. The Diablo Dam Site (41HZ375) includes this shelter (Figure 1) along with hundreds of petroglyphs on nearby sandstone cliffs and boulders. The black coating of the shelter makes for a striking canvas but the dim light, fading imagery, and years of visitation makes the once brilliant mostly white paintings difficult to see and photograph. I remember first visiting the site in 1992 and trying to see the images. My mind tried to connect the dots as my body squirmed to find a comfortable place on the sharp stones of the shelter floor. This shelter is a challenge to photograph and document since you must lie

Margaret Berrier
Jornada Research Institute

Figure 1. Jaguar Cave (photo taken from northeast).

on your back and look across an undulating surface to see the images (Figure 2). The images are on the ceiling directly overhead and back wall on surfaces around the corners of the shelter. You cannot stand up in the shelter so you must maneuver to see all the imagery.

Figure 2. Photographers lying down in Jaguar Cave. Left to right: Evelyn Billo, LeRoy Unglaub, Pam Koegler, and Robert Mark.

Revisiting Jaguar Cave in 2007 I made a note that I needed to do a drawing of this entire shelter. After reviewing published articles and site reports I made a long list of questions to answer and images to be examined. A few of the questions were resolved on subsequent visits but some images remained vague. In the interim years I revisited the shelter many times. In 2013 while using my Canon Power Shot A2000 IS equipped with DStretch I had an "aha" moment when while laying down to look at the ceiling and right hand side of the shelter a vague red pictograph over my head was revealed to be a goggle-eyed anthropomorph which had been painted over a horned serpent. In May of 2016 I was totally surprised when DStretch author Jon Harman visited the site for the first time and sent me an image of a small painted element superimposed that I had never seen. That photo spurred me to finally work on re-documenting the shelter. Using hundreds of my photos and theirs, Robert Mark and Evelyn Billo of Rupestrian CyberServices created several 3-D models for me to examine. With these models and enhanced images I could trace the elements and their relationships to one another. But it wasn't until the photos were traced, field checked, and stitched together that the whole shelter became clearer.

Literature Review

Jaguar Cave was probably known by locals long before A. T. Jackson's initial assessment on a visit before 1937 (Jackson 1938). Jackson referred to the Diablo Dam Site as Hudspeth County Site #11. His report indicated 158 design elements for the entire site with only 18 pictographs from painted shelters (Jackson 1938:35). As with most early surveys these numbers were low. His cursory count of the pecked animal figures indicated that mountain sheep and deer were the most numerous animals at Diablo Dam while he didn't see either of these in the painted shelter. Jackson suggests that this meant the paintings were made at a different, probably later time. Jackson includes a few sketches of the elements of this shelter (Jackson 1938:45, Figure 31).

In 1965 Jack Hedrick completed the El Paso Archaeological Society (EPAS) short form site report (EPAS #35) and Centennial Museum Site Form CM31:105:9:1 for 41HZ375. Both documents were found in the EPAS archives in El Paso. Hedrick suggested the site needed additional photographs and an inventory of elements. The few details about the paintings were included on either the EPAS site form or the Centennial Museum Site Form report. Sometime between when Jackson reported on the site and Hedrick's report, the shelter was named Jaguar Cave or the Feathered Serpent Site (Hedrick 1967). Between 1973 and 1974 the site was recorded and then reported on by Kay Sutherland and Paul Steed (1974). In February of 1986 Hedrick, with the help of Kendra Rumbaugh completed the State of Texas Archaeological Site Data Form and Rock Art Record Information Form which was used for the National Register submission.

Sutherland and Steed's article (1974) indicates 481 petroglyphs and three painted shelters containing 28 pictographs. It was a combination of two separate surveys (six site visits), one done by Steed on December 9, 1973, and visits by Sutherland between February and June of 1974. This report indicates that they felt that the Mexican influence is quite evident, citing one example of a collared jaguar from Tula that vaguely resembles the image in the shelter that they identified as a jaguar. The report also included a quick sketch done by David Parker (Figure 3). From this drawing you would expect that there is one continuous panel that spreads across one surface. Sutherland and Steed state:

> The cave is remarkable for the series of large life-like animals covering the walls of the shelter. They are all painted in white; in several instances they are painted over figures in red. The figures include an impressive plumed serpent (eight feet long), a jaguar (three feet long), a bear (four feet long), a deer head (one and one-half feet) and a mother coyote (six feet long), with her baby nearby. There are at least three square shoulder [sic] kachinas, two in white and one in red underneath the plumed serpent. There is a red snake (18 inches) superimposed by the bear, and there are various other markings. There is a beautiful realistically drawn lady bug [sic] (three inches) that was not discernible the first few visits to the cave. In addition, there are parallel dots in a strange series that begin as the plumed serpent's collar and continue to form the end of the jaguar's tail. All in all, it is an impressive shelter, and the Mexican influence is quite evident… [Sutherland and Steed 1974:39].

Steed (1975:85–88) also presented a shorter summary of the information for the first ARARA meeting in Farmington in 1974.

Other authors have mentioned Jaguar Cave (Schaafsma and Riley 1999:24; Wellman 1979: Figures 361–362, 367). These include photos but not a complete documentation of the site. Polly Schaafsma describes the shelter as:

> An unusual assemblage of large animals painted in white on the soot-blackened roof of a deep rock-shelter occurs at Diablo Dam near Fort Hancock (Sutherland and Steed 1974:39–45). Among them are a deer, two canines (possibly wolves or coyotes), a cat, a large bear, and a very elaborate rendition of the horned serpent [Schaafsma 1980:227].

Schaafsma also notes that "bears and wolves are unusual figures, which among the Pueblos to the north are associated with medicine societies and war."

In 1988 a detailed study was done by Batcho & Kauffman Associates of the petroglyph sites in Western Hudspeth County for the El Paso County Commissioners as part of a study of sites which might be affected by a proposed Low-Level Radioactive Waste disposal facility (Miller et al. 1988). Jaguar Cave was one of these sites and Miller's description is similar to the other authors including the fact that he attributes the images to Puebloan clan or socio-religious themes but doesn't mention Mesoamerican connections.

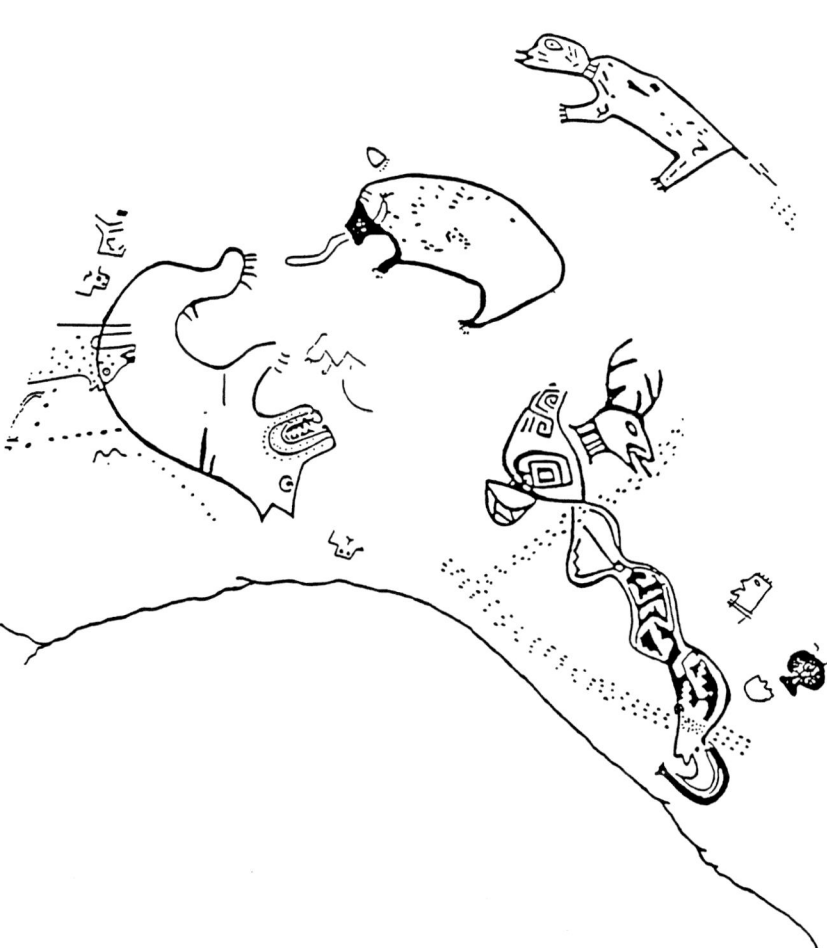

Figure 3. Drawing by David Parker from Sutherland and Steed (1974). Permission to use this drawing by Dave Parker and by Kay Sutherland's husband (Jim McCulloch) was given in 2016.

Kay Sutherland (1998:168–169) labeled David Parker's sketch from Sutherland and Steed 1974 and adds this description of the shelter:

> Beginning with a 3 m long plumed/horned serpent that dominates the view, the vista moves to a deer, a collared jaguar in the recess, a bear, and two magnificent jaguars—one large at 1.5 m and a smaller one at the tail end of the large one. Smaller figures include a goggle-head Tlaloc with no body, a bearded man (head only) in Mimbres profile and other marks, including a series of dots representing seeds. The plumed/horned serpent has been connected to the Hopi Water Clan legend and Hopi Water Serpent ceremony... [Sutherland 1998:168–169].

Sutherland and Steed had noticed part of the red figure revealed with DStretch (Figure 4-4) but not all of it. They called it a square (sic) shoulder kachina. This figure is directly over the head of Robert Mark in Figure 2. Loendorf suggests the red figure over the serpent was a goggle-eyed figure sometimes interpreted as Tlaloc (Miller et al. 2012:202, Figure 8.1). Loendorf discusses Schaafsma and Taube's (2006:250) description of Tlaloc riding the back of a horned serpent, suggesting that this figure from Jaguar Cave may represent that association with rainmaking rituals.

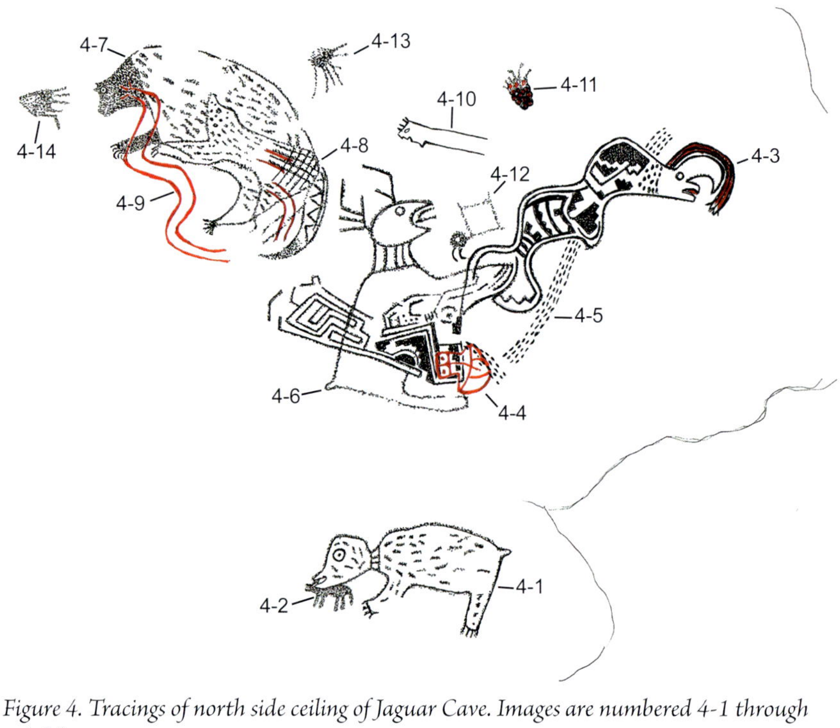

More recently, Jamie Hampson describes the white pictographs of Jaguar cave as

> ...celebrated and remarkable and almost certainly Jornada Mogollon; figures include a bear (painted over meandering red lines, probably a snake), a coyote, a deer, a possible jaguar, and a large plumed serpent with elaborate "stepped" body decoration. All these figures have dots and other entoptics inside and outside their bodies [Hampson 2015:77–78].

Most authors agree that these painted images were created by the Jornada-Mogollon. Despite the numerous descriptions in the literature no author completely described or drew the entire shelter and so readers were left with an incomplete picture.

Site Description

Geology

The Diablo Dam Site is in the Cretaceous sandstone of the Cox formation in the striking fault block escarpment of Diablo Mesa. The formation is a hard, heavily patinated sandstone cliff that is divided into blocks and through time these blocks detach and tumble down the slope. Under some of these fallen blocks shallow shelters, like Jaguar Cave, formed (Miller et al. 1988:11). This east-facing shelter is 2 m high, 4 m wide, and 4.5 m deep.

Several of the authors suggest that the shelter was "smoke-blacked" and there may have been some blackening of the shelter by fires (Jackson 1938; Schaafsma 1980:227; Sutherland and Steed 1974). Most of the images are painted over this black material which might also be either a manganese oxide formed along a metamorphic contact or a carbonate fracture fill (personal communication, geologist Michael McInerney, February 2002). When dating Centipede Cave, a shelter found in the same formation nearby, a similar black coating under the pictographs was dated at an age of 5000+ years B.P. (Marvin Rowe personal communication March 4, 2003). Dr. Rowe dated the coating using AMS and stated that the presence of this black coating in any dating attempts could seriously change the results. The exact nature of the

Figure 4. Tracings of north side ceiling of Jaguar Cave. Images are numbered 4-1 through 4-14.

coating could be determined by using pXRF but I did not have access to this technology.

Land Status and Cultural Affiliation

The National Register of Historic Places indicates that the periods of significances for 41HZ375 are 6999–5000 B.C., 4999–3000 B.C., 2999–1000 B.C., 999 B.C.–A.D. 1000, and A.D. 1000–1499, and the cultural affiliations as Archaic, Shumla, and Jornada Mogollon. The land is currently used for ranching, hunting, and recreation (National Register of Historic Places 1988).

Background

Four distinct rock art styles are found at 41HZ375 including Archaic, Candelaria, Shumla or Diablo Dam, and general Jornada-Mogollon. Although many of the West Texas sites were well known from an early time there is a great deal of rock art on private property that has not been documented except in a cursory matter and reports are a challenge to find. Many spectacular pictograph shelters occur in the Jornada-Mogollon region and, other than Picture Cave (41EP737), these have not been fully recorded. Some of these include Painted Grotto (LA 46313), Thaxton Springs Area (Alamo Canyon Site #13), Centipede Cave, Bobcat Cave, Juniper Shelter, Navar Ranch (41EP10), Wilkey Ranch Sites, and Hueco Tanks (41EP1). Of these only Centipede Cave is painted in a similar way although there is a great difference in the types of zoomorphic and anthropomorphic figures between the two sites (Berrier 2003). Another report is in progress to detail the differences and similarities between Jaguar and Centipede Cave. Detailed comparison with all these nearby painted sites exceeds the scope of this report. The general area must have been a cultural and hunting corridor during various times in the past. The great diversity of images with many unique styles and sites is important to understand and document.

Site Conditions

This site is well known and frequently visited. Vandalism is not rampant but intense visitation may cause erosion and fading of the site. A detailed study of old and new photos may help to understand the rate of deterioration. Unfortunately, the site has been picked over for artifacts and other than the pictographs and petroglyphs, the only remaining artifacts are numerous mortars and cupules.

Field and Lab Methods

Photography is the main tool for recording rock art (Miller et al. 2012) but it is not the only tool necessary to visualize complex panels. Numerous visits were conducted to the site over an extended period to obtain the best photographs. The use of a Canon Power Shot A2000 IS equipped with DStretch and the computer-based application of DStretch was applied to many of the photographs to bring out details.

Because most of the pictographs were white, I also used Photoshop to invert the photo creating black images to bring out the line work in some instances. Notes were taken to determine which areas needed to be revisited, examined, and photographed again. During subsequent visits in the field the DStretch camera was replaced by a smart phone with DStretch. Robert Mark of Rupestrian CyberServices created structure-from-motion models using the multiple photos. Then he used PhotoScan software to create the 3-D models and export them as PDFs. Some areas still needed additional photography to obtain full coverage so Mark and Billo revisited the site in November, 2016. See Mark 2016 for the web address for one of these models.

The next step was to print photos and trace individual motifs using a light table. The drawings were then field checked and modified when necessary. The PDFs of the 3-D models were also printed and traced to create drawings of the two sides of the shelter.

Data Overview

Most of the previous recording work was done to the standards of the day and was valuable in accessing the additional imagery found during this recording. The poor lighting conditions and undulating ceiling of this shelter make photography and documentation a challenge. David Parker's drawing (Figure 3) did not attempt to capture the contours of the shelter. Parker also did not have the benefit of DStretch or 3-D modeling so documentation for this project may vary significantly from his drawing. After using DStretch and 3-D modeling and tracing individual and composite images, I identified a total of 23 images for this shelter. I am using "descriptive names" (such as bear) to help describe figures and not imply interpretations. All paintings are white except where noted in individual descriptions below and many look as if they were created using pigment applied by fingertips.

The shelter has been called "Jaguar Cave" because some researchers thought that a meter-long spotted zoomorph (Figure 5) resembled a jaguar. Jackson (1938) did not mention this figure or include it in his drawing of images at the site. Schaafsma (1980) called it a cat. Prior to 2016 no one noticed the small animal figure under the mouth and chin of this spotted figure because it was invisible without the use of DStretch. Both figures are painted in white. The spotted zoomorph (Figure 4-1) was superimposed over the smaller one (Figure 4-2). These two zoomorphs are around a curved surface that is to the right of the horned serpent (Figure 4-3).

Figure 5. DStretch photo (YWE) of a meter-long spotted zoomorph with a small animal under its chin from Jaguar Cave. Photo courtesy of Jon Harman.

The jaguar interpretation has persisted and has been used to support the theory of Mesoamerican influence among the people of the Jornada-Mogollon (Hampson 2015; Schaafsma and Riley 1999; Wellman 1979). Sutherland and Steed (1974) suggest the lines around the neck are a collar that appears on a jaguar image from the Temple of Tlahuiscalpantecuhtli, Tula, but do not explain the "collars" on the plumed serpent and deer at this site (Figure 4-3 and 4-6). Other researchers have questioned such direct connections between Mesoamerica and the Jornada Mogollon (Berrier 2013; Brody 1991, 2004; Creel 1989; Crotty 1990, 1991; Thompson 2007). The Picture Cave volume (Miller et al. 2012:24–25) also contains a summary of the discussion of diffusion vs independent development with more references.

In comparison with numerous other painted images in this area it appears likely that the "spots" used in Figure 4-1 are used to designate fur rather than actual spots. One example from a newly discovered shelter in Juniper Canyon shows similar spots on an anthropomorphic figure with large horns (Figure 6). Juniper Canyon is about 17.4 kilometers northeast of 41HZ375.

Moreover, upon closer inspection, several other figures in Jaguar Cave also have "spots" including Figures

Figure 6. DStretch LYE enhancement of a figure from Juniper Cave in Hudspeth County, Texas. Original painting is in a dark yellow orange, an unusual color for pictographs from this region.

4-7 and 4-8. There were certainly jaguars in this region (Brown and Lopez Gonzalez 2001) and a few more likely examples of jaguar pictographs have been found at Hueco Tanks State Park and Historic Site near El Paso, Texas (Figure 7a-b). But these figures might just as well have been examples of ocelots, which were far more common. The pattern for their coats sometimes includes a line across the front of their chest that could be what this "collar" is representing.

One of the most dominant figures in this shelter is a 2.5-meter-long plumed and horned serpent (Figure 4-3) painted predominantly in white with red lines between the "plumes" and in the mouth of the serpent. Jackson (1938:45, Figure 31) called this element a conventionalized serpent. This figure goes to the edge of the shelter and looks out towards the northeast.

Some horned serpent images are found in Jornada Mogollon rock art but that combination of plumes and horns is atypical. At Hueco Tanks site 10F, approximately 55 km northwest of Jaguar Cave, there is a face or helmet "mask" (Figure 8). The Hueco Tanks figure

Figure 7. Tracings of possible jaguar images from Hueco Tanks (Site 17-41EP737).

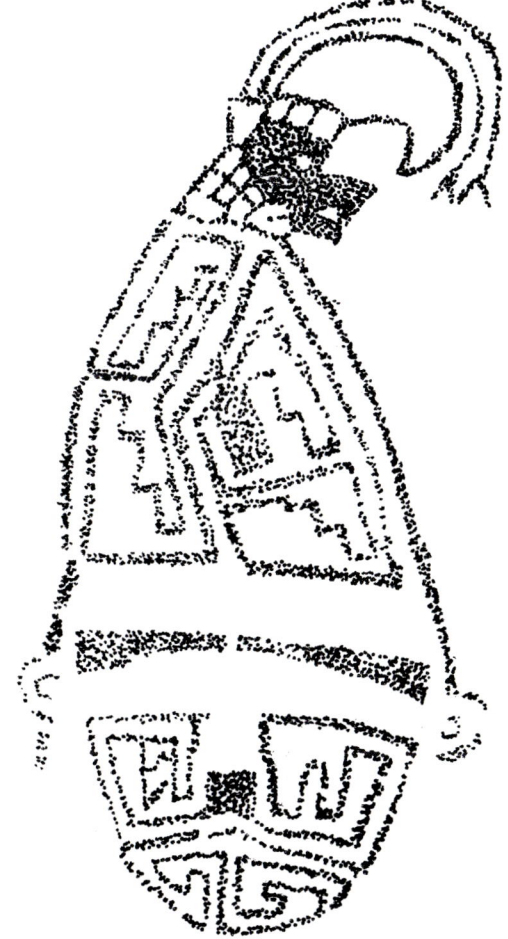

Figure 8. Tracing of a horned and plumed image from Hueco Tanks, Site 10-F. The mask is 58 cm tall.

has a nearly identical configuration except that it resembles a head with the horned and plumed serpent as a headdress. Both images are also decorated with stepped frets and "collars." Schaafsma (1980:229) suggests the stepped motifs in these figures represent clouds.

Undulating across the left-hand side of the shelter and around the curve toward Figures 4-1 and 4-2 is a line of four parallel dots (Figure 4-5). Sometimes the dots are very faint. As noted in the literature search Sutherland (1998) called these "seeds" but doesn't explain why she calls them that. Sutherland suggests that the dots end a few inches from the tail of Figure 4-1 but if they did they have become very faint over time and are no longer visible.

The serpent is superimposed over an open-mouthed deer. Jackson (1938:45) did not include this deer in his drawing. Sutherland and Steed did notice the deer's head but the rest of the body only became visible after using DStretch (Figure 4-6). Schaafsma (1980:227) mentions a deer but does not show a photo or describe it.

Jackson (1938:44) suggested that Figure 4-7 might be an armadillo but subsequent researchers describe this figure as a bear. It is not surprising that there is some confusion since after DStretch there appears to be another spotted and cross-hatched figure (Figure 4-8) superimposed over the "bear." At the back of these images is a "tail" but it is difficult to tell to which zoomorph it belongs. There are two red parallel lines superimposed over the larger figures that may represent an 18-inch-long snake (Figure 4-9) similar to one painted in Bobcat Cave near the far end of Alamo Canyon (Figure 9).

Figure 9. DStretch LRE enhancement of the snake from Bobcat Cave, upper Alamo Canyon, Texas.

Schaafsma (1980:227) notes that bears are rare in rock art of New Mexico but there are certainly many examples of bears on Mimbres pottery and bear effigies were found at sites near Las Cruces, Alamogordo (Lehmer 1948), and on Ft. Bliss (Brook 1982). Bear tracks are frequently found at rock art sites in the region. Bear bones have also been found in archaeological context at Hueco Tanks (Texas Beyond History 2008).

There are five other small images which include a Mimbres style head in profile (Figure 4-10), a possible bird or mountain sheep (Figure 4-12), and three geometric designs (Figures 4-11, 4-13, and 4-14). All of these are painted in white except for Figure 4-11, which is painted red and white. Figure 4-11 is the one that Sutherland and Steed describe as a ladybug. Sutherland called Figure 4-10 a square-shouldered kachina.

I divided the drawing for this shelter into two parts. To accurately see the shelter you have to lie on your back and look up with your head pointing east. Figure 4 shows the right hand side of the undulating ceiling. A crevice in the ceiling approximately 1 m wide divides the two sections of the shelter. When you look left you see the left-hand side of the shelter's ceiling (Figure 10). It is a challenge to depict the undulation of the ceiling. No two-dimensional model can show it accurately.

The most prominent figure on this left side of the shelter is a male zoomorph in profile which is 1.8 m tall (Figure 10-1). Jackson (1938:44) and Wellman (1979:Figure 361) called this figure a coyote. Schaafsma (1980:227) called it a bear. Sutherland and Steed (1974) called it a Mother coyote and later Sutherland (1998:169) called it a jaguar. It could be a composite image of a bear and a canine. The mouth of the bear image is quite unusual, having pointed and curved "fangs." I have seen only one other figure with the combined teeth and fangs—a petroglyph from the Black Mesa Escarpment west of Las Cruces (Figure 11). This figure also features a large inward curving horn so it may also represent a composite anthropomorphized zoomorph.

Approximately 70 km northeast of Jaguar Cave at Alamo Mountain (LA 108976) is another figure that resembles a bear (Figure 12). Although it has pointed ears the rest of

this image does resemble a bear. Its head is very similar to the image in Jaguar Cave but it lacks fangs.

Superimposed over the back of the large Figure 10-1 is a smaller spotted zoomorph with bared teeth and long bushy tail (Figure 10-2 and Figure 13). Sutherland (1998) also suggests that this figure is a jaguar, probably because it too is spotted. Parker drew part of the smaller figure but DStretch brought out more detail so the complete figure could be seen. There are similar coyote or wolf head petroglyphs at the nearby sites of Mullen and Storyteller (41HZ377).

In front of the predominant figure (Figure 10-1) are a number of faint images including a foot with ankle decoration (Figure 10-3), a zoomorph with horns (Figure 10-4), a possible lizard (Figure 10-5), and the out-

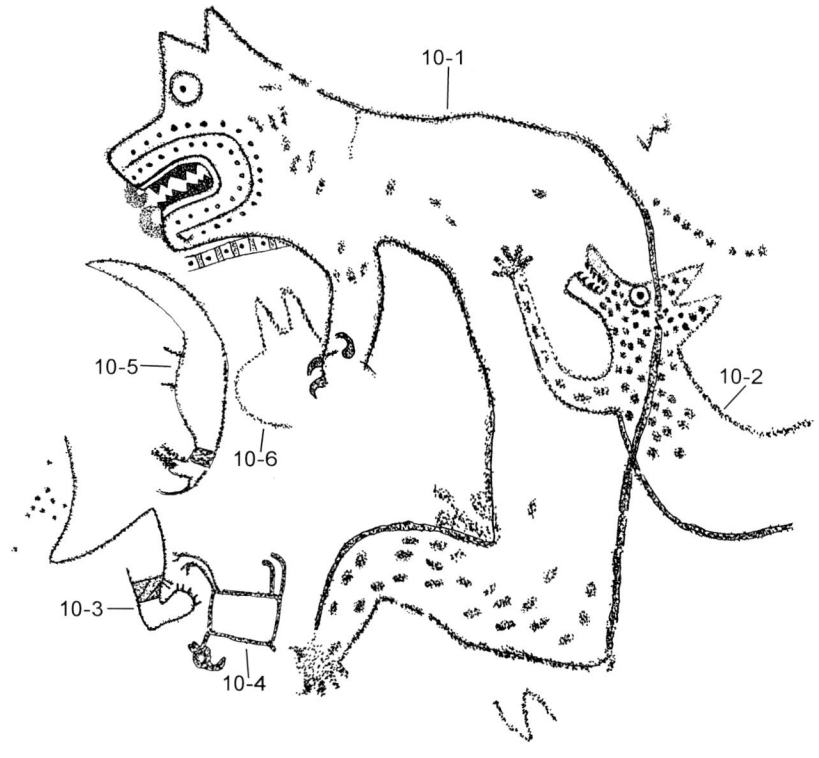

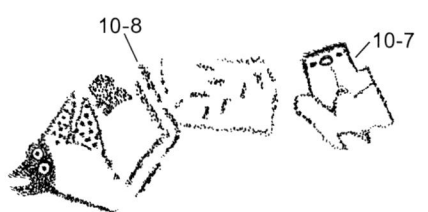

Figure 10. Tracing of south side ceiling of Jaguar Cave. Individual images are numbered 10-1 through 10-8.

Figure 11. Composite figure with fangs and teeth from Black Mesa Escarpment, west of Las Cruces, New Mexico.

Figure 12. Bear from Alamo Mountain, New Mexico.

line of head with pointed ears (Figure 10-6). Parker's drawing (Figure 3) lacks most of this detail.

On another face of the south ceiling is a panel with three elements. One is a square-shouldered anthropomorph (Figure 10-7) that shows up in the Parker drawing. The other two figures are a spotted rectangle and a zoomorphic figure with outstretched arms and spotted muzzle. This stylized sharp-muzzled figure with a mask like a bandit is very striking. These two figures were only discernable using DStretch.

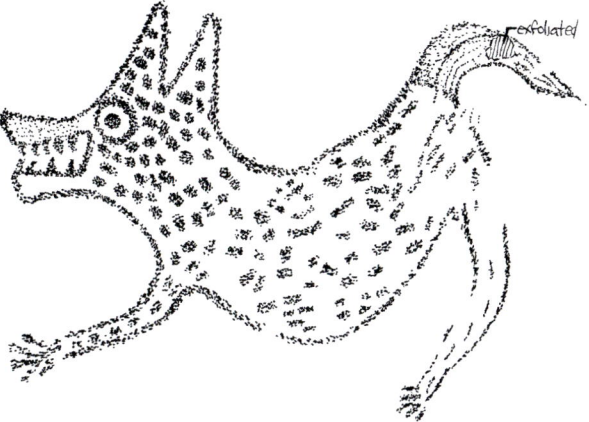

Figure 13. Traced detail of spotted canine figure found behind and superimposed over the largest figure (Figure 9-1) on the south side of the ceiling.

The previous documentation completely missed one panel which is on the outer wall of the shelter, above the head of Evelyn Billo in Figure 2. I had been to the site numerous times but until my field assistant Jeff Kaake pointed it out to me I never noticed the line of white figures that is actually on the south side of the rock face outside the shelter (Figure 14). There is a series of parallel red lines underneath these. Similar figures also appear at nearby Centipede Cave but are inside the shelter and are in much better condition.

Figure 14. DStretch LDS enhancement of the line of figures on the outside of Jaguar Cave.

Conclusions

New applications of technology such as DStretch and 3-D modeling are important tools for documenting rock art sites. The 3-D modeling allowed me to see how the shapes continued around the undulating surfaces of the shelter that were difficult to see in ordinary photos (Figure 15). Robert Mark has published one of these 3-D models online (Mark 2016). New el-

Figure 15. A 3-D model of the ceiling of Jaguar Cave (see Mark 2016). Photo courtesy of Robert Mark.

ements were located with DStretch while additional portions of other images were also added.

Without these new technologies this documentation could not have been completed. At times complex panels require additional steps for a systematic collection of data rather than an incomplete list of elements. As Whitley points out,

> … an important distinction can be made between unsystematic data collection, resulting in anecdotal evidence and systematic data collection that can reveal idiosyncratic behavior or unusual cases. There is nothing about systematic research that precludes the discovery and explication of extraordinary cases or the importance of unusual evidence. But unusual evidence obtained from systematic studies differs from anecdotal data collected unsystematically because, at the outset, we know that it is extraordinary rather than representative, and that would generally be recognized as part of the range of empirical variation that occurs in the archaeological record, thereby potentially providing a more nuanced and detailed understanding of an existing interpretation or theory [Whitley 2011:155].

In order to test my hypothesis about needing more than just photographs, I linked to the 3-D photos and my drawings on Facebook. The following are two of the pertinent responses. Myles Miller (personal communication July 28, 2016) states "I've been there several times and have looked at hundreds of photos, but there are things in this drawing that I've never seen before." During an online discussion one geologist described the experience of comparing the tracings with the enhanced 3-D photographs:

> My expertise in rock art is limited, but I do enjoy seeing it and reading the interpretation/analysis by experts in the field. Rock art enthusiasts have a different "eye" for detail and relationships than the casual observer. I frequently find that seeing a sketch or detailed drawing reveals details that I didn't see in the associated photographs. The ar-

gument that the drawings are the subjective interpretation of a rock art expert and/or artist is self-evident. What is not evident in previous arguments is how important these drawings are in helping people like me see what is not always apparent in a photograph to a non-expert. I find myself going back and forth between the two, seeing details and relationships I hadn't before. Without drawings, much of the meaning and import of this ancient art might escape me. Am I bold to suggest this is also true for many who are considered experts in the field? [Ted Petranoff, personal communication July 21, 2016].

Acknowledgments. A host of people helped with this project including researchers and field assistants LeRoy Unglaub, Jeff Kaake, Myles Miller, Dave Parker, John Davis, Alex Apostolides, and Kay Sutherland. Special thanks go to Jon Harman for his authorship of DStretch and sending me a photo of a figure I had never seen before, and to Robert Mark and Evelyn Billo for their long-term support in everything cyber but especially for the 3-D models of this site.

References Cited

Berrier, Margaret
    2003 Centipede Cave: A Dramatic Mixed-Style Rock Art Site in Western Texas. In *Rock Art Papers, Volume 16*, edited by Ken Hedges, pp. 17–30. San Diego Museum Papers 41. San Diego Museum of Man, San Diego.
    2013 Goggle-eyed Anthropomorphs as Distinctive Component of Jornada Rock Art. Paper presented at the 2013 IFRAO Symposium, Albuquerque, New Mexico. Unpublished manuscript in the possession of the author. Accompanying Powerpoint presentation "Variation and Distribution of Goggle-eyed Anthropomorphic Figures from Southern New Mexico, West Texas and Northern Mexico" available online, https://www.academia.edu/11927334/Variation_and_Distribution_of_Goggle-eyed_Anthropomorphic_Figures_from_Southern_New_Mexico_West_Texas_and_Northern_Mexico, accessed February 15, 2018.

Brody, J. J.
    1991 *Anasazi and Pueblo Painting*. School of American Research, Santa Fe, and University of New Mexico Press, Albuquerque.
    2004 *Mimbres Painted Pottery*. School of American Research, Santa Fe, and University of New Mexico Press, Albuquerque.

Brook, Vernon Ralph
    1982 Some Effigies of the Jornada Branch. In *Mogollon Archaeology, Proceedings of the 1980 Mogollon Conference*, edited by Patrick H. Becket, pp. 211–228. Acoma Books, Ramona, California.

Brown, David E., and Carlos A. Lopez Gonzalez
    2001 *Borderland Jaguars*. University of Utah Press, Salt Lake City.

Creel, Darrell G.
    1989 Anthropomorphic Rock Art Figures in the Middle Mimbres Valley, New Mexico. *Kiva* 55(1):71–86.

Crotty, Helen K.
    1990 Formal Qualities of the Jornada Style and Pueblo IV Rock Art: A Comparison with Implications for the Origins of Pueblo Ceremonialism. In *American Indian Rock Art, Volume 16*, edited by Solveig A. Turpin, pp. 147–166. National Park Service, Del Rio, Texas; American Rock Art Research Association, El Toro, California; and University of Texas, Austin.
    1991 A Consideration of the Formal Qualities of Jornada Style Rock Art with Implications for the Origins of Pueblo Ceremonials. In *Mogollon V: Papers of the Fifth Mogollon Conference 1988*, edited by Patrick H. Becket, pp. 133–145. COAS Publishing and Research, Las Cruces, New Mexico.

Hampson, Jamie
    2015 *Rock Art and Regional Identity A Comparative Perspective*. Left Coast Press, Walnut Creek, California.

Hedrick, John A.
    1967 EPAS Site #35 Report. El Paso Archaeological Society Archives: Unpublished manuscript on file in the Museum of Archaeology, El Paso, Texas.

Jackson, A. T.
    1938 *Picture-Writing of Texas Indians*. Bureau of Research in the Social Sciences Study No. 27, University of Texas Publication 3809. University of Texas, Austin.

Lehmer, Donald J.
    1948 *The Jornada Branch of the Mogollon*. University of Arizona Social Science Bulletin 17. University of Arizona Press, Tucson.

Mark, Robert
    2016 Jaguar Cave (3-D model). Sketchfab.com. Electronic document, https://sketchfab.com/models/a4056742739c467d93fc4dcda81a0a97, accessed February 24, 2018.

Miller, Myles R., Lawrence L. Loendorf, and Leonard Kemp
    2012 *Picture Cave and Other Rock Art Sites on Fort Bliss*. Fort Bliss Cultural Resources Report No. 10-36. GMI Report of Investigations No. 795EP, El Paso, Texas.

Miller, Myles R., Trace Stuart, and Wayne Howell
    1988 *Preliminary Archaeological Surveys and Documentation of Petroglyph Sites in Western Hudspeth County, Texas*. Cultural Resources Report Number 37. Batcho and Kauffman Associates for Texas Historical Commission, Austin, Texas.

National Register of Historic Places
    1988 Alamo Canyon-Wilkey Ranch Discontiguous Archaeological District. Electronic document, http://www.nationalregisterofhistoricplaces.com/Tx/Hudspeth/districts.html, accessed February 21, 2018.

Schaafsma, Curtis, and Carroll L. Riley
    1999 *The Casas Grandes World*. University of Utah Press, Salt Lake City.

Schaafsma, Polly
    1980 *Indian Rock Art of the Southwest*. School of American Research, Santa Fe, and University of New Mexico Press, Albuquerque.

Schaafsma, Polly, and Karl Taube
    2006 Bringing the Rain. In *The Pre-Columbian World*, edited by J. Quilter and M. Miller, pp. 231–285. Dumbarton Oaks, Washington.

Steed, Paul P., Jr.
　1975 The Fort Hancock Rock Art Site. In *American Indian Rock Art: Papers Presented at the 1974 Rock Art Symposium*, edited by Shari T. Grove, pp. 85–88. San Juan County Museum Association, Farmington, New Mexico.

Sutherland, Kay
　1998 Mesoamerican Ceremony Among the Prehistoric Jornada Mogollon. In *American Indian Rock Art, Volume 22*, edited by Steven M. Freers, pp. 161–178. American Rock Art Research Association, San Miguel, California.

Sutherland, Kay, and Paul P. Steed, Jr.
　1974 The Fort Hancock Rock Art Site Number One. *The Artifact* 12(4):1–64. El Paso Archaeological Society, El Paso, Texas.

Texas Beyond History
　2008 Black Bear. Texas Beyond History (website), The University of Texas at Austin. Electronic document, http://www.texasbeyondhistory.net/trans-p/nature/images/bear.html, accessed February 15, 2018.

Thompson, Marc
　2007 Unmasked: Icons of Duality at Hueco Tanks. In *Viva la Jornada: Papers from the 14th Biennial Jornada Mogollon Conference*, edited by Jason Jurgena, Lora Jackson, and Marc Thompson, pp. 87–94. El Paso Museum of Archaeology, El Paso, Texas.

Wellmann, Klaus F.
　1979 *A Survey of North American Indian Rock Art*. Akademische Druck-u. Verlagsanstalt, Graz, Austria.

Whitley, David
　2011 *Introduction to Rock Art Research*. Left Coast Press. Walnut Creek, California.

The Quilcene Petroglyph: A Contact Era Site on the Southern Northwest Coast

Daniel Leen

Located on the edge of Coast Salish territory, the Quilcene petroglyph (45JE235) is a rare example of a site which can be dated, not by subject matter, but by style. Two specific Northwest Coast formline motifs at this site are common in traditional wood, bone, antler, and ivory carvings from the northern Northwest Coast cultures (Haida, Tlingit, Tsimshian, and northern Wakashan) but are not found in Coast Salish mobiliary art. The establishment of Fort Victoria on southern Vancouver Island in 1843 resulted in large numbers of the above northern tribes visiting this fur trading post by the early 1850s. At the same time, the clustering of Coast Salish groups at or near the newly established trading posts resulted in the first non-predatory contact between northern tribes and Coast Salish speakers. Along with furs, some artifacts featuring this northern style of Northwest Coast art (formline executed as positive space) were undoubtedly traded at these gatherings of northern and Coast Salish groups, thus introducing details of the northern style to Coast Salish artists. While there are structural parallels between formline motifs in the Quilcene petroglyph (an ear and a modified ovoid) and some petroglyphs from northern British Columbia and southeast Alaska, the execution of these motifs as positive formline in the Quilcene petroglyph has its only parallel in the mobiliary art of the northern groups, indicating that the artist who carved the Quilcene petroglyph was influenced by mobiliary art from the northern Northwest Coast sometime after 1850.

In 1981 I published "The Rock Art of Western Washington" in *Northwest Anthropological Research Notes*, a description of approximately 20 rock art sites, all but one of them petroglyph sites (Leen 1981). One reported site was based on a sketch drawn from memory by the late Joseph Waterhouse, Jr., former Cultural Resources Program Manager for the Jamestown S'Klallam Tribe. A S'Klallam native, Waterhouse had been shown the petroglyph when a child by his father.

The petroglyph design in his sketch is that of a bird, probably an eagle or mythical bird. Because the subject matter of this design differed fundamentally from all documented sites in Puget Sound and Admiralty Inlet I believed it was a modern carving. I did spend a day searching the reported site location, but when the petroglyph was not found I abandoned further attempts to locate and document the site. This was just as well, as the site was miles away from its reported location. I believe that Waterhouse's memory was of the Quilcene petroglyph and he simply misidentified the site location. While located in Twana territory (Figure 1), the site (45JE235) is known by members of the nearby S'Klallam tribe (Straits Salish). Although differing in detail, the petroglyph design shares significant conceptual similarity (i.e. an eagle profile) with Waterhouse's sketch.

In 1997 the site was visited by Lee Stilson, formerly lead staff archaeologist for Washington Department of Natural Resources. Stilson documented three petroglyphs, the largest on a 70 x 180 cm coarse sandstone boulder situated

Daniel Leen
*Independent Rock Art Researcher,
Seattle, Washington*

Figure 1. Location of Quilcene petroglyph (45JE235) with Coast Salish linguistic boundaries.

Figure 2. Looking north at Quilcene petroglyph (45JE235), located just below higher high water at left center of photograph.

near the high tide line. Lee sent me a copy of the site form, but I again dismissed the design as too modern to be considered prehistoric rock art. Eventually I did visit the site (Figure 2) and documented the petroglyph with photographs and a rubbing (Figures 3a–c). After visiting the site, I modified my opinion regarding the age of the carving, realizing that this design was "not exactly modern" after all, since it shared some similarities with prehistoric petroglyphs of the Island Halkomelem Salish in the vicinity of Nanaimo, on Vancouver Island (Figure 4). More importantly, it also shares some characteristics with classic Northwest coast formline designs as commonly found painted or carved on bentwood boxes and other wooden artifacts.

Formline is defined by Holm (1965:29) as a "continuous grid of relatively even weight and complexity." It is almost always curvilinear, varying in thickness as it alternates between gradual and sharp curves. Holm refers to this aspect of formline design as semiangularity. While formline designs and semiangularity are found in some Northwest Coast petroglyphs and pictographs (Figure 5, see also Hill and Hill 1974; Keyser et al. 2002; Keyser and Poetschat 2012; Leen 1979, 1985), neither characteristic is found in any pre-contact era Coast Salish petroglyph. Thus, while the subject matter of the Quilcene petroglyph has a generic similarity to one Halkomelem Salish petroglyph (Figure 4), the presence of semiangularity and two specific motifs common in northern Northwest Coast formline (Figures 6 and 7) indicate cultural contact with an art style rarely (if ever) encountered by Straits Salish or Halkomelem Salish individuals until the contact period.

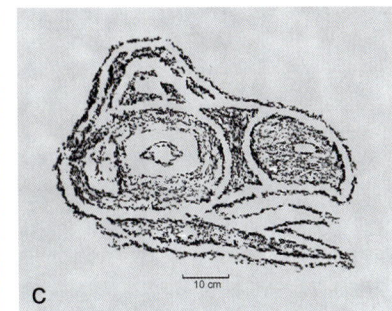

Figure 3. The Quilcene petroglyph (45JE235): (a) before cleaning, (b) after cleaning to expose full design, (c) a rubbing of the Quilcene petroglyph.

Figure 4. A rubbing of a supernatural bird from Gabriola Island site (DgRw201) in Halkomelem Salish territory. Note similarities of head to design at Quilcene.

Although uncommon, examples of formline and semiangularity are found in petroglyphs in Tsimshian and Haisla territory (Figure 8, see also Leen 1979, 1985); and petroglyphs with semiangularity absent

Figure 6. Primary formline with semiangularity from a painted box. Adapted from Holm (1965).

formline—as well as pictographs with formline and semiangularity[1]—are found in Tlingit territory (Figures 6, 9; see also Keyser and Poetschat 2012; Keyser et al. 2002). Three examples of petroglyph formline are illustrated here in Figure 8: Princess Royal Island (FdTd5), Douglas Channel (FjTh1), and Wrangell Narrows, Alaska. The formline in these petroglyphs, as well as every other less obvious example I could readily identify, were all executed as negative space. In contrast, the Quilcene petroglyph features formline as a raised, positive space, identical to formline as traditionally carved in wood. This distinction indicates that the Quilcene petroglyph was made by someone familiar with wood carving traditions of the northern Northwest Coast (and presumably less familiar

Figure 5. Distribution of petroglyphs with semiangularity and formline on the Northwest Coast.

Figure 7. Formline ear on an eagle, replica of carved argillite platter by Charles Edenshaw (Haida) ca. 1885

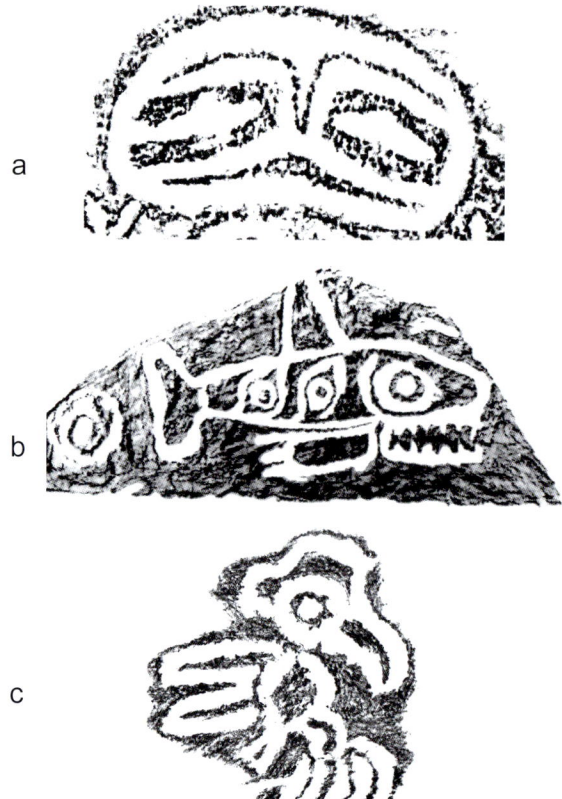

Figure 8. Formline as negative space on petroglyphs. (a) face of frog, Princess Royal Island, British Columbia, FdTd5; (b) whale, Wrangell Narrows, Alaska; (c) eagle crest, Douglas Channel, British Columbia, FjTh1.

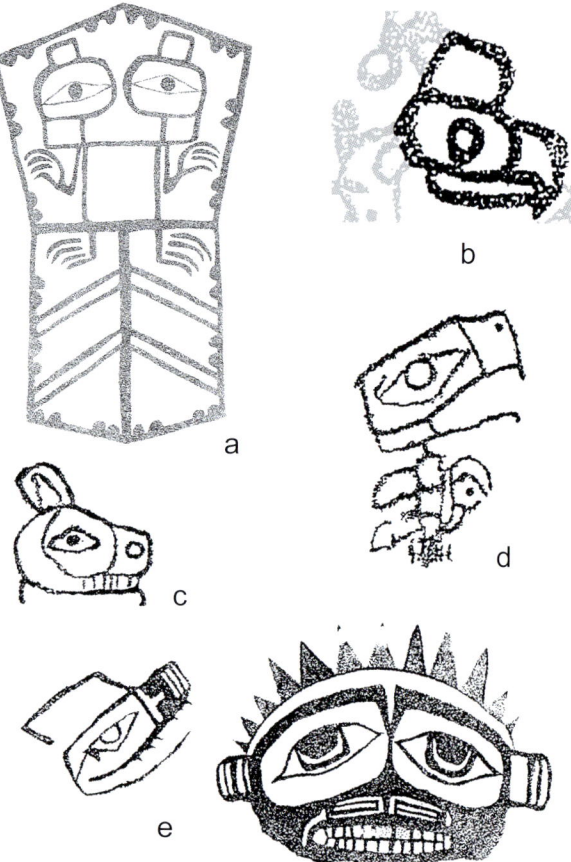

Figure 9. Semiangularity as negative space on petroglyphs. a, copper with bear crest, Kosciusko Island, Alaska, 49PET17; b, eagle, Kosciusko Island, Alaska, 49PET29; c, bear, Kosciusko Island, Alaska, 49PET17; d, eagle, Kosciusko Island, Alaska, 49PET29 (all from Keyser and Poetschat 2012); and semiangularity and formline in pictographs: e, land otter and mask (natural grouping), Pictograph Cave, Southeast Alaska (from Keyser et al. 2002).

Figure 10. Formline as expressed on eagle petroglyph at Quilcene. Ear with both formline and semiangularity, and modified ovoid outlining eye, both shown as as positive space (grey areas added to indicate normal proportions of carved formline on wood).

with the prehistoric traditions of making petroglyphs).

Regarding the presence of formline at 45JE235, two areas of the petroglyph are of particular interest (Figure 10): the semi-angularity of the ear and the modified ovoid surrounding the eye. Formline in Coast Salish mobiliary art is less well known compared to the extremely large amount of documentation which exists for the northern Northwest Coast cultures such as the Tlingit, Tsimshian, Haida, and Haisla. While some design motifs are found in both the formline tradition of mobiliary art and petroglyphs of the Coast Salish, the above two examples of formline motifs in the Quilcene petroglyph are only found in art from the northern Northwest Coast. Modern examples of these northern forms were of course much more precisely executed when painted or carved onto wood, and I have enhanced (with grey shading) irregularities of the Quilcene petroglyph to make the structural parallels of the motifs more obvious.

The Quilcene petroglyph is located approximately four km south of the historic Twana winter village of *qwalsi'd*, near the head of Quilcene Bay (Elmendorf 1992). After the Point-No-Point Treaty of January 1855 was signed with the Twana, Chemakum, and Klallams; the Twana (presumably including the folks living at *qwalsi'd* near the petroglyph site) were removed south to the Skokomish Reservation. Non-native settlement at Quilcene began about 1860, and according to local histories, by 1891 there were about 500 people (non-native settlers) in the Quilcene Valley. Based on the widespread Coast Salish practice of bi-local residence, it seems likely there were residents from *qwalsi'd* who had married into the S'Klallam village to the north. Thus, even if the petroglyph had been carved by a native of *qwalsi'd*, it is not surprising that knowledge of the site extended to the nearby S'Klallam as well.

Although Fort Langley on the lower Fraser River was established in 1827, Fort Victoria was the first non-native establishment near enough to S'Klallam and Twana territory to have a meaningful influence on these groups (Figure 11). Located approximately 100 km north of 45JE235, Fort Victoria was founded in 1843. By the 1850s the higher prices paid for furs there, as well as many other enticements, resulted in increasingly large numbers of the northern tribes visiting that post to trade (Meilleur 1980). Another result of the developing fur trade on the British Columbia coast was the clustering of nearby native groups at various forts and trading posts (Duff 1964). Thus, by the mid 1850s there was an ongoing contact between indigenous southern and central Coast Salish groups and visiting northern tribes in the vicinity of Fort Victoria. The presence of positive formline design elements at 45JE235 are unimpressive at first viewing, but as these elements are only found in northern Northwest Coast art prior to the contact period, they must be seen as borrowings from another cultural tradition, borrowings which are very unlikely to have occurred before the presence of Fort Victoria made such cultural contact possible. Thus, I believe that the Quilcene petroglyph was carved no earlier than 1850, and possibly as late as the early 1900s.

Acknowledgments. I thank Dr. James D. Keyser for his suggestions, advice, and assistance with graphics, and also Rick McClure, who reviewed the paper and made several suggestions that enhanced its clarity.

Note

1. Pictographs with painted formlines (such as those shown in Figure 9e) present a different story than petroglyphs. They are much more common than

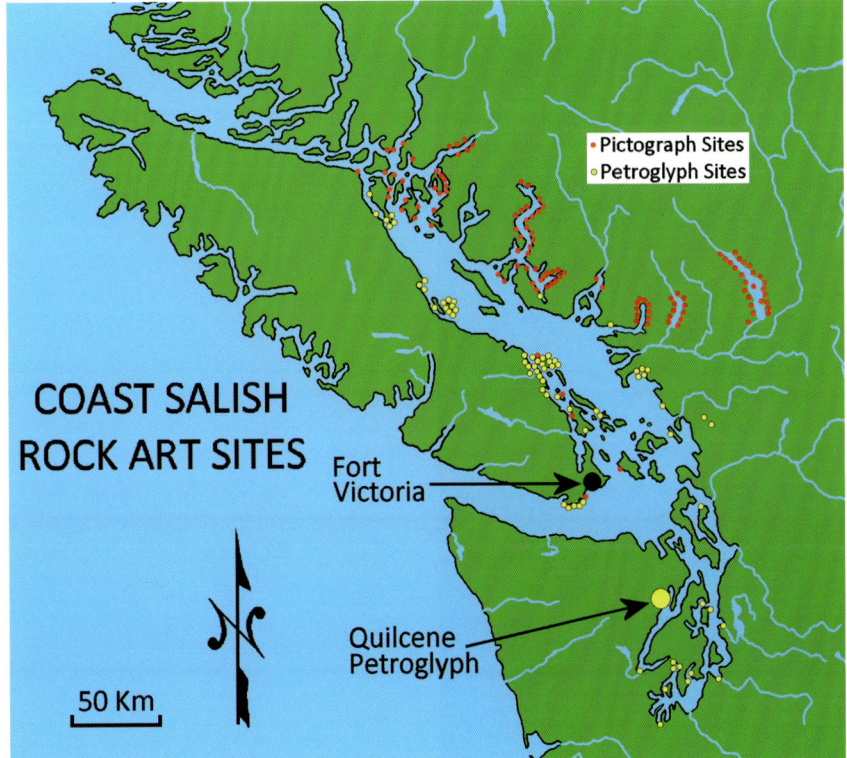

Figure 11. Coast Salish rock art sites with the location of Quilcene petroglyph (45JE235) relative to Fort Victoria.

petroglyphs, but no one has spent the time needed to catalogue where they are found. Thus, without these background data, I am not sure where the southernmost example might be.

References Cited

Duff, Wilson
    1964 *The Indian History of British Columbia, Volume 1: The Impact of the White Man.* Anthropology in British Columbia, Memoir No. 5, Provincial Museum of British Columbia, Victoria.

Elmendorf, William W.
    1992 *The Structure of Twana Culture.* Washington State University Press, Pullman.

Hill, Beth, and Ray Hill
    1974 *Indian Petroglyphs of the Pacific Northwest.* Hancock House, Saanichton, British Columbia.

Holm, Bill
    1965 *Northwest Coast Indian Art: An Analysis of Form.* University of Washington Press, Seattle and London.

Keyser, James and George Poetschat
    2012 *Clan Crests and Shamans' Masks: Petroglyphs in Southeast Alaska.* Indigenous Cultures Preservation Society, Portland.

Keyser, James, George Poetschat, Terry Fifield, and Carolynne Merrell
    2002 Pictograph Cave: Rock Art from Southeast Alaska. *INORA (International Newsletter on Rock Art)* 31:13–22.

Leen, Daniel
    1979 The Meyers Narrows Petroglyphs. Paper presented at the American Rock Art Research Association 5th Annual Meeting, May 26–27, Bottle Hollow, Utah.

    1981 The Rock Art of Western Washington. *Northwest Anthropological Research Notes* 15(1):1–56.

    1985 *A Preliminary Inventory of Haisla and Kitkiata Rock Art.* Kitimat Heritage Advisory Commission, Kitimat, British Columbia.

Meilleur, Helen
    1980 *A Pour of Rain.* Sono Nis Press, Victoria, British Columbia.

Seeing is Finding: The Value of DStretch for Recording Columbia River Rock Art at Spedis Creek and Harris Canyon

David L. Minick and James D. Keyser

Mid-Columbia River Rock art has been documented throughout the twentieth century using a variety of methods and formats. DStretch photo enhancement technology allows a more complete catalog of pictographs to be made than any previously used method. This project documented two sites in the Dalles-Deschutes region that had never been professionally recorded or reported in detail. It marks the first time that DStretch has been extensively used to study Columbia Plateau imagery, and it shows the value of finding and recording Yakima Polychrome Style images. One of our sites—Spedis Creek (45KL81)—has been cited in the rock art literature since the 1920s, but despite this long history of documentation and study, our DStretch recording revealed significant imagery never previously noted. Our work at Harris Canyon (35SH274) is the first organized recording and reporting of that site.

Rock art on the mid-Columbia River is well known, and has been documented since the early twentieth century using a variety of methods and formats. The relatively new technology of DStretch photo enhancement permits a more complete documentation of faded pictographs than ever before possible, thereby enabling a more complete photographic catalog of imagery to be made. This project documented two rock art sites in the Dalles-Deschutes region of the lower Columbia River (Figure 1) that have never been fully professionally recorded or reported in detail. One is the well-

David L. Minick
Oregon Archaeological Society
Portland, Oregon.

James D. Keyser
Oregon Archaeological Society
Portland, Oregon

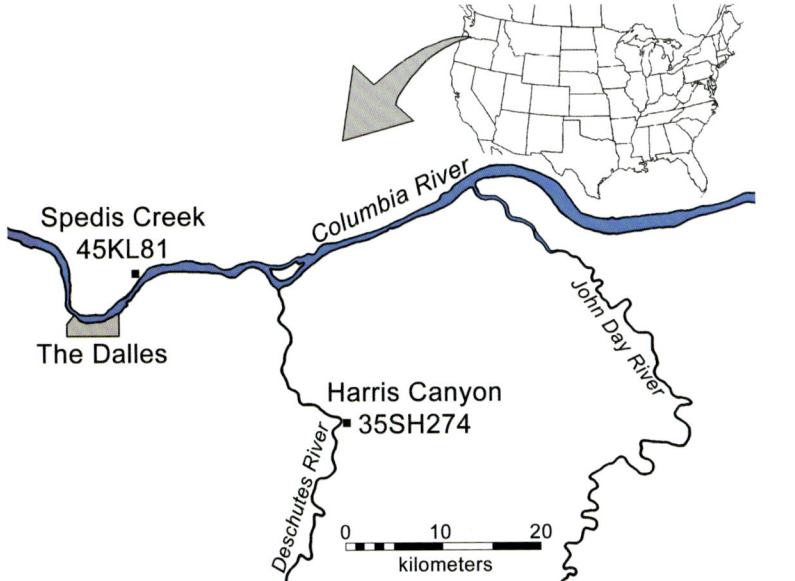

Figure 1. Location of Spedis Creek and Harris Canyon sites in the Lower Columbia River region.

known Spedis Creek site (45KL81) in Washington on the Columbia River, and the other is at Harris Canyon (35SH274) on the Deschutes River in Oregon. The aim of our research is twofold: first, it is to provide as complete a record as possible of the site for use by the agencies responsible for managing them; and second, to foster a better understanding of these sites by analyzing the functional differences between two types of rock art present as expressed by their imagery, location, and other associations. It also marks the first time that DStretch has been used in the detailed study of a site with primarily Yakima Polychrome style imagery.

The Spedis Creek site, located on the Columbia River in Washington's Columbia Hills State Park (Figure 2), has been cited in the region's rock art literature since the 1920s. Despite this long history of documentation and study, our preliminary DStretch photographic assessment in 2015 showed significant imagery that had not been previously noted or recognized. This included examples of Central Columbia Plateau, Yakima Polychrome, and Columbia River Conventionalized style rock art present at the site.

The Harris Canyon site, located on the lower Deschutes River about 15 km (10 miles) upstream from its confluence with the Columbia River (Figure 3), presented a somewhat different opportunity. The site was brought to the attention of the Oregon Archaeological Society rock art interest group by a fishing guide familiar with the lower Deschutes region while we were conducting a different project. When we first visited the site in 2010 we learned that it was not reported in the regional rock art literature so we made arrangements to revisit and photo-document the images there five years later. Our work is the first organized recording and analysis of the Central Columbia Plateau style imagery at that site.

Spedis Creek (45KL81)

The Spedis Creek site is situated in one of the most densely occupied zones of the Lower Columbia River, approximately 10 km (6 miles) downstream from the roaring waters of Celilo Falls and right at the head of Five Mile Rapids, also known as the Long Narrows. Before construction of The Dalles Dam and filling of the reservoir behind it in 1957, this area included the rem-

Figure 2. Overview (to northeast) of Spedis Creek site at Columbia Hills State Park. Pictographs extend from freestanding pillar (arrow at right) to where cliff meets talus slope (arrow at left).

Figure 3. Overview of Harris Canyon site on the Deschutes River. Eight rock art panels located at small white tags.

nants of several large, year-round village sites, some of which had been occupied more or less continuously for the last 6000 years (Butler 1957:161). Located to take advantage of the area's spectacular geology, which created the best salmon fishery on the entire Columbia River, this complex of villages and related sites was the location of an annual trade fair. This gathering attracted people and products from across the Columbia Plateau, but also as far away as the Great Plains, the Northwest Coast region of Vancouver Island, the northern Great Basin, and northern California.

The importance of the area and its relatively urbanized setting is documented by Lewis and Clark, who visited and camped here in October of 1805 and noted that they found the "first wooden houses in which Indians have lived since we left those in the vicinity of the Illinois" (Moulton 1988:333). As part of this native "urban" setting the area has several large and many small rock art sites containing thousands of pictographs and petroglyphs. Among these are three of the largest sites in the region including Petroglyph Canyon (45KL87), most of whose images were drowned by the filling of the Dalles Dam; Atlatl Valley (45KL58), still preserved today; and Spedis Creek, described here. Some Petroglyph Canyon images, rescued in a small-scale salvage effort conducted prior to the 1957 filling of Celilo Reservoir, have been made available for viewing in Columbia Hills State Park along the *Temani Pesh-wa* interpretive trail. The Atlatl Valley site, containing Tsagiglalal ("She Who Watches"), the most well-known of all Columbia Plateau rock art images, is open for visitation on tours guided by Washington State Parks personnel.

The Spedis Creek site itself is located at the base of a high basalt escarpment on the north side of Horsethief Lake (Figure 4), an embayment created by the flooding of Celilo Reservoir and drowning of the Spedis Creek valley. Extending for approximately 100 meters along the base of these cliffs are more than 60 panels of rock art containing hundreds of red and white pictographs and fewer than half a dozen petroglyphs. The rock art here is found from a large freestanding basalt pillar on the east to the area where a steep talus slope finally buries the basalt cliff on the west. Although Keyser had visited the site several times in the past, its full extent was unknown to us and modern site records (e.g., Heddon 1956; McClure 1978; Woodward 1982) were incomplete as far as documenting exactly how many panels and images occurred in the area. What we did know was that many of the larger concentrations of imagery were associated with looted talus-pit burials that had been excavated more than 90 years before our study.

After obtaining permission from Washington State Parks, we first visited the site in June 2015 to do an initial survey with DStretch photography. Because of the complexity of the imagery, the size of the site, and the position of many images high on the basalt cliffs, we had previously decided to record the imagery using DStretch technology rather than tracing like that used in other projects (e.g., Keyser et al. 2004, 2008). Given the utility of DStretch (in combination with close observation during multiple field visits) we felt that this method offered an almost equally good opportunity for recording and documenting the Spedis Creek images. We returned to the site in March of 2016 to continue our documentation effort and to investigate additional panels that had come to light as a result of DStretch analysis in the laboratory. On this second site visit, we were accompanied by Jon Harman, inventor of the DStretch application for rock art photography, who was conducting an advanced DStretch workshop in conjunction with our recording project (Figure 5).

Laboratory work has consisted of DStretch analysis

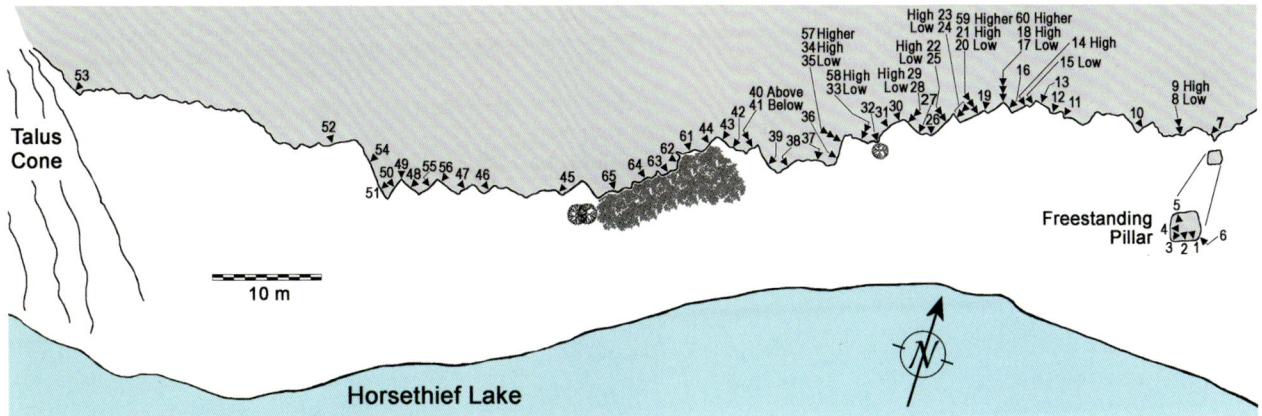

Figure 4. Plan map of Spedis Creek site with 65 rock art panels.

of the site photographs, identification and classification of all motifs visible at the site, mapping of the designated panels, and placing all the resultant information in a format available for use by management of Columbia Hills State Park. Further analysis will include comparison of inter-site and intra-site variation in the recorded motifs with those documented at Harris Canyon. We plan to publish an illustrated volume of the rock art recorded on this project as part of the Oregon Archaeological Society Press publication series.

Figure 5. Jon Harman at the Spedis Creek site.

Harris Canyon (35SH274)

The Harris Canyon site is on the Deschutes River, 15 km from its confluence with the Columbia River. The site is composed of eight, widely dispersed panels of Central Columbia Plateau pictographs painted along a north-facing basalt cliff over a span of about 25 m (Figure 6). This location will be described and discussed in more detail and the imagery found there will be compared and contrasted with that found at Spedis Creek both for style and content in a companion paper by Kaiser and Keyser (2018). The research conducted at Harris Canyon in 2015 involved photo-documentation using DStretch enhancement, with some images traced from DStretch enhancements in the laboratory. This marked the first professional recording of that site.

History of Recording Methods for Columbia Plateau Rock Art

Columbia Plateau rock art images have been depicted since the earliest organized scientific archaeological studies of the nineteenth century. The first recorders used freehand black and white drawings to document the subject (Figure 7), but often these were simply isolated images without panel context (Strong and Schenck 1925:78) Later recorders—often avocationalists—improved on these first efforts by focusing on panel context (Corner 1968), and some (Figure 7b) even recorded the images by hand coloring with pastel watercolors (Cundy 1939).

Rock art recording became increasingly popular following World War II, due to a combination of factors including a growing population involved in leisure-time activities (involving various archaeological subjects), increasingly popularized photographic technology, and the realization that industrialization of the Columbia River region was rapidly destroying much of the rock art resource. In the three decades between 1950 and 1980 there were more people doing more rock art recording than at any time before or since. By the 1940s, photography was regularly included in the mix of recording techniques (Figure 8), though drawing still dominated. The practice of "chalking" petroglyphs became popular to help images stand out and show up better in photographs (Butler 1957:159) and one mis-

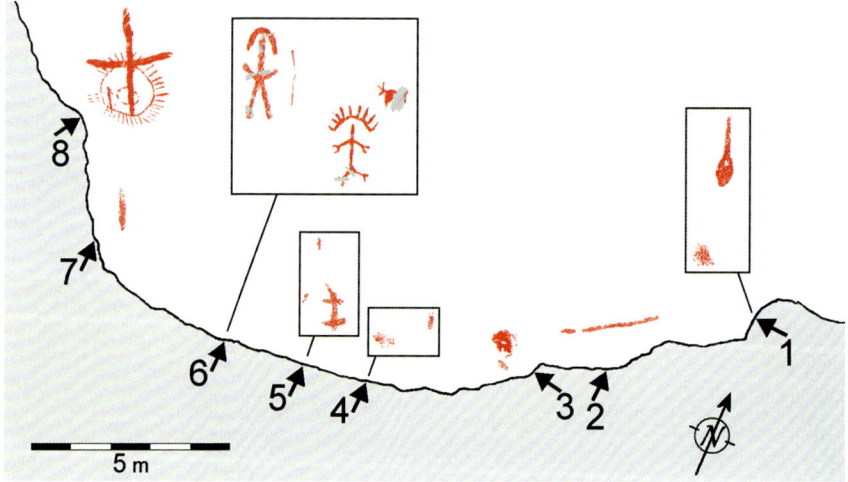

Figure 6. Plan map of Harris Canyon site showing pictographs at eight rock art panels.

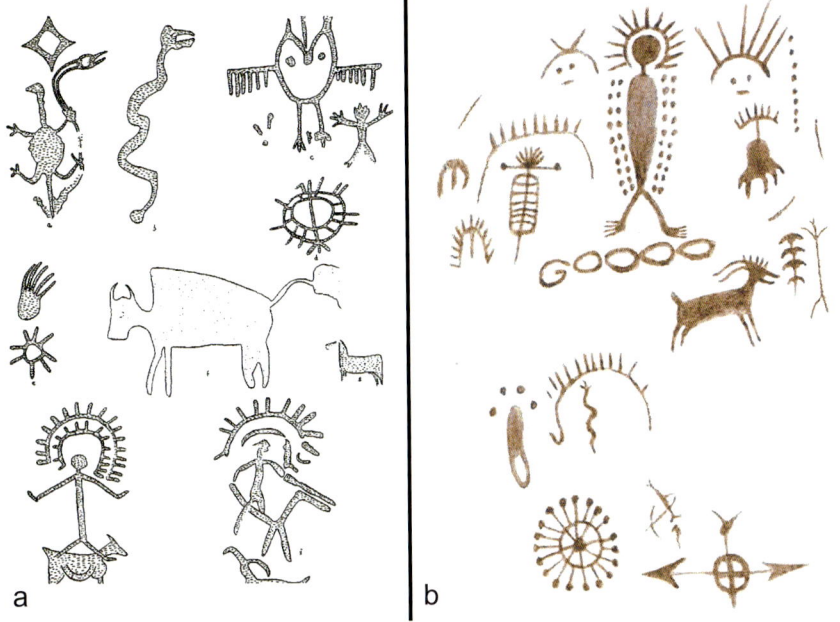

Figure 7. Early recordings of Columbia Plateau rock art utilized freehand drawings. (a) From Strong and Schenck (1925); (b) pastel drawings by Harold Cundy (1939).

Figure 8. Early photography often used chalk to highlight petroglyphs (Petroglyph Canyon, ca. 1940–1950).

guided effort in the Hells Canyon even painted over the actual designs with whitewash for this purpose (Keyser 1992:104). The result usually obscures (and sometimes even completely masks) the actual prehistoric image and is often disastrous for the art itself. Many Hells Canyon sites remain badly damaged today, with pictographs only incompletely visible beneath this historic whitewash overlay.

David Cole and Jack Hegrenes documented rock art at Petroglyph Canyon in 1953 as part of the River Basin Survey sponsored by the National Park Service. Their publication, "Report on Petroglyphs of The Dalles Reservoir," used freehand drawings and photography to record panels and rank significant rock art for removal before the site was inundated (Cole and Hegrenes 1953).

Rubbings were also used to document many petroglyphs in this period (Figure 9). In the 1950s and early 1960s several avocationalists spent many days every summer for several years in advance of reservoir filling making rubbings of petroglyphs threatened with destruction by the rapidly burgeoning dam construction on the lower Columbia River (Keyser 1994). Although this method is no longer widely used because it can have deleterious effects in many cases, the rubbings that have survived provide the best (and sometimes the only reliable) images available for some petroglyphs lost to inundation during that period. Of course, during this period, and even into the 1980s, drawings remained popular, and were still widely used by a few recorders, some-

Figure 9. Rubbings, like this one of the Swallowing Monster at Petroglyph Canyon, were popular in the 1950–1970 period. Many of them were made just in advance of filling of Celilo reservoir. Image of Jeanne Hillis rubbing courtesy of Skamania Lodge.

times aided by use of string grids intended to produce a more accurately scaled image (Churchill et al. 1990 as cited in Keyser 2005:10–20). Although quite time-consuming, these scaled images (Bettis 1987) were certainly better than the crude sketches of past decades (Figure 10). And in one instance (Woodward 1982), some of these images were even published in color.

Starting in the 1970s, professional rock art recorders in the Columbia Plateau began to trace rock art on clear plastic (Figure 11), and illustrations based on this method relatively quickly came to replace hand drawn or sketched images for most professional publications. Rick McClure, who studied the region's rock art for

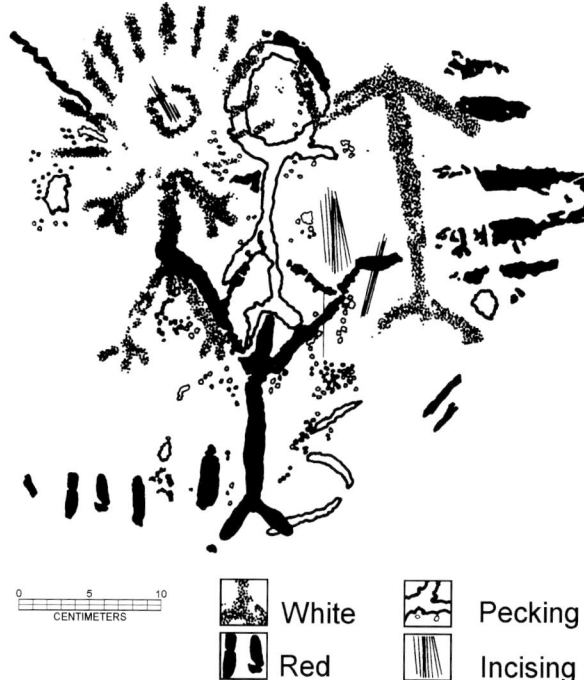

Figure 11. Starting about the mid-1970s, Rick McClure and Dan Leen began to directly trace imagery onto clear plastic. This technique provides exceptional flexibility, and produces a recording that quite closely matches the original image. Note that this tracing of a part of 45KL63, done by Leen and McClure, shows two pigment colors and two petroglyph techniques.

both undergraduate and graduate thesis projects (McClure 1978, 1984), was the first to widely use tracing in the Columbia Plateau, but Keo Boreson (1984) and Dan Leen (1984, 1988; Hann and Leen 2017) also did extensive tracing projects that have produced valuable contributions to the Columbia Plateau rock art record. Tracing is still widely used today (Keyser 2005:23; Keyser et al. 2004, 2008) because the method produces a copy of the image with maximum fidelity to the original and it has the greatest flexibility for use in recording all types of rock art, from the most lightly scratched and abraded petroglyphs to deeply pecked images and even bas-reliefs (Figure 12), and finally to pictographs painted with many different colors.

Photography began to become an even more important part of rock art recording in the digital era, because photographs can now be produced at nearly no cost and these images can be examined in preliminary fashion in the field. The result has been a marked increase in the number of images that are used in recording and the ease with which these can be evaluated during project fieldwork. But the advent of DStretch marks an even more dramatic improvement in the use

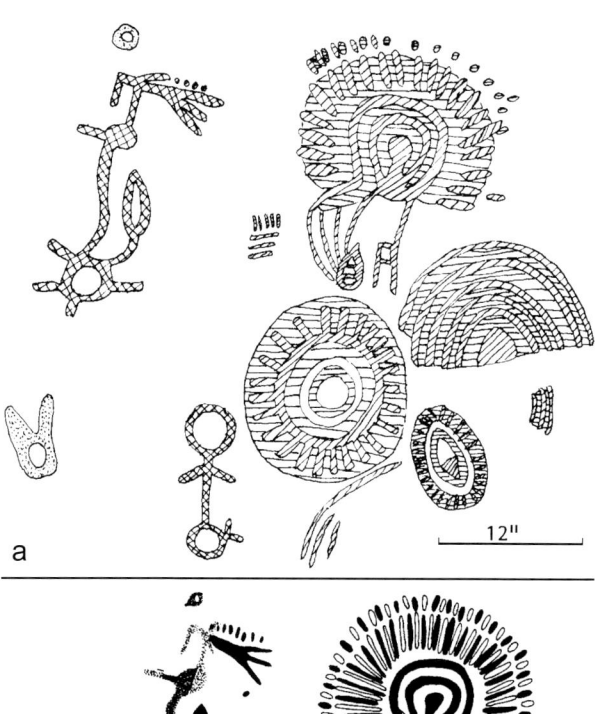

Figure 10. Malcolm and Louise Loring (drawing a) and Greg Bettis (drawing b) recorded much of the rock art in the Lower Columbia region in the 1970s and 1980s. The Lorings recorded with freehand sketches (often made from photographs), while Bettis used string grids to provide a somewhat more accurate rendering whose polychrome imagery is easier to understand. Note discrepancy of scale.

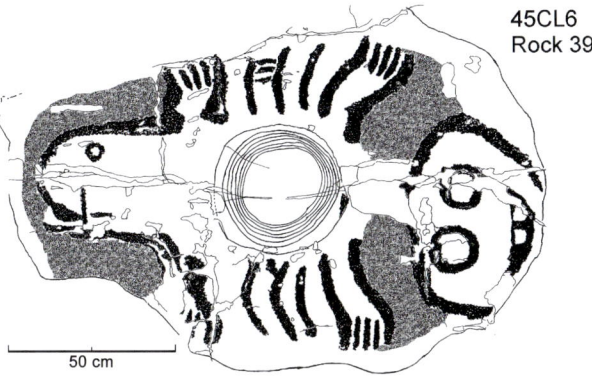

Figure 12. Tracing can even be used to capture bas-relief images like the Beaver Bowl at 45CL6, located in the Portland Basin. Tracing by Angelo Fossati.

a researcher to see and understand images that would generate little interest (if they were even recognizable) in the field without this technology (e.g., Figure 13). Such images can then be completely photographed to ensure that they are not overlooked. Furthermore, in laboratory analysis, the program enables researchers to identify, classify, and catalogue faint images that would otherwise likely be overlooked or misidentified.

Rock Art Recording History at Spedis Creek

Because of proximity to large villages, Petroglyph Canyon, and the Long Narrows fishing sites, the Spedis Creek site has been observed for many years and recorded in "bits and pieces" by several people during that time span. This procession of recorders reveals a history of rock art recording methods and formats more or less paralleling the history of recording in the region. Initial recording by Strong and Schenck (1925) used freehand drawings to document a few images but their primary concern was obtaining cultural materials from the burials at the site.

Thirty years later, Heddon (1956) made relatively detailed records of the Spedis Creek rock art, but these still were only freehand sketches (Figure 14a) and a few black and white photographs. Additionally, his work was never published and is therefore neither widely known nor often cited. The Lorings (1982) included three pages of sketches of imagery from the site, but these are obviously only freehand drawings that range from quite accurate to barely recognizable (Figure 14b).

of photographs coupled with a quantum leap in the ability of researchers to locate and record pictographs. In the field, DStretch technology makes very faint, nearly invisible images recognizable and often permits

Figure 13. Panel 60 at Spedis Creek was found only after DStretch enhancement of the area above a panel nearly three meters above ground surface revealed the circular images at numbers 1–3. Note the difficulty of seeing such small images in photographs, even those enhanced with DStretch. Photograph at right is DStretch enhancement LDS; inset is DStretch enhancement LABI.

McClure (1978:55) provides a general description of the site in his undergraduate thesis, and also references it in his graduate thesis (McClure 1984:152). But other than these general mentions, and a filled-out site form filed with the Washington SHPO, he provides no illustrations. Finally, Woodward (1982:66–76) published eleven color plates of Faye Speciale's scale drawings of imagery from the site. In a description of their methods, Woodward indicates that these were done with the aid of water sprayed on some panels and the use of infrared transparencies in some instances. Some of these reproductions are quite accurate, while others are little more than freehand sketches no better than those done years earlier (Figure 14c).

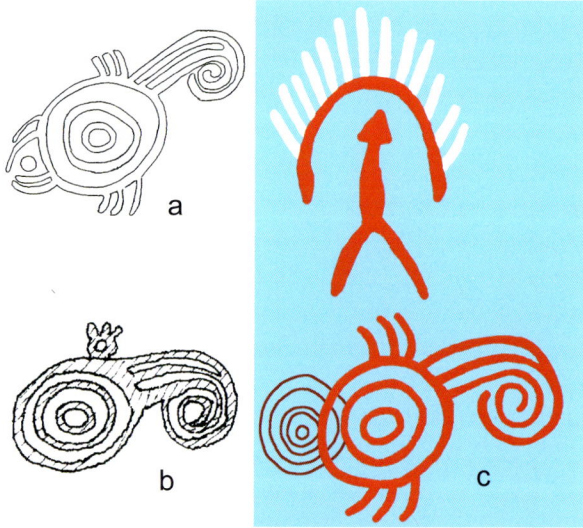

Figure 14. Three versions of the Columbia River Conventionalized style bird on panel 4: (a) Heddon (1956); (b) Loring and Loring (1972); (c) Woodward (1982).

With this as background, we designed our research program at 45KL81 to provide as complete a record as possible of all the rock art we could locate at the site. Our primary purpose was to make this record available to the Columbia Hills State Park staff for their planning purposes, but our research goal was to be able to analyze the site imagery and compare it to that which we had recorded at the Harris Canyon site.

The Value of DStretch to Our Project

Until recently, our research group has used DStretch[1] primarily as a tool for laboratory analysis of rock art images. But in this project we greatly expanded our use of DStretch by recognizing the distinct advantages of having a DStretch camera in the field. The instant feedback that such a camera provides makes for more precise recording and theoretically should guarantee inclusion of the entire panel in photographs taken during fieldwork. Even with this intuitive tool, there are best practices to adhere to when recording that will optimize results. We use DStretch to discern the boundaries of a rock art panel, for placement of scales and panel numbers, and to position the DSLR camera used to produce higher resolution images for later DStretch processing in the laboratory.

Fortunately, since DStretch works so well on red pigment, all but one Spedis Creek panel include red-pigmented pictographs, a significant percentage of which are red and white Yakima Polychrome style paintings. Although many of these pictographs are badly faded because they face directly into the sun throughout the year, we could identify the extent of most panels by using DStretch. And we also used it to find images on some rock surfaces that essentially appeared to be blank in ambient light (Figure 13a). Furthermore, the white pigment used for many Yakima Polychrome images is often fugitive and can be observed only as a negative space where small microscopic pigment traces can sometimes be seen (but often only with the use of a hand lens) where it was used to create the design. What we noted, however, was that previously painted surfaces were sometimes revealed in DStretch, probably because they have a slightly different coloration due to protection from weathering for the life of the white part of the design. Thus, both in our laboratory work and in the field, we were able to identify several images originally painted with white pigment (Figure 15) and we could also recognize several other images as polychrome paintings even though ambient light conditions revealed only the red-pigmented portion of the design or no design at all. In a few instances, to clearly illustrate these "hidden" pictographs, we have made "tracings" of imagery from DStretch photographs (Figure 16).

Even by using the DStretch camera in the field, however, some panels were only partly captured in some photographs. Thus, it was critical that we also took high-resolution, broader-field photographs from a viewpoint showing an entire cliff face. These "overall context" photographs are an important part of the final site record, and we could process them in the laboratory using DStretch to identify the actual boundaries and relative positions of panels that might have been only partly recorded with close-up photographs. By visiting the site multiple times, we could correct the record of close-up photographs so that each panel was fully covered and there was a greater accuracy in recording all of the site images (Figure 17). This would be even more valuable for

Figure 15. DStretch enhancement LDS reveals much more detail for Panel 21 than is visible to the naked eye.

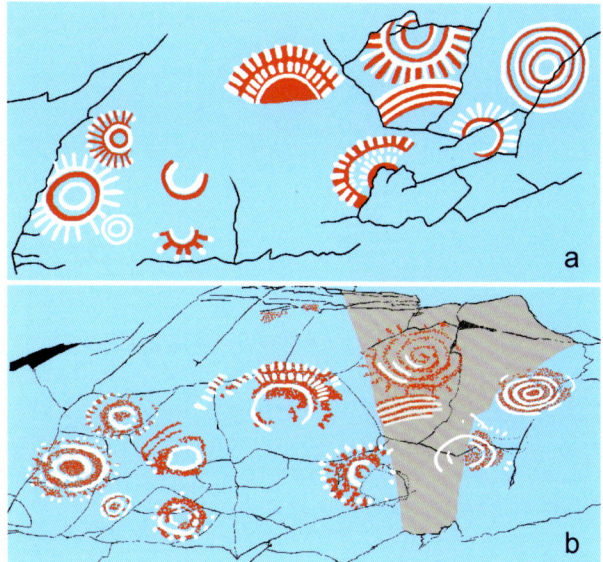

Figure 16. A "photo-tracing" made from DStretched enhancements of Panel 21 (b) enables us to add significant detail to a drawing (a) originally made by Faye Speciale (Woodward 1982:74).

a site that was remote or difficult to access, since this process could be done after a day in the field to avoid having to spend the time to return a long distance to the site.

Spedis Creek Panel 60 is an example of inadvertent discovery, which was corrected on a subsequent site visit (Figure 18). DStretch analysis of the overall context photographs of this area revealed the existence of much higher panels that had not been noticed during our initial visit because they were more than 5 meters (15 feet) above the ground. It is likely that these would not have been found without this laboratory scrutiny. On a subsequent visit to the site, we could target that upper section and fully document the additional Panel 60, which contains three major concentric circle elements (Figure 13).

DStretch also enabled us to discover and document several panels that had been previously overlooked; or only partially or incorrectly recorded, by previous researchers. Panel 28 (Figure 19) is a prime example. It was first noted (as *Sp 42*) by Heddon (1956) and sketched and described in his paper, but only documented with a single rough drawing without scale (Figure 19a).

He did note the bird-like head of the anthropomorph at the left and commented that it appears to be carrying something. But his drawing is rough and incomplete. A quarter century later both the Lorings (1982:53, Figure 14f) and Woodward (1982:73) published versions of this same composition (Figure 19b, c) that are very different from that of Heddon. Unfortunately, both drawings are flawed as well.

Figure 17. DStretch enabled us to clarify and adjust boundaries (white line) of individual panels (a) when close-up photographs (b) revealed data extending off the image (at arrow). DStretch enhancement LRD for both photographs.

Our photographs, enhanced with DStretch, allow us to see much more detail than can be observed with the naked eye, and reveal significantly more detail than any previous recording (Figure 20). They also clarify some of the odd features "seen" by past recorders (e.g. the circular "legs" of the bird-headed anthropomorph in the Woodward/Speciale recording in Figure 19c) and enable any researcher working with the file copy of these photographs to measure and describe many different attributes (e.g., the precise length of elements like the rayed arcs above the figures' heads) much more accurately than any previous recording.

Figure 18. Panel 60 (white arrow) was found while DStretching the broader context photograph of Panel 21 (black arrow). Note white-painted concentric circle highly visible when enlarged in inset. DStretch LDS for photograph and inset (inset contrast-enhanced).

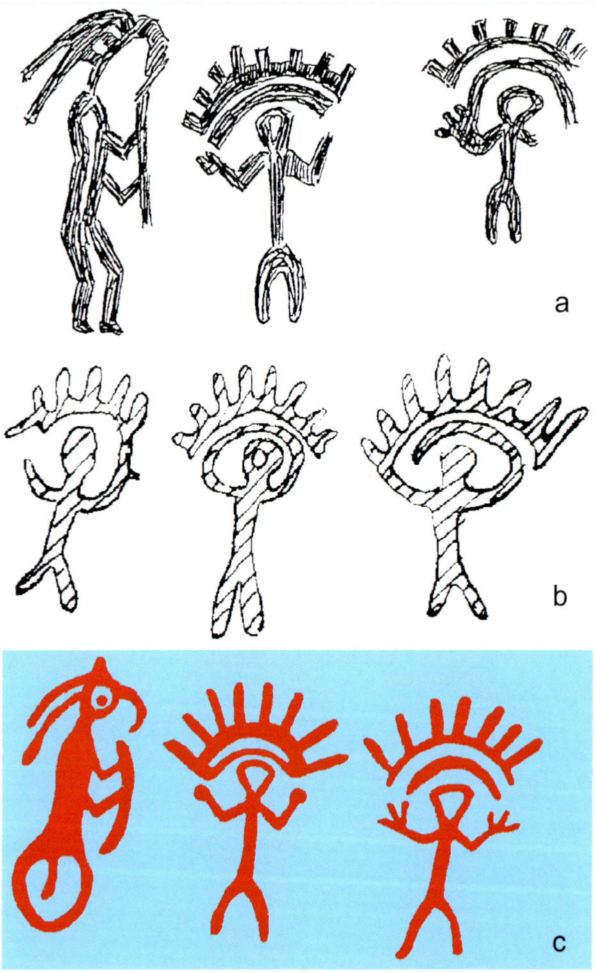

The four recordings of Panel 28 have been made by persons visiting the site over a span of about 60 years. Although we do not know whether Heddon applied water to the image, we suspect that he may have (since it was a common technique at the time), and we have good reason to believe that Speciale did (based

Figure 19. Panel 28 is composed of three figures that have been noted by previous recorders with varying degrees of accuracy. (a) Heddon (1956); (b) Loring and Loring (1982); (c) Woodward (1982).

Figure 20. Panel 28 detail (b) is provided by the use of DStretch enhancement YBR, allowing us to see exact dimensions of the three figures, and to document the bird headdress and the probable flute carried by the figure at left.

on Woodward's [1982:vi] published discussion of her methods). We suspect that the Lorings did not do so for this image, despite their admission that they did use this technique (Loring and Loring 1982:3), based on the incompleteness of their rendering of the figures here. What these differences reflect is that different observers saw different detail at different times. We know, however, that these differences are not primarily a result of weathering (and the resulting slow loss, fading, or "masking" of pigment by accretion of mineral precipitate), because subsequent recordings are different in detail, rather than simply showing a pattern of decreasing pigment visible over time. What these differences do reflect is that different recorders observed the imagery under different ambient conditions (shadow, intensity or angle of sunlight, humidity, application of water, etc.) and brought both different levels of recording experience and ability and presumably somewhat different recording methods to the site.

What this means is that DStretch can essentially factor out these ambient conditions and overcome less than optimal lighting, humidity, shadows, surface textures, or other specific environmental circumstances (e.g., Figure 21). Certainly, one tries to optimize the ambient photographic environment when using DStretch, by enhancing light or shadow depending on the surface and the pigment being photographed (Harman 2015:26). But this is usually no more technical than any field rock art photography, and it certainly obviates the issues arising from such practices as applying water to the panel surface.

In addition to helping arbitrate different recordings of the same motif, DStretch also allowed us to distinguish new motifs and discern patterns across the Spedis Creek site. The Columbia River Conventionalized style bird (Figure 22) was an early surprise. As we moved across the face of Panel 4 at the east end of the site, we were using the DStretch camera to evaluate what was reported (and illustrated) in the published literature variously as a spiral design superimposed on concentric circles or an elongate spiral connected to a concentric circle (Figure 14). With DStretch we quickly recognized that this was, in fact, a bird, with elements like others in the Columbia River Conventionalized style and in the greater Northwest Coast art tradition (Figure 23). It was only later, when we obtained Heddon's unpublished manuscript that we learned that he, too, had identified this as a bird (Heddon 1956:Sp 3).

DStretch helped us recognize three other images that appear to be unique (or nearly so) to this site.

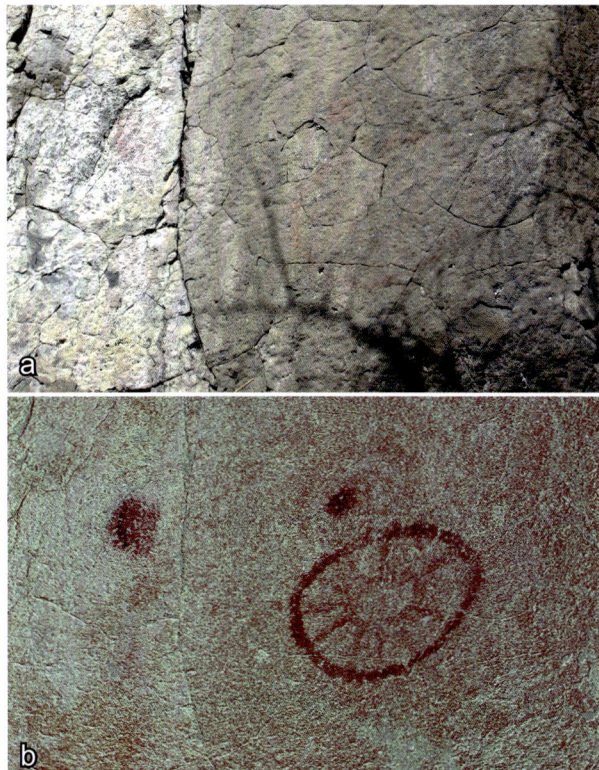

Figure 21. DStretch can be used to overcome visually distracting interference caused by a variety of environmental conditions and uneven rock surfaces (a). Panel 58 is overhead, which limited camera adjustments to eliminate distractions. DStretch enhancement YRE was effective in removing problems of different surface coloration, texture, and tree branch shadows to reveal these images (b).

Figure 22. Columbia River Conventionalized style bird from Panel 4 appears on a freestanding pillar at the east end of the site. DStretch enhancement LRD.

These include a stick-figure human surmounted by a polychrome red and white rayed arc (Figure 24), a distinctive "masted rainbow arc" motif, and a "block-printed" image. DStretch was instrumental either in initially recognizing the first image or recognizing additional examples. While stick-figure anthropomorphs

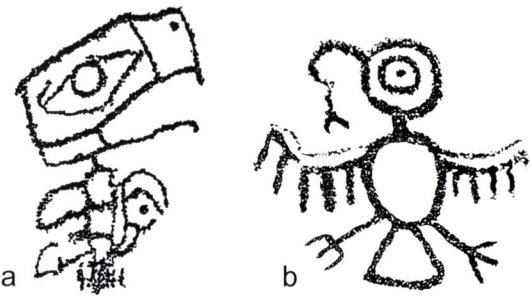

Figure 23. Birds are an important component of various Northwest Coast tradition styles. (a) Classic Conventionalized style eagle at 49-PET-29, Kosciusko Island, Alaska (note attenuated body with outsized head; (b) Columbia River Conventionalized style raptor at Petroglyph Canyon, 45KL87 (note form for head and beak).

Figure 24. A large figure, approximately 30 cm tall, with red and white overhead rayed arc is part of Panel 4, at the base of the pillar on the east end of the site. This Yakima Polychrome image (Dstretch enhancement LRD) is part of the assemblage of Shaman's art that appears across the site on prominent surfaces often associated with burials.

painted in out-of-the-way niches or other places somewhat difficult to access (Keyser et al. 2004:68-73). They are usually best characterized as private art. In contrast, typical shaman's art tends to be larger, more detailed, usually more carefully executed, often painted with more than one color, and typically characterized as public art (Keyser et al. 2004:69-78). From ethnographic reports we know that a shamans' initial contacts with the spirit world were very similar to how laypersons experienced their visions, and thus there is no reason to suspect that the basic pattern would be different for either class of visionaries. Indeed, what sets Columbia Plateau shamans' art apart is the need to "advertise," and the fact that it represents entry into the spirit world to engage a familiar supernatural presence to perform the shaman's bidding. This directly contrasts to a layperson's visit into a frighteningly dangerous spirt world where the goal is to acquire a spirit helper (who is unknown to the supplicant until it reveals itself) and return safely in the shortest time possible.

This particular image at Spedis Creek, despite its basic formal simplicity and resemblance to typical vision quest motifs, appears to better fit the shamanic archetype. Although it is roughly the same size as another stick-figure human on this same panel, both of these are significantly larger than most other stick-figure humans painted at the site. Likewise, the rock face on which it is painted is a large, prominent, billboard-like surface, on the side of a natural pillar facing the rest of the site. This is completely contrary to the small niches and/or low-to-the-ground panels that characterize typical locations of the rest of the stick-figure humans at the site. There is also a Columbia River Conventionalized style bird painted immediately below this image, and certainly spatially associated with it. Although pigment color is not a reliable indicator of such association, there is nothing to indicate that these two images were not painted by the same artist and they both appear to be of about the same relative age. Such an association would be typical of a shaman's painting.

Finally, the use of two colors for this stick-figure human's rayed arc implies significantly more preparation and forethought on the part of the artist who painted it than for those who painted the simpler monochrome red stick figures elsewhere in the site. We infer this greater preparation and forethought because red pigment is readily available in many places in this area of the Columbia Plateau and was widely used by all painters, but white pigment is difficult to find and harder to process, and was used very sparingly—usually only

with rayed arcs are one of the more common and distinctive motifs in the western style zone of the Columbia Plateau (Keyser 1992:61–62; McClure 1980); up to now, polychrome rayed arcs have only been found on rayed arc faces (Keyser 1992:83).[2] The fact that rayed arc faces—as an integral part of the Yakima Polychrome style—are so closely associated with shamans' mortuary and curing rituals both by ethnographic reports and archaeological associations (Hann et al. 2010:13–15) strongly suggests that this stick figure with polychrome rayed arc represents a shaman's vision quest image.

Rayed arc anthropomorphs are one of the most common vision quest motifs in the western style zone of the Columbia Plateau (Keyser et al. 2004:75), and as such they are typically simple, relatively small, and for large "public" paintings that by all other indications have some connection to shamans' work. This association with shamanism is also consistent with Columbia Plateau color symbolism (Hann et al. 2010:14). In summary, this rayed arc stick figure better fits the criteria identified as defining a shaman's painting than it does those indicating a simple vision quest supplicant's painting, so we feel that it most likely represents a shaman's image—possibly a self-image as he interacts with a supernatural being.

The masted rainbow arc motif (Figure 25) is a variant of the polychrome rainbow motif commonly found only in this very restricted area of the lower Columbia River. Other examples of the polychrome rainbow motif typically have from three to a dozen concentric arcs usually painted alternately red and white. Several of these have a solidly painted central "half circle" around which the arcs are concentric. Although the known examples of the polychrome rainbow motif exhibit various sequences of red and white arcs and central painted or unpainted area (e.g., one at Spedis Creek shows a pattern of light red center followed by a sequence of white, red, blank, white, red, white, red, white, blank, white, and red arcs) all appear to represent the same concept. But three examples at Spedis Creek have an additional feature—an upright stem sprouting from the very top center of the rainbow that is painted red at the bottom and white at the top. For all three examples the red portion is shorter than the white. A fourth example at the site (Figure 25d) is probably also a masted rainbow arc, but one that has almost completely faded away (see Kaiser and Keyser 2018). Why this version of the rainbow motif is slightly different than those at other nearby sites is unknown, but the occurrence of three very similar examples strongly suggests that it had some significance to the artist who created it.

Finally, during our DStretch analysis of the pictographs at Spedis Creek we were intrigued by a nested zigzag/arc design painted on one panel that appeared to have been made as a block print designed to emphasize the unpainted spaces rather than the painted ones (Figure 26). The design consists of complex series of nested rectangular arcs that appears to be superimposed by the headdress of a short, angular anthropomorph. The design is centered just above and to the left of the anthropomorph's head. Painted corners on these zigzag arcs range from extremely sharp to quite rounded, but the telltale indication that these are block-printed to emphasize the blank space is that the painted "lines" are of greatly different widths (2 to 6 mm) and densities of pigment. For instance, the pigment marking the more or less solid center of the design is a diffuse smudge whose left edge is very sharp and crisp and clearly delineates the first unpainted zigzag arc around the design's left edge. But on the right edge, the pigment simply feathers out and the blank area is demarcated by a thin line, obviously painted by something thinner than a finger. The second blank zigzag arc is bounded by a similarly thin

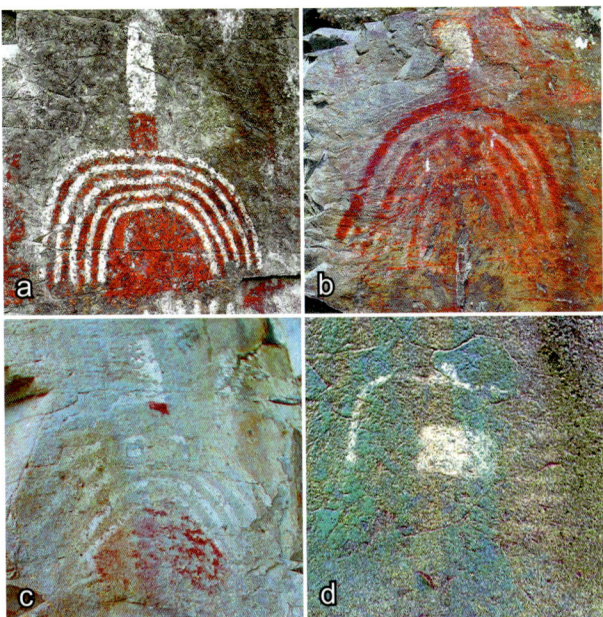

Figure 25. Four examples of the masted rainbow arc motif present at the site. Nested arcs below the mast show a variety of pigments and sequences, but the mast portion remains constant—a red stem with white pigment at the top. Note that d is badly eroded so that no white pigment remains (white color represents red pigment). DStretch enhancements (a) YRD; (b) YBR; (c) YRD; (d) LABI.

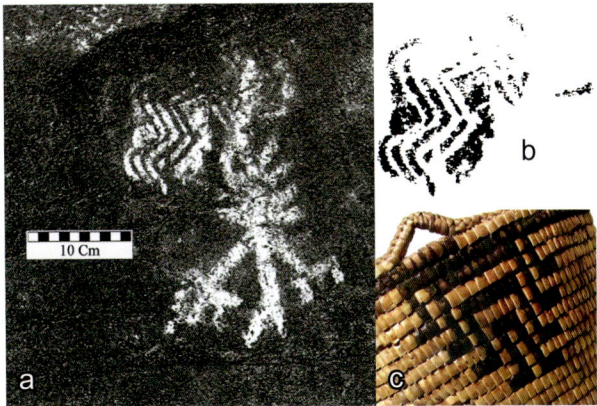

Figure 26. Panel 15 shows a unique stamped pattern (b) superimposed by the human figure (a). This motif is present in Klickitat basketry (c), where it is known as the salmon gill design. For image a, the Dstretch enhancement LABI is converted to grayscale.

line, only about 2 mm wide for most of its extent, but at the lower left the line widens to 6 mm across. Further outward from the presumed center of the design the lines are uniformly between 5 and 6 mm wide, except at the top of the design where they fade out.

The crisp, clean edges of the painted lines indicate that the blank spaces were not scraped away, since there is no feathering or dragging of pigment into the unpainted areas, that are themselves only three to five mm wide. Likewise, the sharp corners of several angles would be almost impossible to paint without having some sort of stamp or stencil to maintain their control. Also, the fact that the paint is blotted, smeared, or feathered out along some parts of the outside edges of the design and occurs as a blob that mars the zigzag pattern at the far left, suggests that the pigment was applied by some sort of stamping rather than painting with a brush. There is no obvious differential erosion to explain the "mostly missing" right side of the figure, but this is exactly what a design looks like that has been made with either an imperfectly "inked" stamp or a stamp that was not applied evenly to the entire surface. The latter seems most likely in this case, since surface irregularities of the cliff would make it difficult for the pigmented surface of the "stamp" to achieve full contact across the breadth of the design.

Exactly what was used to stamp this design remains a mystery. Its size and various attributes clearly show that it was not finger painted, and initially we thought it might have been stenciled. But that did not seem to make sense, given the irregular application of pigment across the design. At that point, we wondered if this could have been stamped on the cliff, much like patterned hand prints that are common in the southwest, but which also occur occasionally here in the Columbia Plateau (Keyser et al. 1998:88). The design is small enough to fit on a large hand, but if applied by a hand, much of it would have had to have been painted across the fingers, and we see no indications of finger prints, palm lines, spaces between fingers, or knuckle "gaps" where they should be visible (e.g., in the very spotty upper right portion of the design). Likewise, there is no indication of the warp and weft that would have remained had this been pressed against the rock using a woven basket or a textile as the stamp.

An important consideration, however, is that stamping this design would have required something that was both flexible and yet voluminous enough to hold its shape. This would seem to rule out a tanned hide, but a hide bag filled with sand or some other substance with suitable heft that would maintain a shape that combined sufficient flexibility with volume might be a possible stamp. Other possibilities are different parts of the body (upper arm, hip, buttock), or the side of a fish, all of which would provide both the required volume coupled with sufficient flexibility. Whatever was used for the "stamp," the artist first painted it, then scraped away the pigment (with a stone flake or fingernail?) to form a negative space composed of lines with notably crisp edges. When the design was finished, the stamp was pressed against the surface, and possibly rolled slightly from one side to the other. During this action the pigment blotted a bit to form the blob in the far leftmost angle of the design. Likewise, unevenness in the rock surface or uneven application of the pigment to the stamp's surface prevented the design from fully imprinting at the top and far right.

While stamping this design on the cliff with a painted fish seems odd at first thought, the design itself lends some credence to this hypothesis. This design, when found on baskets, is named the "salmon gill." The salmon gill design is common motif on Klickitat basketry, which is the predominant basketry type in this area of the lower Columbia (Schlick 1994:96–97). Although the close resemblance of this image to the salmon gill basketry design is not proof that it was stamped on the cliff using a painted salmon, the correspondence of design name and possible stamp applicator is intriguing.

What meaning this design—if it is the salmon gill motif—was intended to convey is also a mystery. It was clearly more than a simple series of nested zigzag arcs, and it does not appear to have been a full cross. Likewise, why it was superimposed by the painted human (Figure 27) is unknown. We do note, however, that rock art elsewhere on the Northwest Coast contains designs (i.e., Woodworm's track) that are better known in basketry (Keyser and Poetschat 2012:48–49), so it is not out of the question that we might have the same "crossover" between art media here. A better understanding of the meaning of this design and how it might have been produced awaits the discovery of additional similar examples or the development of more advanced technology to study this image.

Conclusions

The use of DStretch enhancement, both in the field and in the laboratory, greatly aided our research at the Harris Canyon and Spedis Creek sites. Without this technique, recording these sites to the detail that we have already accomplished would have been impossible

Figure 27. Black and white rendering (at right) of entire painted Panel 15 image made from DStretch enhancement YRD (at left), using color replacement tool in PaintShop Pro graphics program.

without weeks of field effort tracing the imagery. Even had that been done, however, it is unlikely to have revealed the record that we have obtained with DStretch. Motifs would have been misidentified, images would only have been incompletely recognized and recorded, and entire panels would likely have been missed. The record for both sites would still be grossly incomplete.

Conversely, with DStretch we have been able to obtain the first essentially complete recording for both sites. This has enabled us to compare and contrast them and undertake analyses that have yielded new data regarding both the Yakima Polychrome and Columbia River Conventionalized styles. We have identified new motifs in Columbia Plateau rock art, and been able to relate them to the functions of styles as previously disclosed in regional ethnography. Additionally, we have begun to formulate a comparative model that has provided additional information regarding the function of rock art in the region. Comparing this technique to those used throughout the century-long history of rock art recording in the region, it is obvious that we have made a quantum leap forward, both for the management of these sites, and the research potential of the subject matter. With DStretch, the future of Columbia Plateau rock art research looks brighter, and the potential for new discoveries has increased manifold.

Acknowledgments. A variety of people and organizations helped complete the Spedis Creek/Harris Canyon project. Andy Kallinen, Columbia Hills State Park Ranger, supported our recording of the Spedis Creek site in many ways during trips there in four different years. Dennis Griffin, Oregon State Archaeologist, provided the site form for Harris Canyon. Jon Harman consulted on our use of DStretch during one site visit. Some photographs used during our analysis were provided to us by Jean Clottes and François Gohier. David A. Kaiser, Michael W. Taylor, Rebecca Steed, Sueann Jansen, and Carson Hertler assisted us with field recording at these sites. Jack LaFond of Young's Fishing Service in The Dalles, Oregon, first brought the Harris Canyon site to our attention. The Oregon Archaeological Society provided funding for the project.

Notes

1. The DStretch image enhancement program has recently been described in detail by its creator, Jon Harman (2015), so we describe it here only in general. The program uses a decorrelation stretch algorithm originally developed forty years ago to aid in the analysis of Landsat imagery. It was adapted to rock art research by Harman, and released to the research community in 2005. Fortunately for Columbia Plateau rock art study, since the vast majority of pictographs in this region are painted in various shades of red, DStretch is designed for optimum analysis of the red pigment spectrum. Although the program struggles with white pigment, DStretch still produces results far superior to visible light for recording many white images.

2. The only possible exception to this in the published literature is a stick figure at 45KL273 (Keyser et al. 2004:41), which is a superimposed image with both white and red components, but it is difficult to tell what parts were painted at different times. In any case, this figure may have had a similar function to what we propose for the one at Spedis Creek.

References Cited

Bettis, Greg
 1987 *Indian Rock Art Designs from Oregon, Washington, Arizona, and Utah.* Rock Art Research Education, Portland, Oregon

Boreson, Keo
 1984 *The Rock Art of the Lower Salmon River.* Eastern Washington University, Archaeology and Historical Services, Cheney, Washington

Butler, B. Robert
 1957 Art of the Lower Columbia Valley. *Archaeology* 10(3):158–165

Churchill, Thomas E., Paul Christy Jenkins, and Greg Bettis
 1990 *A Damage Assessment of Cultural Resource Sites on the Umpqua National Forest.* Coastal Magnetic Search & Survey Report No. 46. Salem, Oregon

Cole, David L., and Jack R. Hegrenes, Jr.
  1953 *Report on the Petroglyphs of The Dalles Reservoir*. U.S. Department of the Interior, National Park Service, Region Four Office, San Francisco.

Corner, John
  1968 *Pictographs in the Interior of British Columbia*. Wayside Press, Vernon, British Columbia.

Cundy, Harold
  1939 *Petrographs of North Central Washington*. Unpublished manuscript on file with the Washington State Historical Society, Tacoma.

Hann, Don, and Daniel Leen
  2017 *Pushing the Boundaries: The Pictographs and Petroglyphs of Oregon's Harney Basin*. Oregon Archaeological Society Press, Publication No. 24

Hann, Don, James D. Keyser, and Phillip Cash Cash.
  2010 Columbia Plateau Rock Art: A Window to the Spirit World. In *Rock Art of the Oregon Country: Honoring the Lorings' Legacy*, edited by James D. Keyser and George Poetschat, pp. 1–24. Oregon Archaeological Society Press, Publication No. 18

Harman, Jon
  2015 Using DStretch for Rock Art Recording. *International Newsletter On Rock Art* (INORA) 72:26

Heddon, Mark
  1956 *Petroglyphs of The Dalles Area*. Unpublished manuscript on file with the Oregon Archaeological Society.

Kaiser, David A., and James D. Keyser
  2018 A Tale of Two Sites: Comparing Two Columbia Plateau Pictograph Sites. In *American Indian Rock Art, Volume 44*, edited by David A. Kaiser and James D. Keyser, pp. 45–58. American Rock Art Research Association, San Jose, California.

Keyser, James D.
  1992 *Indian Rock Art of the Columbia Plateau*. University of Washington Press, Seattle.

  1994 *Indian Petroglyphs of the Columbia Gorge: The Jeanne Hillis Rubbings*. J. Y. Hollingsworth Co., Portland, Oregon.

  2005 *Pictographs of the High Cascades: Rock Art of Western Oregon*. Umpqua National Forest, Heritage Report No. 1, Roseburg, Oregon.

Keyser, James D., and George Poetschat
  2012 *Clan Crests and Shamans' Masks: Petroglyphs in Southeast Alaska*. Indigenous Cultures Preservation Society, Publication No. 1, Portland, Oregon

Keyser, James D., Carol Pedersen, Greg M. Bettis, George Poetschat, and Helen Hiczun
  1998 Owl Cave. In *Columbia Plateau Rock Art*, edited by James D. Keyser, pp. 81–116. Oregon Archaeological Society Publication No. 11.

Keyser, James D., Michael W. Taylor, and George R. Poetschat
  2004 *Echoes of the Ancients: Rock Art of The Dalles Deschutes Region*. Oregon Archaeological Society Publication No. 14, Portland.

Keyser, James D., Michael W. Taylor, George Poetschat, and David A. Kaiser
  2008 *Visions in the Mist: The Rock Art of Celilo Falls*. Oregon Archaeological Society Press, Publication No. 17, Portland.

Leen, Daniel
  1984 Rock Art Sites. In *Final Report, Archaeological Investigations at Nonhabitation and Burial Sites, Chief Joseph Dam Project, Washington*, edited by Sarah K. Campbell, pp. 13–60. U.S. Army Corps of Engineers, Seattle, Washington.

  1988 *An Inventory of Hells Canyon Rock Art*. USDA Forest Service, Hells Canyon National Recreation Area, Enterprise, Oregon.

Loring, J. Malcolm, and Louise Loring
  1982 *Pictographs and Petroglyphs of the Oregon Country, Part I: Columbia River and Northern Oregon*. Monograph 21 (Part 1), Institute of Archaeology, University of California, Los Angeles.

McClure, Richard H., Jr.
  1978 *An Archeological Survey of Petroglyph and Pictograph Sites in the State of Washington*. Undergraduate Thesis, Evergreen State College, Olympia, Washington.

  1980 Anthropomorphic Motifs and Style in Plateau Rock Art. Paper presented at the 33rd Northwest Anthropological Conference, Bellingham, Washington. Unpublished manuscript on file with junior author.

  1984 *Rock Art of The Dalles-Deschutes Region: A Chronological Perspective*. Master of Arts Thesis, Washington State University, Pullman, Washington.

Moulton, Gary E., editor
  1988 *The Definitive Journals of Lewis and Clark: Through the Rockies to the Cascades, Volume 5*. University of Nebraska Press, Lincoln.

Schlick, Mary Dodds
  1994 *Columbia River Basketry: Gift of the Ancestors, Gift of the Earth*. Second edition. University of Washington Press, Seattle and London.

Strong, William Duncan, and W. Egbert Schenck
  1925 Petroglyphs near The Dalles of the Columbia River. *American Anthropologist* 27(1):76–90.

Woodward, John A.
  1982 *The Ancient Painted Images of The Columbia Gorge*. Acoma Books, Ramona, California.

A Tale of Two Sites: Comparing Two Columbia Plateau Pictograph Sites

David A. Kaiser and James D. Keyser

Rather than analyze rock art sites in isolation, this study compares two Columbia Plateau sites, similar in setting, age, and cultural association. What do their differences and similarities tell us about the two sites' structure and function? How do the types of images and their execution differ between vision quest and shamanic art? Examining how the distribution of multiple art styles within a single site helped reveal their purpose and relation to each other. Also, close examination of the Yakima Polychrome art at one of the sites allowed us to identify new motifs associated with this style.

Rock art in the Columbia Plateau was painted or carved for a variety of reasons, revealed in ethnographic and archaeological studies for over a century (Hann et al. 2010; Keyser 1992; Keyser and Whitley 2006; Teit 1906, 1930). By far the most prevalent reason for rock art's creation was the quest for guardian spirits. Virtually every member of society, male and female, was sent on a vision quest to find his or her spirit helper, often commemorating the event with the creation of rock art. Shamans likewise sought power in a similar fashion, and may have portrayed the acquisition of their spirit helpers in the same way. But when they depicted their visions and specific spirit beings, they usually drew those images in more elaborate detail and size. Shamans, in their spiritual duties to the community, would also create rock art as part of healing or mortuary rituals, for hunting magic, or to commemorate mythological events or places.

Differing constellations of motifs and styles of execution have been associated with the art motivated by these different functions (Keyser et al., 2004:68–82). Our project was designed to investigate two rock art sites from the same region, which are similar in age and cultural association, but found in different specific settings. How does the content of these sites reveal their purpose, and what do the similarities or differences between them tell us about their use, or how they relate to their specific environment?

The two sites chosen were Harris Canyon (35SH274) and Spedis Creek (45KL81). Each site is found at the base of a high basalt rimrock above a talus slope. Both are located along small streams that empty into a large nearby river, which can be seen from the site. The Harris Canyon site is just off the Deschutes River in central Oregon, about 10 river miles (15 km) south of the Columbia River. Spedis Creek overlooks the Columbia in southern Washington about 16 miles (25 km) northwest of Harris Canyon and 10 river miles (16 km) downstream from the mouth of the Deschutes River. The Harris Canyon site stretches along approximately 25 meters of cliff face, while Spedis

David A. Kaiser
Oregon Archaeological Society
Portland, Oregon

James D. Keyser
Oregon Archaeological Society
Portland, Oregon

Creek spans approximately 100 meters (Figure 1). Another difference is in their orientation; Spedis faces south while Harris Canyon faces north.

Figure 1. Overviews of the sites. (a) Harris Canyon; (b) Spedis Creek.

While we knew Spedis Creek provided a denser concentration of pictographs than Harris Canyon, we were surprised by the amount of rock art we discovered through careful survey and the use of D-Stretch to reveal faded images (cf. Minick and Keyser 2018). We recognized 65 panels of pictographs[1] containing more than 300 images at Spedis Creek while there are only eight panels with just 18 total images at Harris Canyon. Therefore, in terms of rock art, the sites are not as similar in size as their physical dimensions would suggest. The concentration of images at Spedis Creek may reflect the site's proximity to the large, year-round villages that occurred in the vicinity of the Long Narrows; whereas Harris Canyon was likely related to seasonal camping. Yet, despite their contrasting sizes, the sites remain appropriate for comparative analysis.

Harris Canyon

The Harris Canyon pictographs are simply executed, with a few small stick figure humans and an animal juxtaposed with lines, dots, rayed circles and arcs, and blobs. Of the three human figures, one is beneath a simple arc, another under a rayed arc is also juxtaposed with a simple animal, and the third human is juxtaposed with a large equilateral cross (Figure 2). Both the human and large cross are superimposed on a simple monochrome concentric rayed circle. All three of these groups involving humans, and also the concentric rayed circle, are classic Columbia Plateau vision quest compositions.

The depiction of an arc, usually rayed, is an indication of spirit power in Columbia Plateau rock art (Keyser 1992:71, 92), and when associated with a human figure likely denotes the successful visionary. This image of the supplicant is frequently juxtaposed with the spirit animal encountered in his or her vision. But to protect the secrets inherent in one's personal power, the animal's specific identity would usually be masked by depicting it in an abbreviated, generic manner without identifying anatomical attributes. Thus, the animal/human conflation would still serve to commemorate the vision, but the animal's anonymity would make it less likely to be taken by a shaman's spirit practicing "black magic." For this reason, we cannot positively identify the

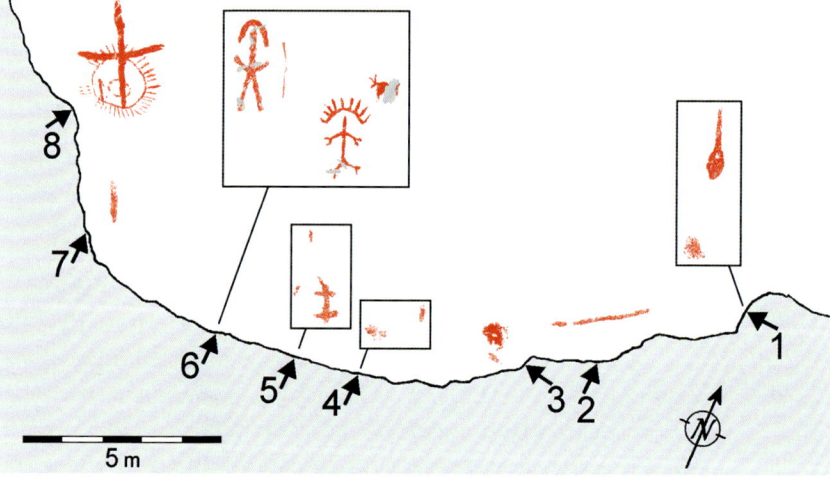

Figure 2. Map of Harris Canyon site showing location of images.

quadruped associated with this Harris Canyon human, but the human itself is depicted with split hooves for hands and feet, implying that the guardian spirit is some species of ungulate. With its distinctly cervid shape, in this area the spirit helper animal could have been a deer (of three different species), an elk, or even a moose.

Another common feature of Columbia Plateau vision quest art is geometric shapes, such as the cross, circles, and arcs found at this site. Arcs and circles are frequently rayed. These shapes likely represent entoptic images seen in early stages of trance. While interpreted and emphasized differently between cultures, such shapes are biological universals, caused by the firing of neurons in the optic nerve (Clottes and Lewis-Williams 1998; Kaiser 2010; Lewis-Williams 2002a; 2002b; Siegel 1977; Whitley 2000). A human image under such an arc, as seen at Harris Canyon, appears to illustrate the transitional stage of trance wherein the supplicant seems to travel down a vortex or tunnel prior to fully interacting with his spirit vision (Kaiser 2010). This is one of the most common compositions found at vision quest sites in the western style zone of Columbia Plateau region (Keyser 1992:61–62).

The simple, free-floating lines and blobs found on six Harris Canyon panels are likely vision quest verifying marks, created by other vision supplicants to prove that they had obtained a spirit helper at this powerful site. Such marks are attested to by several sources in the ethnographic record (Cline 1938:138; Keyser et al., 2004:99–101; Lerman 1954:142; Oregonian 1916; Spier and Sapir 1930:239–240), all of which report that such marks indicated visits to the site that did not result in a fully structured vision quest composition. The various simple finger marks are the clearest indication that the site was visited by multiple people. However, the two humans under arcs on panel 6 are depicted in very different styles, indicating at least two people recording their visions on this particular surface. Elsewhere, the human and cross are superimposed on a concentric rayed circle, indicating multiple uses at this location separated by some significant span of time.

All the imagery at Harris Canyon fits squarely in the Central Columbia Plateau Style (Keyser 1992) and represents what has been interpreted as vision quest motifs. Likewise, the art's position beneath a very shallow overhang is a typical vision quest location: an isolated place, often a rock shelter, with an expansive viewshed. The 18 identified images at the site range from 5 to 45 cm in size, but more than half of them are between 15 and 30 cm in maximum dimension. All of them appear to be finger painted. The art's placement—generally low on the cliff—and the simplicity and small size of these images indicate they were done for private purposes—another hallmark of vision quest art (Keyser et al. 2004:69–72). In summary, Harris Canyon was a vision quest site, visited over the course of many years by between ten and a dozen supplicants.

Spedis Creek

Whereas the art at Harris Canyon is relatively unassuming and simple in execution (though by no means simple in its meaning), much of the art at Spedis Creek is large, detailed, prominently placed, and often polychromatic. Many of the motifs on these panels catch the eye from a distance and demand that the viewer interact with them in a manner completely different than the more modest vision quest art. These images were created by shamans as public art.

Circles and arcs, often rayed, predominate at Spedis Creek, along with other shapes such as zigzags, spirals, and more elaborate or abstract geometric designs. Many of these images are repeated on the same panel, sometimes stacked or nested together to form a multiple-element composition that is truly a work of art.

The large, red and white geometric designs are characteristic of the Yakima Polychrome style (Figure 3). These images are concentrated along the lower Columbia River from The Dalles to Umatilla and in the

Figure 3. Yakima Polychrome designs at Spedis Creek.

Yakima Valley. A few sites are more widely scattered at Priest Rapids, Vantage, along the lower Deschutes River, and at the Steiwer Ranch site in the lower John Day River drainage (Keyser 1992:82–85, 94–95; Keyser et al. 1998:34–35, 49–51, 55). This style also typically includes rayed arc faces and the four-pointed Yakima star. Commonly found associated with talus pit burials, this art was apparently made primarily, though not exclusively, for shamans' mortuary practices. Red and white pigments have extremely significant color symbolism throughout the region as the polarity of life and death (Hann et al. 2010:13–14; Taylor et al. 2008:143–144). Thus, not surprisingly, the bodies or faces of the dead were painted red and white (Hann et al. 2010:14; Keyser et al. 2006:13–16; 2008:58–59) as were wooden grave markers (Hann et al. 2010:13). The spirits of the dead were also said to paint their faces in a similar fashion (Teit 1906:277).

However, in addition to the Yakima Polychrome imagery at Spedis Creek, there are many other images that more closely resemble the Central Columbia Plateau Style, as seen at Harris Canyon. These include many monochrome human figures, especially those depicted beneath a rayed arc; and simple geometric images, such as unelaborated circles, tally marks, and other more random finger marks, dots, and lines (Figure 4).

The site also contains a handful of other images, created as part of shaman's art, which are classified as part of the Columbia River Conventionalized style[2] of the Northwest Coast art tradition (Figures 5 and 6). Columbia River Conventionalized style motifs usually depict spirit figures or mythological beings with complex artistic conventions, including bilateral symmetry, concentric circle eyes, masks, and swollen tongues (Keyser et al. 2008:48; Lundy 1983). All these attributes show a strong connection with Northwest Coast tradition rock art (Keyser et al. 2008:47-52). One of the most distinctive Columbia River Conventionalized motifs at Spedis Creek is a large bird (Figure 6), but other motifs include typical Northwest Coast art tradition faces (Figure 5a, b), an owl, and a rattlesnake image that might be a representation of the land monster based on its similarity to others identified as such (Keyser and Poetschat 2004:122–125).

So, clearly, Spedis Creek is a much more complex site than Harris Canyon, not only in its size and number of images, but in the co-occurrence of three very different and distinctive art styles. Much of the art clearly falls into established classification schema. This is particularly true of the obvious Yakima Polychrome and

Figure 4. Typical layperson's vision quest art at Spedis Creek. Motifs include a person under a rayed arc, person juxtaposed with rayed solid circle, and tally marks at far left. DStretch enhancement YRD.

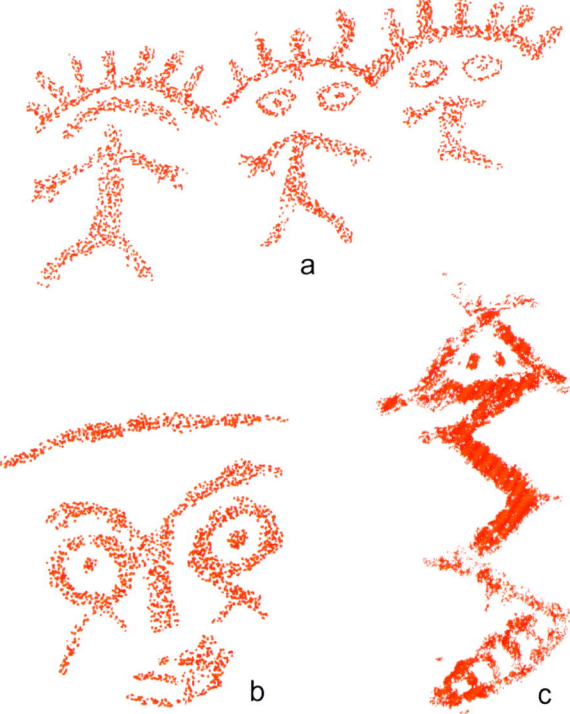

Figure 5. Columbia River Conventionalized images at Spedis Creek. (a) Rayed arc humans morphing into rayed arc faces above stick-figure bodies; (b) Face typical of the style; (c) Snake that may represent the Land Monster. All images produced as photo-tracings.

Figure 6. Panel 4 on the freestanding pillar, showing Yakima Polychrome and Columbia River Conventionalized images. DStretch YRE+FLT+HM combined with original image.

Table 1. Attributes of Vision Quest vs. Shamanic imagery.

Vision Quest	Shamanic
Simple	Complex
Small	Large
Low/Hidden	High/Prominent
Monochrome	Polychrome/Rare Color
Rock as Simple Canvas	Incoporates Rock Features
Blobs/Finger Marks	Complex Geometrics
Quick/Generic	Controlled/Artistic
Juxtaposed	Integrated
Single Episode	Repainting

Columbia River Conventionalized style art. Likewise, some of the vision quest art is clear, such as the juxtaposed simple human and animal images and finger lines. However much of the art falls along a continuum and some images could be assigned to multiple categories.

Many motifs overlap between vision quest art and shaman's art, such as human figures, rayed arcs, and other geometric shapes, since both shamans and lay people had similar visions of the same spirit world, sometimes at the same sites, and used the same basic iconography to express those visions. Thus, archaeological and ethnographic evidence shows that shaman's and layman's art differs mainly in size, location, and complexity. While a lay person's vision quest images tend to be simple, small figures, usually drawn quite low on the cliff face or in a sheltered niche, Central Columbia Plateau style shaman's art tends to be much larger, more elaborately detailed, and placed in prominent, viewable locations (Keyser et al. 2004:60–101). Sometimes these images also incorporate the shape of the rock surface into the overall design (Table 1).

Comparison

So, can we study the execution and placement of the art and tease the different styles and functions apart and see how they may relate to one another? With Harris Canyon as a baseline for vision quest art, Spedis Creek became a prime site to test this hypothesis. We needed to assess the style of execution (simple vs. detailed), location (high/prominent vs. low/hidden), size (large vs. small), and other features differentiating their purpose in order to determine likely classification of the images. Likewise, we sought to determine how these styles might be related.

For example, the tall freestanding pillar at the east end of the site shows all the different styles found there. A large panel on its western face (Panel 4) shows multiple stick figure humans under single or double rayed arcs, one such human with an overhead polychrome rayed arc, concentric circles, other geometric shapes, and a bird drawn in an oddly shorthand form with a large profile head (Figure 6). Placed in a prominent position, several of these detailed images are clearly shaman's art. Two are painted with red and white pigment. One of these, a tall stick figure human whose rayed arc is composed of alternating red and white rays, has been suggested to be a shaman's vision quest image. This panel is classified primarily as having Yakima Polychrome style images, although the elaborate bird image is Columbia River Conventionalized style.

Wrapping around the pillar to the south, Panel 3 includes two circles, one of which is polychrome with appended, nested zig-zags, and another geometric. Again, these more elaborate images are typical shamanic art and classified as Yakima Polychrome. Panel 1 shows multiple rayed arc human figures that vary in size and detail. Clearly this panel was painted during multiple episodes. Although some images may well be vision quest art, their overall size is relatively large and one human shows greater body detail than the usual stick figure, likely indicating a shamanic origin. Thus, this panel is classified as "Vision Quest and/or Shaman's" art. Nearby Panel 2 depicts a simple rayed vertical shape, likely intended to be a human, and some general pigment smudges. Likewise, Panel 5 on the opposite side of the pillar consists only of pigment smudges. These two panels conform closest to a lay person's vision quest art. Finally, at the base of the pillar, slightly downhill and removed from the other panels, is a small rock overhang situated low to the ground. Here Panel 6 shows both simple and concentric circles and two tally marks. Again, the location and motifs are very typical of a neophyte's vision quest.

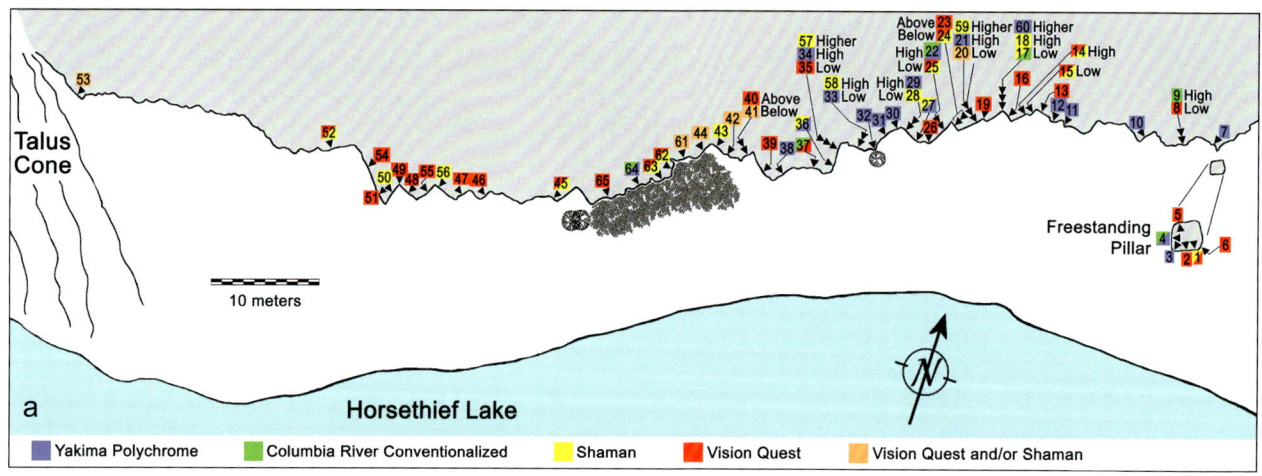
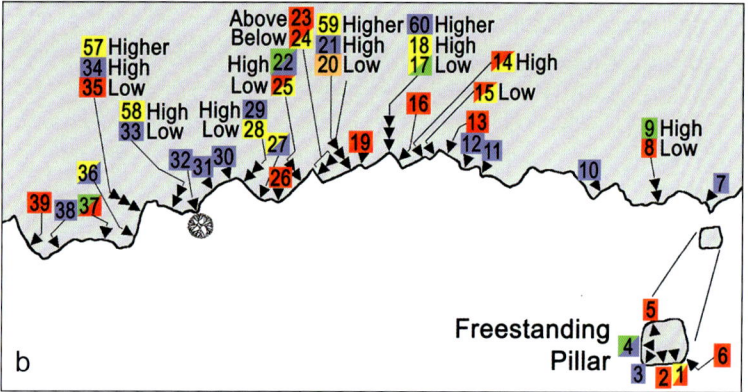
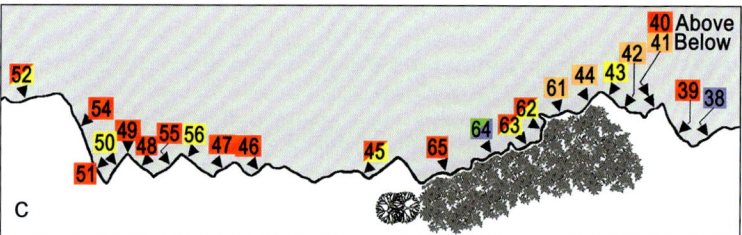

Figure 7. Spedis Creek: (a) Map showing overall distribution of art styles. Detail map views of eastern (b) and western (c) portions of the main site area identify styles and vertical distributions of numbered panels.

This pillar thus shows a microcosm of the interrelation and interaction of the art at the site, repeated multiple times across its entire extent (Figure 7). Large, prominent panels have the most detailed art, much of it Yakima Polychrome, apparently created by shamans for public view. Often flanking these detailed images are smaller, monochromatic panels showing images related to shamanic visions, or simpler vision quest art of the lay person. Many of these latter figures are in low places, beneath small overhangs, or in somewhat hidden niches.

Along the cliff in the Eastern half of the site, the largest panels display Yakima Polychrome imagery and appear to be the primary focus of the art. Occurring in the most prominent locations, and associated with the many looted burials[3] found in this area, this appears to be mortuary art marking spiritually sacred locations used for disposal of the dead. Whether it was the physical location itself, or the fact that burials were interred there and commemorated, this Yakima Polychrome art seemed to then attract additional shamanic art as well as vision quest art, apparently painted both by shamans and lay people on nearby panels. References to exactly this practice—the contemporaneous use of cliffs with Yakima Polychrome images as both a place for shaman's curing/mortuary art and a place for vision quests—were recorded for the Cowiche Creek site, near the city of Yakima. Paintings on this cliff were attributed to shamans' visions of their spirit helpers, and imagery from the site was said to be used in their curing and mortuary ceremonies, but children would be left at this same cliff to have their visions (Bagley 1930:120; Hines 1992:106, 1993:103–104). In fact, a local tribal member told one of us that his initial vision was obtained as a child at a site dominated by Yakima Polychrome style imagery that he later learned was associated with mortuary rituals.

The few Columbia River Conventionalized images found at the site are all associated with Yakima Polychrome art. This supports the previously noted association between these two styles (Hann et al. 2010:13–15; Keyser 1992:94; Keyser et al. 2004:63), and reinforces the notion that both were primarily shamanic art. It seems to us that these different styles may well have served just slightly different functions. This is supported by the fact that the nearby Atlatl Valley site (45KL58) shows essentially the same overall pattern as at Spedis Creek, but the imagery there is primarily Columbia River Conventionalized style, with only a few Yakima Polychrome style motifs scattered among the numerous panels.

Columbia River Conventionalized art is often associated with mythological images. Recognizable mythic figures such as Swallowing Monster, Owl, Land Monster, She Who Watches, and Cannibal Woman have been identified in the region's rock art (Curtis 1911:ii, 145–146; Hann et al. 2010:15–18; Kaiser 2017; Keyser 1992:88–89; Keyser and Poetschat 2004:122–126; Keyser et al. 2006:19–23, 2008:66–69; McClure 1979; Strong et al. 1930:136; Strong and Schenck 1925:85). We suggest that two such mythic figures can be identified at Spedis Creek. Repeated images of a Columbia River Conventionalized style bird's head are found at the site (Figure 8). The largest and most striking of these occurs on the freestanding pillar at the east end of the site (Figures 6 and 8a). Another very similar image was illustrated by Mark Heddon (1956), reportedly near the western end of the site (Figure 8b). Heddon, who conducted a broad-scale survey of rock art in the area surrounding The Dalles in 1956, did an intensive examination of the Spedis Creek site and provided a relatively accurate record of some of the rock art located there. While some of his panel descriptions can be quite confusing, and a few of his specific locations and descriptions are notably vague, his illustrations of individual images have proven to be relatively quite accurate. Unfortunately, he located and recorded this second bird image, which he specifically related to the larger, more complex version on Panel 4, on a "secondary" examination of the site, noting that it had been "overlooked in first survey" (Heddon 1956:72, 73). Using his description of its location (in relation to known panels and images that we had relocated with certainty), we made a concerted effort to find this image during three separate site visits, but we were unsuccessful. Nonetheless, given the fidelity of his other recordings, we believe that this image was originally at the site, and we have included it in our report. We cannot explain why it can no longer be located.

The third bird head image is recognized as part of a composition consisting of two front-view human figures with multiple overhead rayed arcs standing next to a therianthrope drawn as a profile human with a bird's head (Figure 8c). This figure has bent knees and a long sash or tail trailing behind and holds a long, vertically-oriented object out in front of his body in both hands. It has a large eye in the open head and a down-curving beak. While the beak does not spiral in the same form as the other two bird heads at the site, it does conform to other bird images found nearby (Figure 9).

Traditional Northwest Coast iconography would identify these bird heads as Thunderbird. In Northwest Coast tradition art Thunderbird (Figure 10) is dif-

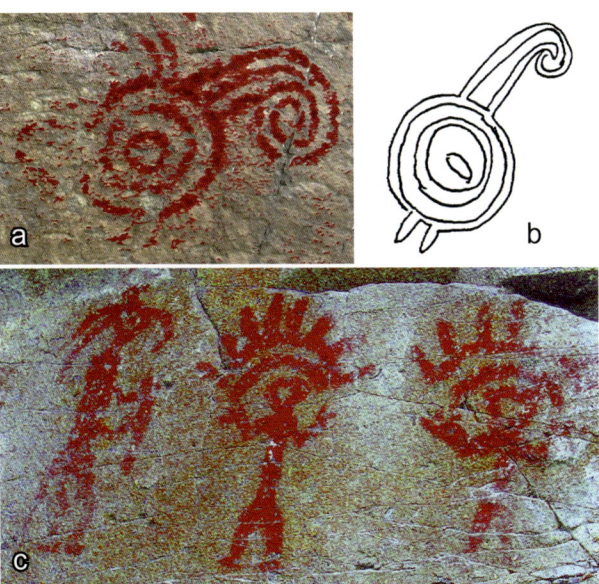

Figure 8 Spedis Creek bird images. (a) Bird head on Panel 4, DStretch YRE+FLT+HM combined with original image; (b) Bird head (not currently located), illustrated in Heddon (1956); (c) Bird-headed therianthrope in composition with two rayed arc human figures, Panel 28, DStretch enhancement YRD.

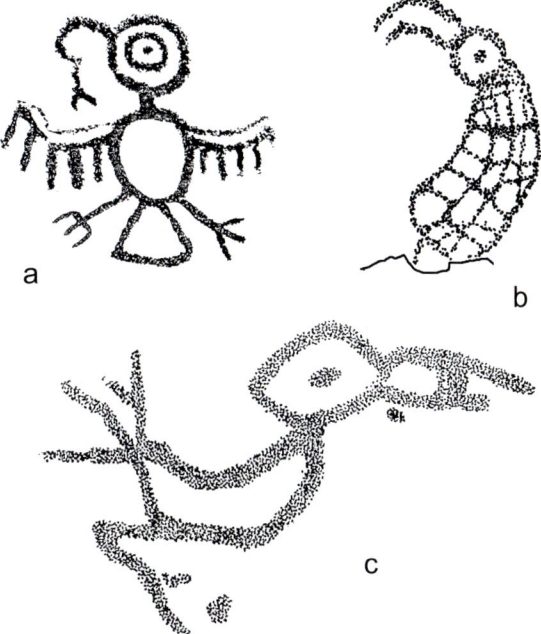

Figure 9. Columbia River Conventionalized bird images. (a, b) Petroglyph Canyon (45KL87); (c) Site 45KL1196 (see Keyser et al. 2008).

ferentiated from other birds by its recurved beak, and two curved appendages coming from its head (Stewart 1979:65–67). The two unattached heads clearly depict this recurved beak, but lack the curved rearward-extending appendages. The therianthrope has two long head appendages and the recurved beak. However, unlike the coast and the plains where great storms frequently occurred and Thunderbird was a prominent figure, Thunderbird is not a common mythic character in mid-Columbia River tales. Eagle and Raven, on the other hand, often appear. While being strongly influenced by the art of the Northwest Coast, the Columbia River Conventionalized style incorporates local variation in depiction and subject matter. Lacking further specific diagnostic elements, the depictions at Spedis could be any of these birds. However, these three bird images in such proximity to one another presumably depict the same mythic avian.

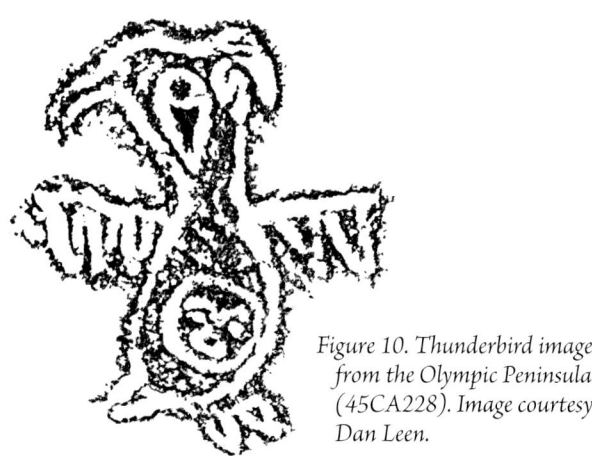

Figure 10. Thunderbird image from the Olympic Peninsula (45CA228). Image courtesy Dan Leen.

Raven is often depicted as a doctor in mythic tales, where he is asked to heal people (Sapir 1909:12–13, 149). Healing and mortuary practices were related functions of shamans. Along the Columbia River, Indian doctors and their assistants also used time-beating sticks in healing ceremonies. With these instruments, they kept time by pounding on a plank (Sapir 1909:180–181) or on the underside of a plank house ceiling (Strong 1901). While one might argue that such an activity could account for the therianthropic image and the object it is holding, one key defining feature of Raven in Northwest Coast art is its straight beak (Stewart 1979:57), and the object being carried by the bird-headed man is neither held like a drumstick (or pounding implement) nor does it appear long enough to touch the ceiling of a plank house.

Instead, it seems more likely to us that this figure could be identified as Eagle, which is generally shown with a curved beak and could easily be confused with Thunderbird (Stewart 1979:54). The main difference is the occurrence of curled appendages extending from the rear of the head of this figure. But such appendages appear to be symbols of spirit power (Stewart 1979:65) and occur on other, non-bird, images in the Columbia River Conventionalized style (Keyser et al. 2008:47-48). Thus, we feel that they might well have been painted here on a bird that was not intended to represent Thunderbird.

A tale which may account for this image is the story of Eagle and Coyote's visit to the world of ghosts (Sapir 1909:107–117):

In this tale, the wives and sons of Eagle and Coyote died. Eagle avows that he knows where the dead go and asserts they can retrieve them. They then travelled to a great river and Eagle blew his flute while saying, "Look across yonder. You will behold the (ghost) people." Despite Eagle blowing his flute numerous times, Coyote could not see the Ghost people. Eventually Eagle carries Coyote over the water where they meet the dead. During their visit to the land of the dead, Coyote kills *Nikciamtca'c* (the one who kills people and traps their souls in the land of the dead). Then Coyote and Eagle place their wives and sons in a box and head back toward the land of the living. However, despite warnings, Coyote opens the box and the wives' and sons' spirits escape, dooming future spirits to forever remain in the land of the dead, instead of returning each fall and spring.

The association with Eagle and his ability to see and travel to the land of the dead seems metaphorically appropriate to a site such as Spedis Creek, which has such prominent mortuary associations. Even the image itself lends credence to this proposed relationship. The object depicted in the hands of the therianthrope is carried much like a flute would be—and is strikingly reminiscent of Kokopelli and his instrument (Slifer 2016). The painting itself could easily be seen as Eagle metaphorically sharing his vision through the playing of his flute.

Although there are very few superimpositions at Spedis Creek, the location of the two primary styles in the eastern half of the site suggests that the Central Columbia Plateau style is later in that area than the Yakima Polychrome paintings. Most Central Columbia Plateau style art in the area from Panel 39 to the east[4] seems to be painted near larger panels of Yakima Polychrome pictographs, but the simple red pictographs do not overlap the polychrome images. Instead, the smaller vision quest art clusters on irregular stone surfaces near or surrounding the large Yakima Polychrome images, which are placed on smooth primary rock faces that make ideal rock art canvases. While the lack of superimpositions fails to offer direct evidence of the sequence, such a structural relationship suggests that the vision quest art likely came later, attracted by the larger images which were already painted on the best surfaces.

Along the western half of the site, from Panel 44 to the west the situation is completely different. In this area, panels are far more widely scattered, and there are only single Yakima Polychrome and Columbia River Conventionalized images (adjacent images on the same panel). Instead, all images along the western end of the site (except these two) are simple red pictographs of anthropomorphs, animals, and geometric motifs. These appear in relatively low places on the cliff face, and two-thirds of the panels in this part of the site have five or fewer images. Even though there are just 26 percent of the total number of panels in this area, they contain 40 percent of the anthropomorphs and 60 percent of the animals. In short, all the art in the western half of the site appears to be associated with vision questing, and the panels are quite similar in structure and motifs to the art at Harris Canyon, though there are many more individual images at Spedis Creek. These images vary in complexity, but the simplest ones (like those at Harris Canyon) are interspersed with slightly more complex renderings, on neighboring panels or even the same panel. This slightly exacerbates the difficulty in differentiating between lay person's and shaman's vision quest art.

The similarity of the motifs and co-occurrence of images of shamanic and lay people's vision quest art in this part of the site indicate how flexible and adaptable these images can be. Both shamans and laypersons use essentially the same restricted suite of imagery. Shamans tend to combine these into more complex compositions, to use more forms in a single composition, and to use somewhat larger forms in any one composition. So often, on a single panel, a shaman's vision quest composition will be a large series of zigzags with rays and multiple human figures, while what we interpret as a lay person's vision image will be a small person with a rayed arc, a human with an animal, or a pair of humans with a zigzag line or a series of tally marks (Figure 11).

While shamans contacted the spirits on a more regular basis, the evidence suggests to us that the recording of their initial vision (or simpler visions later in life) shared a common visual vocabulary—as well as location—with the visions of lay people. In these instances, differentiating between the two origins of vision quest art is simply a matter of degree. This suggests that for many figures their differences may be more a result of modern classification schema and they might not have been seen as significantly different to the culture who created them.

So, it appears that there were two main foci for the art at Spedis Creek. The Eastern half is focused on Mortuary and other Shamanic art, which attracted some vision quest art as well. In contrast, the Western half appears solely devoted to vision questing, though some of the imagery could have been painted by shamans to commemorate their visions. In terms of the different functions for the two parts of the site, it may be significant that the far Western panels have a clear view of Mt. Hood at sundown. Mt. Hood was a powerful symbol in Columbia Plateau mythology, and one that figured importantly in vision questing. Likewise, sunset was a particularly sacred time of day (Keyser and Whitley 2000:15).

New Discoveries

As this is the first major study to investigate a site with Yakima Polychrome as the primary rock art component we have recognized new things about the style through assessing the content and placement of the images at Spedis Creek. One of the traits of Yakima Polychrome was thought that it was "rarely drawn at the smaller 'private' sites and never in small niches or nooks" (Keyser et al. 2004:63). Likewise, the images were said to generally be drawn high up a surface so people would have to look up at them (Keyser et al. 2004; Wood-

Figure 11. Panel 53. Humans juxtaposed with animals in typical layperson's vision quest composition, contrasted with the complex geometrics which typify the art of a shaman's vision. DStretch YRD.

ward 1982). But while many Yakima Polychrome images fit these characteristics, Yakima Polychrome art at Spedis Creek frequently occurs at or near the former ground level. For instance, numerous examples, while still relatively large, were drawn low to the ground or in little nooks, where they were not easily viewed. This seems due to their association with the now-looted burials along the base of the cliff. Some of these images are directly above looted graves and must have been at ground level before the interments were disturbed.

In general, Yakima Polychrome art is arresting in both size and color. It draws the viewer's attention and inspires awe, even without an understanding of the meaning behind it. However, the impact on the viewer aware of its cultural implications, including its strong color symbolism, the fact that it memorialized the dead, and perhaps also that it served as a permeable boundary between this world and the next, would have been remarkable.

Typically placed high on the cliff, this striking art looms over the viewer more than any other Columbia Plateau tradition style, perhaps with the exception of some Columbia River Conventionalized style images. From ethnography, we know that Yakima Polychrome was a monumental art style, intended to commemorate and assist the passage of the dead, while inspiring and consoling the living. Being so spiritually powerful, we propose that the art was placed both on prominent panels for the living to witness, but also low to the ground, directly above these graves, to assist the dead.

Surprisingly, no unquestionable depictions of the Yakima Star motif are found at this site. There are two conjoined diamond shaped images on Panel 52, and a third star-shaped image on Panel 4 that could be interpreted as Yakima Stars if one adopted a very broad definition. However, all three of these would be atypical, since they lack the clearly defined central circle, and have only a ragged void in their center. Likewise, instead of broad triangular arms, each possesses narrow arms that hardly taper. Finally, at other sites, the motif is found only as petroglyphs or white pictographs, so these would be the only known red painted examples. Thus, we have not classified these as Yakima Stars. The two linked Panel 52 images have been classified, along with several other pairs of circular images, as "eyes" and the Panel 4 image as a cross.

Since the Yakima Star is a frequent component of Yakima Polychrome art, the motif's absence cannot be readily explained at this site, especially since examples are found at several nearby sites, including Atlatl Valley (45KL58). Perhaps the star is a component of the Yakima Polychrome art style that had some other function not directly associated with mortuary practices. Further research might shed light on this issue.

But, at Spedis Creek, we identified two previously unrecognized motifs associated with the Yakima Polychrome style. While they had been illustrated in a past report (Loring and Loring 1982:52–54,75; Woodward 1982:51, 72–76), they had not previously been recognized as repeated motifs that likely relate specifically to shamanic mortuary practices. The first of these is the spiral. While arcs and circles, frequently rayed, have long been recognized as primary Yakima Polychrome style components, spirals had not previously been noted as a repeated motif on the Columbia Plateau. Four spirals occur at Spedis Creek, three of which are rayed (Figure 12a, b). One rayed example is also a red and white polychrome. While now submerged beneath the backfill of the dams on the Columbia, a further example has been recognized in an illustration of the art at John Day Bar (Loring and Loring 1982:75) (Figure 12c).

Figure 12. Spirals. (a) Tracing of Panel 21; (b) Panel 27, DStretch LRE; (c) John Day Bar, adapted from Loring and Loring (1982).

Spirals on the Columbia Plateau may have escaped scrutiny due to their relative scarcity; however, they are common in Northwest Coast rock art (Keyser and Poetschat 2012:56; Lundy 1974:211–212). The Columbia River Conventionalized Style, often found in conjunction with Yakima Polychrome art, shows strong Northwest Coast artistic influences (Keyser 1992:96–97; Lundy 1974:272–277), and the appearance of the spiral may be further indication of this connection. All the spirals found at Columbia River sites are associated with circles and arcs (sometimes rayed), as well as human figures. Whether the spiral motif was intended to convey a different meaning than the numerous concentric circles found at the site is unknown, but it should now be recognized as a component of the Yakima Polychrome style.

Likewise, another newly recognized motif at Spedis Creek is the masted rainbow arc (Figure 13). Clearly occurring three times at the site, this motif has a tall, slender "mast" protruding directly upward out of the top of a rainbow motif formed of concentric arcs. All examples are polychrome, with a solid red half-circle topped by multiple arcs, either all white or alternating red and white in different arrangements. The mast is also polychrome, with a red base and a white top.

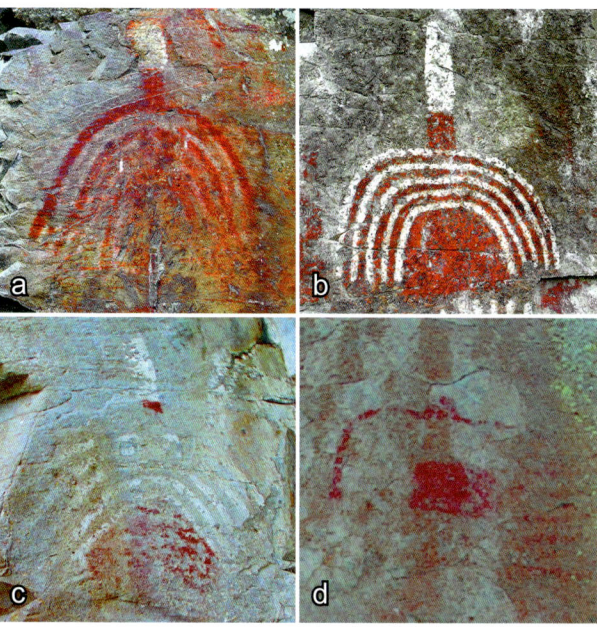

Figure 13. Masted Rainbow Arcs at Spedis Creek. (a) Panel 11, DStretch LDS; (b) Panel 33, DStretch YRD; (c) Panel 34, DStretch YRD; (d) Panel 12, DStretch LRE.

A probable fourth example at the site is very faded, seen primarily through the use of DStretch enhancement (Figure 13d). However, while this image has the central red half circle and knob-like protuberance rising from what would have been the uppermost arc, it lacks the long vertical extension typical of the mast. We suspect that the white pigment that likely completed this image is fugitive and we now only see the remaining red pigment, which itself is extremely faded. The number of white arcs that might have been painted between the red central half circle and the topmost arc is conjectural. Likewise, the relationship of the image and the horizontal rays along its right side cannot be clearly determined. Possibly the right half of the motif was rayed, but it is equally likely that this is some sort of superimposition. Demonstrating which of these alternatives is the case is impossible at present.

Three other masted rainbow arcs have been recognized in this area and there are two additional images that may represent the same motif. Two of the verifiable examples of this motif (Figure 14a) occur at the Upper Spearfish site (45KL90) and are illustrated in Woodward (1982:51). Painted side by side, both are composed of white rays. In one case the rays surmount a red center, but the center of the second example is apparently lost to erosion. Both have the typical mast, although the white top of one is either missing or was not sufficiently visible to have been recorded. The other clear example (Figure 14b) is also illustrated in Woodward (1982:91). Unfortunately, he does not identify the site, but through context it appears to be in the Wishram area. It shows a multicolored arc with a red center, red and white arcs, and is topped with a red mast. As above, it is possible that the white portion of the mast was not observed due to fugitive pigment. Additionally, both of these sites contain other typical Yakima Polychrome imagery whose motifs are nearly identical to those at Spedis Creek.

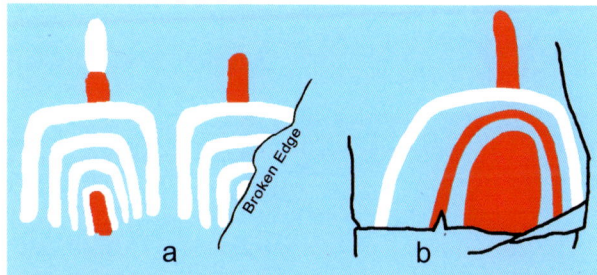

Figure 14. Other Masted Rainbow Arcs in The Dalles area rock art. (a) Upper Spearfish (Woodward 1982); (b) Unknown site (Woodward 1982).

Two other "possible" examples further upstream on the Columbia River must be mentioned, because they are illustrated in the literature. The first one, more than 300 km upstream at Picture Rocks Bay (45KT11), located in the Vantage site complex, is now submerged beneath the waters behind Wanapum Dam. This figure is part of a large site containing many Yakima Polychrome images including numerous red and white rayed arcs and circles among others. Drawings of the site made by Harold Cundy in 1936, show one possible masted arc (Layman 2002:36), depicted as a tall column rising above a single red spoked arc without accompanying white pigment. The authors contacted Bill Layman, who published the illustration, and were directed to historical photographs of the panel in the Wenatchee Valley Museum and Cultural Center. Though black and white, these images clearly show a red and white polychrome rainbow arc seemingly topped with a vertical mast-like appendage. However, upon further careful examination of all existing photographs we concluded that the "mast" illustrated by Cundy was an artifact of a superimposition, since lines in the same orientation extend below the arc as well. Unless better photographs can be obtained, the relationship of this image to those near The Dalles remains unclear.

The second possible example is a petroglyph at the Roosevelt site (Figure 15), now under the backwaters of John Day Dam on the Columbia River about 70 km upstream from Spedis Creek. Illustrated in Loring and Loring (1982:118), this image shows an arc with a single line emerging from its top. However, as illustrated, it is neither a rainbow arc nor a polychrome pictograph. In the absence of photographs, we cannot verify if it is related to this motif.

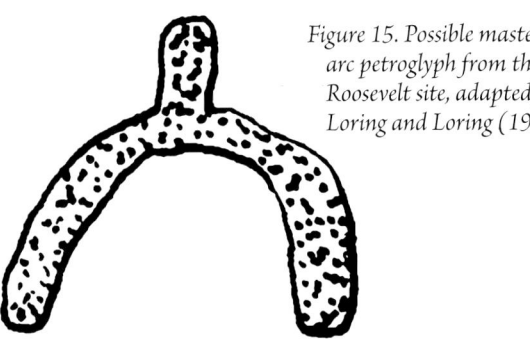

Figure 15. Possible masted arc petroglyph from the Roosevelt site, adapted from Loring and Loring (1982).

So, in summary, the masted rainbow arc motif occurs in conjunction with Yakima Polychrome images at three relatively closely clustered sites in The Dalles area. Two other published images, at far distant sites, which have limited formal similarity may be related but this cannot be demonstrated with the available evidence. The association with other Yakima Polychrome art strongly reinforces the connection of this masted arc motif to mortuary rituals, and its repeated use with just enough variation to suggest that examples were painted by several different artists implies that it had a specific meaning. Unfortunately, the absence of references to this motif in the ethnographic record suggests that the meaning of this image is apparently lost.

Conclusion

Detailed comparison of Harris Canyon and Spedis Creek highlights some of the differences between a complex multipurpose site and a simpler vision quest location. However, it also confirms the consistency of the rock art associated with Columbia Plateau vision questing, by both shamans and lay people. Examination of differing art styles at a single site also gives insight into how these images are interrelated. Additional multi-site and intra-site comparisons will undoubtedly reveal further information concerning the structure and purpose of Columbia Plateau rock art.

Acknowledgments. The authors thank Jack Lafond for introducing us to the Harris Canyon site. Andy Kallinen facilitated research at Spedis Creek and provided boat transport to the site. Becky Steed, Sue Ann Jansen, David Minick, George Poetschat, Mike Taylor, Carson Hertler, and Jon Harmon assisted with site recording. François Gohier and Jean Clottes each provided photographs for us to use in our analysis. Dan Leen graciously permitted use of the Thunderbird rubbing in Figure 10. Bill Layman helped us to obtain source material for the 45KT11 image and the Wenatchee Valley Museum and Cultural Center for the photograph of that figure. The Oregon Archaeological Society funded the project through a Loring Grant.

Notes

1. All 18 images at Harris Canyon are pictographs, as are the overwhelming majority of the more than 350 images at Spedis Creek, where we recorded only two petroglyphs.

2. Elsewhere referred to as the Long Narrows Style (Keyser 1992) or the Dalles Style (Hill and Hill 1974).

3. Two burials at the site were professionally excavated in 1924 (McClure 1984:55; Strong et al., 1930:10, 18–19), but numerous others were looted both before and after that date until the 1970s. Keyser has been visiting the site since the mid-1980s and has not noted any obvious new looting since his initial visit.

4. A single outlier with one Yakima Polychrome style image adjacent to one Columbia River Conventionalized style image occurs at Panel 64 approximately 10 meters west, where the associated Central Columbia Plateau rock art interacts in a similar fashion.

References Cited

Bagley, Clarence B.
   1930 *Indian Myths of the Northwest*. Lowman & Hanford, Seattle, Washington.

Cline, Walter
   1938 Religion and World View. In *The Sinkaietk or Southern Okanagon of Washington*, edited by Leslie Spier, pp. 133–182. General Series in Anthropology 6. Menasha, Wisconsin.

Clottes, Jean and David Lewis-Williams
   1998 *The Shamans of Prehistory*. Harry N. Abrams, New York.

Curtis, Edward S.
   1911 *The North American Indian*. Volume 8. Plimpton Press, Norwood, Massachusetts.

Hann, Don, James D. Keyser, and Phillip Cash Cash
   2010 Columbia Plateau Rock Art: A Window to the Sprit World. In *Rock Art of the Oregon Country – Honoring the Lorings' Legacy*, edited by James D. Keyser and George Poetschat, pp. 1–24. Oregon Archaeological Society Press, Publication 18, Portland.

Heddon, Mark
　1956 Petroglyphs of the Dalles Area. Unpublished Manuscript on file with the Oregon Archaeological Society, Portland.

Hill, Beth, and Ray Hill
　1974 *Indian Petroglyphs of the Pacific Northwest*. University of Washington Press, Seattle.

Hines, Donald M.
　1992 *Ghost Voices: Yakima Indian Myths, Legends, Humor, and Hunting Stories*. Great Eagle Publishing, Issaquah, Washington.
　1993 *Magic in the Mountains, The Yakima Shaman: Power and Practice*. Great Eagle Publishing, Issaquah, Washington.

Kaiser, David A.
　2010 Tunnel Vision: The Rayed Arc Motif in Columbia Plateau Rock Art Interpreted as Transitional Entoptic Imagery. In *Rock Art of the Oregon Country – Honoring the Lorings' Legacy*, edited by James D. Keyser and George Poetschat, pp. 25–34. Oregon Archaeological Society Press, Publication 18, Portland.
　2017 Cannibal Woman on the Columbia—Exploring a Mythological Motif. In *American Indian Rock Art*, Volume 43 edited by Ken Hedges and Mark Calamia, pp.1–9. American Rock Art Research Association, Glendale, Arizona.

Keyser, James D.
　1992 *Indian Rock Art of the Columbia Plateau*. University of Washington Press, Seattle.

Keyser, James D., and George Poetschat
　2004 The Canvas as Art: Landscape Analysis of the Rock Art Panel. In *The Figured Landscapes of Rock-Art: Looking at Pictures in Place*, edited by Christopher Chippindale and George Nash, pp. 118–130. Cambridge University Press, Cambridge.
　2012 *Clan Crests and Shamans' Masks: Petroglyphs in Southeast Alaska*. Indigenous Cultures Preservation Society, Portland, Oregon.

Keyser, James D., George Poetschat, and Michael W. Taylor
　2006 *Talking With the Past: The Ethnography of Rock Art*. Oregon Archaeological Society Press, Publication 16, Portland.

Keyser, James D., George Poetschat, Phillip Minthorn Cash Cash, Don Hann, Helen Hiczun, Roz Malin, Carol Pedersen, Cathy Poetschat, and Betty Tandberg
　1998 *Columbia Plateau Rock Art, The Butte Creek Sites: Steiwer Ranch and Rattlesnake Shelter*. Oregon Archaeological Society Press, Publication 11, Portland.

Keyser, James D., Michael W. Taylor, and George Poetschat
　2004 *Echoes of the Ancients: Rock Art of the Dalles-Deschutes Region*. Oregon Archaeological Society Press, Publication 14, Portland.

Keyser, James D., Michael W. Taylor, George Poetschat, and David A. Kaiser
　2008 *Visions in the Mist: The Rock Art of Celilo Falls*. Oregon Archaeology Society Press, Publication 17, Portland.

Keyser, James D., and David S. Whitley
　2000 A New Ethnographic Reference for Columbia Plateau Rock Art: Documenting A Century of Vision Quest Practices. *INORA (International Newsletter On Rock Art)* 25:14–20.
　2006 Sympathetic Magic in Western North American Rock Art. *American Antiquity* 71(1):3–26.

Layman, William D.
　2002 *Native River*. Washington State University Press, Pullman.

Lerman, Norman
　1954 Okanogan (Salish) Ehtnography. Field Notes and Manuscript, Melville Jacobs Collection, University of Washington Library Archives, Seattle.

Lewis-Williams, J. David
　2002a *A Cosmos In Stone*. Alta Mira Press, Walnut Creek, California.
　2002b *The Mind in the Cave*. Thames and Hudson, London.

Loring, J. Malcom, and Louise Loring
　1982 *Pictographs and Petroglyphs of the Oregon Country: Part 1: Columbia River and Northern Oregon*. Monograph XXI, University of California, Los Angeles

Lundy, Doris
　1974 *The Rock Art of the Northwest Coast*. Master of Arts Thesis, Department of Archaeology, Simon Fraser University, Burnaby, British Columbia.
　1983 Styles of Coastal Rock Art. In *Indian Art Traditions of the Northwest Coast*, edited by Roy L. Carson, pp. 89–97. Archaeology Press, Simon Fraser University, Burnaby, British Columbia.

McClure, Richard H., Jr.
　1979 The Tsagiglalal Motif in Rock Art of the Lower Columbia River. In *American Indian Rock Art, Volume 5*, edited by Frank G. Bock, Ken Hedges, Georgia Lee, and Helen Michaelis, pp. 173-189. American Rock Art Research Association, El Toro, California.
　1984 *Rock Art of The Dalles-Deschutes Region: A Chronological Perspective*. Master of Arts Thesis, Washington State University, Pullman.

Minick, David L., and James D. Keyser
　2018 Seeing is Finding: The Value of DStretch for Recording Columbia River Rock Art at Spedis Creek and Harris Canyon. In *American Indian Rock Art, Volume 44*, edited by David A. Kaiser and James D. Keyser, pp. 29-44. American Rock Art Research Association, San Jose, California.

Oregonian
　1916 Indian Tells Story of City Hall Rock. *The Oregonian*, Monday, January 24, page 3.

Sapir, Edward
　1909 Wishram Texts. In *Publications of the American Ethnological Society, Volume 2*, edited by Franz Boas, pp. 1–235. Late E. J. Brill, Leyden, Holland.

Siegel, Ronald K.
　1977 Hallucinations. *Scientific American* 237:132–140.

Slifer, Dennis
　2016 *Kokopelli: The Magic, Mirth, and Mischief of an Ancient Symbol*. Gibbs Smith, Layton, Utah.

Spier, Leslie, and Edward Sapir
　1930 Wishram Ethnography. *University of Washington Publications in Anthropology* 3(3):151–300, Seattle.

Stewart, Hilary
　1979 *Looking at Indian Art of the Northwest Coast*. Douglas and McIntyre, Seattle.

Strong, Thomas N.
　1901 How the Indians Were Decimated. *The Oregonian Newspaper*, Sunday, November 17, page 32.

Strong, William Duncan, and W. Egbert Schenck
　1925 Petroglyphs near the Dalles of the Columbia River. *American Anthropologist* 27(1):76–90.

Strong, William Duncan, W. Egbert Schenck, and Julian H. Steward
  1930 *Archaeology of the Dalles-Deschutes Region.* University of California Press, Berkeley.

Taylor, Michael W., James D. Keyser, and Phillip Cash Cash
  2008 The Role of Women in Columbia Plateau Rock Art. In *American Indian Rock Art, Volume 34,* edited by James D. Keyser, David A. Keyser, George Poetschat, and Michael W. Taylor, pp. 133–154. American Rock Art Research Association, Tucson, Arizona.

Teit, James A.
  1906 The Lillooet Indians. *Publications of the Jesup North Pacific Expedition* Part 2, No. 5. Memoirs of the American Museum of Natural History 4(5). G. E. Stechert & Co., New York.
  1930 The Salishan Tribes of the Western Plateau. *Bureau of American Ethnology Annual Report* 45:23–396.

Whitley, David S.
  2000 *The Art of the Shaman.* University of Utah Press, Salt Lake City.

Woodward, John A.
  1982 *The Ancient Painted Images of the Columbia Gorge.* Acoma Books, Ramona, California.

Exploring the Use of an Idaho Cave by an Antelope Charmer

Carolynne L. Merrell

Numerous references in ethnographic literature describe the specialized role of an antelope shaman or charmer in antelope hunting procedures by the indigenous peoples of the Great Plains, Great Basin, and the southwestern United States. One cave at the base of the Lemhi Range in south-central Idaho contains pictographs related to ritual activity, artifacts, and physical remains of antelope origin. A detailed investigation is building a connection between what is described in the literature, the archaeological contents of the cave, and the cave's pictographs. Scientific analysis of hair, bone, and fiber objects, coupled with a unique interior surface coating of the cave, strongly suggests that this location may have, at one time, been used by someone who possessed unique powers for procuring antelope.

Research on the communal procurement of antelope has contributed substantially to supporting the case that an Idaho cave, 10BT1, was a place where an antelope charmer prepared mentally, physically, and spiritually to lead a successful communal hunt.

Antelope Characteristics

The North American antelope is correctly called a pronghorn (Figure 1). The North American pronghorn (*Antilocapra americana*) is the surviving member of a group of animals that evolved in North America during the past

Figure 1. North American antelope, Antilocapra americana *(courtesy naturespicsonline, Wikimedia Commons public domain license).*

Carolynne L. Merrell
Archaeographics
Hamilton, Montana

20 million years. It is not a true antelope. The use of the term "antelope" seems to have originated when the first written description of the animal was made during the 1804–1806 Lewis and Clark Expedition. Pronghorn are the fastest mammal in the Americas and are able to run at a sustained speed of over 60 miles per hour. The pronghorn has true horns, similar to bison and bighorn sheep. The horns are made of modified, fused hair that grows over permanent bony cores, but they differ from those of other horned animals in two major ways: the sheaths are shed and grown every year and they are pronged on the male (National Park Service 2017). Pronghorns form herds in late fall until late spring. The coat consists of hollow hairs. The males have a dark throat patch; females do not (Coffman 1973:23). They rarely jump or leap like deer; when confined, they will run in circles until exhausted. They have keen eyesight, are extremely curious, and have a sense of smell for their own kind for over a mile. Because some of these characteristics presented a challenge to hunting the animals, the early cultures secured the talents of a specialist who had the ability to manipulate the antelope's behavior to ensure a successful hunt.

These characteristics influenced the methods needed to successfully hunt antelope in greater numbers than a single kill. For the aboriginal groups of the Great Basin and Great Plains, pronghorn were a consistent resource (Lubinski, 1999). In the Great Basin, this animal was the largest game available and was of considerable significance as food and source of material items (Arkush 1986; Steward 1938). Generally, a successful kill of numerous pronghorn involved channeling a herd through a drive line into a circular corral where the animals were run to exhaustion and killed by clubbing, or with bow and arrow. Over time, using a person with "magical" skills and knowledge of the pronghorn to lead the hunt was found to ensure a successful drive and kill. The details of preparation by the select person leading to a successful drive varied with each indigenous group, but certain similarities were consistent and were maintained for generations. This changed significantly with the introduction of the horse in the 1700s.

Ethnographic Background

Ethnographies related to pronghorn procurement in the western North America are extensive, with details describing practices by the Hopi, Cheyenne, Northern and Eastern Shoshone, Northern Paiute tribes, and Canadian aboriginal societies, to name a few. Antelope hunting is known from the Washoe to the Eastern Shoshone and involves the singing and hypnotizing power of a medicine man (Hultkrantz 1986:635). The name used for the person with special abilities to bring antelope into a trap or circular corral varied with the culture group. In northern Paiute, he was called tin'a timadaidi or "antelope wonder-worker" (Liljeblad 1986:645). The most common name used is "antelope charmer".

A review of the literature on the subject of antelope shamans or charmers and hunting practices shows the wide range of possibilities for defining the role of an antelope charmer (Fowler 1986; Kelly 1932; Liljeblad 1986; Lowie 1909, 1924 1963; Malouf 1940; Park 1938; Shimkin 1986; Steward 1938, 1941). Malouf (1940) stated that shamans "need to charm the souls of the antelope." Park explains that the preparation for a hunt is highly variable, but the basic belief in the control of the antelope by supernatural means is clear; the success of an antelope drive is dependent upon a ritual performance, which precedes the drive, in which "the shaman, who is the leader of the drive, must have the spirit of the antelope as his source of power....In the spring when food supplies are exhausted, there is often a strong public demand for the antelope shaman to exercise his power" (Park 1938:62, 63). Generally stated, communal antelope hunts were directed by individuals with specific powers over these animals. The shaman, who acquired his power through dreams, "could capture the antelopes' souls…rendering them subservient to his will, and thus bring them into the corral" (Steward 1941:219). Shamans sought control by possessing items touched by or related to the animals, such as sticks broken by antelope, thought to have "antelope essence, which the shaman could activate to influence the animals. In this way, he could cause them to be sympathetic to his desires. They would, then, become willing victims of the hunt" (Pavesic 1993:57). Linea Sundstrom (2000) stated that the ceremonial pronghorn drive of historic times appears to derive from prehistoric practices. The accumulated evidence, including the information reported here supports this statement and suggests practices may date to at least 3500 years ago or more.

Cave 10BT1 Archaeological History

Located in southern Idaho, at the southeastern tip of the Lemhi Range, the limestone solution cave, 10BT1, overlooks the sinks of the Little Lost River (Figure 2). The site is located on the northern fringe of the Great Basin and the western edge of the Great Plains of

Wyoming and Montana. It is in the ancestral domain of the Northern Shoshone and Northern Paiute.

The cave looks south across an alluvial fan to the fertile plain (Figure 3). This plain formerly provided roots, plants and plentiful game for the indigenous people who would have returned to the area in the spring of the year from their winter camps closer to the Snake River.

Figure 2. Location of Cave 10BT1.

Figure 3. View from Cave 10BT1 south across the sinks of the Little Lost River.

Known as the Little Lost River Cave, 10BT1 is one of Idaho's first archaeological sites to be scientifically excavated in 1954 (Butler 1981; Fichter et al. 1955). Another excavation followed in 1990 by Ruth Gruhn (Gruhn and Bryan 1990). This work was followed in 1999 with the rediscovery and recording of the cave's pictographs by Archaeographics (Merrell 2000, 2001). Prior to the first official excavation, this "old Indian Cave," as it was known to locals, was looted of unknown materials and evidence of digging holes continues to be ongoing.

An outstanding natural feature of this cave is a shiny black semi-transparent coating covering the ceiling and much of the walls in the back section of the cave (Figure 4). This coating covers most of the red and yellow ochre pictographs.[1] An analysis of the coating was conducted by Marvin Rowe and Karen Steelman (Steelman et al. 2002), in an effort to identify its properties. In summary, Rowe and Steelman suspected that the residue was due to cooking residues from human activity which was mixed with a naturally occurring geological deposition of calcite, sulfate, chloride, and borate accretion. Rowe and Steelman obtained a ^{14}C date for the coating of 3340 to 990 B.P. This provides a minimum date for the pictographs that lie below the coating.

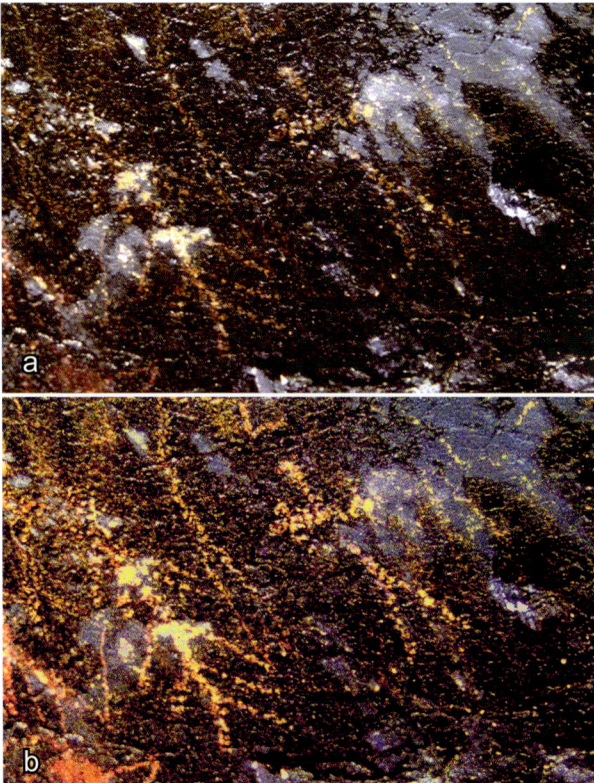

Figure 4. (a) Example of shiny semi-transparent coating over pictographs; (b) DStretch enhancement YBK.

Notes from the 1954 project indicate that the excavations "yielded cultural materials and big game animal bones. Among the latter were the remains of several species of artiodactyls—deer, mountain sheep and antelope, with the last preponderant" (Butler 1981:6). They also stated that deer hair was frequently found mixed with the cultural materials from the excavation. Questioning this identification, several samples of the hair were sent to specialists at Sam Houston State University who have specifically identified the hair as antelope rather than deer. The technology they used for the identification was not available at the time of the 1954 report. At one place in the excavation the 1954 researchers found considerable "deer" (now confirmed to be antelope) hair closely associated with a small ring of juniper bark (Figure 5). The significance of pronghorn hair as it relates to hunting antelope is described for the Cheyenne in Cheyenne Memories (Stands in Timber and Liberty 1967:85), where it describes the ritual of striking the pole of an antelope-hide tipi in an attempt to dislodge some hairs, which would portend a successful hunt.

Figure 5. Dated ring of juniper bark that was found covered with antelope hair.

Samples of both the antelope hair and the ring were tested by Ruth Ann Armitage (Armitage et al. 2012) and ^{14}C dates are 3370 to 3090 B.P. for the juniper ring and 3360 to 3080 B.P. for the hair. These results confirm that the ring and the hair are contemporaneous. Because these were excavated from an undisturbed layer it may be assumed that they were not placed in this relationship by accident but that there may be some significance to them being placed near each other. These dates work well with the dates for the coating determined by Rowe and Steelman.

These dates compare favorably to the dating of the Laidlaw aboriginal antelope trap site in southeastern Alberta at ca. 3280 B.P. reported by Brumley in 1984. Brink (2013) has reported on the Barnett site, another similar aboriginal game trap, in the general vicinity of the Laidlow trap that he believes is within the same time frame. Frison (1991:241–246) also confirms the use of pronghorn traps as early as 3000 years ago based on archaeological data.

Cave 10BT1 Pictographs

The research continues with the study of the pictographs found in the cave and adjacent area. The majority of the pictographs are located on the rear east wall of the cave near the ground. There are also individual images scattered on the ceiling and slanted projections of rock extending from the ceiling throughout the back section of the cave. Most of the art appears drawn with a crayon type stick in either red-orange or yellow ochre (Figure 6). A few may have been painted because they are very smooth and solid in color.

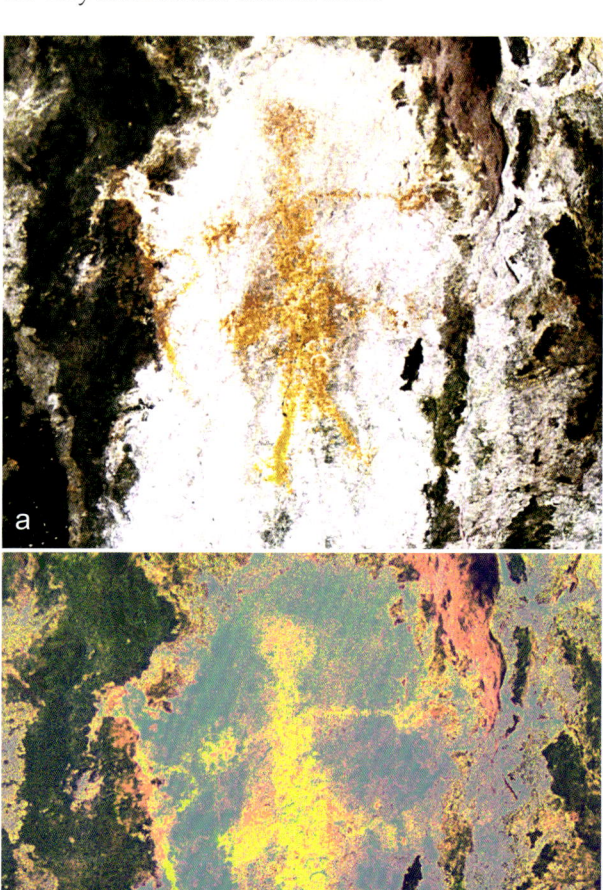

Figure 6. (a) Yellow ochre pictograph of an anthropomorph; (b) DStretch enhancement YBK.

The subject matter varies but there are some very distinct motifs. For example, the only animal shown appears to be an ungulate (Figure 7), likely an antelope. In two cases, a human figure is seen with the animal. One example is found just inside the cave entrance and is not covered with the black coating (Figure 8). The other example is located outside the cave, directly above the opening on the steep cliff facing southeast, next to a small "one person alcove" (Figure 9).

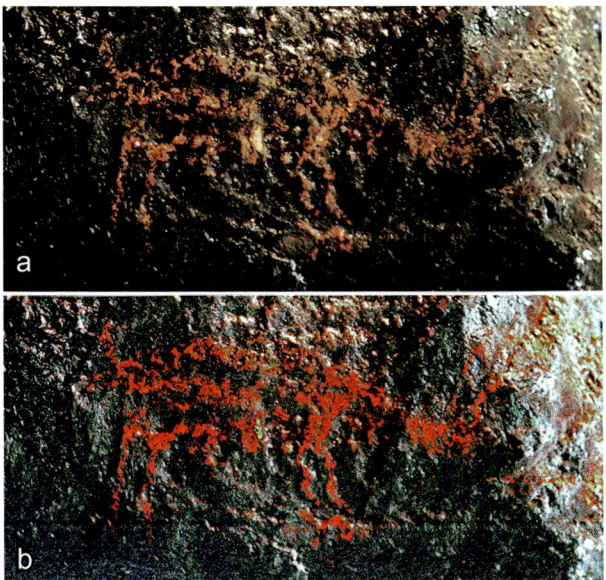

Figure 7. (a) Ungulate pictograph; (b) DStretch enhancement YWE.

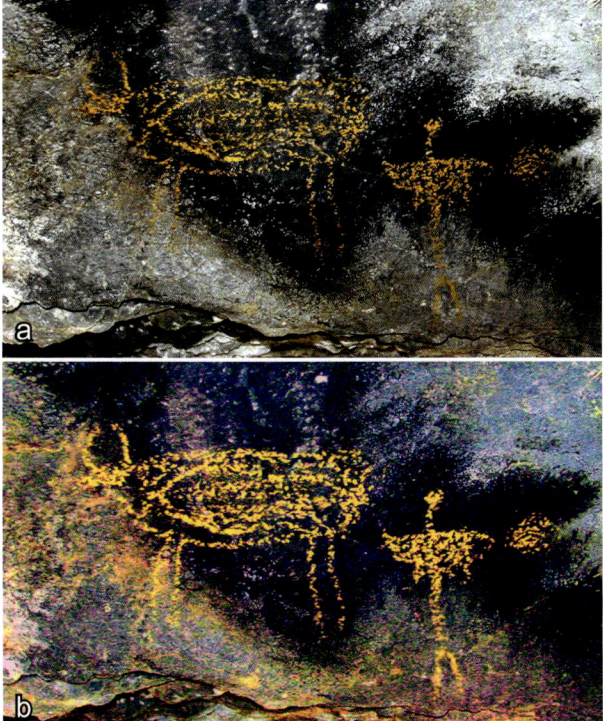

Figure 8. (a) Yellow ochre pictograph showing shamanistic figure driving an ungulate; (b) DStretch enhancement YBK.

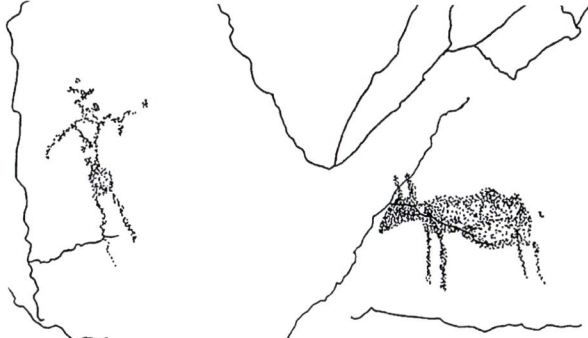

Figure 9. Panel above cave exterior showing shaman confronting an antelope.

Figure 10. Photo of "monolithic" rock located below cave showing how it would be seen in an upright position.

Below the ascent to the cave, one unique pictograph was painted on a monolithic rock that was blown up in the 1970s (Figure 10). In the prehistoric past, the two exterior pictograph panels may have helped further identify the cave as being related to a charmer or shaman.

An interesting observation compares an antelope in the Short Bull winter count (Figure 11) with the image on the monolithic rock. Note the similarity between the bun or bump on the top of the head of the pronghorn with that on the element on the monolithic rock. Does this "bun" hold some special meaning? Perhaps, because it is found not only on the head of the historic ledger art pronghorn, but it is also found on the head of the human seen in the cave (Figure 12) and is a focal point at the end of drive corrals (Figure 13). These interesting similarities call for more study beyond the scope of this paper, but there is the possibility the bun

Figure 11. Antelope figure enlarged and redrawn from the Short Bull winter count ledger (Journey Museum, Rapid City, South Dakota, Courtesy of the U.S. Department of the Interior, Indian Arts and Crafts Board).

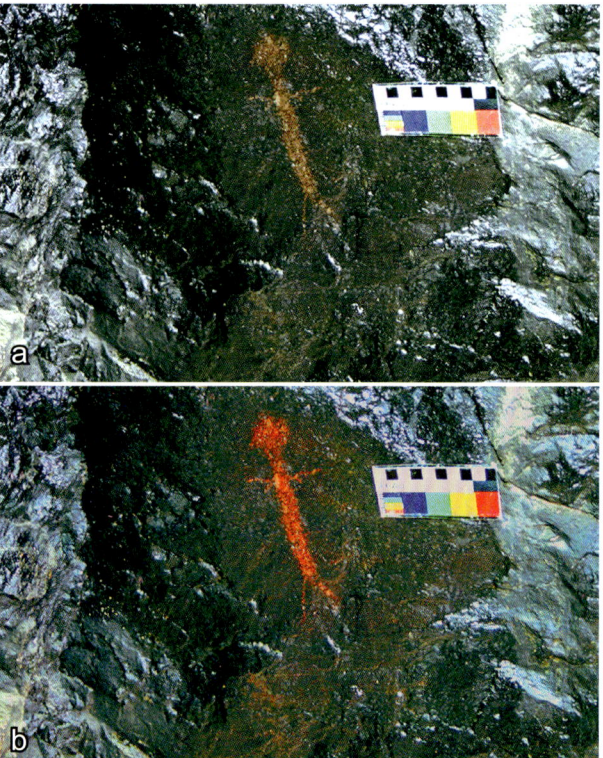

Figure 12. (a) Example of shaman in rear of cave in red ochre covered with transparent coating; (b) DStretch enhancement LAB.

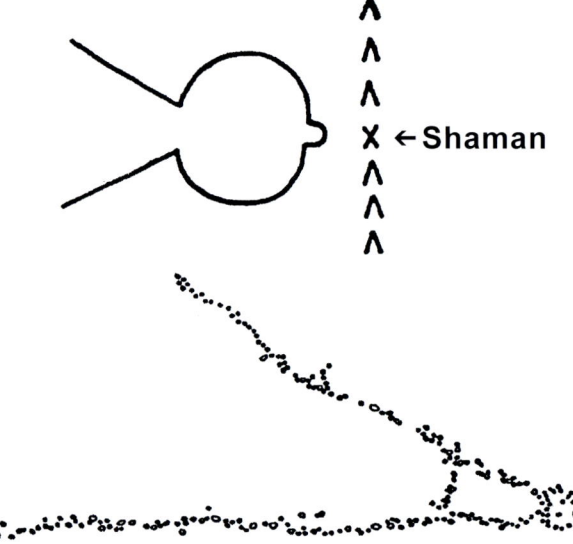

Figure 13. Examples of two corral drives showing circular corral at vertex of the drive: (a) Pronghorn corral, Ruby Valley, Nevada (Steward 1941:Figure 1f); (b) the Laidlaw site trap, Alberta Canada (after Brumley 1984:Figure 32).

or bump demonstrates some spiritual connection between the pronghorn prey and the shaman or charmer who seeks control over the animal.

There are several single stick type anthropomorphs scattered throughout the cave interior. On a lower back section of smooth rock, near the ground, a carefully drawn and painted person is seen under the coating, with a ball shape above and connected to his head (Figure 12), which may represent a shaman with his *mu'gua*. This type of figure is found at other locations in the general vicinity of this cave and throughout the ancestral territory of the Northern Shoshone. I suggest this figure represents a shaman because the ball may be an example of a hair knot, documented in early historic times as being worn only by shamans or medicine persons (Figure 14). This ball may represent the *mu'gua* or soul of the individual as described by Robert Lowie in *The Northern Shoshone* (1909:226). In discussing the soul of a person, Lowie states "the principle of life which departs at death is called mu'gua. During life its seat is in the head." At death, this life principle, *mu'gua*, which resides in the head, rises cloud-fashion to the land of Wolf and Coyote, visible only by a medicine-man until it is washed by Wolf. Further details from Lowie's informants make it clear that the *mu'gua* can also leave the body when one experiences a trancelike state or has an out-of-body experience (Lowie 1909:226, 301–302).

Also seen are at least two stick type figures (Figures 15 and 16) that appear to be holding a skin and/

Figure 14. Example of shaman with his hair knot or "bun," identified as a Blackfoot Medicine Pipe carrier (photograph by Edwad S. Curtis, in the Rare Book Division, New York Public Library).

Figure 15. Shamanic figure holding wand or stick type implement.

Figure 16. Another shamanic figure holding a hide.

or some type of wand or stick type implement. Carrying articles like this has been reported as having ritualistic "magical" or spiritual significance that assists the "charmer" by attracting and leading the animals into the trap. Although these objects were considered to have some supernatural power, they really worked by piquing the curiosity of the pronghorns.

Other significant abstract appearing pictograph panels located on the eastern side wall appear at first to be entoptic motifs (Figure 17), which compare favorably with those shown in illustrations by David Whitley (2000) (Figure 18). Although the entoptic comparisons can be made, another way to look at these motifs is by comparing them to trap designs that have been reported by Lubinski (1999:163) (Figure 13). Another example from 10BT1 appears to show a person, perhaps an antelope shaman, incorporated within a series of lines and maze-like patterns (Figure 19). These can be compared to descriptions of antelope drives and the shaman performing acts that will charm the animals, causing them to enter a circular enclosure where they are killed. Keyser (2016:49) shows some of these in a hunting magic site on the Green River. Loendorf shows an example of a corral site in *Thunder and Herds: Rock Art of the High Plains* (2008:126,127). A pictograph showing a circular enclosure containing two animals, easily identified as pronghorn by the markings on the body and neck, has been recently photographed by Bill Woodland in southern Utah (Figures 20 and 21). We can also see an antelope portrayed in Short Bull Winter Count ledger art (Figure 11) where it appears that the antelope is entering an enclosure represented by a ring encircling the antelope.

Conclusion

Herds of antelope existed on the upper Snake River plains for centuries. They were especially concentrated in the spring of the year. Characteristics of the antelope required special techniques to subdue the herd for

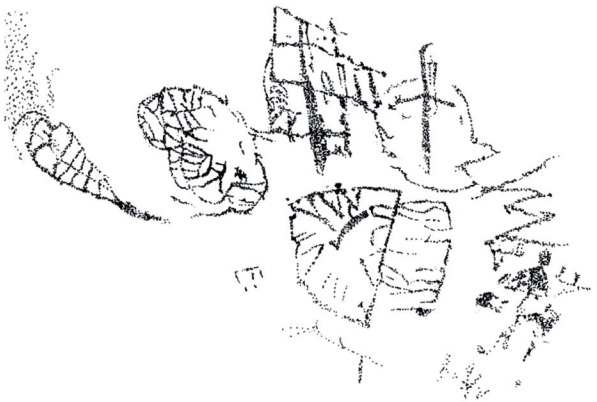

Figure 17. Cave Panel showing possible entoptic motifs that may also represent antelope traps.

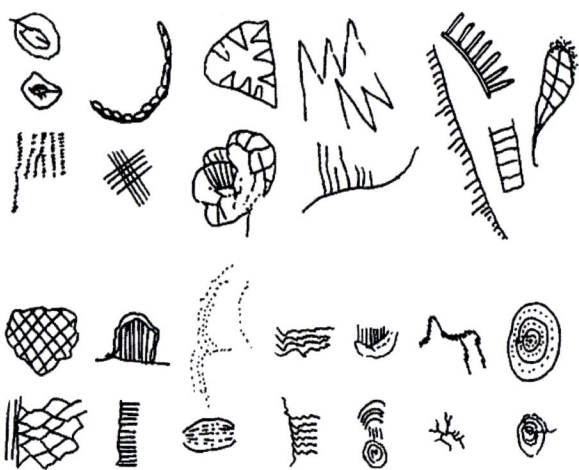

Figure 18. Possible entoptic elements from cave 10BT1 (top) compared with examples of entoptics from David Whitley (bottom) (redrawn by author after Whitley 2000:107).

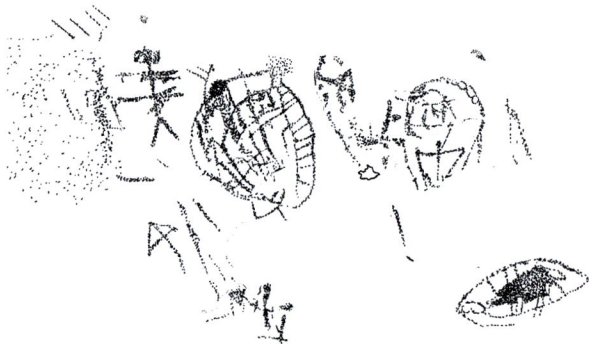

Figure 19. Cave panel showing maze-like patterns that likely represent an antelope drive that includes a presumed antelope charmer.

Figure 20. Recently reported circular enclosure containing two presumed antelopes, one naturalistic in red showing neck marking and one in white with traces of red at knee joints, neck, and on head (photograph courtesy of Bill Woodland).

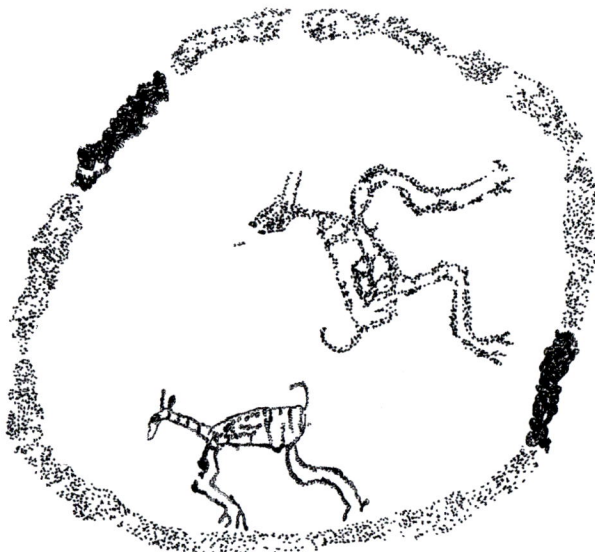

Figure 21. Tracing of photograph (Figure 20) to clarify images.

harvest. These techniques were the specialty of an antelope charmer or shaman who was sought out to lead the hunt. Like others in his cultural group, this specialist moved around on the landscape, taking steps to prepare himself for his select role. Following the tradition-al seasonal round, the antelope charmer from 10BT1 would have returned to this cave from winter camp locations in the spring of the year to prepare himself for a possible hunt. He would do this through dreams and self-induced trances that would inspire pictographs. In preparation to charm the antelope, the shaman would surround himself with "essence"; antelope material such as bone, hair, feces, or other items touched or scented by antelope. From these items, he selected those that served him best for the select rituals needed to lead a successful drive. For example, the juniper ring covered with antelope hair discussed earlier may have represented the round corral or enclosure into which the antelope are driven. The antelope hair placed over the ring would represent the antelope to be charmed by the shaman into entering the ring. A song like this one attributed to the Northern Paiute (Lowie 1963:15–16) might be sung: "Don't get scared antelope, slowly come here. Come in to your house, Don't get scared. Your house it is. Obey me."

The immediate area around Cave 10BT1 shows no remains of a drive or trap but that is not unusual given that the historic settlement, fires, and development of the land would have removed any semblance of a drive construction. There is one option that has yet to be explored. Along the base of the Lemhi range in the location of the cave, the mountains divide and break down into many toes forming shallow dead end canyons (Merrell 2000). It is conceivable that the people with the help of the charmer or shaman could have driven the antelope through the narrow openings, closing the way behind them, and killed them in the confined arena of rocky cliffs. To confirm this possibility, field surveys would have to be conducted for the most likely canyon entrances and explored for any evidence of a pronghorn kill site.

Looking at the possible use of Cave 10BT1 by a shaman or antelope charmer at some time in its ancient past at first seemed unlikely and somewhat speculative. But when all the evidence was viewed, evaluated, and put in perspective with all that has been written about the ceremony surrounding communal pronghorn hunts, it becomes plausible. Yes, this cave has the appropriate body of rock art, location, excavated artifacts, dates, and material evidence that fit together, to have been a place where a person achieved the stature and spiritual presence to lead his people on a successful communal antelope hunt.

Acknowledgements. The documentation and research for Little Lost Cave was accomplished through Challenge Cost Share Agreements with the Bureau of Land Management, under the direction of Richard Hill, BLM archaeologist. Also, a special thank you goes to volunteers who donated time and services including: Marvin Rowe, Karen Steelman, Ruth Ann Armitage, Richard Furman, Sylvia Miller, Carol Hearne, Gene Merrell, Vicky Varnum, and Lisa Wisnant. Comments by the reviewers were appreciated. My thanks to Ken Hedges for editorial review and DStrech processing.

Note

1. The reflective coating covering the pictographs and the lack of light in the cave interior created a serious challenge for the photography. Applying Adobe Photoshop enhancement technology greatly improved the subsequent photographic results, with DStretch enhancements clarifying sigificant details.. Tracings of enlarged photographs of the rock art combined with field drawings produced the final illustrations.

References Cited

Arkush, Brooke
    1986 Aboriginal Exploitation of Pronghorn in the Great Basin. *Journal of Ethnography* 6(2):239–255.

Armitage, Ruth Ann, Mary Ellen Ellis, and Carolynne Merrell
    2012 New Developments in the Nondestructive Dating of Perishable Artifacts Using Plasma-Chemical Oxidation. *American Chemical Society Symposium Series*, Volume 1103, Chapter 8:143–154.

Brink, Jack W.
    2013 The Barnett Site: A Stone Drive Lane Communal Pronghorn Trap on the Alberta Plains, Canada. *Quaternary International* 297:24–35. Royal Alberta Museum, Edmonton, Alberta, Canada.

Brumley, John H.
    1984 The Laidlaw Site: An Aboriginal Antelope Trap from Southeastern Alberta. In *Archaeological Survey of Alberta Occasional Paper 23*, edited by D. Burley, pp. 96–127. Edmonton, Alberta.

Butler, B. Robert
    1981 Little Lost River Cave No.1, the Birch Creek Project and the Antiquity of the Northern Shoshoni. In *When Did the Shoshoni Begin to Occupy Southern Idaho?: Essays on Late Prehistoric Cultural Remains From the Upper Snake and Salmon River Country* by B. Rob ert Btler, pp. 4–17. Occasional Papers of the Idaho Museum of Natural History 32, Pocatello.

Coffman, Carl
    1973 The Pronghorn Antelope. *Montana Outdoors* 4(6): 22–25.

Fichter, Edson, Marie Hopkins, Andre Isotoff, Sven Liljeblad, Rufus A. Lyman, Mary Strawn and Albert E. Taylor
    1955 Exploratory Excavation in Little Lost River Cave No.1 (Site 10-BT-1): A Progress Report. Report on file at Idaho Museum of Natural History, Division of Archaeology. Pocatello., and at BLM Field Office, Idaho Falls.

Fowler, Catherine S.
    1986 Subsistence. In *Handbook of North American Indians, Volume 11: Great Basin*, edited by Warren L. D'Azevedo, pp. 64–97. Smithsonian Institution, Washington, D.C.

Frison, George
    1991 *Prehistoric Hunters of the High Plains*. Second Edition. Academic Press, San Diego.

Gruhn, R., and A. Bryan
    1990 Report on a Test Excavation at Little Lost River Cave No. 1 (10BT1) in 1990. Cultural Resource Use Permit ID-I-27727. Unpublished report on file with the Idaho Falls District Bureau of Land Management, 1 October 1990. Idaho Falls, Idaho.

Hultkrantz, Ake
　1986 Mythology and Religious Concepts. In *Handbook of North American Indians, Volume 11: Great Basin*, edited by Warren L. D'Azevedo, pp. 630–640. Smithsonian Institution, Washington, D.C.

Kelly, Isabel T.
　1932 Ethnography of the Surprise Valley Paiute. *University of California Publications in American Archaeology and Ethnography* 31(3):67–210. Berkeley.

Keyser, James D.
　2016 Site 48SW85: A Hunting Magic Petroglyph on the Green River. In *American Indian Rock Art, Volume 42*, edited by Ken Hedges and Mark A. Calamia, pp. 41-59. American Rock Art Research Association, San Jose, California.

Liljeblad, Sven
　1986 Oral Tradition: Content and Style of Verbal Arts. In *Handbook of North American Indians, Volume 11: Great Basin*, edited by Warren L. D'Azevedo, pp. 641–659. Smithsonian Institution, Washington.

Loendorf, Lawrence L.
　2008 *Thunder and Herds: Rock Art of the High Plains*. Left Coast Press, Walnut Creek, California.

Lowie, Robert H.
　1909 *The Northern Shoshone*. Anthropological Papers of the American Museum of Natural History, Volume 2, Part 2. New York.
　1924 *Notes on Shoshonean Ethnography*. Anthropological Papers of the American Museum of Natural History, Volume 20, Part 3.
　1963 Washo Texts. *Anthropological Linguistics* 5(7):1-30

Lubinski, Patrick M.
　1999 The Communal Pronghorn Hunt: A Review of the Ethnographic and Archaeological Evidence. *Journal of California and Great Basin Anthropology* 21(2):158-181.

Malouf, Carling
　1940 The Gosiute Indians. *University of Utah Archaeology and and Ethnology Papers* 3. Salt Lake City.

Merrell, Carolynne L.
　2000 Black Canyon Wilderness Rock Art Inventory. A Cost Share Project between the BLM, Idaho Falls Resource Area, and Archaeographics, Agreement No. DDP990013. On file with the Idaho Falls District Bureau of Land Management, Idaho Falls, Idaho.
　2001 Pictograph Documentation from the Little Lost River Cave No. 1 (10BT1). A Cost Share Project between the BLM, Idaho Falls Resource Area, and Archaeographics, Agreement No. DAA000103. On file with the Idaho Falls District Bureau of Land Management, Idaho Falls, Idaho.

National Park Service
　2017 Horns versus Antlers. Yellowstone National Park. Electronic document, http://wwwnps.gov/articles/yell-hors-vs-antlers.htm, accessed August 23, 2017.

Park, Willard Z.
　1938 *Shamanism in Western North America: A Study in Cultural Relationships*. Northwestern University Studies in the Social Sciences 2. Evanston, Ill.

Pavesic, Max G.
　1993 Ancient Art in Southern Idaho: An Archaeological Perspective. In *Backtracking: Ancient Art of Southern Idaho*, edited by Max G. Pavesic and William Studebaker, pp. 9–36. Idaho Museum of Natural History, Pocatello.

Shimkin, Demitri B.
　1986 Eastern Shoshone. In *Handbook of North American Indians, Volume 11: Great Basin*, edited by Warren L. D'Azevedo, pp. 308–335. Smithsonian Institution, Washington, D.C.

Stands in Timber, John, and Margot Liberty
　1967 *Cheyenne Memories*. University of Nebraska Press, Lincoln.

Steelman, Karen L., Marvin W. Rowe, Thomas W. Boutton, John R. Southon, Carolynne L. Merrell, and Richard D. Hill
　2002 Stable Isotope and Radiocarbon Analyses of a Black Deposit Associated with Pictographs at Little Lost River Cave No. 1, Idaho. *Journal of Archaeological Science* 29(10):1189–1198.

Steward, Julian
　1938 Analysis of Data. In *Basin-Plateau Aboriginal Sociopolitical Groups*, by Julian A. Steward, pp. 230–258. Bureau of American Ethnology Bulletin 120. Facsimile reprint with original pagination in *A Great Basin Shoshonean Source Book*, edited by David Hurst Thomas. Garland Publishing, New York.
　1941 *Cultural Element Distributions 13: Nevada Shoshone*. University of California Anthropological Records 4(2).

Sundstrom, Linea
　2000 Cheyenne Pronghorn Procurement and Ceremony. In *Pronghorn Past and Present: Archaeology, Ethnography, and Biology*, edited by Jana V. Pastor and Patrick M. Lubinski, pp. 119–132. *Plains Anthropologist*, Memoir 32, 45(174):1–139.

Whitley, David S.
　2000 *The Art of the Shaman: Rock Art of California*. University of Utah Press, Salt Lake City.

Investigating the Co-occurrence of Petroglyphs and Pictographs on the Volcanic Tablelands of Northeastern California

Eric W. Ritter, Jon Harman, Jennifer Rovanpera, Devin Snyder, Elisa Correa, and Sheila Harman

As our methodological and theoretical approaches to the study of rock art improve, new discoveries and insights into the past behavior of various Native American Indian and other cultural participants are possible. Rock art on the volcanic tablelands of the Modoc Plateau of northeastern California is found to be more complex than previously thought through DStretch technology and careful observations. Faint or indistinct pictographs are sometimes found to be directly interacting with petroglyphs or occur adjoining. This pattern has also been reported in southern Oregon. This co-occurrence and likely connectivity as well as heritage, environmental associations, and informant information are explored in terms of their explanatory value from an archaeological perspective.

Within the vast semi-arid volcanic reaches of northeastern California, there are scores of rock art sites, considerably more than generally recognized by archaeologists and rock art scholars. The principal focus of our study is two-fold: (1) recognition of the abundance of rock art sites in California's very northeastern corner, specifically the Devil's Garden and Likely Tablelands, and, (2) improve the recognition of the rock art's diversity and complexity. Part of the recognition comes with the application of a range of investigative techniques and detailed analyses and subsequent interpretive efforts. Central sites within the study include complex archaeological sites known as the F Site (CA-MOD-19), M Springs (Bureau of Land Management [BLM] number 40.13.12.01), P Canyon (BLM number 40.14.30.01), and N Site (CA-MOD-4738). While not discussed in detail, a nearby site labeled the B Site (CA-MOD-161) is of a similar character (Figure 1). Localized site names have been omitted from this paper due to concerns from federal archaeologists and tribes (Modoc Tribe of Oklahoma, personal communication 2017; Pit River Tribe, personal communication 2015) that revealing too much detailed geographical information may lead to detrimental activities at these sites. Furthermore, the presentation of rock art images and science-based interpretations are presented in this paper in the interest of scholarly communication, although we are aware that there is some unease on the Modoc tribal representative's part in doing so.

Local Environment

The study area is situated within the eastern half of the Modoc Plateau, a broad, volcanic tableland of scarp-step topography broken by isolated volca-

Eric W. Ritter
Bureau of Land Management
Redding, California.

Jon Harman
DStretch.com, Pacifica, California

Jennifer Rovanpera
Bureau of Land Management
Cedarville, California

Devin Snyder
Bureau of Land Management
Alturas, California

Elisa Correa
Las Californias Heritage Research Group, Red Bluff, California.

Sheila Harman
Independent Researcher
Pacifica, California

Figure 1. Map of study site locations.

Figure 2. Modoc Plateau with view of Warner Mountains to the east (P Canyon vicinity).

as "Warner Basalts" as well as later extrusions of rhyolitic pyroclastic rocks of the "Cedarville Series" (Alt and Hyndman 2000; Norris and Webb 1990). Such rocky landforms, dominated by prominent bedrock and rimrock outcrops, provided a more than suitable canvas for rock art creation.

Prior to Euro-American arrival within the study area, the Likely Tablelands and Devil's Garden were home to the Hammawi and Hewesidewi bands of the Pit River Tribe, respectively, and the Modoc tribe to the north (Figure 3). These lands, according to tribal narrative, have been occupied by the Pit River since

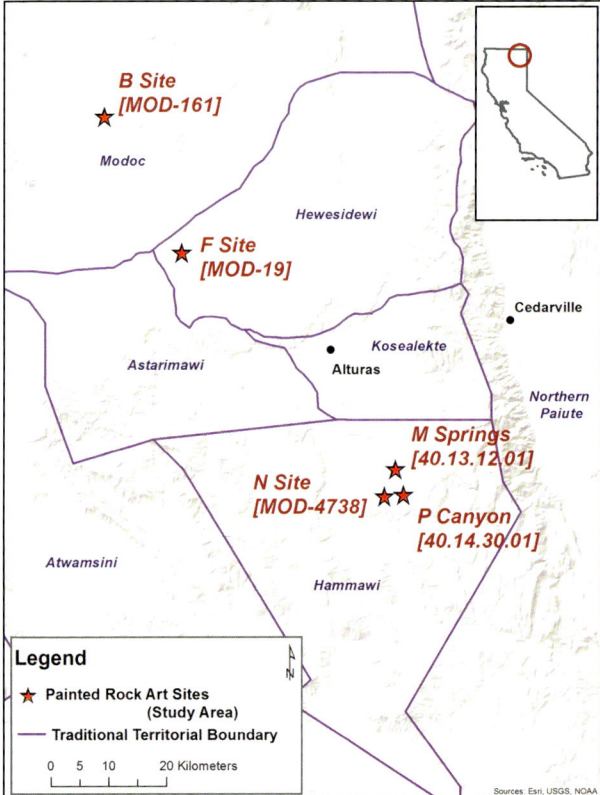

Figure 3. Map of study site locations and tribal boundaries.

time immemorial, and some tribal members continue to reside locally and call the greater area home.

Most of the Modoc Plateau is sagebrush-steppe habitat, comprised of large swaths of sagebrush and grassland vegetation (big and low sagebrush, bitterbrush, rabbitbrush, perennial bunch grasses, and non-annual grasses), with sometimes dense stands of western juniper (*Juniperus occidentalis*) along rockier substrates and hillsides. Significant aboriginal plant food resources in this area include primarily geophytes (roots, bulbs, and tubers) such as *ba'ha* (alternatively known as yampa or epos elsewhere) (*Perideridia* spp.), biscuitroot (*Lomati-*

nic cones, numerous rimrock benches, and deeply incised canyons just beyond the westernmost reaches of the Great Basin (Figure 2). Sites included in this study are more specifically located on the Likely Tablelands and Devil's Garden, two separate but similar volcanic plateau features that embody the Modoc Plateau and form the western foothills of the South Warner Mountain Range. These landforms are comprised predominately of Miocene-age basalts commonly referred to ium spp.), camas (*Camassia quamash*), brodiaea (*Brodiacea* spp.), and sego or lily (*Calochortus macrocarpus*). Seeds such as sunflower, lambsquarter (*Chenopodium* spp.), and wild rye (*Leymus cinereus*) were of dietary importance (Barrett 1910; Kniffen 1928). Other non-food plant resources, as known commonly, include but are not limited to bulrush, cattail, willow, bentgrass, other various rushes and sedges, wild rose, peppergrass, mustard, and thistle. Due to long, cold winters, seasonal food storage was of the upmost importance.

In addition to a vibrant vegetative community, the area also has a diverse array of both terrestrial and aquatic game. Antelope and mule deer are especially prevalent in the study area vicinity, and were important game resources that were hunted by the Pit River along with hares, rabbits, sage grouse, and marmots. The nearby Pit River, its tributaries, and adjacent seasonal wetlands, marshes, and lakes also provided habitat for migratory waterfowl and for non-migratory waterfowl and fish. Ducks, geese, coots, grebes, pelicans, suckers, tule perch, pike-minnow, and trout represent some of the most significant aquatic games resources, most of which were available predominately in the spring. Overall, the Modoc Plateau is most appropriately characterized as a landscape of seasonal abundance.

History of Previous Studies

The scholarly and local community following Euro-American settlement has been directly or indirectly aware of rock art in the study locality for many decades beginning with the documentation of the F Site by University of California anthropologist Julian Steward in 1929 based on a 1923 letter from Will W. Awl of Alturas, California. The general area of the Modoc Plateau and Klamath Basin, or southwest extension of the Columbia Plateau, has a rich history of archaeological and, more specifically, rock art studies. In California's Modoc County alone there are over 8500 archaeological sites documented as of April 2017 of which there are 134 petroglyph sites and 19 pictograph sites following attribute lists queried from data files of the Northeast Center of the California Historical Resources Information System, California State University, Chico.

After Steward's early documentation and that of Luther Cressman in nearby Oregon in 1937, Heizer in 1942 briefly discusses the rock art at Tule Lake, part of the Klamath Basin. Then, following World War II there was a gap of nearly 20 years until the work of Swartz (1960), and Heizer and Baumhoff (1962). There followed thereafter into the present a long list of over 30 regional rock art scholars. These include, among others, Armitage et al. (1997), Benson and Buckskin (1985), Crotty (1979, 1981), David (2005, 2010, 2012), David and Keyser (2008), Gates (1980), Grant (1967), Hann and Bettles (2006), Hann et al. (2010), Heizer and Clewlow (1973), Hyder and Lee (1990), Johnson (2003), Lee et al. (1988), Loring and Loring (1983), Loubser et al. (1999), Ricks (1996), Ricks and Cannon (1993), Ritter (1999), Ross (2000), Silver (1982), Swartz (1963, 1978, 1998), Wellmann (1979), Whitley (2000a), and Whitley et al. (2004).

The Problem

When visiting the F Site in the Devil's Garden it became apparent that the petroglyphs as previously documented were more complex than stated on the site record and within the published literature. In fact, faint traces of red pigment were noted within pecked motifs and on nearby faces along with an unreported black pictograph. Such occurrences were observed also at the other study sites described herein.

The mostly red pigments in many of the pictographs described in this paper have faded almost to the point of invisibility. Often faint traces of red paint can be discerned with effort, but design patterns cannot be perceived. The familiar computer program DStretch has been used to detect and enhance the painted designs. DStretch uses the Decorrelation Stretch algorithm specially modified for use in rock art (Harman 2015). In addition to the (desktop or laptop) computer version, there are portable versions available for Apple iPhones and iPads, Android phones and tablets, and certain Canon cameras. Portable versions were used in the fieldwork for this paper. When pictographs were detected, high quality digital photos were taken and later enhanced using DStretch on a desktop computer. DStretch enhancements are given three or four letter names, mimicking the names (e.g., RGB, YUV) given to color spaces used in color imaging. These color spaces are then modified for DStretch and given names. Certain enhancements work well for specific pigment colors. The YRE and YRD enhancements were used to enhance red pigments in the study area, while YBK was used on black pigments. DStretch can give good results for petroglyphs in some cases and the enhancement LBK was used to visualize a petroglyph in P Canyon (Figure 4).

While Steward (1929:59) was the first to note the co-occurrence of petroglyphs and pictographs in northeast California, as stated above, he failed to note pictographs over petroglyphs at the F Site since he did

Figure 4. DStretch image (LBK) of petroglyph at P Canyon.

not personally visit the site, nor was this co-occurrence observed on the other study sites discussed herein by later workers. Steward (1929:61, Figure 3) does mention the combination petroglyph-pictograph from Tule Lake at his Site 11, and the combined site at Tule Lake is also mentioned by Heizer (1942:123), and Heizer and Clewlow (1973:103–104). These latter authors also refer to the nearby red painted petroglyphs at Gillem Bluff (CA-SIS-210).

Just across the California border into Oregon, Cressman (1937:Site 27, Figure 21, 26–27) very early discusses the production of grooves in the rock that were painted red. Loring and Loring (1983:47) relate 31 sites in southern Oregon's Klamath and Lake counties with pictographs over petroglyphs, adjoining pictographs and petroglyphs, integrated petroglyph with a pictograph, and several other combinations (Also see David [2012:89], Ricks [1996:66], and Ross [2000:32] for other southern Oregon examples). Swartz's Klamath Basin rock art work has led to the recognition of pigment over petroglyphs at three sites (1960:18).

Loubser et al. (1999:29) note scratching over black pictographs at Lava Beds National Monument in the greater study area. Whitley (2000a:69) relates that in the Klamath Basin, some engraved sites have paintings and some of the painted sites have scratched and abraded motifs.

Although Gates (1980:84) did not observe the pictographs at the F Site, he does relate (1980:85) the nearby occurrence of "painted petroglyphs" in Devil's Garden at CA-MOD-161 or the B Site. Johnson (2003:110) reports the presence of pigment applied to pecked designs at CA-MOD-194, also in Devil's Garden, and at several sites to the south of the study area in adjoining Lassen County near Susanville, California.

Woody's 2000 study of nearby Nevada's rock art sites found 62 sites with both pictographs and petroglyphs in the state, with 11 in neighboring Washoe County bordering northern California. However, she does not elaborate on the connection of these two techniques noting (Woody 2000:186) "the relationship between petroglyphs and pictographs is not clear, and should be a focus for further research." Gilreath (2007:280), in her synthesis of California rock art studies, relates that "though not common anywhere, there are examples throughout the state where pigment has been applied to petroglyphs." She also mentions further that pigments in petroglyphs might disappear, lessening our knowledge of the actual frequency of this practice.

Definitely, our study in the volcanic tablelands of California's Modoc County is augmented by applying technology-assisted procedures as related to the fugitive nature of open site pictographs in association with petroglyphs at various levels of interplay in one locality. If we are to better understand and document these vestiges of the past here and in similar situations, we need to apply as many technological aids as reasonably feasible. Generally, rock art motifs, associated site components, and the greater landscape interplay have not been given the attention they deserve (but see Van Tilburg and Backes Jr.'s 2012 study of southern California Desert's Little Lake rock art for an example of a detailed study like attempted here). Our research is a start at a reasonable approach to recognizing the information complexities of the sites in this northern California region.

Site Descriptions

F Site

This site is located along a volcanic rim adjacent to large wetlands within the Modoc Plateau's Devil's Garden (Figure 5). The one-half hectare site contains three rock alignments, a rockshelter, a bedrock milling slick, and rock art. The rock art is located along the face of a large, steep rim overlooking the wetlands and an upland habitation site several hundred meters to the east at an elevation of 1524 meters above sea level (asl).

M Springs

M Springs is composed of three arbitrarily designated loci: two prehistoric sites and one historic homestead dating to the early 1900s. The prehistoric loci are located along a north-south trending volcanic rim between two seasonal creeks at

Figure 5. F Site and Devil's Garden view northwesterly.

an elevation of 1555 meters asl (Figure 6). There are small waterfalls and rock tanks where the northern and southern seasonal drainages of the

Figure 6. M Springs site view.

site flow over the volcanic rim. In two places, water flows from beneath the basalt rim creating springs. Prior to the introduction of non-native annual grasses, the vegetation of the site would have been predominantly sagebrush, bunch grasses, and western juniper. A field of biscuitroot still blooms here in the late spring. A majority of the rock art on-site is located along prominent basalt rims that border both sides of an ephemeral drainage that feeds a seasonal creek. Archaeological features are predominantly situated above or upslope of the rimrock outcrops. The 34 hect-

are site contains approximately eight rock rings or enclosures, 27 other rock alignments (possible hunting blinds or of unknown function), 158 rock stacks, four talus pits, three bedrock mortars, 20 small rockshelters or overhangs, a midden, lithic scatters, milling stones, and more than 160 rock art panels. Artifacts include corner-notched and contracting stem obsidian projectile points that date from the mid to late Archaic (3800 cal B.P. to 600 cal B.P.).

P Canyon

This site is also located on the Likely Tablelands, approximately 3.5 kilometers south of M Springs. The site is situated along an east west trending seasonal drainage within a volcanic trench or collapsed lava tube at 1585 meters asl (Figure 7). A seasonal creek flows over the lava rim creating a small rock tank. Vegetation is predominately sagebrush and western juniper along the volcanic rimrock. The 12 hectare site contains approximately two rock rings or enclosures, one U-shaped rock alignment (possibly a prayer seat), 11 other rock alignments (possible hunting blinds or of unknown function), 20 rock stacks, one bedrock mortar, one bedrock milling slick, three small rockshelters, lithic scatters, a few pieces of ground stone, and approximately 74 rock art panels. Diagnostic artifacts date from the Late Archaic (1300 cal B.P. to 600 cal B.P.) to the Terminal Prehistoric (600 cal B.P. to Contact), although one non-diag-

Figure 7. P Canyon site view.

nostic larger dart-size obsidian projectile point of a presumed earlier period was also noted.

N Site

The N Site is interpreted as a large, long-term habitation and food-processing locality. The site is located along an unnamed seasonal drainage along a north-south oriented rimrock (Figure 8). Notable are five large rock rings or enclosures interpreted to reflect house structures, a separate

Figure 8. View of N Site looking southwesterly.

multi-compartment rock ring/enclosure complex, and five additional smaller rock enclosures of indeterminate function, at least 65 panels of rock art, a dense associated flaked and ground stone scatter, a locus with midden development, and the presence of freshwater mussel shell. Rose Spring or Rosegate, Humboldt Concave Base, Elko Series, and Cottonwood triangular point types are represented in the site assemblage, suggesting a date range spanning roughly between 4,500 years BP and historic contact. The site was test excavated revealing intact deposits ranging between 20 and 100 centimeters below surface. According to Roybal and Evans (1982), the site was identified by Pit River informants as a "good luck spring" that also likely served as a village location.

Nature of the Rock Art

The following paragraphs summarize the various rock art motifs occurring at three of the four study locations (F Site, M Springs, and P Canyon) where we have the most complete information. The material was established from a GIS rock art database compiled by the BLM Applegate Field Office. The motif key used is based on the template provided by the American Rock Art Research Association's *A Basic Guide for Rock Art Recording* (2007:9) with additions of locally re-occurring motifs. The GIS database also tracks the type of rock art for each motif (e.g., petroglyph, pictograph, or painted petroglyph) in addition to the technique used to create the motif (e.g., for petroglyphs: carved, solid pecked, stippled pecked, abraded, or scratched). For pictographs, the color of each motif is also noted. The GIS database was designed to study where certain motifs occur across the landscape rather than to track their quantity (i.e., if a rock art panel had five pecked "dot" motifs, the "dot" motif is only listed once for that panel). The names given the motifs are arbitrary and the significance of these subjective names should not be used for analysis. "Generations" of rock art on an individual rock art panel are identified by superimposition and/or differences in the rock coatings of the motifs.

F Site

The F Site is dominated by petroglyphs: 83 percent of the motifs are petroglyphs and the majority are stipple pecked (91%). Unlike the other study sites, the F Site has the largest, most elaborate rock art panel with an estimated 51 to 60 figures (Figure 9). The rock art panels at the F Site have a slightly greater re-use per panel: 55 percent of the panels have two or more generations compared to 48 percent at P Canyon and 38 percent at M Springs. Four different petroglyph techniques are represented: one panel includes a carved motif, one panel includes a scratched motif, 12 motifs are solid pecked, and 129 motifs are stipple pecked.

Figure 9. F Site main panel (ca. 1.5 m across).

Although the F Site is the smallest, it contains the most painted rock art motifs of all three sites, an estimated 14 painted petroglyphs and 16 pictographs spanning six individual rock art panels (Figures 10 and 11). While some of the painted rock art features are discernible to the naked eye, many are severely faded suggesting that natural weathering has deteriorated or erased much of the painted rock art at the site. Two different types of pigment—red and black—were used to create the motifs. In addition, similar to the other two sites, red pigment was the preferred. All but two of the painted rock art motifs occur on the exposed volcanic rimrock with the most appearing on the largest, elaborate rock art panel. A red "amoeba" motif occurs in a small alcove created by large collapsed boulders near the rimrock and two black sub-rectangles occur in a small rock overhang located below the rimrock (Figure 12). Non-rock art features near the painted rock art include three rock alignments (the largest rock align-

Figure 12. F Site black pictograph enhanced with DStretch LBK.

ment is located directly above the largest, most elaborate panel). A rockshelter with a bedrock milling slick is located about 40 meters below the rim.

M Springs

At this site there are more than 487 motifs spanning 160 individual rock art panels, which represent a long tradition of site use. While the volcanic rim was used intensively for rock art, most panels appear to represent individual events. Thus, almost three-fourths (63%) of the panels only contain one "generation" of rock art, while 36 percent contain two "generations," and three panels contain three "generations" of use as evidenced by rock coating variations and superimpositioning. Furthermore, most of the panels (93%) contain one to 10 motifs, while only 10 panels are more elaborate.

Similar to the F Site, while there is some variation in rock art type and technique at the site, the majority of the rock art is composed of petroglyphs of the stippled pecked technique (93 percent of the petroglyph motifs). Six of the motifs—all located in a single panel—are carved or deeply pecked (most likely the Great Basin Carved Abstract style) and are possibly the oldest at the site. Twenty-three of the motifs are solid pecked (there is very little space between the pecks or dints), and only five motifs are scratched.

There are 15 painted rock art motifs on four individual rock art panels: 14 pictographs and one painted petroglyph (Figure 13). Red pigment was used for 13 images, while black pigment was used for the remaining two pictograph motifs (Figure 14). The painted petroglyphs occur at two locations on the site: on a

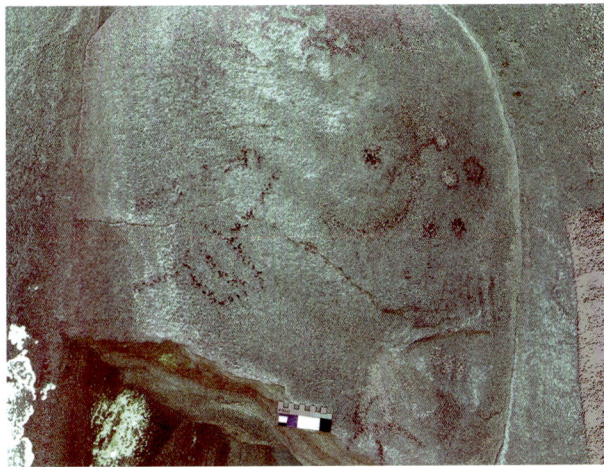

Figure 10. F Site painted petroglyphs visible with DStretch YRE.

Figure 11. F Site painted petroglyphs visible with DStretch YRE.

Figure 13. M Springs obscure pictograph and petroglyphs enhanced with DStretch YRE.

Figure 15. N Springs cupules and grooves—boulder ca. 1.5 m across.

Figure 14. M Springs black pictograph enhanced with DStretch LBK.

monumental boulder in the middle of a seasonal drainage near the southern end of the site, and in a small overhang near one of the springs that emerges below the volcanic rim. The painted petroglyph consists of red pigment painted into a stipple pecked dot on an elaborate rock art panel containing other petroglyphs and pictographs near the spring. The monumental boulder is located about 35 meters away from three bedrock mortars and 25 meters from a series of rock rings or enclosures and rock alignments. While the spring is surrounded by 20 rock art panels (including the possible Great Basin Carved Abstract panel with cupules, Figure 15), no other features were observed within its vicinity.

P Canyon

Similar to M Springs, the rock art at this site is dominated by petroglyphs on panels that experienced a single generation of use. Most of the rock art is at the north end of the site. There are 74 panels containing 276 motifs with 70 percent of the panels containing a single "generation" of rock art, and 97 percent of the panels containing one to ten figures. Unlike M Springs, only two petroglyph techniques are represented: solid pecked (14%) and stipple pecked (86%).

There are nine red painted rock art motifs on six individual rock art panels: three painted petroglyphs (Figures 16, 17 and 18) and six pictographs including a lizard figure with a superimposed petroglyph (Figure 19). The panels occur in a cluster along the volcanic rimrock approximately 80 meters from the rock pool. Three panels occur near a small alcove created by large, collapsed boulders along the rimrock. Two other panels are located under slight rock overhangs in the rimrock. While the painted rock art panels occur in a cluster surrounded by 22 other rock art panels, the nearest non-rock art features include a few rock stacks along the top of the rim and a bedrock-milling slick located five meters northeast of the pictograph panels.

N Site

The data from this site are incomplete. In general, there are at least 65 known rock art panels with all but three of the motifs being petroglyphs. The majority of the rock art occurs in three clusters: on a rock rim below the rock rings and along a seasonal creek; on a smaller rock rim near a spring; and along a west-facing rim near a midden deposit and smaller rock rings or enclosures. The rock art at this site is similar to M Springs and P Canyon—common petroglyph motifs include abstract designs and quadrupeds.

Three painted rock art motifs were identified during a cursory exploration of the site: two red "dots" on

Figure 16. DStretch image (YRE) of P Canyon painted petroglyph.

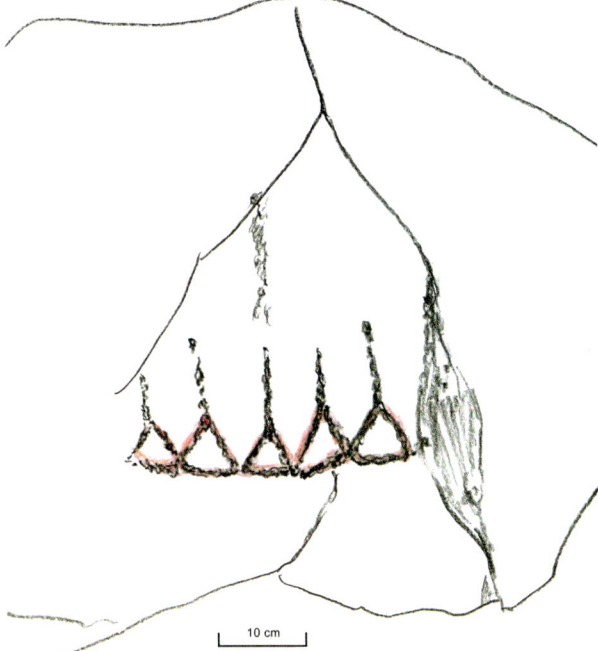

Figure 17. P Canyon painted petroglyph.

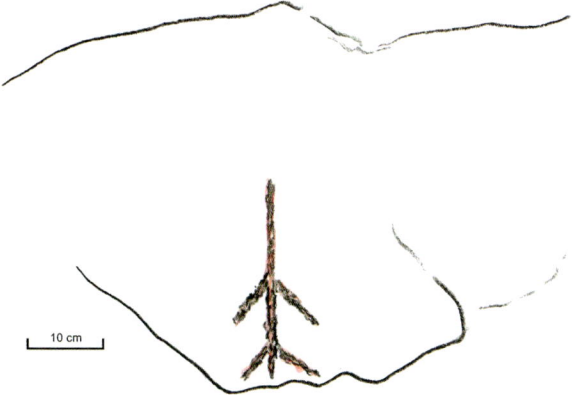

Figure 18. P Canyon painted lizard-like petroglyph.

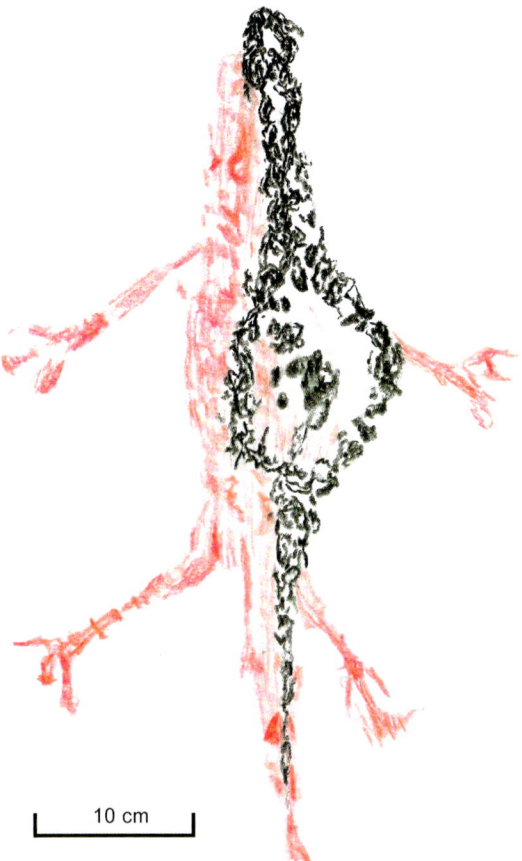

Figure 19. P Canyon painted lizard with superimposed petroglyph.

two individual rock art panels near the spring, a large red swath, and a painted groove complex (Figure 20). Two of the pictographs co-occur with stipple pecked petroglyphs.

B Site

Painted petroglyphs at this site in the Devil's Garden are largely geometric with one anthropomorph with cephalic projections and several lizard figures (Heizer and Clewlow 1973:Figures 161a and b, Steward 1929:Figure 5b, and Swartz 1978:Plate 4a-d). Which figures are painted is unreported.

Although located just outside the Great Basin (technically as close as 22 km away at the crest of the Warner Mountains), the study sites are very similar to Great Basin rock art to the east as discussed in the style section of this paper. At all three sites with detailed data, the petroglyphs far outnumber the painted rock art (M Springs, 97%; P Canyon, 97%; F Site, 83%). The two examples of carved petroglyphs occur at the M Springs site and the F Site. The panel at M Springs very likely is a classic example of Great Basin

Fivgure 20. B Site painted petroglyph.

Figure 21. F Site with hidden deep grooves with scratching (grooves about 15 cm in length).

Figure 22. P Site anthropomorph petroglyph cluster.

Carved Abstract; the motifs are composed of abstract lines, dots/cupules, and circles that are completely re-patinated or re-coated and the figures are dispersed across the panel so that there is very little "white space" (Cannon and Ricks 1986). The probable Great Basin Carved Abstract example at the F Site is smaller and consists of parallel grooves carved into the rock panel near the ground surface (Figure 21). Interestingly, superimposing the grooves are scratched lines that also have a heavy rock coating.

At the three well-studied sites, the majority of the petroglyphs are stipple pecked (M Springs, 93%; P Canyon, 86%; F Site, 91%), followed by solid pecked. At all three sites, the pecked abstract motifs comprise more than 80 percent of the motifs. Common re-occurring solid pecked and stipple pecked motifs include circles, dots, hearts, wavy lines, rectangles, triangles, grids, lines, chevrons, and their variations. A small portion of the pecked motifs can be referred to as representational figures. These include anthropomorphs (both stick figures and solid bodies) (Figure 22), quadrupeds (including deer, bighorn sheep, and a possible mountain lion), lizards, and other figures (e.g., snakes or insects). At all three sites there are more stipple pecked representational figures than solid pecked figures. However, beyond that the similarities between the sites decreases. The two sites on the Likely Tablelands have anthropomorphic figures and more quadrupeds, but the F Site has a much higher proportion of lizard motifs.

Only two of the sites (M Springs and the F Site) have petroglyphs that have been scratched into the rock surface. The five scratched cases at M Springs include one lizard and four rectilinear abstract figures. Except for the F Site example, these appear to be the youngest figures at the site based on rock coating development and superimposition.

Nearly half of the rock art panels at the three sites have multiple generations (based on repatination or superimposition) of rock art (M Springs, 38%; P Canyon, 48%; F Site, 55%). An even smaller portion of the rock art panels (M Springs, 3%; P Canyon, 9%; F Site, 8%) show figures being re-worked (i.e., re-pecked) or modified (i.e., figures added onto the original figure to create a more elaborate, integrated design). Not only were people repeatedly returning to the same site, in many cases they were re-using individual rock art panels and motifs.

The painted rock art at the three sites is divided into two categories: pictographs and painted petroglyphs. For the two sites located on the Likely Tablelands, painted rock art comprises three to four percent of the figures at the sites. At the F Site, the proportion is higher (17%). All the painted rock art directly coincides with petroglyphs or is located within the vicinity of petroglyphs. At all three sites, red pigment was the preferred (or enduring) pigment, and only red pigment was used to paint petroglyphs (or have superimposed petroglyphs).

Between the three sites, there are 17 examples of painted petroglyphs (M Springs, 1; P Canyon, 2; F Site, 14). All are abstract designs on stipple pecked petroglyphs except for four examples at the F Site, and one possible lizard-like figure at P Canyon. All the painted solid pecked petroglyphs are abstract curvilinear designs, and about half of the painted stipple pecked petroglyphs (54%) are curvilinear abstract, while the remaining examples (46%) include rectilinear abstract designs (Table 1).

There are 37 examples of pictographs between the three sites (M Springs, 14; P Canyon, 7; F Site, 16). While red pigment is more common, at two sites (M Springs and the F Site) black pigment was used for pictographs (all abstract designs). Most of the red pictographs are abstract; on the Likely Tablelands, the abstract designs are roughly half-curvilinear and half-rectilinear, whereas there are slightly more painted curvilinear abstract designs at the F Site. However, on the Likely Tablelands there are four examples of painted representational figures: two anthropomorphic figures at M Springs and two lizards at P Canyon (Table 1).

In general, the painted rock art appears to be located near water (springs, rock tanks or pools, wet meadows) but not necessarily immediately adjacent to it. In some instances, the painted rock art occurs on natural monumental or unique features—small alcoves created by collapsed boulders such as at P Canyon and the F Site, a large boulder at M Springs, and a spring/creek emerging from underneath a volcanic rimrock. Furthermore, they

co-occur on large petroglyph panels ("human modified monuments") that are visible from a good distance (such as at the F Site) (Figure 23). They are similar to the pecked petroglyphs in design and execution; similar motifs are used and their placement on the rock art panel is similar to the pecked petroglyphs—not necessarily centered on the panel, symmetrical, or equally dispersed in relation to the other designs, and an abundance of "white space" is left on the panel. In some instances, the pecked petroglyphs are painted; in one case, a stipple-pecked curvilinear abstract design is pecked over a red lizard pictograph (Figure 19), and several other examples of petroglyphs over red pictographs are known including one at the N Site. While the scratched petroglyphs appear to be the youngest based on the lightest repatination, this may not necessarily be the case: one pictograph at M Springs dates to 1936 (Figure 24), and almost all of the petroglyphs of historic motifs (e.g., cowboys, horses, and cows) nearby in Surprise Valley, California, are stipple pecked.

Figure 23. F Site view of rimrock with rock art.

Table 1. Comparisons of Motif Categories.

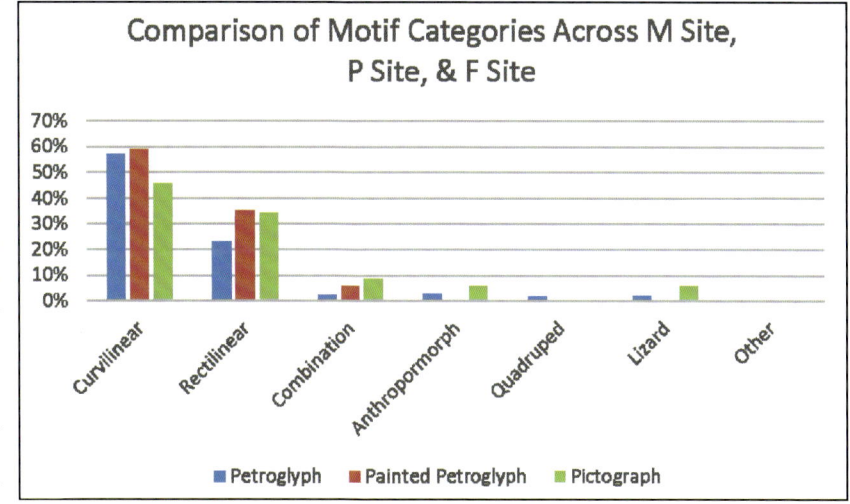

Figure 24. M Springs—hidden red painted date visible with DStretch YRE.

The dominance of red in the pictographs is apparent and such pigment may have been derived from hematite or ochre. Munsell colors were taken from pictographs at the P Canyon and the M Springs sites. The first site includes weak red (10R 4/4), light red to pale red (10R 6/6), to red (10R 5/6) pictographs with reddish black (10R 2.5/1), dark reddish gray (10R 4/1), and very dusky red (10R 2.5/2) rock backgrounds. A pecked figure has a color reading of light gray (2.5Y 7/2). At M Springs there are pictograph readings of dark red (10R 3/6) and red (10R 5/6) with a rock color of gray (5Y 5/1). A hematite rock from Nevada has a red streak Munsell reading on a geologist's white plate of 10R 5/8, close to some of the pictograph colors. A weathered pebble of ultramafic vesicular rhyolite with garnets and pyrrhotite from the nearby Warner Mountains left a color streak of pink red (10R 6/4). A piece of cinnabar from the Warner Mountains left a streak color of light red (2.5YR 6/6). Any of these rock types could have been used in the pictograph manufacture. Gates (1980:86) mentions Forest Service site number FS-05-09-55-297, a petroglyph site in the Devil's Garden near Alturas, California, where there was a fine-grained "hematite" mined. Kelly (1932:151 notes that the Surprise Valley Paiute traded red ochre to the Pit River people, the source found near Big Valley to the north of Mount Bidwell in the Warner Mountains (Kelly 1932:116).

In a very preliminary attempt to identify the mineral used in the pictograph manufacture, a hand held Thermo Scientific Niton XL3t GOLDD+ XRF Analyzer was used on a dozen plus of the pictographs, the rock background where minimal rock coatings were observed by eye, on solid-pecked petroglyphs, and on select natural rock samples. The machine was calibrated using the soil/mineral setting with 90 second runs. For the most part, only one to three readings were rendered preventing adequate averaging. Furthermore, the pigments were often not solid in application, and they certainly are weathered and likely veneered with rock coatings of unknown composition. Attempts were made to place the reading lens over the more robust pigment coatings. Huntley (2014:27, 160-161) has commented on various problems with the technique including issues of the thin paint application and incorporation of rock substrate into the spectra.

There is a suggestion of a higher iron count in parts per million on a few of the pictographs than both the mother rock and the petroglyph readings. For example, there is an average of two readings of base rock at the P Canyon of 57573 ppm with one red pictograph reading 112104 ppm and a lizard pictograph from the same site at 99613 ppm. However, the average from three readings on a piece of hematite was 18986 ppm. Overall, without more complete testing the best that can be said is that the red pictographs may be derived from iron-rich hematite.

Expanding Perspectives

Through our study and using comparative information from neighboring rock art sites and literature examples, there are numerous permutations of pictograph and petroglyph associations. There are undoubtedly others not listed here. For our four study sites, we see the following:

1) Pecked petroglyph motifs with red paint added within the pecked lines (partial and whole integration?).
2) Petroglyphs with pictographs immediately adjoining.
3) Petroglyphs with nearby pictographs within the greater archaeological site.
4) Pictograph with an overlying petroglyph (also see Little Lake, California, examples in Van Tilburg and Backes 2012).
5) Isolated pictograph panels near other petroglyph/pictograph combined panels, including both red and black examples.
6) Variations in pigment application and selection of pecked images or portions of images, including pigment continuing off the pecked motif.

In addition, not within the study sites there is:

7) Petroglyphs outlined with paint (William Cannon, Bureau of Land Management, Lakeview, Oregon, personal communication 2017).
8) Pictographs between petroglyph lines.

9) Rubbed petroglyphs with pigment added.
10) Combined petroglyph and pictograph with no apparent overlap.

Style Considerations

Stylistic definitions are often instilled with subjective evaluations, are an ongoing development in the search for heuristic categories with spatial, temporal, and behavioral meaning, and are often subject to lumping or simplification. Motif complex variation should be examined in the light of group interaction, idiosyncratic representation, functional variation displayed through variable presentations, and temporally overlapping or even multiple cultural use of the same location.

Malotki (2007:17) has stated that in style analysis one looks to "...recurring similarities of design and motif, technique, distinctness of expression, overall aesthetic quality, artistic attributes, and material considerations." Conkey and Hastorf (1990:2) believe that "Style is also ideas, intentions, and perceptions...highly variable, polysemic, and ambivalent."

There has been no absence of stylistic assignments to the rock art of the greater region by researchers. Early writers such as Steward (1929), Heizer and Baumhoff (1962), Grant (1967), and Gates (1980:89) lump the regional rock art into a Great Basin Tradition of styles. Steward (1929:219) has noted the similarity in design in his sample of petroglyphs and pictographs in northeastern California. Wallace and Holmlund (1986:85) would perhaps place the art in the Western Archaic Tradition. Heizer and Clewlow (1973:34–37), focusing on those sites in the Klamath Basin, argue for a Northeast (California) Painted Style with Great Basin affinities for the pictographs of the region. Wellmann (1979:69) has defined a Northeast Painted Style to include the study location with the same approach as Heizer and Clewlow. Crotty (1979, 1981), Hyder and Lee (1990), and Lee et al. (1988) argue for a Modoc Style for petroglyphs and pictographs—primarily in the Klamath Basin—composed primarily of parallel lines, wavy or zig-zag lines, dot designs, and circles, both plain and elaborate. Swartz (1998) has outlined a Klamath Basin pictographic design. These authors were seemingly looking beyond the painted figures of the tablelands studied herein, a pattern not well recognized before this study.

In Whitley's (2000a:48) rock art study of California, he places the Klamath Basin rock art into a Plateau Tradition and the volcanic tablelands encompassing our study sites in the Great Basin Tradition noting there is a Great Basin Painted Variant primarily confined to the southern California deserts. Hann et al. (2010:2) designate the corpus of painted and petroglyph motifs in the Klamath Basin as the Klamath Basin Style of the Columbia Plateau rock art tradition. As noted by David (2012:1), this style is characterized by a frequency of circular designs associated with zigzag, abstract, and triangular motifs. Even Steward (1929:235) early on noted, "A connection with the Columbia region with Area A is probable." Unmistakably, what we have in our study locality is something more complicated with an unquantified portion of the motif assemblages similar to those of the Klamath Basin (cf. Figure 14).

What is apparent is that the study sites incorporate a series of motif complexes with an elevated level of Great Basin or Basin and Range Tradition affinities but also with cupules, what Whitley (2000a:47) would see as a variant of the Far Western Pit and Groove Tradition. There is as well presumed Great Basin Carved Abstract figures (see Ricks and Cannon 1993) at the F Site and M Springs (an apparent extension of the style from the adjoining Great Basin), and panels and motifs not easily classified, such as a series of anthropomorphs on several panels at P Canyon (Figure 22).

Chronological Reflections

Assigning an age to the rock art at these sites must rely on cultural associations (e.g., projectile points) and stylistic comparisons to regional sites of similar character. The three primary sites exhibit re-use spanning hundreds to thousands of years. The possible Great Basin Carved Abstract style at two of the sites can be at least 7,000 years old (Cannon and Ricks 1986) and in some areas has been dated to as old as 14,800 cal B.P. (Benson et al., 2013:4476). Heizer and Clewlow (1973:36), with little direct dating information, place the regional painted rock art in the A.D. 500-circa A.D. 1600 range. Ross's (2000:75) southern Oregon excavations at sites with painted petroglyphs provided midden feature dates associated with the Late Archaic, the last 1000 years or so. David (2012:89) discusses a painted petroglyph site near Bly, Oregon, in the Klamath Basin with associated projectile points he dates between A.D. 500 and 1300. Swartz (1960:19) states: "The faint traces of pigment found on clear pecked petroglyphs also suggest that pictographs are probably of recent date due to the lack of permanency of the marking substance. Adhering pigments more rapidly disappear than defacement of markings by erosion, especially on hard surfaces." Steward (1929:234) earlier remarked on the "perishability of pictographs." Logically, there is no information that demonstrates how far back this painted practice was carried out in the region, preservation issues being a main consideration. Nevertheless, it seems almost certain that painting is at least late prehistoric in age.

The focus sites in this study have projectile points in proximity (within the greater site) that date from approximately 1,500 B.C. (Elko series) to A.D. 1300 and later (Rosegate and Desert Side-notched) following Thomas' narrative (2013). Of course, this association is at best tenuous between those who made the rock art and those who left the points behind.

It is pertinent to the discussion of dating the pictographs at the sites to note the red date visible to us only through DStretch at M Springs, a location of an older historic ranch. This date is "4/11/36," in red pigment, on its own panel (Figure 24). A reading with the pXRF machine was inconclusive, and the color does not appear to differ from that applied to the petroglyphs. However, the applied pigment to form the date appears to have been saturated or water solvent as it has dripped downward from its original application. This would suggest a later application of paint much like that discussed by Crotty (1981:146) at CA-MOD-1 along Tule Lake to the west. However, the iconography of red and black pictographs at this site suggests some, if not all of the pictographs are earlier in time than the historic period. Nevertheless, we leave open the possibility of later, even historic application of red pigment to the study locality petroglyphs by Pit River or even Northern Paiute people descended from new populations of the hypothesized Numic expansion (cf. Bettinger and Baumhoff 1982).

Interpretation Possibilities

We profess no certainty in the meaning or function of the rock art within the study sites. It is also clear that care must be communicated when using the ethnographic record and contemporary informant discussions regarding graphic expressions that go back hundreds and thousands of years.

Cressman (1937:Site 27, Figure 21, 26–27) discusses the production of grooves in the rock in nearby Oregon that were painted red leading him to suggest that this was done to give contrast to the light rock. Van Tilburg and Backes, Jr. (2012:135, 149) from work at Little Lake in Southern California also observed that in cases there was a clear intent to enhance petroglyphs with painting, "…to associate with the group or person who authored the original motif and to retain, renew, or revive its symbolic meaning.." Whitley (2000a:69) states: "Combined with the general equivalence in motif types, this suggests that the distinction in origin and meaning between painted and engraved art may not have been great on the Modoc Plateau, as also suggested for the Great Basin Tradition." David (2012:99) relates that for painted petroglyphs in the Klamath Basin "Just like the telling and re-telling of myths over winter campfires, the re-painting of rock art probably served to keep alive group ideology and at the same time maintain the power foundations of shamans." In Australia, Edwards (1979) shares that Aborigine repainting was related to either power renewal or a request for supernatural intervention of the power in the motif being repainted. We have no doubt that the application of pigment to petroglyphs and pictograph and petroglyph associations was communicative for more than the maker, and, for the most part, visible to those present, often at a distance. It was likely ritually and non-ritually multi-functional, multi-personal, and multi-generational and may have been influential in ritual and non-ritual behavior on a day-to-day basis, perhaps even in mediating social changes.

In cross-cultural studies of hunter-forager religion, ethnographer Mathias Guenther (1999:426) said, "Underneath all of the contextual and cultural diversity, there indeed is a substrate of ritual, cosmological, and symbolic commonality. This is fundamentally shamanistic (and sometimes totemistic)." We would add animistic to Guenther's list.

With this generality of Guenther's in mind, it is worthwhile to review briefly some of the previous regional and broader interpretations for the rock art. Voegelin (1942:204), based on her 1930 ethnographic work, notes that Pit River Atsugewi (Hat Creek) informants considered pictographs as a cultural element, while the Pit River Achomawi (Hammawi) deemed petroglyphs as a cultural element. Voegelin (1942:219) notes that during Hammawi girls' puberty ceremonies (including dancing) red stripes were painted on the initiates face including cheeks, chin, and nose. Whether there is any relationship of the puberty ceremonies, use of facial red designs, and red pictograph manufacture is undetermined but thought provoking.

Buckskin (1985:50), a Pit River cultural representative and elder, based on information from other Pit River elders, states: "One function of rock art is to communicate to the observer his or her location on earth in relationship to the stars. This can be determined by those who know how to interpret the symbols in the rock art. Rock art also relates knowledge about the location of springs, food resources, and sacred place."

Benson and Buckskin (1985:135–137, 139–140) have offered interpretations of rock art at CA-MOD-75 in the Devil's Garden, a location partially occupied into historic times by the Modoc in its southerly recesses and by the Pit River people in its northern portions with some interaction and variations in the extent of the tribal boundaries (cf. Benson and Buckskin 1985:134). The junior author of the article, Floyd Buckskin, as mentioned above, is a Pit River cultural representative and authority. He interpreted one group of symbols as resembling the Pit River mythological being World's Heart, *te-qa-te hataji*, in his sky lodge, and the circular images below possibly symbolizing social groups or geographical locations. Benson and Buckskin (1985:137) state that the panel "metaphorically unites concepts from both Pit River and Modoc mythology." Voegelin (1942:209) and Olmsted and Stewart (1978:230–231) note the hostility on part of the Modoc who raided Achomawi country for slaves. The introduction of guns and horses may have initiated or accelerated such practices (cf. Stern 1998:456–457). Friendly interactions, such as marriage unions (Stern 1998:454) and trade (Davis 1961:15) also occurred during the past. In this regard, it is evident that during the historic past, if not earlier, tribal interactions varied in scope.

Benson and Buckskin (1991:53) describe an association of rimrock petroglyphs just to the north of the study locality in Oregon with association with lightning strikes and magnetic anomalies. This is a situation possibly analogous to one or more of our study sites. Benson and Buckskin (1991:58) relate, "The Achumawi, Atsugewi, Modoc, and Northern Paiute all regard thunder as a powerful being as well as a source of power. We suggest that a person seeking power may attempt to obtain power by painting or carving a picture of her (or his) *damaagome* (e.g., a lizard) directly over a rock struck by lightning." Since a number of lizard figures (painted and pecked) are present at the study sites it is worth noting that among the Pit River groups, and neighboring Klamath and Northern Paiute, the lizard was a spirit helper (Benson and Buckskin 1991:57–58, Garth 1953:187, and Spier 1930:142–143), drawn under shamanistic influence as stated by Spier for the Klamath.

It is also noteworthy that the rock art locations are near major water sources and habitation locales. Pit River peoples, as related in the Voegelin (1940:158) ethnography, recognized the weather shaman who made rain by formula and song and in cases required supernatural experience. Park (1986:36) notes that among the Atsuge Pit River "some doctors can make rain. They travel in the daytime and they travel very far." Such shamans or religious formulators/doctors were likely instrumental spiritually in maintaining the water sources for day-to-day living and for providing rain to soften the ground for the important root digging (Garth 1953:196).

In Australia, as likely in the Modoc Plateau, Taçon (1999:34) remarks that rock art activity "....is most directly linked to early perceptions of landscape—the very location and organizational structure of rock art speaks of human relationships to places and spaces." With more archaeological inventory in this locality of the Modoc Plateau we may eventually be able to better link these rock art sites and others with a superior defined pattern of prehistoric and, perhaps, protohistoric use and behavior. Following Troncoso et al.'s (2016:166–167) study of hunter-forager rock art in Chile, we see the similarity in the site's dominance of non-figurative motifs, the dominant use of red paint, and perhaps similarity in symmetry patterns on the rock panels that "created a shared horizon for these communities, integrating the whole region through a same practice, and similar process of semantization of space....associated with the process of territorialisation and demarcation of space by hunter-gatherer groups."

One of the most common interpretations of abstract-geometric rock art (and iconic-abstract combinations) among American hunter-forager groups is derived from the neuropsychological model that has been described at length in many rock art publications (see David 2012:46–51 for a recent review). This model—even in this region (see David 2012, Loubser et al. 1999, Ritter 1999)—distinguishes some of the graphic presentations in a ritual or ceremonial context. They are most often associated with the religious formulator, shaman, vision seeker, dreamer, and perhaps the mentally impaired seeking or affirming his or her power, initiation into manhood or womanhood, or perhaps improved health as examples. This model continues to be debated and refined (cf. Bahn 2001, Dronfield 1996, Hedges 1992, 2001; Helvenston and Bahn 2005, Lewis-Williams 2001, 2002; Lewis-Williams and Dowson 1988, Malotki 2007, McFall 2006, Pearson 2002, Quinlan 2000, 2001; Whitley 1998:15, 2000b; Wright 2014:166, and others)

Campbell (2007:28) notes for the California Indians that "the sacred quality that red ochre imparted through time likely came from its association with the red of blood, the life force...the Atsugewi say red *ishuri ta' wi*, 'blood colored.' Red ochre was their most valued pigment according to Campbell (2007:28). With regard to trance state imagery, Campbell (2007:11) offers this interpretation for California pictographs: "On rock walls, shamans painted an opposite world, an altered state, a trance or dream. The answers came, but they were answers impossible to explain—the dreamer ground pigments and left signs and metaphors linking to a parallel universe beyond measure." While this is likely an oversimplification of the world of California pictographs, such a practice may have been the case for some of the Modoc Plateau pictographs. However, final answers are elusive and the purposes of image production was likely multivocal and polysemous as can be read in the paragraphs below.

Malotki (2007:32–34) has offered still another interpretation of some abstract/geometric art following the work of Dissanayake (1992). In this proposal abstract/geometric figures are placed on the rocks as a means to obtain life's necessities, to make order out of disorder, to provide "markings of magic and power" and thereby creating rock art "shrines" that help individuals "feel that they exercised a certain control over an unpredictable and dangerous world"—"art for life's sake," or "artification" with adaptive and selective survival value.

Van Tilburg (2012:173), based on the Little Lake study previously mentioned with similar imagery and painting over petroglyphs, suggests that portions of the body of educational symbols are representatives of memories of dreams, of embodied wealth related to shamans and other storytellers in graphic form.

Hann et al. (2010) have discussed the mortuary-related aspects of rock art production in Columbian Plateau rock art. However, there is no clear-cut association of the study sites with mortuary practices or mortuary-related behavior. Steward (1929:59), based on a report from Paul J. Fair, does note, "Painted picture writing was found on the rimrock of Snake Island, on the south shore of Tule Lake. Burial places were located in crevices under and between large fragments of rock which had split off and fallen from the rim of the island." Such an association at Snake Island may be fortuitous or mortuary relationships to the paintings could apply to a differing regional expression of rock art and/or ethnic groups.

David (2012:2) has concluded that rock art in the adjoining Klamath Basin at settlement sites probably included cases of ritual curing, while rock art at frequently used areas may have been produced for public display, "concentrating and advertising the power of the surrounding landscape as well as that of shamans." This agrees with Rick's (1996:vii) conclusions for rock art just north into Oregon where the images were associated with human aggregation centers focused on food producing plant communities, not solitary vision quest or hunting-related locales.

In terms of the earlier proposals by such authors as Heizer and Baumhoff (1962), Heizer and Clewlow (1978), and Gates (1980) that the Hunting Magic hypothesis has tenancy at least in a broad sense with regard to the Likely Tablelands' rock art sites, the reader should examine Keyser and Whitley's (2006) discussion of the hunting magic interpretation, an assertion often made without empirical evidence. On the Modoc Plateau, possible hunting blinds, projectile point presence, antelope herding zones, and rock art in close approximation could substantiate a hunting magic or game animal fertility and take function for some of the art, at least in a multi-functional context. (Also, see Garfinkel and Austin's 2011 animal reproduction symbolism discussion for an area to the south with a much greater concentration of game animal images.)

With regard to a hunting association, a study of the sites' rock enclosures and features such as undertaken by Dalton (2011) in a nearby area might provide evidence that these locations with features and rock art were used as part of a hunting strategy for killing large game, assuming contemporaneity of feature use and rock art production.

The religious formulator connection or influence on at least some of the multi-technique rock art manufacture and use at the subject sites seems likely in our estimation, not only from the widespread ethnographic narratives but also from the images, the symbols portrayed--some of which seem to fit well with the neuropsychological theory. These include many complex curvilinear, integrated, and isolated geometric images, of special note the co-occurrence of petroglyphs and pictographs in various combinations.

These rock art locations were likely places of ritualization and immediate or not-too-distant (hundreds of meters) domestic settlement, not necessarily congruent. We believe that the motifs were for the most part open, non-secluded, signs or symbols of religious meaning and knowledge, at least in part derived from visions and dreams, in cases amplified or reified by paintings.

Almost certainly, the sites and the rock art had many functions and contexts likely related to different age grades, gender, societal roles, and even to differing culture groups such as an expanding Paiute population. The places are still revered as likely in the past, locations respected and consecrated to many and left as an enduring artistic and communicative record to aid in individual and societal health and persistence over the generations. Painting patterns are apparently relatively long-standing cultural traditions imbued with ritual and decorative aspects, and the application of programs such as DStretch to rock art studies must continue to be well considered in both comprehensive and more focused rock art research.

Acknowledgments. Our appreciation is extended to David "Jack" Scott (retired) of the Applegate BLM office for assistance in fieldwork and other aspects of the project. We also thank the Modoc National Forest's Dr. M. Pamela Bumsted and Vicki Adkinson for processing the permit to work in the Devil's Garden area. The Pit River Tribe and Modoc Tribe of Oklahoma offered insightful comments and opinions that we respect, even if our approach to the rock art's study differs from their concepts.

References Cited

Alt, David D., and Donald W. Hyndman
 2000 *Roadside Geology of Northern and Central California*. Mountain Press Publishing Company, Missoula, Montana.

American Rock Art Research Association
 2007 A Basic Guide for Rock Art Recording. Electronic document, www.arara.org/Recording_Manual.pdf, accessed December 21, 2017.

Armitage, Ruth Ann, Marian Hyman, John Southon, Chandri Barat, and Marvin W. Rowe
 1997 Rock Art Image in Fern Cave, Lava Beds National Monument: Not the AD 1054 (Crab Nebula) Supernova. *Antiquity* 71:715–719.

Bahn, Paul G.
 2001 Save the Last Trance for Me: An Assessment of the Misuse of Shamanism in Rock Art Studies. In *The Concept of Shamanism: Uses and Abuses*, edited by Henri-Paul Francfort and Robert N. Hamayon, pp. 51–94. Akadémiai Kiadó, Budapest.

Barrett, Samuel K.
 1910 *The Material Culture of the Klamath and Modoc Indians of Northeastern California and Southern Oregon*. University of California Publications in American Archaeology and Ethnology 5(4):239–292.

Benson, Arlene, and Floyd Buckskin
 1985 Modoc-75. In *Rock Art Papers*, Volume 2, edited by Ken Hedges, pp. 133–142. San Diego Museum Papers No. 18. San Diego.
 1991 Magnetic Anomalies at Petroglyph Lake. In *Rock Art Papers*, Volume 2, edited by Ken Hedges, pp. 53–64. San Diego Museum Papers No. 27. San Diego.

Benson, Larry V., Eugene M. Hattori, John Southon, and Ben Aleck
 2013 Dating North America's Oldest Petroglyphs, Winnemucca Lake Subbasin, Nevada. *Journal of Archaeological Science* 40:4466–4476.

Bettinger, Robert L., and Martin A. Baumhoff
 1982 The Numic Spread: Great Basin Cultures in Competition. *American Antiquity* 47(3):485–503.

Buckskin, Floyd
 1985 Racing Simlek's Shadow. In *Earth and Sky*, edited by Arlene Benson and Tom Hoskinson, pp. 49–54. Slo'w Press, Thousand Oaks, California.

Campbell, Paul Douglas
 2007 *Earth Pigments and Paint of the California Indians, Meaning and Technology*. Privately published, Los Angeles.

Cannon, William J., and Mary Ricks
 1986 The Lake County Oregon Rock Art Inventory: Implications for Prehistoric Settlement and Land Use Patterns. In *Contributions to the Archaeology of Oregon 1983–1986*, edited by K. M. Ames, pp. 1–22. Department of Anthropology and University Foundation Occasional Papers No. 3. Portland State University and the Association of Oregon Archaeologists, Salem.

Conkey, Margaret W., and Christine A. Hastorf
 1990 Introduction. In *The Uses of Style in Archaeology*, edited by Margaret Conkey and Christine Hastorf, pp.1–5. Cambridge University Press, Cambridge, England.

Cressman, Luther
 1937 *Petroglyphs of Oregon*. University of Oregon Monographs, Studies in Anthropology 2. Eugene.

Crotty, Helen .K.
 1979 Rock Art of the Modoc Territory. In *American Indian Rock Art*, Volume 5, edited by Frank G. Bock, Ken Hedges, Georgia Lee, and Helen Michaelis, pp. 22–35. American Rock Art Research Association, El Toro, California.
 1981 Petroglyph Point Revisited—A Modoc County Site. In *Messages from the Past*, edited by Clement W. Meighan, pp. 141–168. Monograph 20, Institute of Archaeology, University of California, Los Angeles.

Dalton, Kevin D.
 2011 A Geospatial Analysis of Prehistoric Hunting Blinds and Forager Group Size at Cowhead Slough, Modoc County, California. Master's thesis, Department of Anthropology, California State University, Chico.

David, Robert James
 2005 Rock Art as Shamans' Tools: Testing and Refining Landscape Symbolism Models in the Klamath Basin. Master's Thesis, Department of Anthropology, Portland State University, Oregon.
 2010 The Archaeology of Myth: Rock Art, Ritual Objects, and Mythical Landscapes of the Klamath Basin. *Archaeologies: Journal of the World Archaeological Congress* 6(2).
 2012 The Landscape of Klamath Basin Rock Art. Ph.D. Dissertation, Department of Anthropology, University of California, Berkeley.

David, Robert J., and James D. Keyser
 2008 A New Ethnographic Reference for Klamath Basin Rock Art: Shamans' Incantations and Sacred Rock. In International Newsletter on Rock Art (INORA), edited by Jean Clottes, No.50:26–27.

Davis, James T.
    1961. *Trade Routes and Economic Exchange among the Indians of California.* University of California Archaeological Survey Reports No. 54. Berkeley.

Dissanayake, Ellen
    1992 *Homo Aestheticus: Where Art Comes From and Why.* The Free Press, New York.

Dronfield, Jeremy
    1996 The Vision Thing: Diagnosis of Endogenous Derivation in Abstract Arts. *Current Anthropology* 37:373–391.

Edwards, Robert
    1979 *Australian Aboriginal Art: Art of the Alligator River Region, Northern Territory.* Australian Institute of Aboriginal Studies, Canberra.

Garfinkel, Alan, and Donald R. Austin
    2011 Reproductive Symbolism in Great Basin Rock Art: Bighorn Sheep Hunting, Fertility and Forager Ideology. *Cambridge Archaeological Journal* 21:3:453–471.

Garth, Thomas R.
    1953 Atsugewi Ethnography. *University of California Anthropological Records* 14:2. Berkeley.

Gates, Gerald R.
    1980 A Preliminary Report on the Prehistoric Rock Art of the Modoc National Forest. *The Journal of the Modoc County Historical Society* 2:69–103.

Gilreath, Amy J.
    2007 Rock Art in the Golden State: Pictographs and Petroglyphs, Portable and Panoramic. In *California Prehistory, Colonization, Culture, and Complexity*, edited by Terry L. Jones and Kathryn A. Klar, pp. 273–290. Altamira Press, Lanham, Maryland.

Grant, Campbell
    1967 *Rock Art of the American Indian.* Thomas Y. Crowell Co., New York.

Guenther, Mathias
    1999 From Totemism to Shamanism: Hunter-Gatherer Contributions to World Mythology and Spirituality. In *The Cambridge Encyclopedia of Hunters and Gatherers*, edited by Richard B. Lee and Richard Daly, pp. 426–433. Cambridge University Press, Cambridge.

Hann, Don, and Gordon Bettles
    2006 House of the Rising Sun: Using the Ethnographic Record to Illuminate Aspects of Klamath Basin Rock Art. In *Talking with the Past, the Ethnography of Rock Art*, edited by James D. Keyser, George Poetschat, and Michael W. Taylor, pp. 176–192. Oregon Archaeological Society, Portland.

Hann, Don, James D. Keyser, and Phillip Cash Cash
    2010 Columbia Plateau Rock Art: A Window to the Spirit World. In *Rock Art of the Oregon Country: Honoring the Lorings' Legacy*, edited by James D. Keyser and George Poetschat, pp. 1–24. Collected Papers in Oregon Rock Art, Oregon Archaeological Society Press Publication No. 18. Portland, Oregon.

Harman, Jon
    2015 Using DStretch for Rock Art Recording. *International Newsletter on Rock Art (INORA)*, 72:24–30.

Hedges, Ken
    1992 Shamanistic Aspects of California Rock Art. In *California Indian Shamanism*, edited by Lowell John Bean, pp. 67–88. Ballena Press, Menlo Park, California.

    2001 Traversing the Great Gray Middle Ground: An Examination of Shamanistic Interpretation of Rock Art. In *American Indian Rock Art*, Volume 27, edited by Steven M. Freers and Alanah Woody, pp. 123–136. American Rock Art Research Association, Tucson, Arizona.

Heizer, Robert F.
    1942 Massacre Lake Cave, Tule Lake Cave and Shore Sites. In *Archaeological Researches in the Northern Great Basin*, edited by Luther S. Cressman, pp. 121–134. Carnegie Institution of Washington, Publication 538.

Heizer, Robert F., and Martin A. Baumhoff
    1962 *Prehistoric Rock Art of Nevada and Eastern California.* University of California Press, Berkeley.

Heizer, Robert F., and C. William Clewlow, Jr.
    1973 *Prehistoric Rock Art of California.* Ballena Press, Socorro, New Mexico.

Helvenston, Patricia A., and Paul G. Bahn
    2005 *Waking the Trance-Fixed.* Wasteland Press, Louisville, Kentucky.

Huntley, Jillian A.
    2014 Messages in Paint, An Archaeometric Analysis of Pigment Use in Aboriginal Australia Focusing on the Production of Rock Art. Ph.D dissertation, University of New England, Australia.

Hyder, William D., and Georgia Lee
    1990 Modoc Rock Art: A Reevaluation. In *American Indian Rock Art*, Volume 16, edited by S. A. Turpin, pp. 237–252. A joint publication of the National Park Service; American Rock Art Research Association; and Texas Archaeological Research Laboratory, The University of Texas at Austin.

Johnson, Jerald Jay
    2003 Prehistoric Human Remains, Petroglyphs, Structures, and Miscellaneous Features from Northeastern California. Draft report on file with the Institute of Archaeology and Cultural Studies, Department of Anthropology, California State University, Sacramento.

Kelly, Isabel
    1932 Ethnography of the Surprise Valley Paiute. *University of California Publications in American Archaeology and Ethnology* 31(3):67–210.

Kniffen, Fred B.
    1928 Achomawi Geography. *University of California Publications in American Archaeology and Ethnology* 23(5):297–332.

Keyser, James D., and David S. Whitley
    2006 Sympathetic Magic in Western North American Rock Art. *American Antiquity* 71(1):3–26.

Lee, Georgia, William D. Hyder, and Arlene Benson
    1988 The Rock Art of Petroglyph Point and Fern Cave, Lava Beds National Monument. Report submitted to Lava Beds National Monument, Tulelake, California.

Lewis-Williams, J. David
    2001 Brainstorming Images: Neuropsychology and Rock Art Research. In *Handbook of Rock Art Research*, edited by David S. Whitley, pp. 332–357. AltaMira Press, Walnut Creek, California.

    2002 *A Cosmos in Stone, Interpreting Religion and Society through Rock Art.* AltaMira Press, Walnut Creek, California.

Lewis-Williams, J.D., and Thomas A. Dowson
    1988 The Signs of All Times: Entoptic Phenomena in Upper Paleolithic Art. *Current Anthropology* 29:201–245.

Loring, J. Malcolm, and Louise Loring
  1983 *Pictographs & Petroglyphs of the Oregon County, Part II: Southern Oregon.* Monograph 23, Institute of Archaeology, University of California, Los Angeles.

Loubser, Johannes H. N., David S. Whitley, T. Greiner, Dan Leen, and Joseph Simon
  1999 Recording Eight Places with Rock Art Imagery, Lava Beds National Monument, Northern California. New South Associates Technical Report 604. Submitted to the National Park Service. Copies available from the National Park Service, Arcata, California.

Malotki, Ekkehart
  2007 *The Rock Art of Arizona, Art for Life's Sake.* Kiva Publishing, Walnut, California.

McFall, Grant S.
  2006 Add Shamans and Stir? A Critical Review of the Shamanism Model of Forager Rock Art Production. *Journal of Anthropological Anthropology* 26(2007) 224–233.

Norris, Robert M., and Robert W. Webb
  1990 *Geology of California*, Second Edition. John Wiley & Sons, New York.

Olmsted, D. L., and Omer Stewart
  1978 Achumawi. In *California, Handbook of North American Indians*, Volume 8, edited by Robert F. Heizer, pp. 225–235. Smithsonian Institution, Washington, D.C.

Park, Susan
  1986 *Samson Grant, Atsuge Shaman.* Occasional Papers of the Redding Museum, Number 3. Redding, California.

Pearson, James L.
  2002 *Shamanism and the Ancient Mind.* AltaMira Press, Walnut Creek, California.

Quinlan, Angus R.
  2000 The Ventriloquist's Dummy: A Critical Review of Shamanism and Rock Art in Far Western North America. *Journal of California and Great Basin Anthropology* 22(1):92–108.
  2001 Smoke and Mirrors: Rock Art and Shamanism in California and the Great Basin. In *The Concept of Shamanism: Uses and Abuses,* edited by Henri-Paul Francfort and Robert N. Hamayon, pp. 189–206. Akadémiai Kiadó, Budapest.

Ricks, Mary Francis
  1996 *A Survey and Analysis of Prehistoric Rock Art of the Warner Valley Region, Lake County, Oregon.* Technical Report 96-1. Department of Anthropology, University of Nevada, Reno.

Ricks, Mary F., and William J. Cannon
  1993 A Preliminary Report on the Lake County, Oregon, Rock Art Inventory: A Data Base for Rock Art Inventory. In *American Indian Rock Art*, Volume 12, edited William D. Hyder, pp. 93–100. American Rock Art Research Association, San Miguel, California.

Ritter, Eric W.
  1999 Boundary, Style and Function: Extrapolations from the Keno, Oregon Pictographs. In *American Indian Rock Art*, Volume 25, edited by Steven M. Freers, pp. 81–100. American Rock Art Research Association, Tucson.

Ross, Michelle Antonia
  2000 Test Excavations at Three Mid-Elevation Rock Art Sites, Warner Valley, Oregon. Master's thesis, Department of Anthropology, Washington State University, Pullman.

Roybal, Gerald, and Thomas Evans
  1982 Sites with Cultural Significance for the Upriver Bands of the Pit River Tribe. Report prepared for the Bureau of Land Management, Susanville, California.

Silver, Constance S.
  1982 The Pictographs of Fern Cave, Lava Beds National Monument: Agents of Deterioration and Prospects for Conservation. Report submitted to the National Park Service, San Francisco.

Spier, Leslie
  1930 Klamath Ethnography. *University of California Publications in American Archaeology and Ethnology* 30. Berkeley.

Stern, Theodore
  1998 Klamath and Modoc. In *Plateau, Handbook of North American Indians*, Volume 12, edited by Deward E. Walker, Jr., pp. 446–466. Smithsonian Institution, Washington, D.C.

Steward, Julian H.
  1929 Petroglyphs of California and Adjoining States. *University of California Publications in American Archaeology and Ethnology* 24(2):47–238. Berkeley.

Swartz, Ben K. Jr.
  1960 A Bibliography of Klamath Basin Anthropology with Excerpts and Annotations. Research Papers No. 3. Klamath County Museum, Klamath Falls, Oregon.
  1963 Klamath Basin Petroglyphs. Archives of Archaeology 21. University of Wisconsin Press, Madison.
  1978 Klamath Basin Petroglyphs, Revised and Abridged. Ballena Press Anthropological Papers No. 12. Socorro, New Mexico.
  1998 A Comparative Design Element Analysis of Klamath Basin (Modoc), Southern Sierra (Yokuts), and Santa Barbara (Chumash) Pictograph Styles, California-Oregon. In *Rock Art Studies in the Great Basin,* edited by Eric W. Ritter, pp. 113–125. Coyote Press Archives of Great Basin Prehistory No. 1. Salinas, California.

Taçon, Paul S.
  1999 Identifying Ancient Sacred Landscapes in Australia: From Physical to Social. In *Archaeologies of Landscape,* edited by Wendy Ashmore and A. Bernard Knapp, pp. 33–57. Blackwell Publishers, Malden, Massachusetts

Thomas, David Hurst
  2013 Great Basin Projectile Point Typology: Still Relevant? *Journal of California and Great Basin Anthropology* 33(2):133–152.

Troncoso, Andres, Francisca Moya Cañoles, and Mara Basile
  2016 Rock Art and Social networks among Hunter Gatherers of North-Central Chile. *Journal of Anthropological Archaeology* 42:154–168.

Van Tilburg, Jo Anne
  2012 Rock Art, Aesthetics, and Belief. In *Rock Art at Little Lake, An Ancient Crossroads in the California Desert,* edited by Jo Anne VanTilburg, Gordon E. Hull, and John C. Bretney, pp. 151–175. The Costen Institute of Archaeology, University of California. Los Angeles.

Van Tilburg, Jo Anne, and Clarus Backes, Jr.
  2012 Painted Rock Art and Stahl Site Pigments. In *Rock Art at Little Lake, An Ancient Crossroads in the California Desert,* edited by Jo Anne VanTilburg, Gordon E. Hull, and John C. Bretney, pp. 134–150. The Costen Institute of Archaeology, University of California. Los Angeles.

Voegelin, Erminie W.
  1942 Culture Element Distribution, 20: Northeast California. *University of California Anthropological Records* 7(2):47–251.

Wallace, Henry D., and James P. Holmlund
  1986 Petroglyphs of the Picacho Mountains, South Central, Arizona. *Institute for American Research Anthropological Papers* 6. Tucson.

Wellmann, Klaus
  1979 *A Survey of North American Indian Rock Art*. Akademische Druck-w. Verlagsanstalt, Graz, Austria.

Whitley, David S.
  1998 Finding Rain in the Desert: Landscape, Gender and Far Western North American Rock-art. In *The Archaeology of Rock-Art*, edited by Christopher Chippindale and Paul S.C. Taçon, pp. 11–29. Cambridge University Press, Cambridge, England.

  2000a *The Art of the Shaman, Rock Art in California*. The University of Utah Press, Salt Lake City.

  2000b Use and Abuse of Ethnohistory in the Far West. In *1999 International Rock Art Congress Proceedings*, Volume 1, edited by Peggy Whitehead and Lawrence Loendorf, pp. 127–154. American Rock Art Research Association, Tucson.

  2006 Rock Art and Rites of Passage in Far Western North America. In *Talking with the Past, the Ethnography of Rock Art*, edited by James D. Keyser, George Poetschat, and Michael W. Taylor, pp. 295–325. Oregon Archaeological Society, Portland.

Whitley, David S., Johannes H. N. Loubser, and Don Hann
  2004 Friends in Low Places: Rock Art and Landscape on the Modoc Plateau. In *Pictures in Place: Landscape of Rock-Art*, edited by C. Chippindale and G. Nash, pp. 217–238. Cambridge University Press, Cambridge, England.

Woody, Alanah J.
  2000 How to Do Things with Petroglyphs: The Rock Art of Nevada. Ph.D. Dissertation, Department of Archaeology, University of Southampton, England.

Wright, Aaron M.
  2014 *Religion on the Rocks, Hohokam Rock Art, Ritual Practice, and Social Transformation*. The University of Utah Press, Salt Lake City.

Dating Western Message Petroglyphs with Aztec and Maya Glyphs

Judy F. Hilbish

Western Message Petroglyphs (WMP) can be dated in part by oral history from the 1880s that implies the carvings were made in or before the 1880s, and by the founding dates (predominately mid to late 1800s) for the town closest to the site. These dates correlate well with when the symbols from various cultures appeared in U.S. and European literature as the result of the decipherments of many writing systems in the 1800s. I discuss 15 WMP panels with Aztec and Maya symbols. The decipherment dates of these symbols are helpful in suggesting the earliest construction date for these petroglyphs. The context of one glyph as used in WMP refines the definition of the Aztec glyph that has several possible meanings, and narrows the time frame for panels using this symbol from 1831 to 1903, while Maya symbols place carvings containing them to 1864 and later.

A group of petroglyph symbols known as Western Message Petroglyphs (WMP) are characterized by their locations close to mining towns and supply centers of the Gold Rush era and later, the linear arrangement of the culturally diverse but limited number of symbols used, and the limited size range of the symbols. The word "Message" in the name implies that WMP can be read. Since the collection of symbols used for these carvings does not correspond to any known writing system, it is important to determine the time frame in which they were created in order to establish a cultural reference point for their eventual decipherment.

The locations of the sites are given in Figure 1 along with the earliest known dates for prospecting or settlement of nearby locations. Other than one site near a mission in California, the sites were generally prospected before settlement starting with the Gold Rush in 1848 and continuing to 1901 with the silver strike in Tonopah, Nevada. The WMP are usually found within a mile of the towns and in some cases are now within city limits.

Oral history for some of the sites suggests a time frame in which these carvings might have been done: no later than the late 1800s to early 1900s (Table 1). The source of the symbols may provide a *terminus post quem*. The unusual combination of symbols from several cultures, including Egyptian, Mesoamerican, Chinese, European, and the predominance of Ojibwa and Sioux (Figure 2) found in WMP creates the issue of how the carver(s) may have learned of these symbols.

One way for the creators of the images to learn of the symbols used in the WMP would have been to travel to Central America, then to Egypt, and on to China to learn the few non-Indian symbols in WMP. The problem with this is that travel took time and was fraught with risk including disease. Then there still remained the time needed to travel to the eight western states of the U.S. to create the sites. The hieroglyphs of Mesoamerica and Egyptian cultures

Judy F. Hilbish
Private Researcher

Figure 1. Map of the Western Message Petroglyphs and the approximate dates of first prospecting or settlement.

Figure 2. Silver City, New Mexico. Western Message Petroglyph located on a limestone bluff, illustrating some of the cultural sources of the symbols.

the scripts from these two areas occurred in the early 1800s and later in Europe and the Americas.

Multiple sources about newly interpreted writing systems were available in the 1800s ranging from encyclopedias, travel books such as John Stephens' travels through Central America, journals published by scientific organizations, the U.S government's series on ethnology, and countless publications from Europe. As early as 1819 Thomas Young's article in the Encyclopaedia Britannica (Young 1819) included decipherment of Egyptian hieroglyphs subsequently used in WMP, and Champollion published his Grammaire Egyptienne in 1836. This sets the earliest possible date for WMP to the early 1800s.

Dates for WMP that contain Aztec and Maya glyphs (Figure 3) can be further narrowed by the dates these symbols first appeared in the literature. The symbols of interest started appearing in the literature with their decipherment as early as 1810 (von Humboldt 2012) and continued to 1876 (Rosny 1876) and beyond. Decipherment of the Aztec and Maya documents and monuments has been corrected, refined, and expanded since that time, but the focus here is the state of knowledge prior to the dates indicated by oral histories.

The first symbol to consider is an ellipse that had multiple interpretations starting in the early 1800s. The ellipse in question closely resembles the Aztec symbol *tecpatl*, meaning "flint" (von Humboldt 2012:171). It is used in different ways in the codices and has multiple forms (Figure 4). One definition is a designation in the calendar system, and in other instances it is used as a descriptive element in the pictorial representations of various entities per discussions found in Kingsborough, as discussed below. There is no discussion in early pub-

were virtually dead writing systems as far as the indigenous people were concerned. An easier way to acquire the knowledge of the various writing systems would be to read about their translations. The deciphering of

Table 1. Oral history for WMP with Aztec/Maya symbols.

Rockville, California	Late 1800s to early 1900s[1]
Durango, Colorado	Late 1800s to early 1900s[2]
Del Norte, Colorado	Late 1800s[3]
Silver City, New Mexico	1880s[4]
Ogden, Utah	1880[5]

[1]Interview with Ken Stark, 1996. [2]Interview with Tod Stoddard, 2004.
[3]General consensus of town historians per Ken Frye(?).
[4]Interview by Gary Hobson of grandson of discoverer of the site.
[5]Mark Stuart's interview about 1975 with Ezra Nelson.

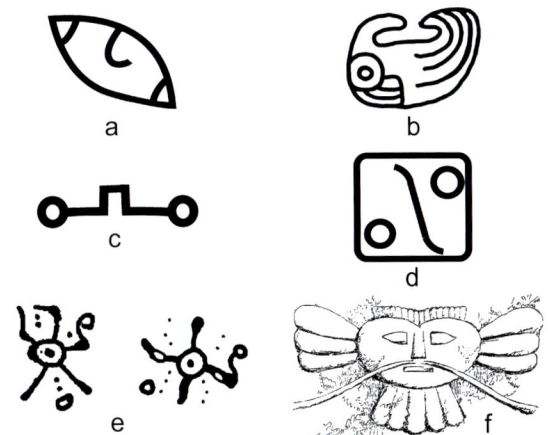

Figure 3. Mesomerican glyphs in the WMP: (a) tecpatl, (b) manik, (c) ma, (d) cimi, (e) crater spewing rocks, (f) a deity.

Figure 4. Forms of tecpatl in the codices: (a) Duran 1971:36; (b) von Humboldt 2012:Plate 23; (c) von Humboldt 2012:Plate 13; (d) Codex Vaticanus 3773 (Kingsborough 1831b:Plate 17); (e) Codex Vaticanus 3773 (Kingsborough 1831b:Plate 45; (f) Codex Vaticanus 3773 (Kingsborough 1831b:Plate 75); (g) Codex Fjérváry (Kingsborough 1831d: Plate 39); (h) Codex Laud (Kingsborough 1831c:Plate 30).

lications of the form of *tecpatl* found in WMP so it is necessary to follow the discussions of the various forms of the glyph to arrive at its meaning.

Fray Diego Duran described *tecpatl* in the 1500s in a document called the Codex Duran. It was divided into three parts, History, Book of The Gods and Rites, and The Ancient Calendar (Duran 1971:xviii). Spanish authorities and the Church feared the spread of paganism through such works and suppressed his work as well as works of others on the Mesoamerican cultures. Jose Fernando Ramírez salvaged the manuscript three centuries later and it was published by Eduardo Gallo in 1873. In the section on the calendar, Duran described the ellipse (Figure 4a), the eighteenth day sign, as Flint Knife (Duran 1971:395). Considered the worst sign, it was "hard as flint, and harsh" and anyone born under this sign would "be fortunate [in many things] except in being fertile and in engendering children" (Duran 1971:403, Plate 36). The Flint Knife symbolized the years associated with north, depicted by *tecpatl*. *Tecpatl*, with its implication of harshness, indicated these times were cold, fraught with ice and times of hunger (Duran 1971:392).

Von Humboldt traveled through the Americas in the late eighteenth century. A product of these excursions was *Views of the Cordilleras*, printed in French between 1810 and 1813 as a series of articles. The basalt relief Aztec calendar (von Humboldt 2012:155, Plate 23) shows another form of the eighteenth day glyph, *tecpatl*, which he calls "flint or gun flint" (von Humboldt 2012:165) (Figure 4b). Another form of the glyph recognized by von Humboldt is displayed in his Plate 13, from the Codex Vaticanus 3773 (von Humboldt 2012:87, 16) (Figure 4c).

Continuing with Codex Vaticanus 3773, there is a discussion of the Aztec calendar. It states "the third sign was a razor or stone knife, by which are meant the wars and dissensions of the world: they call it Tequepatl" (Kingsborough 1831e:197). From Plates 17, 45, and 75 of the Codex Vaticanus 3773, some of the various forms of *tecpatl* are seen. Each of the plates is discussed in volume 6. In Plate 17 (Figure 4d) we see "This man and woman...the first pair who existed in the world...Between them is placed a knife or razor" (Kingsborough 1831e:198). Plate 45 (Figure 4e) pictures the god Yxpapalotl, "a knife of butterflies," and "on this account they paint him surrounded by knives, and wings of butterflies" (Kingsborough 1831e:210). Finally Plate 75 (Figure 4f) leads to a discussion of glyphs associated with various body parts where *tecpatl* represents the teeth (Kingsborough 1831e:223). Kingsborough identifies the "Mexican hieroglyphic for...knives or flints to denote its sharpness" in reference to Clavigero's reference to a depiction of "Itzehecajan, the place of the wind of razors or flint" (Kingsborough 1831e:158).

Finally, by their association with other calendric glyphs, it is easy to discover *tecpatl* in the Codices Fejérváry and Laud (respectively, Kingsborough 1831d:Plate 39, 1831c:Plate 30) (Figures 4g, h). It is the Codex Laud form of *tecpatl* that is found in the WMP. Extrapolating from the type of *tecpatl* in Plate 45 of Vaticanus 3773 and the interpretation of the central figure: "they paint him surrounded by knives" (Kingsborough 1831e:210) (Figure 4e), it is a simple matter to interpret the ellipse at the end of the speech scroll in the Codex Selden (Kingsborough 1831a:Plate 7) (Figure 5) as *tecpatl* and therefore indicating sharp speech. The appearance of *tecpatl* at the end of the speech bars at Tonopah confirms the interpretation of this glyph as "sharp, harsh" (Figure 6). Also, WMP have two Maya

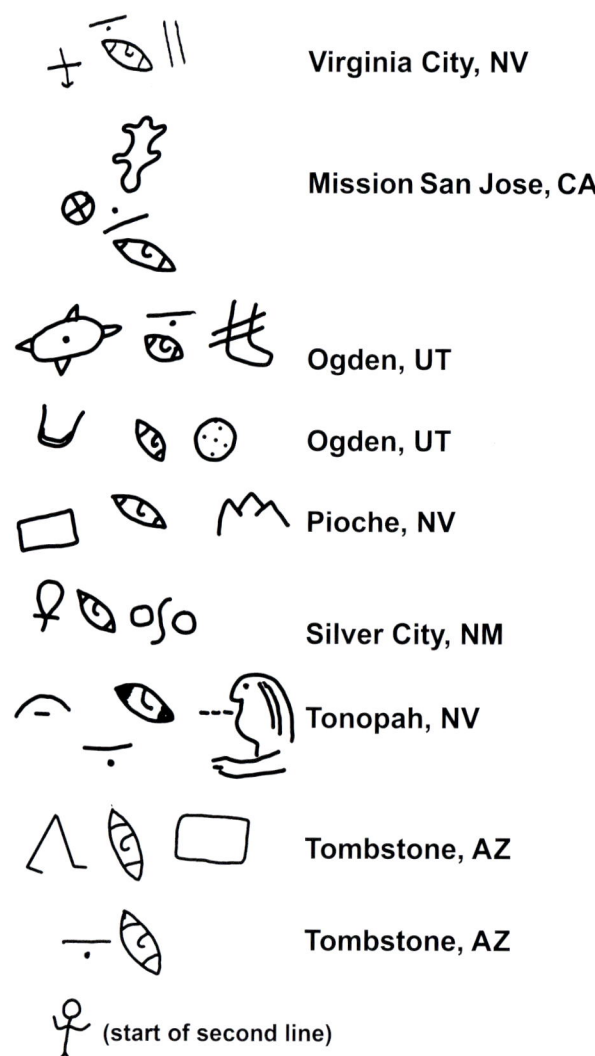

Figure 6. Tecpatl *shown in context in the Western Message Petroglyphs.*

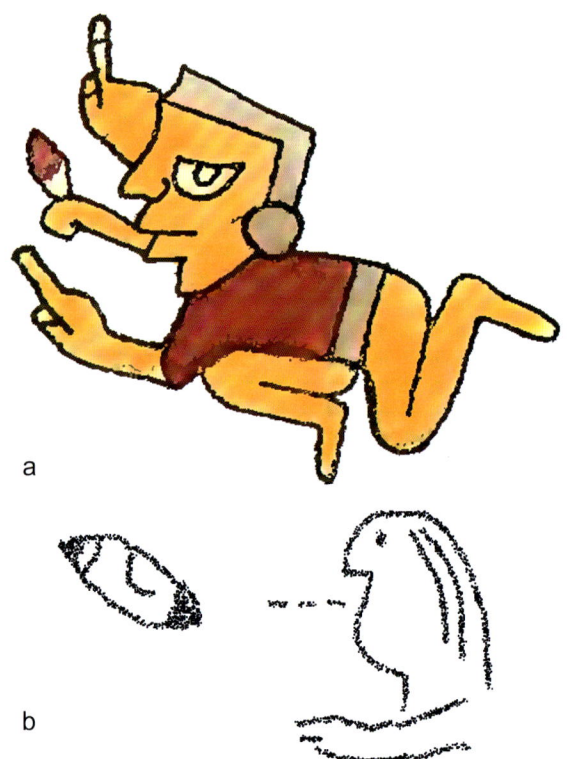

Figure 5. (a) Codex Selden, Leaf 7, line 3, demonstrating tecpatl *next to a speech scroll; (b)* tecpatl *next to a speech bar at Tonopah, Nevada.*

symbols that come from the calendar systems. As calendric notations, they would be accompanied by bars and dots to indicate a date. In the WMP this does not happen for the two Maya glyphs. There is only one WMP site where a date is clearly indicated. At St. George, Utah, a glyph designating the "Thunder moon" (August) shows a thunderbird over a crescent moon as found in Indian writing systems (Tomkins 1931:83). It appears that designations for dates were not important to the carver(s) and that *tecpatl* and the calendric Maya symbols had other meanings in WMP, as discussed later. Thus *tecpatl* in the WMP is probably a descriptive term indicating harsh, sharp, flint, or even possibly north.

A critical issue with Edward King's 1831 publications as a source for this decipherment of *tecpatl* is that there were less than 100 copies printed of his nine volume series and these were distributed to notable persons in Europe. But it was not unheard of in the U.S. After the Gold Rush, the Bay Area became a major financial center in the West. Entrepreneurs from the east coast brought with them their culture. Libraries were in demand and copies of King's works were not left out. The California State Library in Sacramento obtained a complete set of the *Antiquities* in 1863 for $1600 (Gary Kurutz, electronic communication, 2010). Another set was purchased by the San Francisco Mercantile Library prior to 1874 as indicated in their third catalog now published on the Web (Whitaker 1874:32). This confirms that certain WMP (Tonopah, Virginia City, and Pioche, Nevada; Ogden, Utah; Silver City, New Mexico; and Mission San Jose, California) were carved no earlier than 1831 but possibly after 1863 or 1874 if the California libraries were the source of Kingsborough's works used by the carver(s) of the WMP.

Two other Maya glyphs help narrow the timeframe further. The Franciscan bishop to the Yucatan, Fray Diego de Landa, did interviews and wrote his findings in 1566. His works as well as those of other historians were subsequently suppressed by the Church until the 1800s. A copy of his works was found and translated by another priest, Abbe Brasseur de Bourbourg, who published his translation in 1864. The longer he wrote, the more his writings fell into disfavor due to his lack of scientific methods and his conclusions that became more far fetched as he aged. However, he was still a prominent authority on the Maya writing system in the mid 1800s and made the first significant inroads to decipherment of the Maya script. His translation (Brasseur de Bourbourg 1864:318, 494) of Landa's work, *Relation des Choses de Yucatan de Diego Landa*, produced the translation of "no, none, negative" for the symbol *ma* (Figure 3c), which is found slightly modified from Brasseur's rendition of the symbol in WMP sites at Del Norte, Colorado, and Tombstone, Arizona (Figure 7).

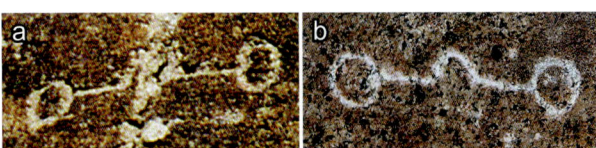

Figure 7. The Maya symbol ma in (a) Del Norte, Colorado, and (b) Tombstone, Arizona.

Another glyph of Landa's in Brasseur de Bourbourg's translation (1864:373) was for a hand, known as *manik* (Figure 3b), a day sign used in the Maya calendar. *Manik* was deciphered by Landa as "the wind that passes" ("le vent qui passe") and had different forms. Brasseur later described this symbol as *main que se ferme*, the "hand that closes" (Brasseur de Bourbourg 1869:78). As a definition, "the hand that closes" fits the context for this symbol in the WMP. It is used in a reversed manner (Figure 8), with palm down, at Grand Junction, Colorado, with a symbol that may be modified from the Egyptian symbol for "revolve" or "turn." This suggests Brasseur's later description of the "the hand that closes" as the correct decipherment and upside down it may represent a hand in the process of dropping something. Daniel Brinton (1895:111) reiterated Brasseur's description of *manik* and states that the glyph is a rebus for the word mach meaning "to grasp." Thus, the panels containing *manik* suggest that they may have been carved in 1869 at the earliest.

Figure 8. Manik *as used in the Grand Junction Western Message Petroglyph.*

The final Maya symbol to be considered is *cimi* (Figure 3d), a symbol for "death or dead." It has two basic forms, the most common of which is a skull, seen, along with its Aztec counterpart *miquiztli*, in the calendar systems of both cultures, and found in the Fillmore, Utah, WMP. The other form of *cimi*, found at Silver City, New Mexico, and Fillmore and St. George, Utah, is the Maya symbol shown here in Figure 9. This form

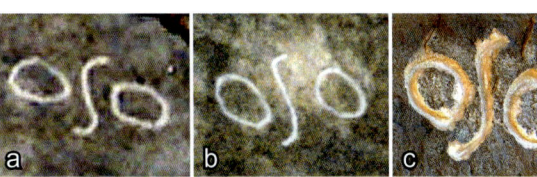

Figure 9. Cimi *as seen in the Western Message Petroglyphs. (a) Silver City, New Mexico; (b) Fillmore, Utah; (c) St. George, Utah.*

is found in the codex Troano, which is now known to be a part of the codex Madrid, along with the codex Cortesiano. Leon de Rosny (1876) deciphered this alternate form of *cimi* and noted that it appeared with different orientations. Thus the three WMP with this second form of *cimi* were carved in or after 1875.

A symbol that may be Maya is a five-rayed glyph (Figure 3e) with a central circle and four dots placed in various locations between the rays and is found at Tempe and Tombstone, Arizona, and Silver City, New Mexico. It also somewhat resembles an alchemy symbol for verdigris, a copper compound (Frutiger 1998:300). Unfortunately most references on alchemy symbols do not give source information. A Maya symbol is noted by Brasseur de Bourbourg (1869:219) in his book on the Codex Troano that closely matches the WMP symbol. He recognizes two forms of "an open crater spurting rock and gas" (*symboles d'un cratère ouvert d'où s'élancent des pierres et du gaz*). One has five rays and the other four rays, each with dots interspersed between the rays (Figure 10). Either interpretation of the symbol may be relevant to these WMP sites. There is evidence of extensive lava fields and craters in New Mexico and from mid to southern Arizona. These areas are also notable for copper mining.

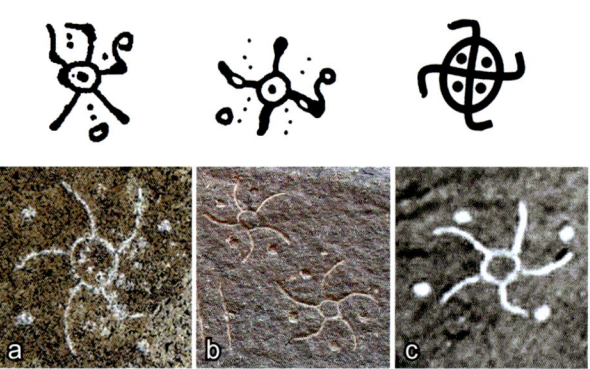

Figure 10. Symbols at (a) Tombstone and (b) Tempe, Arizona, and (c) Silver City, New Mexico, compared to two Maya symbols on the upper left (Brasseur de Bourbourg 1869:219) and the alchemy symbol on the upper right. Tempe photo by Alvin McLane. Silver City photo by T. Carter.

Finally, a symbol at the Genoa, Nevada, WMP is almost identical to an illustration (Pim and Seemann 1869:128) of a portion of a sculpture found in a cave near Limon, New Segovia, in Nicaragua (Figure 11). This illustration sets the earliest date, 1869, that the Genoa WMP could have been carved. Their illustration was subsequently published in *Native Races* (Bancroft 1883). Pim and Seemann described the figure as "a human face representing the sun, the hair doing duty for the rays." They felt that the "long appendages" represented moustaches, thus suggesting that the culture there had contact with a bearded race. However, considering the importance of serpents and snakes among various Indian tribes, the appendages might represent a snake.

Figure 11. Drawing of a portion of a sculpture found in New Segovia, Nicaragua (Pim and Seemann 1869:128), compared to the glyph in Genoa, Nevada (Elsasser and Contreras 1958:13).

As an aside, Garrett Mallery's *Picture-Writing of the American Indians*, printed in 1893, has been a popular source of North and Central American Indian symbols. It also contained a smattering of symbols from other cultures. Was his work a source for the Aztec and Maya glyphs discussed here? Probably not since his work was published after the dates indicated by oral history for the WMP with the symbol *ma*. The only other pertinent Maya symbols from Mallery are "flint," which was not the same style as seen in WMP (Mallery 1893:614, Plate 49), and a "turtle" that was a misdrawn representation of *manik* (Mallery 1893:756, Figures 1281a through 1281d).

It has been shown that the dates for prospecting and settlement of the areas where WMP are located, dates given by oral histories, and publication dates for Aztec and Maya symbols are consistent with each other (Table 2), thus narrowing the time frame for the creation of the this unique group of petroglyphs from 1831 to the latter 1800s, and possibly as late as 1901. With this time line, I suggest the culture and times the carver(s) chose to "write" about were the early days of mining and settlement of the West in the latter 1800s. This cultural setting may help us understand the nature of the "messages" in WMP. Narrowing the time line will also help further investigations of these carvings relative to their historical setting and may lead to the identity of the carver(s).

References Cited

Bancroft, Hubert Howe
   1883 *Native Races: The Works of Hubert Howe Bancroft, IV*. A. L. Bancroft & Co., San Francisco.

Table 2. Earliest possible dates for some of the Western Message Petroglyphs according to the publication dates of certain Aztec and Maya Symbols.

Symbol	Site	PD	OH	GD
Tecpatl		1831	1880	
	Ogden, UT			1847
	Mission San Jose, CA			1797
	Tonopah, NV			1901
	Pioche, NV			1864
	Virginia City, NV			1859
Ma		1864	late 1800s	
	Del Norte, CO			1871
	Tombstone, AZ			1871
Manik		1869	late 1800s–early 1900s	
	Rockville, CA			
	Grand Junction, CO			1881
	Virginia City, NV			1859
	Fillmore, UT		1879	1851
	Manti, UT			1849
	Provo, UT			1849
Cimi		1876		
	Silver City, NM		1880s	1862
	Fillmore, UT		1879	1851
PD = Publication Date for Symbol OH = Oral History GD = General dates for Prospecting/Township				

Brasseur de Bourbourg, Charles Étienne
 1864 *Relation Des Choses de Yucatan de Diego de Landa*. Trubner and Co., London and Paris.
 1869 *Manucrit Troano: Etudes sur le Systeme Graphique et la Langue Des Mayas*. Imprimerie Imperiale, Paris.

Brinton, Daniel G.
 1895 *A Primer of Mayan Hieroglyphics*. University of Pennsylvania Series in Philology Literature and Archaeology. Ginn and Company, Boston.

Champollion, J. F.
 1836 *Grammaire Egyptienne*. Firmin Didot Freres, Paris.

Duran, Fray Diego
 1971 *Book of the Gods and Rites and the Ancient Calendar*. Translated and Edited by Fernando Horcasitas and Doris Heyden. University of Oklahoma Pres, Norman, Oklahoma.

Elsasser, Albert B., and Eduardo Contreras
 1958 Modern Petrography in Central California and Western Nevada. Papers on California Archaeology 65. *Reports of the University of California Archaeological Survey* 41:12–18.

Frutiger, Adrian
 1998 *Signs and Symbols: Their Design and Meaning*. Watson-Guptill, New York.

Kingsborough, Lord (Edward King), editor
 1831a Fac-Simile of an Original Mexican Painting Preserved in the Selden Collection of Manuscripts in the Bodleian Library at Oxford (Marked Arch. Seld. A. 2. MSS Ang. 3135). In *Antiquities of Mexico: Fac-Similes of Ancient Mexican Paintings and Hieroglyphics, Preserved in the Royal Libraries of Paris, Berlin, and Dresden, in the Imperial Library of Vienna, in the Vatican Library, in the Borgian Museum at Rome, in the Library of the Institute at Bologna and in the Bodleian Library at Oxford, Together with the Monuments of New Spain by M. Dupaix, with Their Respective Scales of Measurement and Accompanying Descriptions, the Whole Illustrated by Many Valuable Inedited Manuscripts, by Lord Kingsborough, the Drawings, on Stone, by A. Aglio, in Seven Volumes*, Volume 1, Part 5. Robert Havell, 77, Oxford Street, and Colnaghi, Son, and Co., Pall Mall East, London.

 1831b Copy of a Mexican Manuscript, Preserved in the Library of the Vatican: 149 Pages (Marked No. 3738). In *Antiquities of Mexico: Fac-Similes of Ancient Mexican Paintings and Hieroglyphics, Preserved in the Royal Libraries of Paris, Berlin, and Dresden, in the Imperial Library of Vienna, in the Vatican Library, in the Borgian Museum at Rome, in the Library of the Institute at Bologna and in the Bodleian Library at Oxford, Together with the Monuments of New Spain by M. Dupaix, with Their Respective Scales of Measurement and Accompanying Descriptions, the Whole Illustrated by Many Valuable Inedited Manuscripts, by Lord Kingsborough, the Drawings, on Stone, by A. Aglio, in Seven Volumes*, Volume 2, Part 1. Robert Havell, 77, Oxford Street, and Colnaghi, Son, and Co., Pall Mall East, London.

 1831c Fac-simile of an Original Mexican Painting, Given to the University of Oxford by Archbishop Laud, and Preserved in the Bodleian Library: 46 Pages (Marked Laud. B. 65. Nunc 678. Cat. MSS. Angl. 546). In *Antiquities of Mexico: Fac-Similes of Ancient Mexican Paintings and Hieroglyphics, Preserved in the Royal Libraries of Paris, Berlin, and Dresden, in the Imperial Library of Vienna, in the Vatican Library, in the Borgian Museum at Rome, in the Library of the Institute at Bologna and in the Bodleian Library at Oxford, Together with the Monuments of New Spain by M. Dupaix, with Their Respective Scales of Measurement and Accompanying Descriptions, the Whole Illustrated by Many Valuable Inedited Manuscripts, by Lord Kingsborough, the Drawings, on Stone, by A. Aglio, in Seven Volumes*, Volume 2, Part 2. Robert Havell, 77, Oxford Street, and Colnaghi, Son, and Co., Pall Mall East, London.

1831d Fac-simile of an Original Mexican Painting in the Possession of M. De Fejérváry, at Pess, in Hungary. In *Antiquities of Mexico: Fac-Similies of Ancient Mexican Paintings and Hieroglyphics, Preserved in the Royal Libraries of Paris, Berlin, and Dresden, in the Imperial Library of Vienna, in the Vatican Library, in the Borgian Museum at Rome, in the Library of the Institute at Bologna and in the Bodleian Library at Oxford, Together with the Monuments of New Spain by M. Dupaix, with Their Respective Scales of Measurement and Accompanying Descriptions, the Whole Illustrated by Many Valuable Inedited Manuscripts, by Lord Kingsborough, the Drawings, on Stone, by A. Aglio, in Seven Volumes*, Volume 3, Part 3. Robert Havell, 77, Oxford Street, and Colnaghi, Son, and Co., Pall Mall East, London.

1831e The Translation of the Explanation of the Mexican Paintings of the Codex Vaticanus. In *Antiquities of Mexico: Fac-Similies of Ancient Mexican Paintings and Hieroglyphics, Preserved in the Royal Libraries of Paris, Berlin, and Dresden, in the Imperial Library of Vienna, in the Vatican Library, in the Borgian Museum at Rome, in the Library of the Institute at Bologna and in the Bodleian Library at Oxford, Together with the Monuments of New Spain by M. Dupaix, with Their Respective Scales of Measurement and Accompanying Descriptions, the Whole Illustrated by Many Valuable Inedited Manuscripts, by Lord Kingsborough, the Drawings, on Stone, by A. Aglio, in Seven Volumes*, Volume 6, pp. 155–232. Robert Havell, 77, Oxford Street, and Colnaghi, Son, and Co., Pall Mall East, London.

Mallery, Garrick
1893 *Picture-Writing of the American Indians*. Tenth Annual Report of the Bureau of Ethnology, 1888–1889. Facsimile reprint 1972, Dover Publications, New York.

Pim, Bedford, and Berthold Seemann
1869 *Dottings on the Roadside, in Panama, Nicaragua, and Mosquito*. Chapman and Hall, London.

Rosny, Leon de
1876 *Sur le Dechiffrement de Ecriture Hieratiqui de L'Amerique Centrale*. Imprimerie et Librairie de Mme V. Bouchard-Huzard, Paris.

Tomkins, William
1931 *Universal Sign Language of the Plains Indians of North America*. 5th edition. William Tomkins, San Diego, California. Facsimile reprint 1969, published under the title *Indian Sign Language*, Dover Publications, New York.

von Humboldt, Alexander
2012 *Views of the Cordilleras and Monuments of the Indigenous Peoples of the Americas: A Critical Edition*. Edited by Vera M. Kutzinski and Ottmar Ette, translated by F. Ryan Poynter. University of Chicago Press, Chicago. Originally published as *Vues des Cordillères et Monumens des Peuples Indigènes de l'Amérique* in various editions, Paris, 1810–1816.

Whitaker, A. E., editor
1874 *Catalogue of the Library of the Mercantile Library Association of San Francisco*. Mercantile Library Association, San Francisco.

Young, Thomas
1819 Egypt. In *Supplement to the Fourth, Fifth, and Sixth Editions of the Encyclopaedia Britannica, Volume Fourth*, pp. 38–74 and Plates 74–78. Archibald, Constable and Company, Edinburgh.

Becoming Human: Rock Art Depictions of Transformation in Landscapes of Emergence

Janine Hernbrode and Peter Boyle

Two circles connected by a straight line form a common Hohokam petroglyph motif often referred to as a "barbell." At the Sutherland Wash Rock Art District near Tucson, we observed this motif is often elaborated with additional components similar to those present in anthropomorphs. In addition, we noted that some petroglyphs that are clearly anthropomorphs resemble barbells because they have characteristics such as bowed legs and uplifted arms forming a circle. Our analysis of 90 such glyphs at Sutherland Wash suggests that there is a continuum of glyphs from clear barbells to clear anthropomorphs with a range of transitional images in between. We observed a similar pattern at the Cocoraque Butte Complex, another site near Tucson, as well as a different set of motifs resembling anthropomorphs arranged in groups in a very linear fashion. Coupled with landscape features suggesting places of origin, we propose that these glyphs represent human transformation following emergence from another level in a tiered universe, analogous to the transformations described in some creation stories in the American Southwest.

This paper focuses on petroglyphs located primarily at two sites near Tucson, Arizona that include motifs we believe are related to each other and, to our knowledge, have not been previously described in the literature. We offer an interpretation of this imagery based on landscape features common to the two sites and ethnographic information regarding tribal origin stories in the Southwest. We suggest that the images relate to human emergence from a lower world to the present world and, in some cases, involve a physical transformation of the emergent beings.

The two sites are the Sutherland Wash Rock Art District (Figure 1) and The Cocoraque Butte Complex (Figure 2), two large rock art sites located in the Sonoran Desert at the foot of the Santa Catalina Mountains and the Roskruge Mountains, respectively. Both sites include multiple clusters of large boulders with extensive rock art dating largely to the portion of the Hohokam time frame from A.D. 950 to 1300; there are earlier archaic and possible proto-historic petroglyphs as well. We have reported previously that the rock art at these two sites includes a significant amount of Flower World imagery, and both have unusual acoustic features (Hernbrode and Boyle 2013b, 2016, 2017). We have suggested that both sites include habitation and ceremonial components (see also Wallace 2012). The plant community at Sutherland Wash is much more diverse than at the Cocoraque Butte Complex, but the major food source plants for gathering (saguaro, cholla, and prickly pear fruits as well as mesquite beans) are abundant at both sites. As we discuss below, both sites have significant sources of water.

Janine Hernbrode
Arizona Archaeological and Historical Society

Peter Boyle
Arizona Archaeological and Historical Society

Tiered Cosmos

There are a number of commonalities shared by native cultures of North America including the importance of the four directions, assigning colors to the four directions, serpent symbolism, and, of particular interest to this paper, a belief in a tiered cosmos (McGuire 2011; Wilcox et al. 2008). Belief in a tiered cosmos is a worldwide phenomenon, summarized by Lewis-Williams (2002, 2008:31) as "at its simplest, the cosmos is believed to have three levels: a realm above inhabited by beings and spirit animals; the daily world in which people live; and an underworld where beings and spirit animals dwell." Among people in the American Southwest, the number of layers of the cosmos varies, sometimes encompassing discarded worlds where the people were evil and their world was destroyed. But the three levels Lewis-Williams describes generally represent the cosmologies of Southwestern cultural groups who frequently depict the underworld (also referred to as lower world) as a watery, sometimes chaotic place where the water cycle begins and the spirits of the ancestors dwell.

Among the people of North and South America, belief in a tiered cosmos is quite ancient. The Olmecs (2500 B.C. to A.D. 400) of Mexico's Yucatan are the oldest culture identified in the New World that left a record suggesting belief in a tiered Cosmos. Their world was composed of sky, earth, and underworld; was defined by four directions; and had a central axis-mundi through the tiers where shamans in a trance could travel to contact the ancestors and seek the power to influence forces beyond human control (Diehl 2004:100). More complex multi-tiered structures have been described among the Aztecs and Maya (Carrasco 2014:69; Markman and Markman 1992:93–94).

Figure 1. Landscape setting at Sutherland Wash Rock Art District showing the canyon with water in the foreground and, in the upper left, the group of large boulders covered with petroglyphs creating a cave-like opening.

That the tiered cosmos was also reflected in ancient architecture of the Puebloans, Mimbres, Mogollon, and Hohokam, has been noted by researchers for at least a century from Fewkes (1911) to the present (Wright and Russell 2011.) Structures of kivas and houses were built as symbolic manifestations of the people's world view. People buried under the floor were literally being placed back into the underworld and access to the exterior via a lad-

Figure 2. Part of the Cocoraque Ranch boulder-covered hill located within the larger Cocoraque Butte Complex. Note the high density of petroglyphs.

der through an opening in the ceiling was a reenactment of emergence into the daily world (Shafer 1995). During the Hohokam Classic Period when inhabitants built platform mounds, the mound itself and the structures on top have been interpreted as symbols of the sky world (Bostwick 1992; Wright and Russell 2011), while the partially subterranean pithouse symbolized the underworld (Preucel 1996).

Origin Stories

In cultures where there is emphasis on altered states of consciousness, people believe they can move between the layers of the cosmos (Hedges 2006; Lewis-Williams 2002). But of particular importance for the present discussion is that origin stories frequently involve emergence of either people, or beings who eventually become people, from the lower world.

In many origin stories, fully-formed people emerge into the current world through a hole in the earth, sometimes a hole covered by a lake (Helms 1998:77). For example, the Hopi speak of their emergence through a sipapu, a hole in the earth which was subsequently covered by water by Spider Grandmother so that it resembled an ordinary pond (Courlander 1971:29–30). People emerged from a lake in the origin story of the Tewa Pueblo people at Ohkay Owingeh (San Juan) Pueblo in New Mexico (Parsons 1994:9). The origin story of the Tohono O'odham, who are descendants of the Hohokam, describes crawling through a hole bored by Gopher near Casa Grande, Arizona (Underhill 1946:11).

Other origin stories describe not only emergence but also transformation from one form to another. In the origin story of the Tewa living at Hopi in Arizona, people originally lived "way down underneath" and were in the form of ants. They then came up to the earth and turned into creatures with tails. Finally, they came up to a third world where they began to turn into people (Parsons 1994:172). An additional example comes from the Zuni origin story where the people emerge in a semiaquatic form and, after bathing in a spring, transform to a fully human state (Benedict 1935:1–5; Parsons 1923).

In an article comparing the creation stories of the O'odham with their neighbors, the Maricopa and the Yavapai, Donald Bahr (2009) notes that all three tribes either originated from or replaced the Hohokam in their home area. All three stories say that the gods and humans come or go from the underworld. Two of the stories have frog-like beings that are not quite human: the Yavapai chief who leads his people from the underworld is a frog-man, and the Maricopa have two gods who create humans, but one of them makes people with webbed hands and feet. Both the O'odham and the Yavapai emerge, not singly, but as a group of people (Bahr 2009, Underhill 1938:14).

Of the tribes mentioned above, the O'odham, Hopi, and Zuni are believed to have ancestral links to the Hohokam. O'odham people are considered direct descendants of the Hohokam (Bahr 2008; Lopez 2008; Loendorf and Lewis 2017) and today live on land that was once part of the Hohokam culture area. Traditional stories and archaeological data indicate that both the Hopi and Zuni peoples migrated through the Hohokam culture area (Clark 2008; Clark et al. 2012; Wallace 2014:474) and the migration stories of some Hopi clans state that they came to Hopi from the South, perhaps the Hohokam culture area, and more specifically the Tucson Valley, Casa Grande and the Salt-Gila Basin (Bernardini 2005). In contrast, Loendorf and Lewis (2017) have argued that it is not necessary to invoke migrations by other groups to account for Hohokam archaeology in the Phoenix basin portion of the Hohokam culture area, currently occupied by the Akimel O'odham.

Representation of Tiered Cosmos in Rock Art Imagery

Wright and Russell (2011) identified the "pipette" (Figure 3) as a specific rock art element depicting the tiered cosmos in the American southwest. The pipette is a series of stacked boxes with a central portal, or "axis mundi", connecting the boxes that are either plain or with a number of variations and attachments. The form of the pipette is not unlike the crenelated lines and other related patterns described by Boyd (2003:60) and Hedges (1994), which both authors relate to altered states of consciousness and the related experience of movement between layers of the cosmos. The pipette motif is found widely in Arizona, New Mexico, and California along with a few sites in Utah and northern Mexico. The Cocoraque Butte Complex has four such pipettes, whereas Sutherland Wash has none that we could identify.

Another common rock art motif suggesting movement from one tier in the cosmos to another is depictions of anthropomorphs that incorporate openings in the rock surface such as cracks or holes (Clottes and Lewis-Williams 1996:85–86; Wright and Russell 2011:375). Two Hohokam examples are shown in Figure 4. Ladders have also been interpreted as metaphors for the axis mundi (Wright and Russell 2011:366), and cal properties of the rock itself to seemingly indicate a differentiation between an upper and lower world. This can be a change in either texture or color of a portion of the boulder, dividing the panel distinctly into two areas. Lawrence Loendorf (personal communication 2017) has also observed a change in texture used in this way.

However, the rock art elements at Sutherland Wash and the Cocoraque Butte Complex described in the following sections of this paper are quite different from these motifs and, we suggest, represent both human emergence and transformation.

Landscape Considerations

Hohokam ideology attributed special significance to features of the landscape that were maintained by the repetition of sacred rituals. Mountains, caves, and streams were celebrated as sites where passage to the underworld was possible (Preucel 1996). Emergence stories often refer to a particular site acknowledged as "The Emergence Site," but other places symbolically represent access to the underworld. As mentioned above, for the Hopi, each kiva has a commemorative opening to the underworld, but presumably each of these is not considered the original one covered with water by Spider Grandmother. The same appears true of landscape features that serve as metaphors for emergence sites or otherwise represent passageways to the underworld.

Both Sutherland Wash and the Cocoraque Butte Complex have landscape features that could serve as metaphors for the watery underworld and for the axis mundi. The first feature is a prominent cave-like opening at Sutherland Wash (Figure 5) created by huge boulders that could commemorate a portal to the lower world. The boulders include extensive rock art panels containing many of the elements we describe below, which we suggest depict human emergence and transformation. This panel overlooks the second feature, a periodic stream through the center of the district with tinajas eroded into the granitic bedrock that store water much of the year. This stream is actually a canyon drainage fed by the Santa Catalina Mountains and at least two springs in the foothills. Inhabiting the pool are canyon tree frogs (*Hyla arenicolor*), which have a transformational life cycle.

The Cocoraque Butte Complex, likewise, has both features that could have been metaphors for the axis mundi and a source of water. Figure 6 shows a rock art-covered fissure formed by a split in what was once a single large boulder that is located centrally on a large hill. The cleft goes beyond the split and into the earth itself

Figure 3. Four-tiered "pipette" at Cocoraque Butte. This motif is widespread in the American Southwest and may represent a tiered cosmos (Wright and Russell 2011).

Figure 4. Two examples of Hohokam anthropomorphs incorporating cracks or holes in the boulder, thus appearing to travel through a portal or axis mundi: (a) Sutherland Wash; (b) Tumamoc Hill in Tucson.

are a common rock art motif. Finally, flute players are depicted in Hohokam imagery (Bostwick and Krocek 2002:109; Haury 1976:239–240) and, according to Taube (2010:113), are associated with emergence among the Hopi and the Navajo.

On rock art panels that appear to be compositions, we have observed utilization of the changes in the physi-

Figure 5. Extensive rock art panels containing emergence imagery, discussed in this paper, surrounding the cave-like opening formed by huge boulders at Sutherland Wash Rock Art District. It is possible this formation commemorates a passage to the lower world.

Figure 6. One of the fissures created by split boulders at Cocoraque Ranch that may also represent a portal to the lower world. The rock art includes element types we suggest relate to emergence.

suggesting an opening into another world. Nearby is a possible one-tier pipette with openings both top and bottom, similar to some of the renderings of other pipettes recorded by Wright and Russell (2011:60). There is also a second, less-used fissure, upslope and more northerly than the first, with the same general characteristics: a split of a huge boulder with a narrow passage between the halves and rock art imagery that will be discussed below. The Cocoraque Butte Complex had a continuous water source as well. As reported by T. J. Ferguson (2008), the O'odham name for the Butte is "Shontok" which has two meanings: a "source or beginning" in reference to the water supply; and "to pound," perhaps referring to the thousands of petroglyphs. Currently, water at Cocoraque Ranch is available from a shallow hand-dug well with water standing just 20 feet below the surface. This indicates an aquifer below that would have provided water at ground level prior to modern depletion of the water table. The aquifer thus provided surface water to indigenous people to support their seasonal habitation, agriculture (Suzanne K. Fish personal communication 2015), and ceremonial activities. Water coming to the surface here, in an otherwise dry desert, may have been a powerful materialization of the watery underworld to the native people.

Methods and Results

The information presented below is from two rock art recording studies conducted by the authors and a sizable group of dedicated volunteers. Site numbers are listed in the end note.[1] The recording work at Sutherland Wash Rock Art District in the Coronado National Forest involved a total of 15 recorders working from 2006 to 2012. The recording work at the Cocoraque Butte Complex has involved 31 recorders; it began in 2014 and is nearing completion. Archaeologically, the Cocoraque Butte Complex is considered a single site, but for practical reasons is generally referred to using two different site names. The first, commonly called "Cocoraque Butte", is within the Ironwood National Monument and was the subject of a report by the authors (Hernbrode and Boyle 2016). The second, usually termed "Cocoraque Ranch," is on private ranch land immediately adjacent to Cocoraque Butte and has been described by Ferguson (2008). Our recording project at the Ranch is ongoing and nearly complete. In all cases recording included digital photography, sketches, and the completion of a detailed recording form providing GPS information, element type, patination information, and various dimensional data. Additional data recorded included artifacts, structures, trails, and certain acoustic features of the landscape. More detailed information regarding methods can be found in Hernbrode and Boyle (2013a; 2013b; 2016).

Petroglyphs Depicting Human Transformation and Emergence: From Barbells to Anthropomorphs

Figure 7 presents two anthropomorphic stick figures from Sutherland Wash. Figure 7a is a form that is very common in Hohokam rock art and is seen in depictions of humans worldwide. However, the glyph in Figure 7b differs in important ways. Both the arms and legs are bowed and are circular in form. Bowed arms could represent a body position that humans might normally assume, but bowed legs are another matter. Many (N = 51) anthropomorphs at Sutherland Wash have bowed legs, but this is a difficult, if not impossible, way to stand, leading us to wonder why these glyphs take this form.

Figure 7. Two different styles of stick-figure anthropomorphs from Sutherland Wash: (a) a relatively common form with straight legs; (b) a less common form with both circular upraised arms and bowed legs.

Another common Hohokam motif is the "barbell." There are 12 of these at Sutherland Wash, two of which are shown in Figure 8. We noted that there are 27 additional barbell-like elements that are elaborated,

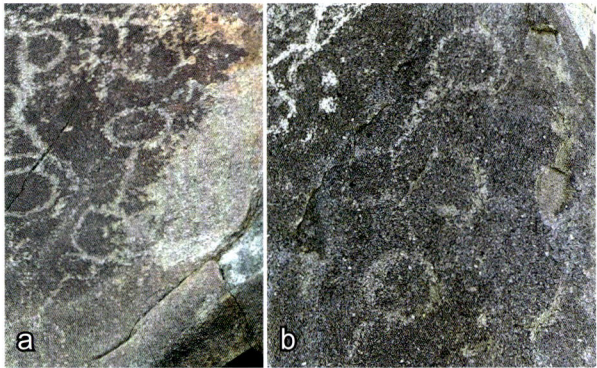

Figure 8. Two barbell petroglyphs from Sutherland Wash; the basic structure of this common motif resembles that of the anthropomorph shown in Figure 7b: (a) barbell, without elaboration, at the edge of an extensive panel; (b) another example of an unelaborated barbell (in upper half of image).

i.e., they include additional components. Often these elaborations are suggestive of the human form and, at times, we had difficulty deciding if we should classify a given glyph as a barbell or an anthropomorph. This conundrum suggested the hypothesis that barbells, the elaborated forms of barbells, and anthropomorphs with bowed arms and legs depict stages of human transformation. As discussed below, because of their positioning on the landscape, we suggest that these glyphs represent transformation during emergence from a lower world.

For purposes of this analysis we have grouped these elaborated, intermediate images into two groups. The two groups divide the glyphs into one group more similar to barbells and a second group more similar to anthropomorphs with bowed legs and arms. Therefore, our analysis resulted in four groups: barbells, elaborated barbells, elaborated barbells resembling humans, and bowed-leg anthropomorphs.

Figure 9 provides examples of the first of the two intermediate steps, barbells with elaborations that are not strongly suggestive of human form (transitional barbells). Note that both circles are fully closed and that the elaborations in these cases are either lines or dots. The figures in Figure 9c and 9d have elaborations on the torso, suggestive of human forms but not so strongly that we would classify these as humans instead of barbells.

Examples of the second group of intermediate stages between barbells and anthropomorphs where the glyphs appear more like anthropomorphs than barbells (transitional anthropomorphs) are provided in Figure 10. The three glyphs shown in the figure have closed circles on top and bottom and yet have enough other characteristics that these appear quite human-like, including the image of a baby being delivered from a straight-armed and straight-legged mother. In contrast to the glyphs in Figure 9, these glyphs were recorded as anthropomorphs (not barbells) even though they have closed arms and legs. But these glyphs retain a barbell-like character, and we suggest represent a transitional stage of the transformation from barbell to human. Wallace (2008) has reported a few anthropomorph-like glyphs with similarly closed circular legs at several sites near Tucson; he comments that the repetition of this figure type is probably significant.

Figure 11 presents several glyphs that most observers would classify as anthropomorphs without laboring over the decision. But, in all cases they have bowed and raised arms and bowed legs reminiscent of barbell origins.

Figure 12 provides additional support for our proposed interpretation of these barbell-like petroglyphs. This Hohokam composition panel from Sutherland Wash, shows three elongate barbell-like figures in different stages of transformation. It includes a barbell in the center, a transitional barbell with fingers on the upper circle on the right, and a transitional anthropomorph on the left with fingers, a head that is possibly not connected to the body, and toes. Each of the glyphs is similar in length and width, giving the impression that they are a composition showing different stages of transformation for the same figure.

The graph presented in Figure 13 shows the frequency of the four categories of glyphs at Sutherland Wash. The counts range from 12 to 16 in each of the first three categories and 51 anthropomorphs with bowed arms and legs. For perspective, at Sutherland Wash we recorded 419 anthropomorphs; put another way, 15 percent of the anthropomorphs are of the transformational type as shown in the two right-most bars of the graph.

Figure 9. Examples of elaborated barbells from Sutherland Wash where the elaborations are not strongly suggestive of the human form (transitional barbells): (a) elaborated with lines; (b) elaborated with dots and lines; (c and d) more extensive elaborations, not strongly human-like. These glyphs are characteristic of the first of two intermediate steps between barbells and anthropomorphs.

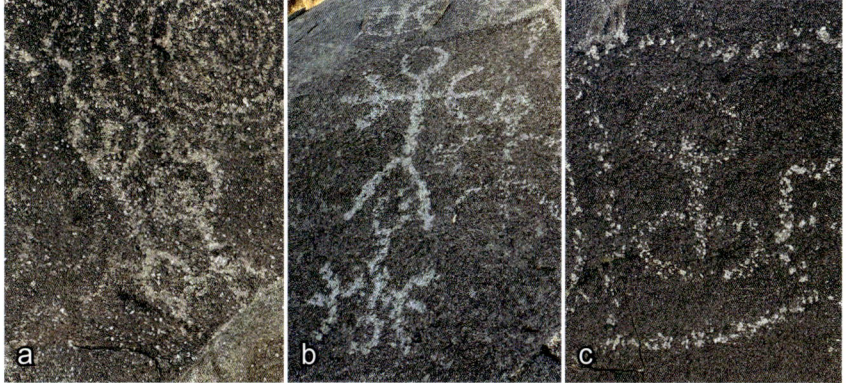

Figure 10. Three Sutherland Wash examples of the second intermediate step between barbells and anthropomorphs, strongly suggestive of the human form (transitional anthropomorphs). Note that, although human-like, both top and bottom circles are connected: (a) left figure has an obvious head and possible feet; (b) the "baby" being delivered in lower half of image has arms and digits like its "mother"; (c) elaborated with a head and sex characteristics.

Figure 11. Examples of fully-formed anthropomorphs at Sutherland Wash with bowed arms and legs. Note that the arms and legs are not connected but still retain a barbell-like character.

The petroglyphs discussed thus far have been from Sutherland Wash. At the Cocoraque Butte Complex we see the same progression from barbells through the two transitional forms, to anthropomorphs with bowed arms and legs. Figure 14 includes an example of

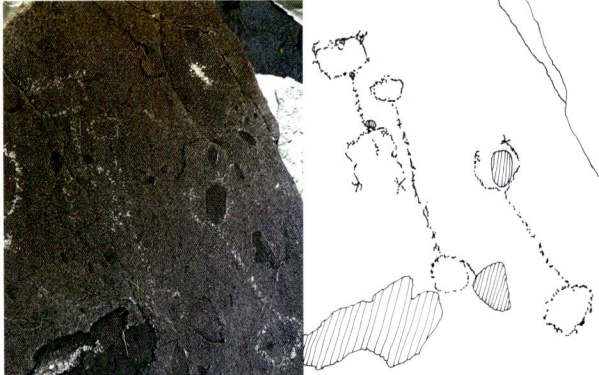

Figure 12. Hohokam panel that includes a barbell (center), transitional barbell (right), and transitional anthropomorph (left).

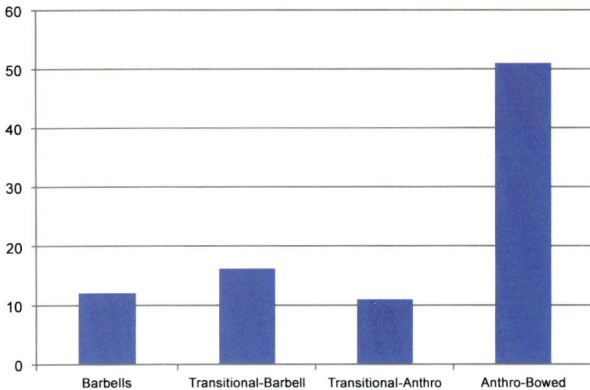

Figure 13. Histogram showing the frequency of the four element categories at Sutherland Wash that may represent human transformation during emergence from a lower world. Taken together there are a total of 90 elements.

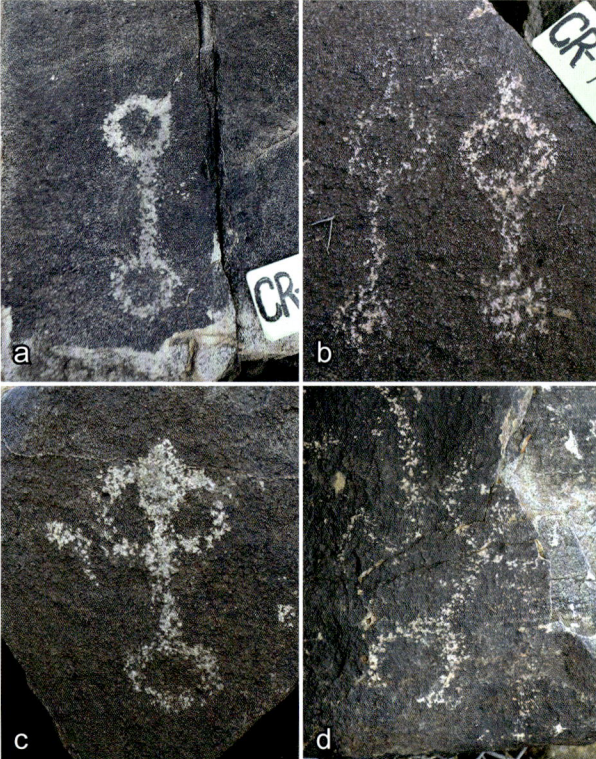

Figure 14. Cocoraque Ranch examples of the same four element categories identified at Sutherland Wash: (a) unelaborated barbell; (b) transitional barbell; (c) transitional anthropomorph; (d) anthropomorph with bowed arms and legs.

each of the four categories from our current work at Cocoraque Ranch. One panel at Cocoraque Butte juxtaposes an image of a pipette, which Wright and Russell (2011) have suggested illustrates the tiered universe, with three other elements relating to emergence and transformation: barbells, a bowed-leg anthropomorph, and snakes that act as messengers to the lower world (Clottes and Lewis-Williams 1996; Whittlesey 2008).

Petroglyph Panels Depicting Groups of Emerging and Transforming Humans

There are two panels at Sutherland Wash showing rows of humans holding hands. One panel has been published previously which depicts a row of six anthropomorphic stick figures that probably represent singers and/or dancers (Hernbrode and Boyle 2013b). The other panel, shown in Figure 15, includes four anthropomorphic stick figures holding hands. But all four anthropomorphs have bowed legs like the glyphs discussed above, perhaps relating these anthropomorphs to emergence and transformation. The idea of anthropomorphs or more abstract images relating to transformation configured side-by-side is important and is a very prominent feature at the Cocoraque Ranch portion of the Cocoraque Butte Complex.

Thus far in this paper we have primarily been considering many individual figures, but at Cocoraque

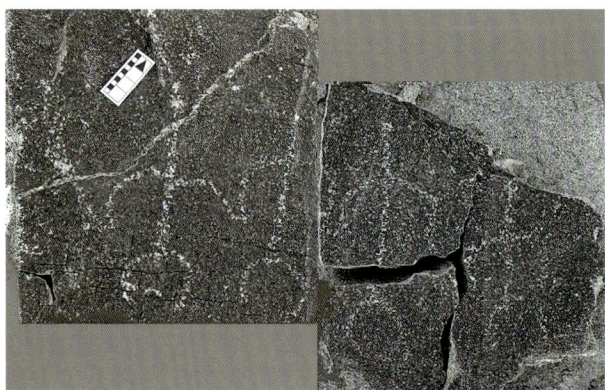

Figure 15. Reassembled broken panel at Sutherland Wash with a line of bow-legged, hand-holding anthropomorphs. Linear groups of anthropomorphic figures are rare at Sutherland Wash in contrast to Cocoraque Ranch.

Ranch there are many panels where we see groups of the same element types arrayed side-by-side in a very linear way. At Cocoraque Ranch, we have the same kind of barbells discussed above, but we also have rows of solid barbells such as those shown in Figure 16. In this example, the barbell images are on the underside of a boulder possibly suggesting existence in the lower world, strengthening the case that barbells can represent unformed or incomplete humans prior to emergence from the underworld.

Figure 17 shows additional rows of barbell-like images, but in these cases the lower part is forked, suggesting legs. Another variant is shown in Figure 18, which again is a row of figures, but now these figures have forks both top and bottom suggesting arms and legs. In Figure 19, similar figures are connected at the top with forked legs at the bottom possibly suggesting anthropomorphs holding hands while dancing or singing. The two panels in Figures 20 are additional examples of abstract panels at Cocoraque Ranch that remind us of the fairly common Hohokam motif of anthropomorphs in a line holding hands as if dancing and/or singing together.

A number of these images are present on the boulders that form the two fissures at Cocoraque Ranch, which we have suggested may represent the point of emergence. One of these features (Figure 6) includes a row of forked lines (Figure 17b) as well as barbells and a

Figure 16. *Rows of barbells with fully pecked circles located on the underside of a boulder at Cocoraque Ranch, suggesting existence in the lower world.*

Figure 17. *Two panels at Cocoraque Ranch containing barbell-like images with the lower portion forked, suggestive of developing legs.*

Figure 18. *Line of unattached figures at Cocoraque Ranch with forks at both top and bottom suggesting arms and legs.*

Figure 19. *Line of figures at Cocoraque Ranch showing attachments at the top and forked legs at the bottom.*

Figure 20. *Two additional examples of connected linear figures perhaps suggesting hand-holding dancers or singers. Both are from Cocoraque Ranch.*

snake. The second fissure includes barbells, snakes, and juxtaposed to the opening of the fissure is a possible pipette glyph. The pipette is a series of stacked rectangular boxes connected and bisected by a vertical line. The presence of these images of transformation on the two strikingly similar fissures, set in a landscape evocative of a watery underworld, suggests to us that the transformational imagery is related to stories of human origin.

The petroglyphs showing rows of figures resembling humans are reminiscent of the origin stories describing the emergence of groups of people as told in O'odham and Yavapai narratives (Bahr 2009; Underhill 1938:14). This emphasis on the group, versus individuals, is much stronger in the rock art at Cocoraque Ranch than it is at Sutherland Wash. Of the petroglyphs that we have interpreted as relating to emergence and transformation, the glyphs at Sutherland Wash primarily represent individuals, whereas the glyphs at Cocoraque Ranch not only depict individuals but also represent groups of people. Perhaps this reflects differences in the social structure of the people at these two sites or may simply indicate variation in the particulars, or points of emphasis, in origin stories.

Frogs as a Metaphor for Human Transformation

Water is inextricably connected to concepts of origin and creation, but it is also a practical need in the desert at the large ceremonial and ritual sites that are the focus of this study. Frogs possess an obvious connection to water so it is not surprising that the material culture of the Hohokam includes imagery of frogs on stone censors, carved shell bracelets and pendants, and shells with or without mosaic turquoise overlay (Haury 1976:314–315, 320–21; Whittlesey 2008). Among the Puebloans, frogs begin the water cycle (Hays-Gilpin 2011). The O'odham sing about frogs' connections to rain (Bostwick and Krocek 2002:49; Shaw 1968:80). James Bayman (2008:81) has summarized evidence that frog-shaped pendants were part of rituals to bring rain to agricultural fields. As noted above, emergent humans possess various frog-like features in several origin stories. Wallace (2014:479) has pointed out that "toads in the desert environment likely symbolize water, but also life, rejuvenation, and transformation."

In our work at Sutherland Wash, we have observed that canyon tree frogs (*Hyla arenicolor*) inhabit the pools in the canyon and, since they require continuous water to survive, it is likely that the frog habitat at this petroglyph site drainage has been in place for a very long time. There are three frog-like petroglyphs located near the landscape feature shown in Figure 5 and the canyon immediately below (Figure 1). Figure 21a appears to depict a tadpole with a translucent tail, suggesting awareness of the detailed life cycle of these frogs. Figure 21b shows an image of a frog at the developmental stage where the tail is still present. Both petroglyphs bear a strong resemblance to actual tadpoles and frogs. We suggest that the barbell-to-human continuum presented above may be modelled on this phenomenon of nature, possibly serving as a metaphor for becoming human. This way of thinking is consistent with David Whitley's (2001:132) concept of "natural models" wherein "natural phenomena...structure the logic underlying aspects of religious symbolism."

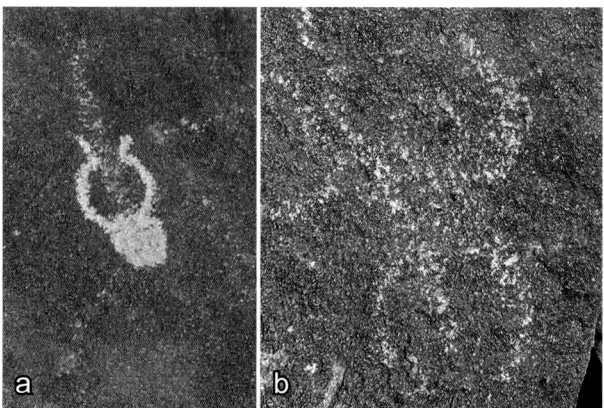

Figure 21. Depictions of the frog life cycle: (a) a tadpole image showing the translucent tail; (b) frog image showing stage of development with tail still present. These images are located at Sutherland Wash in the canyon overlooking the stream and near the landscape features and imagery suggestive of emergence.

Discussion

The life cycle of frogs encompasses vast transformations in form during a gradual development from an egg to a total larval stage where the tadpole looks like a spot with a tail and breathes with gills in the water. Ultimately, the tadpole acquires adult frog characteristics. It grows limbs and eventually the long tail is absorbed and its lungs develop to a stage where air breathing is possible, and it can live on the land (Reid and Zim 1967).

This life cycle is not dissimilar from the development illustrated as the barbell to human sequence. At first the barbell is two circles connected by a line that gradually adds human parts like arms, legs, fingers, a separate head, facial features, and sex characteristics until it is a fully developed human being. It should not be surprising then that creation stories include a not-quite-human, slimy chief interpreted as a "frog-man" to lead the people from the underworld (Bahr 2009:6); or a group of not-quite-humans who bathe in the waters of the first spring they encounter that makes them lose their tails and other non-human characteristics (Parsons 1923:138–139, 1994:170–172; Young 1988:122–123); or that two gods are making humans and one of them makes only beings with webbed hands and feet (Bahr 2009).

It is reality that women tending to women for childbirth and all forms of miscarried fetuses would have given the ancients a familiarity with human development that we reserve for our medical practitioners today. A fetus develops inside a liquid-filled sac with varying human parts being added through growth and maturity until a fully formed baby can work its way to an air-breathing layer of the tiered cosmos. Men too would have been aware of this process, at the very least through their experience in butchering animals. We do not think the parallels between human development and the life cycle of frogs were lost on the makers of the rock art imagery under discussion, and may well have provided a basis for the importance amphibious creatures play in traditional narratives relating to fertility, creation, and emergence.

As noted above, the barbell-to-human imagery is dominant at Sutherland Wash and seems to represent the transformation of individuals. In contrast, although barbell-to-human transformation is also present at Cocoraque Ranch, there is additional embellishment of the story to depict groups of barbells, groups of enhanced barbells, groups of almost humans, and groups of people attached to one another, emerging and transforming in unison. Perhaps this difference reflects a greater emphasis at Cocoraque Ranch on the cohesion of the social group at this site versus at Sutherland Wash. Based on their study of late Basketmaker III rock art imagery, Robins and Hays-Gilpin (2000) have proposed a shift in iconography from single, static anthropomorphs to rows of anthropomorphs engaged in active association. They suggest that this communal imagery reflects shared stories emphasizing the unified identity and cohesion of the social group and a possible connection to "cosmic realms." Based on the data we have presented, it appears that a similar change in iconography occurred among the Hohokam in Southern Arizona that also appears connected to the inhabitants' views of the cosmos. However, at this point we cannot say whether this differing iconography resulted from temporal or spatial differences, a conundrum that further research could address.

We want to emphasize the repetition and striking consistency of the linked figures at Cocoraque Ranch discussed in this paper. When on the ground at the site, one is struck by the many panels characterized by linearity and orderliness. Some examples have been presented in this paper, but there are many others. The salience of this imagery must have been as clear to the Hohokam as it is to modern observers; to us, this suggests that the imagery had powerful meaning to ancient people, whether or not our particular interpretation of the meaning of the imagery is correct.

We have not observed such repetition or uniformity at other sites throughout the Hohokam culture area. We note with interest that the examples in the literature of groups of human figures holding hands depicted in Hohokam rock art and ceramics are relatively rare, and their compositions are highly variable. Examples of variation include: an attached zoomorph (Figure 22); elaborate headgear (Fish and Fish 2008:40; Schaafsma 1980:95); legs in motion (Fish and Fish 2008:40; Haury 1976:239); arms in motion (Schaafsma 1980:93); production of sound (Hernbrode and Boyle 2013b:1088); bowed legs (Figure 15 this paper). At least in the case of Hohokam rock art, we know of no instances where groups of humans are depicted in a given way multiple times at the same site except those reported here at Cocoraque Ranch.

Figure 22. Panel at Tumamoc Hill with hand-holding anthropomorphs, perhaps dancing. In this variation of the "hand-holder" motif, one figure is connected to a quadruped.

Notwithstanding the difference in emphasis on individuals versus groups, our overarching thought is that Sutherland Wash and the Cocoraque Butte Complex have much in common. Both appear to be ceremonial places where water was available year-around with landscape features that may represent the axis mundi. Although different in detail, both sites have a suite of interrelated rock art imagery that we interpret as depicting human emergence and transformation, imagery that reflects transformations in the natural world and which finds parallels in traditional origin stories of

Southwestern peoples. In our view, these images made by the Hohokam are fully consistent with the origin stories of modern groups including the O'odham, the Hopi, and the Zuni. The imagery appears to reflect the widely held belief in the emergence of tribal peoples from a lower world to the present often including not only a change in location but a change in physical form as well. Furthermore, the imagery is located on or near landscape features consistent with origin stories containing both sources of water and physical features that may represent emergence points from the lower world to the present.

Mary W. Helms (1998) and Stephen Plog (2011) have urged that we consider belief systems and meanings in order to understand culture history and change in the Southwest. We believe that rock art research can contribute to this effort, because rock art often is an expression of deeply held religious beliefs (Bostwick and Krocek 2002; Whitley 2005; Wright 2014). For example, given the importance of origin stories to modern descendants of the Hohokam, one would anticipate that these stories would be represented in the imagery of their ancestors. There is much to be gained by attempting to determine meaning of rock art to its makers in the context of other information such as traditional knowledge and details of the landscape. While it is true that we can never know with certainty what images communicated to the Hohokam, it is also true that we can deepen our understanding of Hohokam ideology by relating Hohokam imagery to that of their descendants and the meanings such imagery has to those descendants.

Conclusion

The origin stories of many tribes in the American Southwest describe emergence from a lower world to the present world, typically through an opening in the earth that is often associated with water. In some of these stories, humans emerged from the lower world in an incomplete state, consistent with living in a watery underworld. Emergent creatures sometimes have features such as slimy skin, tails, or webbed feet and hands. Subsequently, these creatures transformed to their present human form.

The landscapes at both Sutherland Wash and the Cocoraque Butte Complex include access to water and rock formations that may represent a portal to the underworld. Against this backdrop, the rock art at both sites includes a number of element types that we believe are interrelated and that we have interpreted as representing human emergence and transformation in a fashion consistent with the origin stories narrated by several contemporary tribes. The emphasis at Sutherland Wash is on individual elements that include "barbells," anthropomorphs with bowed arms and legs, and intermediate forms that progressively more closely approximate the typical anthropomorphic motif. This same pattern is apparent at the Cocoraque Butte Complex, but other motifs with linear arrangements of groups of human-like elements are numerous. This difference may reflect local variation in the details of origin stories, perhaps indicating differences in the social structure of the two sites.

Note

1. Site numbers: Cocoraque Butte Complex AZ AA: 15:3 (ASM); Sutherland Wash AZ BB:9:66 (ASM), AZ BB:9:59 (ASM), AR03-05-05-111, 112, 117, 118, 119, 120, 121, 122, 123, 146, 147, 169, 186, 208, 320, 359, 368, 370, 377, 378, 379, 382, 384, 386, 387, 389 (USFS).

Acknowledgments. The research presented here would not have been possible without the enthusiastic support of the many volunteer rock art recorders. All these people dedicated many hours and provided expertise to this project. We thank them for their effort and friendship.

The recording project at the Cocoraque Butte Complex has been supported by the Arizona Archaeological and Historical Society (AAHS) whose members are the volunteers and whose financial contribution will provide a means to archive the project records. AAHS members associated with the recording of Cocoraque Ranch portion from 2015 to the present include Mary Andersen, Steven Boley, Barbara Casimir, Katherine Cerino, Carl Evertsbusch, William Gillespie, Gordon Hanson, Bob Hernbrode, Laura LePere, Timothy Loftus, Karen Lominac, Jean Mabry, Fran Maiuri, Marilyn Marshall, Brad Paxton, Gail Roper, Lance Trask, Joseph Watkins, Esther White, Logan T. White, and Donna Yoder. The following volunteers recorded rock art at the Cocoraque Butte portion of the Cocoraque Butte Complex from 2014 to 2015: Patrick Brooks, Marc Calis, Katherine Cerino, Carl Evertsbusch, Bob Hernbrode, Marie Lynn Hunken, Fran Maiuri, David McLean, Jack Nichols, Myra Nichols, Lynn Ratener, Jaye Smith, Lance Trask, and Donna Yoder.

The following volunteers for Coronado National Forest participated in the recording project at Sutherland Wash Rock Art District from 2006 to 2012: Judith Billings, Bruce Billings, Joyce Boyle, Katherine Cerino, Valerie Davison, Bob Hernbrode, Marie Lynn

Hunken, David McLean, Judy Oyen, Vicky Palmer, Kit Schweitzer, Joel Woppert, and Donna Yoder. Forest Archaeologist William Gillespie's support, encouragement, and participation made the project possible. The authors are also members of AAHS and were volunteers on all of these projects.

Photographs reproduced in this paper were taken by: Lance K. Trask - Figures 2, 3, 14b, 14c, 14d, 16, 17a, 17b, 18, 19, 20a; Gordon Hanson - Figure 20b; Logan T. White - Figures 6, 14a; Janine Hernbrode - Figures 1, 4a, 4b, 5, 7a, 7b, 8a, 8b, 9a, 9b, 9c, 9d, 10a, 10b, 10c, 11a, 11b, 11c, 12, 15, 21a, 21b, 22.

Access to the extensive petroglyph site at Cocoraque Ranch was kindly granted by the owner, Jesus Arvizu. Historical protection of the site by the owners of this ranch before and after the land was patented in 1911 has preserved many features and the integrity of the petroglyphs over time. Every day we were on site we felt privileged and grateful to have been allowed this access.

References Cited

Bahr, Donald
  2008 O'odham Traditions about the Hohokam. In *The Hohokam Millennium*, edited by Suzanne K. Fish and Paul R. Fish, pp. 117–121. School of American Research Press, Santa Fe.
  2009 Tribal Perspectives on the Hohokam. *Bulletin of Old Pueblo Archaeology Center* 60:1–9.

Bayman, James M.
  2008 Artisans and Their Crafts in Hohokam Society. In *The Hohokam Millennium*, edited by Suzanne K. Fish and Paul R. Fish, pp. 75–81. School of American Research Press, Santa Fe.

Benedict, Ruth
  1935 *Zuni Mythology*. Vol. 1. Columbia University Press, New York.

Bernardini, Wesley
  2005 *Hopi Oral Tradition and the Archaeology of Identity*. University of Arizona Press, Tucson.

Bostwick, Todd W.
  1992 Platform Mound Ceremonialism in Southern Arizona: Possible Symbolic Meanings of Hohokam and Salado Platform Mounds. In *Proceedings of the Second Salado Conference, Globe, Arizona*, edited by Richard C. Lange and Stephen Germick, pp.78–85. Arizona Archaeological Society, Phoenix.

Bostwick, Todd W., and Peter Krocek
  2002 *Landscape of the Spirits: Hohokam Rock Art at South Mountain Park*. University of Arizona Press, Tucson.

Boyd, Carolyn E.
  2003 *Rock Art of the Lower Pecos*. Texas A&M University Press, College Station.

Carrasco, David
  2014 *Religions of Mesoamerica*. Second Edition. Waveland Press, Long Grove, Illinois.

Clark, Jeffery J.
  2008 A San Pedro Valley Perspective on Ancestral Pueblo Migration in the Hohokam World. In *The Hohokam Millennium*, edited by Suzanne K. Fish and Paul R. Fish, pp. 117–121. School of American Research Press, Santa Fe.

Clark, Jeffrey J., J. Brett Hill, Patrick D. Lyons, and Stacey N Lengyel
  2012 Of Migrants and Mounds. In *Mounds and Migrants: Classic Period Archaeology of the Lower San Pedro Valley*, edited by Jeffery J. Clark and Patrick D. Lyons, pp. 345–405. Anthropological Papers 45, Archaeology Southwest, Tucson.

Clottes, Jean, and David Lewis-Williams
  1996 *The Shamans of Prehistory: Trance and Magic in the Painted Caves*. Harry N. Abrams, Inc., New York.

Courlander, Harold
  1971 *The Fourth World of the Hopis: The Epic Story of the Hopi Indians as Preserved in their Legends and Traditions*. University of New Mexico Press, Albuquerque.

Diehl, Richard A.
  2004 *The Olmecs: America's First Civilization*. Thames and Hudson Ltd., London.

Ferguson, T. J.
  2008 *Cocoraque Butte: Signs of History in the Storied Landscape of the Tohono O'odham*. Report for the Arizona Open Lands Trust, Tucson.

Fewkes, Jesse Walter
  1911 *Antiquities of the Mesa Verde National Park: Cliff Palace*. Bureau of American Ethnology Bulletin 51. United States Government Printing Office, Washington, D.C.

Fish, Suzanne K., and Paul R. Fish
  2008 Community, Territory, and Polity. In *The Hohokam Millennium*, edited by Suzanne K. Fish and Paul R. Fish, pp. 38–47. School for Advanced Research Press, Santa Fe.

Haury, Emil W.
  1976 *The Hohokam: Desert Farmers and Craftsmen*. University of Arizona Press, Tucson.

Hays-Gilpin, Kelley
  2011 The Flower World: The Time Depth of Ecological Knowledge. Archaeology Southwest, Tucson. Electronic document (video), http://www.archaeologysouthwest.org/what-we-do/information/video/, accessed July 9, 2017.

Hedges, Ken
  1994 Pipette Dreams and the Primordial Snake Canoe: Analysis of a Hallucinatory Form Constant. In *Shamanism and Rock Art in North America*, edited by Solveig Turpin, pp. 103–124. Special Publication 1. Rock Art Foundation, San Antonio.
  2006 Images of the Spirit World: Vision Imagery and Spirit Beings in North American Rock Art. In *American Indian Rock Art, Volume 21*, edited by Frank Bock, John Clegg, Edwin Krupp, and Georgia Lee, pp. 541–558. International Rock Art Congress (IRAC) 1994 Proceedings, Rock Art–World Heritage, Volume 3. American Rock Art Research Association, Phoenix, Arizona.

Helms, Mary W.
  1998 *Access to Origins: Affines, Ancestors, and Aristocrats*. University of Texas Press, Austin.

Hernbrode, Janine, and Peter Boyle
  2013a Gender in Hohokam Imagery and Landscape: Sutherland Wash Rock Art District, Coronado National Forest, Arizona. In *American Indian Rock Art, Volume 39*, edited by William D. Hyder, pp. 43–54. American Rock Art Research Association, Glendale, Arizona.
  2013b Flower World Imagery in Petroglyphs: Hints of Hohokam Cosmology on the Landscape. In *American Indian Rock Art, Volume 40*, edited by Peggy Whitehead, pp. 1077–1092. International Rock Art Congress (IRAC) 2013 Proceedings. American Rock Art Research Association, Glendale, Arizona.

2016 Petroglyphs and Bell Rocks at Cocoraque Butte: Further Evidence of the Flower World Belief Among the Hohokam. In *American Indian Rock Art, Volume 42*, edited by Ken Hedges, pp. 91–105. American Rock Art Research Association, San Jose, California.

2017 Broad Distribution of Flower World Imagery in Hohokam Petroglyphs. In *American Indian Rock Art, Volume 43*, edited by Ken Hedges and Mark A. Calamia, pp. 75-83. American Rock Art Research Association, San Jose, California.

Lewis-Williams, David
 2002 *The Mind in the Cave: Consciousness and the Origins of Art*. Thames and Hudson, Ltd., London.

 2008 Religion and Archaeology: An Analytical, Materialist Account. In *Belief in the Past, Theoretical Approaches to the Archaeology of Religion*, edited by David S. Whitley and Kelley Hays-Gilpin, pp. 23–42. Left Coast Press, Walnut Creek, California.

Loendorf, Chris, and Barnaby V. Lewis
 2017 Ancestral O'odham: Akimel O'odham Cultural Traditions and the Archaeological Record. *American Antiquity* 82(1):123–139.

Lopez, Daniel
 2008 Huhugam. In *The Hohokam Millennium*, edited by Suzanne K. Fish and Paul R. Fish, pp. 117–121. School of American Research Press, Santa Fe.

Markman, Roberta H. and Peter T. Markman
 1992 *The Flayed God: The Mesoamerican Mythological Tradition: Sacred Texts and Images from Pre-Columbian Mexico and Central America*. Harper Collins Books, New York.

McGuire, Randall H.
 2011 Pueblo Religion and the Mesoamerican Connection. In *Religious Transformation in the Late Pre-Hispanic Pueblo World*, edited by Donna M. Glowacki and Scott Van Keuren, pp. 23–49. University of Arizona Press, Tucson.

Parsons, Elsie Clews
 1923 The Origin Myth of the Zuni. *Journal of American Folk-Lore* 36:135–162.

 1994 *Tewa Tales*. University of Arizona Press, Tucson. Reprint edition, original publication 1926 as Volume 19 of the Memoirs of the American Folk-Lore Society.

Plog, Stephen
 2011 Ritual and Cosmology in the Chaco Era. In *Religious Transformation in the Late Pre-Hispanic Pueblo World*, edited by Donna M. Glowacki and Scott Van Keuren, pp. 50–65. University of Arizona Press, Tucson.

Preucel, Robert W.
 1996 Cooking Status: Hohokam Ideology, Power, and Social Reproduction. In *Interpreting Southwestern Diversity: Underlying Principles and Overarching Patterns*, edited by Paul R. Fish and J. Jefferson Reid, pp. 125–131. Anthropological Papers 48, Arizona State University, Tempe.

Reid, George K. and Herbert S. Zim
 1967 *Pond Life*. Golden Press, New York, and Western Publishing Company, Racine, Wisconsin.

Robins, Michael R., and Kelley A. Hays-Gilpin
 2000 The Bird in the Basket: Gender and Social Change in Basketmaker Iconography. In *Foundations of Anasazi Culture: The Basketmaker-Pueblo Transition*, edited by Paul F. Reed, pp. 231–247. University of Utah Press, Salt Lake City.

Schaafsma, Polly
 1980 *Indian Rock Art of the Southwest*. School of American Research, Santa Fe, and University of New Mexico Press, Albuquerque.

Shafer, Harry J.
 1995 Architecture and Symbolism in Transitional Pueblo Development in the Mimbres Valley, Southwest New Mexico. *Journal of Field Archaeology* 22(1): 23–47.

Shaw, Anna M.
 1968 *Pima Indian Legends*. University of Arizona Press, Tucson.

Taube, Karl
 2010 Gateways to Another World: the Symbolism of Supernatural Passageways in the Art and Ritual of Mesoamerica and the American Southwest. In *Painting the Cosmos: Metaphor and Worldview in Images from the Southwest Pueblos and Mexico*, edited by Kelley Hays-Gilpin and Polly Schaafsma, pp. 73–120. Museum of Northern Arizona Bulletin 67, Flagstaff, Arizona.

Underhill, Ruth M.
 1938 *Singing for Power: The Song Magic of the Papago Indians of Southern Arizona*. University of Arizona Press, Tucson.

 1946 *Papago Indian Religion*. Columbia University Press, New York.

Wallace, Henry D.
 2008 The Petroglyphs of Atlatl Ridge, Tortolita Mountains, Pima County, Arizona. In *Life in the Foothills: Archaeological Investigations of the Tortolita Mountains of Southern Arizona*, edited by Deborah L. Schwartz, pp 159–231. Anthropological Papers 46, Center for Desert Archaeology, Tucson.

 2012 The Architecture of Honey Bee Village. In *Life in the Valley of Gold: Archaeological Investigations at Honey Bee Village, A Prehistoric Hohokam Ballcourt Village, Part 2*, edited by Henry D. Wallace, pp. 709–766. Anthropological Papers 48, Archaeology Southwest, Tucson.

 2014 Ritual Transformation and Cultural Revitalization: Explaining Hohokam in Pre-A.D. 1000 Southeastern Arizona. In *Between Mimbres and Hohokam: Exploring the Archaeology and History of Southeastern Arizona and Southwestern New Mexico*, edited by Henry D, Wallace, pp. 433–500. Anthropological Papers 52, Archaeology Southwest, Tucson.

Whittlesey, Stephanie
 2008 Hohokam Ceramics, Hohokam Beliefs. In *The Hohokam Millennium*, edited by Suzanne K. Fish and Paul R. Fish, pp. 65–73. School for Advanced Research Press, Santa Fe.

Whitley, David S.
 2001 Science and the Sacred: Interpretive Theory in U.S. Rock Art Research. In *Theoretical Perspectives in Rock Art Research*, edited by K. Helskog, pp. 130–157. Novus forlag, Oslo.

 2005 *Introduction to Rock Art Research*. Left Coast Press, Walnut Creek, California.

Wilcox, David R., Phil C. Weigand, J. Scott Wood, and Jerry B. Howard
 2008 Ancient Cultural Interplay of the American Southwest in the Mexican Northwest. *Journal of the Southwest* 50(2):103–206.

Wright, Aaron M.
 2014 *Religion on the Rocks: Hohokam Rock Art, Ritual Practice, and Social Transformation*. University of Utah Press, Salt Lake City.

Wright, Aaron M., and Will G. Russell
 2011 The Pipette, the Tiered Cosmos, and the Materialization of Transcendence in the Rock Art of the North American Southwest. *Journal of Social Archaeology* 11(3) 361–386.

Young, M. Jane
 1988 *Signs from the Ancestors: Zuni Cultural Symbolism and Perceptions of Rock Art*. University of New Mexico Press, Albuquerque.

Ritual and Rock Art in Basketmaker Ceremonies from Butler Wash to Atlatl Rock

William D. Hyder and Dorothy Bohntinsky

In September 2016, we presented a research paper at the Utah Rock Research Association Symposium in Utah: Ritual and Rock Art in Basketmaker Ceremonies: Butler Wash Revisited (2016). It discusses our re-evaluation of the Big Kachina Panel and the Procession Panel based on an approach William Strange introduced thirty-one years ago at the American Rock Art Research Association conference in Santa Barbara, California. Strange contended that interpretation often requires a layered, textured, and complementary blend of voices aligned to tell a coherent story. He identified the poetic voice as an essential component for expanding perception in order to develop the ability to see anew without blinders imposed by current canon. Inspired by Strange and building on Rappaport's (1999) theory of ritual and humanity, we presented new perspectives of how certain Basketmaker anthropomorphic imagery can be seen as a documentation of ritual and ceremony. This new conclusion was built by blending academic considerations from our different fields of expertise with the exploratory poetic voice.

Inspired by Rapport's (1999) treatise on ritual and religion, Hyder (2002) explored selected Basketmaker sites in Utah's Grand Gulch. Hyder proposed that

> Taking a more general approach to rock art analysis based on the nature and function of ritual allows one to explore how rock art assumes its role within ceremony, how it acquires and communicates symbolic information, and why it evolves with social change. The focus on ritual also emphasizes the importance of the archaeological context when ethnographic information is lacking. Rock art takes its meaning from the rituals or other social contexts associated with its creation; meaning is not inherent in the symbols themselves [Hyder 2002:86]

Building on our previous exploration of layered multivocal interpretations of ritual and Basketmaker/Pueblo rock art, we turned our attention to the well-known images of atlatls, darts, and ceremonial staffs or wands. While we focused on the Four Corners region of the Southwest, we recognize that the images discussed are well documented across a wider area with a time depth that predates Basketmaker. As we studied these rock art sites from a layered perspective, specific questions began to form. Can the representation of a utilitarian item evolve into an icon of ritual, ceremony, and identity in addition to its functional use? More specifically, did the atlatl and dart evolve into such an icon? Can the study of this specific iconic image contribute to our understanding of Basketmaker cultural development? With these questions in mind, Atlatl Rock at Valley of Fire in Nevada (Figure 1) inspired a fresh look at Puebloan images of the atlatl and dart.

William D. Hyder
Independent Archaeologist
Scotts Valley, California

Dorothy Bohntinsky
Speech Language Pathologist
Hayward, California

Figure 1. The Puebloan atlatl and dart petroglyphs from Atlatl Rock in Nevada's Valley of Fire are at the top of the large panel.

What would you think if you imagined depictions
of a young man's head severed,
a baby elephant slain and head dismembered,
followed by the assailant affixing the elephant's head
to the young man's shoulders?
Would you shudder at its seeming insanity?

Yet, that is what came into my mind
when I saw the image of a pachyderm's head
sculpted by Nature upon a rocky hill
near the temple-like projection of Atlatl Rock.
Images of elephant heads returned again
as I began focusing more deeply upon the designs.
Memories of other rock art with darts piercing sheep
and hail creating the twins' hats from the teats
of a large beast penetrated by a dart in the rear
could make one shudder over such primitiveness.

However, the images of the beheadings in my mind's eye
reminded me of the sacred religious story
about the creation of Lord Ganesha
and the enlightened state of mind his followers strive for.
Most simply put, his human body and elephant head
serve as an iconic reminder to avoid hardheadedness
in order to expand observations and perceptions.
So, what I am telling myself as I take Atlatl Rock in?
Maybe, it is to absorb both setting and art
through the exploration of universality and metaphor
rather than struggling with meaning.

This new intention moved such panels to the level of sacred art
adorning the Sistine Chapel and other great religious structures,
where images serve as icons that hold sacred narratives.

Scanning the myriad of petroglyphs from this perspective
invites awareness from a dimension that dispels judgement.
Then, I can avoid asking questions borne upon prejudice
such as what magic, myth, or trance states are being revealed.
Instead, I asked myself if I can imagine some ancient faith
being shared within icons etched upon this rock.

Our different perceptions became aligned by proposing that the image of atlatl and dart evolved from a symbol of weaponry that required highly developed physical and mental skills into icons of ritual and ceremony. Then, while reviewing the literature, we focused on two philosophical layers of "interpretative concerns" used successfully by archaeology when engaging in cultural analysis: etic versus emic. Etic involves the perspectives by investigators outside the culture; emic brings in the perspectives of those inside the culture being investigated.

If I can entertain rock art as a sacred artistic representation—
of ritual as a peoples' interaction with something nonempirical
such as powers, beings, qualities, and states of mind;
of religious sacred stories about these interactions;
of individuals experiencing altered dimensions of consciousness;
of individuals having specific religious roles and positions;
and of symbols that were understood to encapsulate ideas—
then how might I find myself scanning the images differently?

The atlatl, or throwing stick (Figure 2), is a device that enhanced the hunter's ability to launch a spear-like dart at game animals (or human enemies when needed). It has been an integral element of the prehistoric toolkit for nearly 20,000 years. Atlatls and atlatl frag-

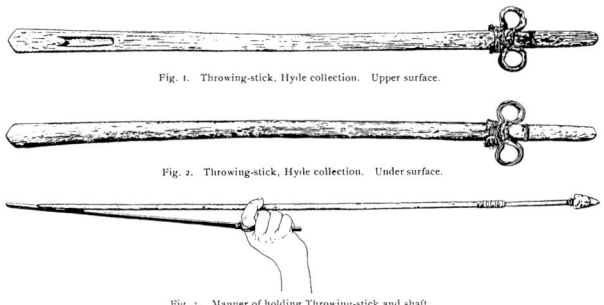

Figure 2. Plate I from Pepper's (1902) essay on Southwestern throwing-sticks. The illustrated specimen was found in a burial site in Grand Gulch, Utah, and collected by McLoyd and Graham in 1894.

ments are well known from Basketmaker sites in the Four Corners region, and five nearly intact examples were the basis for Garnett's (2015) guide to the Basketmaker atlatl.

Garnett's in-depth description of Basketmaker atlatls and their construction provides as close an insider's or emic understanding as is possible after nearly 1,500 years or more since the atlatl's arrival in the Southwest. If we look at the atlatl in rock art from an etic view, we certainly recognize it as a weapon and understand its use in hunting. Images can be entertained as representing successful hunts, desires for successful hunts, or symbols of male prowess (assuming hunters were men). But Garnett's proficiency with the atlatl enabled him to offer a careful analysis that reveals deeper details that refined our thinking. For example, the Broken Roof Cave atlatl (Guernsey 1931) has a large seed incorporated into the fingerloop binding and a small translucent moonstone bound adjacent to the seed (Figure 3). The atlatl also has a weight still attached closer to the spur than the fingerloops. Atlatl weights have long been considered non-functional ceremonial attachments or simple weights to increase the mass of the atlatl and thereby the power of a throw.

Figure 3. Profile view of the Broken Roof Cave atlatl. The seed and moonstone are situated to the right of the fingerloops on the left end of the atlatl. The atlatl weight is located two-thirds of the way from the left end. The extreme curvature is a product of warping over time (after Guernsey 1931:Plate 50).

We can appreciate that the seed and crystal bound to this particular atlatl fulfilled a ceremonial rather than functional purpose. Although some disagree with him, Garnett (2015:57) continues to propose that the atlatl weights serve a complex functional purpose. Rather than increasing the mass of the atlatl and therefore its power as many argue, Garnett contends that the placement of the weight adjusts the balance of the atlatl in the hand, which increases the accuracy of the aim. If we acknowledge Garnett's explanation, then the construction, balancing, and use of the atlatl required a technical skill level heretofore unexamined. What does this tell us about examining atlatl images? Realistic images can be identified for what they are drawing from archaeological evidence, but there can also be a deeper, technological, and ceremonial meaning that may not be accessible to us as at the etic level.

Anthropologist Wesley Bernardini (2006) integrated a multilayered process of research to study how people of the Southwest may have come together to form communities in the later prehistoric period. He blended results from his scientific analysis of artifacts with evidence from ethnology through oral traditions. He identified two types of oral traditions of the Hopi peoples that anthropologists draw upon to study Puebloan culture. One is traditional knowledge (*navoti*) and the other is folklore (*tuuwutsi*). *Navoti* played an important role in his investigation regarding northerly migrations and clan verses lineage. "Oral tradition is a germane source of this information because it is concerned with preserving information about the past that is relevant to the present" (Bernardini 2006:21).

Hopi society sees *navoti* as a
> ...system of knowledge that includes philosophy, science, and theology and incorporates conceptual models for explaining the past and predicting, or 'prophesying' future events...a sort of Hopi hermeneutic. To the Hopi, *navoti* has historical veracity, and as such differs from *tuuwutsi*, or folklore, which does not [Bernardini 2006:23].

In regard to using Hopi consultants to obtain traditional knowledge, *navoti* is "transmitted primarily in ceremonial contexts" with the "most complete and reliable accounts...restricted to high-ranking clan members of that clan" (Bernardini 2006:23). In regard to others outside the clan attempting to obtain knowledge, it can more often than not result in inaccurate or incomplete information being provided by the source.

Archaeologist John Ware (2014:xiii, xvii) writes that understanding "the present requires a deep history that only archaeology can provide. Similarly, the past can be understood socially by linking it with ethnographic studies that document humans' lived experiences…[T]he direct historical approach starts with the ethnography as the end result of historical developments and then upstreams into the past through a combination of historical documents and archaeology" (Earle 2014:xiii). Yet, regarding the acquisition of *navoti*, there "are societies so secret in the east[ern Pueblos] that to even acknowledge their existence would be a betrayal of society secrets" (Ware 2014:xvii).

The study of rock art is an exercise in reconstructing the behaviors—frequently ritual and ceremonial behaviors—which led to the creation of the art. Where there is reason to suspect that rock art is the result of ceremonial or ritualistic activities, Rappaport's model provides a theoretical basis for making the linkage between rock art, ritual, and ceremony. According to anthropologist Elsie Clews Parsons (1996a:489), to the Pueblo a "large number of ceremonial objects are representative…Such representations are in varying degrees forms of compulsive magic insuring the presence or imparting the power of the thing represented, and they are referred to by the very name the thing represents." The depiction of the atlatl and dart in both realistic circumstances (*navoti*) and in unrealistic representations (possibly *tuuwutsi*) suggests that it is an example of restructuring objects to serve a broader function, which is best documented within art.

Atlatl and Dart: A Multilayered Icon

How can we recognize the atlatl in rock art and distinguish it from a dart or some other object? Scattered throughout the Cedar Mesa region in the Four Corners are examples of an anthropomorphic figure throwing a dart with an atlatl at a bighorn sheep. The sheep is significant (note the bighorn above the atlatl in Figure 1), but not a topic for discussion here with the exception of noting that it provides a link to a broader, regional ceremonial meaning found across the Southwest. A panel found near the mouth of Johns Canyon where it meets the San Juan River helps open the discussion. Two anthropomorphs in the lower right hand edge of the panel are holding atlatls. The upper figure has just thrown a dart that struck a bighorn sheep in the chest. The lower figure has an atlatl in his hand with his arm back in a throwing stance. He holds two darts in his other hand (Figure 4).

Figure 4. An instructive Basketmaker panel with two anthropomorphs with atlatls and darts in the lower right corner (photograph courtesy Leon Yost).

A second Basketmaker panel from the Music Note site near the Narrows in Grand Gulch (Figure 5) can be seen as a simple representation of a hunt (an etic view based on assumed hunting imagery). However, it may carry a deeper, ceremonial meaning not immediately obvious to the modern observer (an assumed emic view deferring to Basketmaker ethnography no longer accessible or inferred from modern Pueblo ethnography). The anthropomorph on the right has his arm raised in the action of throwing one of the darts that impaled the bighorn sheep on the left. The difference in scale of the bighorn compared to the human and its sharp teeth could indicate a mythical being (*tuuwutsi*) rather than a simple representation of a sheep kill. Or, the image could represent a ceremonial significance to the scene that cannot be known in the absence of ceremonial knowledge (*navoti*).

Figure 5. A seemingly uncomplicated representation of a sheep kill could have several different meanings that are no longer accessible today.

A popular etic view of many rock art images with bird heads classifies them as shamanistic. A prominent Basketmaker III painting of a procession of bird-headed figures in the Ghost Panel near the mouth of Dripping Canyon in Grand Gulch would therefore represent shamans carrying darts in procession (Figure 6). Using Rappaport's terminology, rock art was created as a self-referential statement about the actors portrayed or the artist. In time, the images acquired symbolic meaning based on their permanence. While Basketmaker III rock art continues to record ritual activities, panels become more narrative in their construction and individual elements become imbued with more symbolic meaning. An alternative emic explanation might argue instead that bird-head figures could represent a ceremonial social class or lineage that enjoyed a wide distribution throughout the Basketmaker Southwest.

Parson's ethnographic study of Pueblo religion supports the possibility that images came to represent lineage as well as an ideology within ritual. It may have

Figure 6. A procession of bird-headed figures carrying darts from the Ghost Panel in Grand Gulch. The panel takes its name from the fact that most of the paintings were executed in what is now a fugitive white pigment. The black and grey tones in the illustration represent different shades of white.

been the pre-alphabet way to conserve what was held to be most essential and/or sacred in order to preserve traditions and honor lineage.

> Possession of ceremonial paraphernalia which exact careful guardianship, being potent for good or ill, is a factor for conservatism. Ritual wealth, like other forms of wealth, renders a person conservative or sets him up a conservative standard…Any group property is a stabilizing influence, binding together the propriety unit and leading to all kinds of communal practices and customs. The Zuni way of placing a man by saying he came out of such and such house, and Zuni and Hopi lineage or clan ownership of house, lands, springs, or fetishes are illustrations. Indeed property, more particularly houses and ritual property, seems to be the source of Hopi or Pueblo clanship, the means by which the fiction of kinship is maintained after connection by blood is lost track of [Parsons 1996b:1158–1159].

From this perspective, it is possible that the artistic depiction of atlatl and dart alone upon the rocks and within panels came to serve the process of conserving some form of social unity through remembrance of what is most important in history, ritual, lore, and lineage (possibly as the "players" within the drama of life).

Several panels in the so-called Music Note site near the Narrows in Grand Gulch illustrate the variability in the form of the atlatl in Basketmaker rock art. These variations could be the result of artistic convention or it could be the deliberate intention to illustrate specific paraphernalia. One panel illustrates what might be four distinct items found in Basketmaker rock art in the region stretching from Canyon de Chelly to Cedar Mesa (Figure 7). The three figures on the right illustrate an anthropomorph, an atlatl, and a dart in approximately proper proportion to one another. The atlatl has elliptical fingerloops and the dart has a large oval form representing the fletching.

The atlatl is illustrated in a second panel at the Music Note site (Figure 8). This atlatl is held in a position as it might appear when the dart has left the device.

Figure 7. One of several Basketmaker painted panels at the Music Note site near the Narrows in Grand Gulch. The figures, from right to left, include an anthropomorph, an atlatl, and a dart in roughly correct scale. The next four figures may be darts with distinctive fletching or ceremonial wands. The last figure maybe a dart, again with distinctive fletching, or a ceremonial staff. We do not know if the final five images were painted in the same scale as the first three.

On the other hand, we are identifying the distinctive oval form to represent the dart. Darts, as defined by the oval, appear more frequently in rock art. The trailing darts in the Ghost Panel (Figure 6) are found in a small charcoal drawing of a procession (without bird heads) at this site (Figure 9). A later Basketmaker III small painting located in a site in the area of Jailhouse Ruin in Bullet Canyon illustrates a single anthropomorph with 19 darts (Figure 10).

Paired darts appear frequently, either with an anthropomorph or isolated as an intentional image. The oval indication of fletching as opposed to the elliptical depiction of fingerloops define the figures as darts (Figure 11). A pair of fancier darts is found in a Music Note panel (Figure 12). The paired polychrome darts on the left are an example of a more detailed depiction of the oval fletching.

Figure 11. Paired darts painted on an eroding cliff face opposite the Jailhouse Ruin in Bullet Canyon.

Figure 8. An anthropomorph with an atlatl held upright as if he has just thrown a dart. The birds may be later additions, although the human figure has talon-like feet.

Figure 9. A small panel of a charcoal drawing at the Music Note site illustrates a procession of figures holding darts trailing behind them.

Figure 12. (a) Paired polychrome darts with oval fletching at the Music Notes site; (b) DStretch modified LAB enhancement to highlight the polychrome fletching.

Another example of a dart with fancy fletching is the image on the left side of Figure 7. It appears to be a dart in some settings (Figure 13) and a ceremonial staff in others (Figure 14). The use of the dart-like figure

Figure 10. A later Basketmaker III painting shows a single anthropomorph with 19 darts.

as a possible staff is best illustrated in the Butler Wash Wolfman Panel (Figure 15). These elaborate darts depicted as staffs are also found paired (Figure 16), much as the example in Figure 11. While we suspect the paired images represent the evolution of the dart into a ceremonial sacrosanct artifact, paired darts that are too large in comparison to one another to represent an actual atlatl and dart are depicted in the later Basketmaker III Procession Panel in Butler Wash (Figure 17). Does the ambiguity reflect their dual nature as weapon and ceremonial staff?

Returning to Figure 7, the last element is the group of four darts or wands. The detailed fletching is much like that of the two darts in Figure 12. We single them out because other examples of four similar dart-like

Figure 15. The Wolfman Panel in the lower end of Butler Wash includes two elements on the left end of the image that might be a dart (with the oval fletching) and a ceremonial staff (at the left tip of the bird's wing). The purpose of the dart is ambiguous and may be an example of a ceremonial staff.

Figure 13. An atlatl and dart are highlighted in the photograph of the heavily eroded Basketmaker petroglyph panel located near the mouth of Butler Wash on the San Juan River.

Figure 16. The two examples of paired darts or staffs painted not far from the isolated figure in Figure 14 further blur the meaning of the dart image.

Figure 14. A single, large dart or ceremonial staff painted as an isolated image in the Narrows stranded oxbow in Grand Gulch.

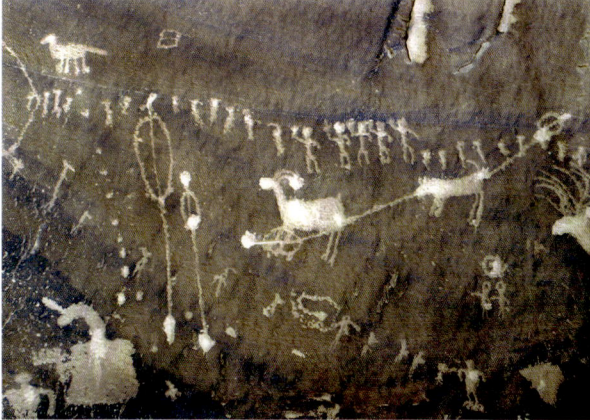

Figure 17. A pair of darts with the oval fletching in the Basketmaker III Procession Panel. They are of two sizes, much like the earlier Basketmaker figures in Figure 16. We would label these as an atlatl and dart if the smaller image had elliptical instead of oval loops. Two darts impale either end of a probable feline figure to the right.

items are found elsewhere in Grand Gulch. Two instances are represented in Figure 18, one from the Narrows paintings and the second from the Big Panel further downstream in Grand Gulch.

Figure 18. Two examples of clusters of four darts. The dart shafts are eroded away in the top image from the Narrows. White pigment is the most commonly encountered in Grand Gulch and the most likely to be eroded away with time. The four from the Big Panel in the lower half of the image have the red dots in the middle of the fletching as opposed to the bottom of the fletching in the Narrows example.

How did we move our thinking from the dart to ceremonial staff or wand? A painted panel located on a high ledge between the Narrows and the Big Panel integrates the dart image, the cluster of four, and ceremonial activities (Figure 19). We suggest further that the painting records an actual ceremony although we do not know its purpose. On the left are four figures. They may be male since an appendage shows between their legs, although it might be a representation of an animal tail hanging from a waist sash. On the right are four figures with headdresses indicated by crowns of dots. The figures on either end of the group of four on the right are holding staffs with the oval shape we interpret as fletching when discussing darts. Paired images are painted between the two groups of figures. The one on the left has the classic form of a dart. It may have a point at the end although the fugitive nature of the white pigment leaves the question open. The one on the right could be a dart, but the triangular nature of what would be the fletching may represent something else. The paired images resemble the two items in Figure 15. The presence of handprints superimposed on the figures suggests that visitors held the panel in veneration.

It is not difficult to imagine the early hunters
being highly trained in ceremonies and rituals
surrounding use of the atlatl.
There may have been specified petitions to Hunting Spirit
for a successful hunt while tracking and waiting
for the prey's surrender,
while preparing for the throw,
and during the throw for release of the prey's spirit
through a prayer of gratitude.
If so, the entire hunt was a ritualized body prayer.

Did the added newcomers to the hunt
require more time to be spent developing proficiency
with the atlatl
than in mastering traditional rituals and ceremony
for engaging prey with indoctrinated reverence?
The concentration required for a new dexterity
may have even changed the flow of the "old" prayers.
Such might have caused concern among elders
that the new atlatl restricted the breath of mutuality
between natural elements and humankind.

Figure 19. A painting of an apparent ceremony in Grand Gulch that includes the use of ceremonial staffs and perhaps a pair of ceremonial staffs, one of which may be a dart.

*Dilemma innately moving the mind into creativity,
a solution might be to elevate the status of the atlatl and dart
from weapon to partners in personal ritual and ceremony.
Might there have evolved a belief that weapons could pray?*

We have come to accept that there are at least two components to the rock art of atlatls and darts. One is as weaponry and the other is as ceremonial staffs and wands. This second component to rock art fits into the Hopi oral traditions previously mentioned: traditional knowledge *(navoti)* and folklore *(tuuwutsi)*. Understanding becomes part of the process of distinguishing between the two. The images of the atlatl and wand can be both representational of something that actually existed, events—real or imagined—that happened, and symbolic of an ideology it represents. Distinguishing these differences within oral traditions enables us to perceive an important alignment within those works through images. We can see within the rock art that there is a coming together of tradition, aligned side-by-side through a unified artistic documentation of history that blends facts with beliefs in a way that not only preserves but very likely advances wisdom in order to evolve with change.

Conclusion

The evolving Basketmaker culture became the foundation for the Puebloan cultures that continue to inhabit the Southwest. Little is known of their actual roots other than their movement north from the southern deserts onto the Colorado Plateau. We can assume they confronted the problems of environmental stress, resource conflicts, and episodic intra-group violence with rituals designed to reduce the impacts of conflict and to enhance ethnic similarities that bound them as an emerging cultural identity. They certainly carried their rituals and ceremonies with them as they came into sporadic contact with the Archaic culture that moved through the same environment. With small isolated populations loosely tethered to experimental agricultural plots, one can assume they interacted and intermarried with the Archaic people well versed in the traditional hunting and gathering resources of the region.

Can we find evidence for the blending of the two cultures in rock art images of the atlatl and dart? The evidence for an indigenous bighorn sheep cult integrating the importance of the atlatl and dart can be found in the Archaic Period art and archaeology at Newberry Cave in California (Garfinkel et al. 2016). The artifact inventory from Newberry Cave includes 11 complete and 1049 fragmentary split-twig figurines, 1019 dart shaft fragments, and 310 projectile points. Sixty-six rock art panels are found outside and inside the cave. Radiocarbon dates range from 2175 to 1179 B.C.E. indicating use over roughly 1,000 years. These artifacts are primarily related to men's hunting and ritual activities. Garfinkel, et al. (2016:205) concluded that Newberry Cave was the site of increase rituals for bighorn sheep. Notable for our argument is the presence of the dart fragments alongside the split-twig figurines.

Coulam and Schroedl (2004) examined the distribution of 30 Late Archaic sites with split-twig figurines and argue that they served two different functions. The Grand Canyon style is evidence of increase totems while the Green River style functioned as social totems. Cole (2009:45) notes the correlation of split-twig figurines with Glen Canyon Style 5 petroglyphs and their similarities and juxtaposition with Basketmaker II rock art. Grant (1979) plotted the distribution of atlatls in his early survey of the occurrence of the image. He (Grant 1978:210) noted the co-occurrence of atlatls and bird images in Canyon de Chelly, but it appears he was less familiar with the significant numbers present in the Cedar Mesa region.

We plot the overlapping distributions of split-twig figurines, Glen Canyon Style 5 rock art, atlatls in the western Southwest, and the Puebloan cultural area in Figure 20. The Basketmaker rock art examples illustrated in Figures 2 through 19 are found in the area defined by the overlap of the Glen Canyon Style 5 and the occurrence of atlatls above the Utah/Arizona border on the right side of Figure 20. The area includes the Cedar Mesa region, Butler Wash, and the San Juan River corridor. The Basketmaker atlatl/dart imagery continues down Chinle Wash into Canyon de Chelly as noted by Grant.

Rock art in the San Juan River Basin in the Four Corners region offers the opportunity to explore the cultural interactions and blending of ritual practices among the indigenous Archaic population and the agricultural immigrants. The Basketmaker roots of later Puebloan cultures emerged from the melding of the two cultures. We have focused on one class of image here, but our study could be expanded to consider the bighorn and the bird as they are other key elements in the rituals, ceremonies, and rock art that evolved from the cultural melting pot. Nor have we explored Coulam and Schroedl's (2004) functional dichotomy defining split-twig figurines in habitation sites as social totems and in non-habitation settings as increase totems. We

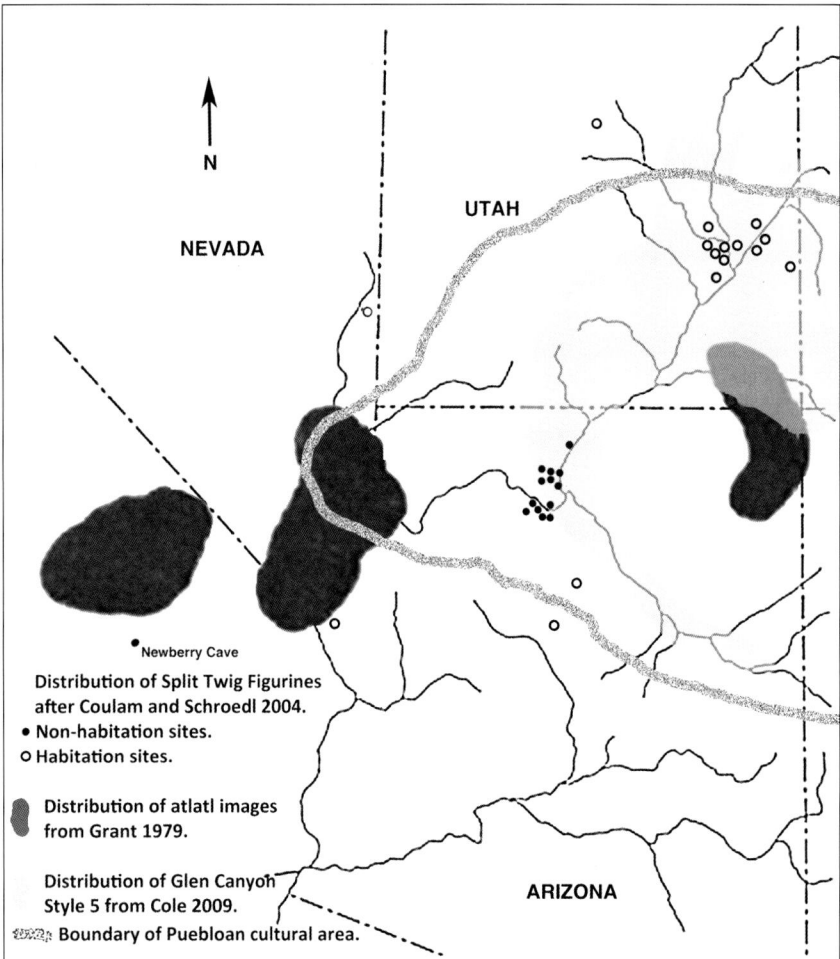

Figure 20. The overlapping distributions of split-twig figurines, atlatl images, Glen Canyon Style 5 rock art, and the Puebloan cultural area in the region of the western Basketmakers.

align the atlatl and dart with ceremonies and rituals without further interpretation. This enables us to consider that, as sacrosanct icons, they may have evolved to set the underlying intent of narratives graphically depicted by artists to represent an important aspect of life in the culture. Such considerations allow modern viewers to engage such panels with a broader and even multilayered perspective of appreciation.

According to speech language pathologists Barbara Shadden and Fran Hagstrom and sociologist Partrica Kiski, narratives are important at different levels, from the individual to the entire culture.

> Our perceptual self is the product of an accumulation of life experiences, and the meaning we have forged out of these experiences, the knowledge of our typical patterns of acting and reacting, our memories, the roles we play, our biographic realities, and our perceived status in the society. Although we may feel that this self exists in a very private domain, it does not exist in a vacuum...This self is socially situated or constructed [Shadden et al. 2008:4].

In the realm of communication, humans are highly driven by the need to make sense of experience, and this is accomplished by creating stories (narratives) that reflect our selective understanding of our lives. Narrative also refers to the communicative exchanges through which we share aspects of our life stories.

Bohntinsky (2016:84–86) discusses the levels of communication, and explains how the most basic level of communication is internal communication (self talk). It is the foundation for all other levels of communication (interpersonal, group, organizational, and social). "This is where we interact with ourselves in interpreting reality and creating messages for communicating with others (interpersonal communication). The central communicative processes of sending out information (encoding) and receiving information (decoding) are performed at the internal level." According to Bohntinsky, messages are being created and interpreted by the individual. One's memories of experiences and feelings, based on cultural influences, create his/her personal view of communication from automatic associations to higher critical thinking. The more people learn to abide with feelings in a non-judgmental manner the better "communication then becomes a medium for Self-understanding that flows over to mutual understanding" (Bohntinsky 2016:64). Perhaps, this is how we come to experience the sacred in some rock art: there is the universal perception of some immutable essence at the internal level despite cultural differences and varied approaches to critical thinking.

Simple drawings have the ability to circumvent the judgmental mind. Frugality of design, whether etched or painted, can expand an image's potential for triggering internal communication that bypasses the rational literal mind in order to create an immediate automatic association. Basic designs are especially useful for understanding and recalling religious teachings from creation stories and doctrines to higher truths (*tuuwutsi* to *navoti*). A broad example is the line drawing symbol serving as an icon for each major world religion's beliefs, ceremonies, and practices, such as the fish or cross for Christianity. The evidence that we presented here highly supports our proposal that the atlatl and dart in Basketmaker rock art evolved from documenting literal utility to serving as icons for communicating ideology within ceremony and ritual. Something old was repurposed into something new by creating a symbol that communicated an important "practice" at a personal and cultural level in order for the teachings to survive after the weapon was replaced by the bow and arrow.

Finally, after all of this, what I can best surmise
is that here lies early evidence of preservation.
Did these ancient artists entertain the idea
their designs would have such far-reaching implications
into a new millennium?
Lines blended so astutely in mediums that outlast time,
painted upon or etched deeply into eternal stone,
invite the mind and body into some creative dance.
Yet, unlike being mesmerized by a spiral spinning,
rather than falling into entranced suggestibility,
these images elicit something quite the opposite.

There must have been something important about interactions
that evolved into a science and theology
once enough trials demonstrated validity of consequences.
Ethology describes the philosophy of "like causes like."
It stimulated the imagination for metaphor and analogies
that accommodates change by assimilating new facts
into the ancient creation story.
Yet, something very important was to remain constant,
and I suspect this is how these lines touch us.

When viewing rock art images from different perspectives,
such as weapons to icons,
I also begin to see static postures that provoke analysis
move into fluid processions that invite my participation.
Then it is as if I lose my mind, or become unenculturated,
by being dropped right in the middle of the action
and experiencing what the ancient ones were expressing
without any linguistics for backstory or conclusion.

Suddenly, I do remember a conclusion in Pueblo tuuwutsi.
"That is how they learned to make their ceremony.
When they were underground maybe they were asleep
and did not pay attention.
This is why they did not bring their ceremonies with them"
and started their own.
Maybe rock art invokes an attentive level of mind
where deep appreciation aligns with aspiration.
Both blend to ignite a fundamental need for discovery
especially when navoti knowledge is believed obtainable.
Does this all serve to awaken sacred creativity?
If so, then maybe, this would be something to be preserved.

References Cited

Bernardini, Wesley
 2006 *Hopi Oral Tradition and the Archaeology of Identity*. University of Arizona Press, Tucson.

Bohntinsky, Dorothy
 2016 *Transformational Healing through the Integration of the Self*. In-Word Bound, Hayward, California.

Cole, Sally J.
 2009 *Legacy on Stone*. Revised and Updated Edition. Johnson Books, Boulder, Colorado.

Coulam, Nancy J., and Alan R. Schroedl
 2004 Late Archaic Totemism in the Greater American Southwest. *American Antiquity* 69(1):41–62

Earle, Timothy
 2014 Foreword. In *A Pueblo Social History: Kinship, Sodality, and Community in the Northern Southwest*, edited by John A. Ware, pp. ix–xiv. School for Advanced Research Press, Santa Fe.

Garfinkel, Alan P., Donald Austin, Adella Schroth, Paul Goldsmith, and Ernest H. Siva
 2016 Ritual, Ceremony and Symbolism of Archaic Bighorn Hunters of the Eastern Mojave Desert: Newberry Cave, California. *Rock Art Research* 33(2):193–208.

Grant, Campbell
 1978 *Canyon De Chelly*. University of Arizona Press, Tucson, Arizona.

 1979 The Occurrence of the Atlatl in Rock Art. In *American Indian Rock Art, Volume 5*, edited by Frank G. Bock, Ken Hedges, Georgia Lee, and Helen Michaelis, pp. 1–21. American Rock Art Research Association, El Toro, California.

Garnett, Justin
 2015 *Practical Atlatlry of the Four Corners: A Complete Guide to the Basketmaker Atlatl*. CreateSpace Independent Publishing, Kansas City.

Guernsey, Samuel J.
 1931 Explorations in Northeastern Arizona: Report on the Archaeological Fieldwork of 1920-1923. *Papers of the Peabody Museum of American Archaeology and Ethnology, Harvard University* 8(2). Cambridge.

Hyder, William D.
 2002 Basketmaker Ceremonial Caves of Grand Gulch, Utah. In *Rock Art and Cultural Processes*, edited by Solveig A. Turpin, pp. 67–89. Special Publication 3, Rock Art Foundation, San Antonio.

Hyder William D., and Bohntinsky, Dorothy
 2016 Ritual and Rock Art in Basketmaker Ceremonies: Butler Wash Revisited. URARA 2016 Symposium. http://www.utahrockart2.org/pubs/proceedings/papers/36-11-Hyder_and_Bohntinsky_Basketmaker_Ceremonies_B.pdf, accessed January 22, 2018.

Parsons, Elsie Clews

    1996a *Pueblo Indian Religion: Volume One.* University of Nebraska, Lincoln. Reprint edition, original publication 1939, The University of Chicago, Chicago.

    1996b *Pueblo Indian Religion: Volume Two.* University of Nebraska, Lincoln and London. Reprint edition, original publication 1939, The University of Chicago, Chicago.

Pepper, George H.

    1902 The Throwing-stick of a Prehistoric People of the Southwest. In *Proceedings of International Congress of Americanists, Thirteenth Session Held in New York 1902*, pp. 107–130. Eschenbach Printing Co., Easton, Pennsylvania.

Rappaport, Roy A.

    1999 *Ritual and Religion in the Making of Humanity.* Cambridge University Press, Cambridge.

Shadden, Barbara, Fran Hagstrom, and Patricia Koski

    2008 *Neurogenic Communication Disorders: Life Stories and the Narrative Self.* Plural Publishing, San Diego.

Ware, John A.

    2014 *A Pueblo Social History: Kinship, Sodality, and Community in the Northern Southwest.* School for Advanced Research Press, Santa Fe.

Pipe Spring: Fremont-Anasazi Interaction in Southeastern Utah

Kevin Conti, James D. Keyser, David A. Kaiser, and David L. Minick

Site 42SA27325, Pipe Spring, is a small Anasazi four-room pueblo farmstead in southeastern Utah. The ceramic assemblage suggests occupation between A.D. 750 and 1175. A T-shaped door is typical of Mesa Verdean architecture. Anthropomorphs on associated rock art panels indicate BM II–III through early P III period activity (A.D. 200–1150), but during the late part of this sequence four large Fremont anthropomorphs were carved and/or painted at the site. These show formal attributes consistent with both the Classic Vernal and Southern San Rafael styles found to the north and west, and suggest a cultural interchange between Fremont and Mesa Verde peoples.

Traditionally, the Fremont cultural area has been neatly demarcated by the Colorado River to the west (where it is separated from the Anasazi culture area located further east and southeast) and the Wyoming state line to the north (Schaafsma 1971; 1980; 2008). Many contemporary Fremont scholars still accept these traditional borders as originally defined (Richards 2014). However, in recent years rock art research has identified sites with a strong Fremont signature that sit "out of bounds" of this area (Horn et. al. 1994; Keyser and Poetschat 2017; Neal 2010). Pipe Spring is one such site that has a heavy Fremont signature but that falls well outside what has traditionally been defined as the Fremont homeland (Figure 1).

In this paper, we first describe the environmental setting and surface features present at Pipe Spring. Then we describe our research approach and detail the documentation methods we used to record the rock art. Finally, we describe the imagery on rock art Panels 1 to 4. Following that we discuss the chronology and associations of the rock art, and present some ideas as to its meaning. In this section we provide a brief overview of the Fremont "problem" in this area, and summarize how the Fremont figures on Panel 2 may possibly have functioned.

Site Description

The Pipe Spring Site sits at an elevation of 5,900 feet in the West Central Mesa Verde Cultural Region, on land administered by the Monticello District of the Bureau of Land Management (BLM). In this area, pinion and juniper slopes of the Abajo Mountains give way to slick rock drainages whose canyon-bottom cottonwood stands collect runoff. Pipe Spring itself sits below a slick rock pour-off, within an alcove at the head of one such drainage (Figure 2). A substantial waterfall can be the effect of seasonal precipitation and snow melt at this pour-off, and several hundred meters of slick rock below the plunge pool have large natural tanks that retain this excess water. Located at the base of

Kevin Conti
Independent Researcher
Monticello, Utah

James D. Keyser
Oregon Archaeological Society
Portland, Oregon

David A. Kaiser
Oregon Archaeological Society
Portland, Oregon

David L. Minick
Oregon Archaeological Society
Portland, Oregon

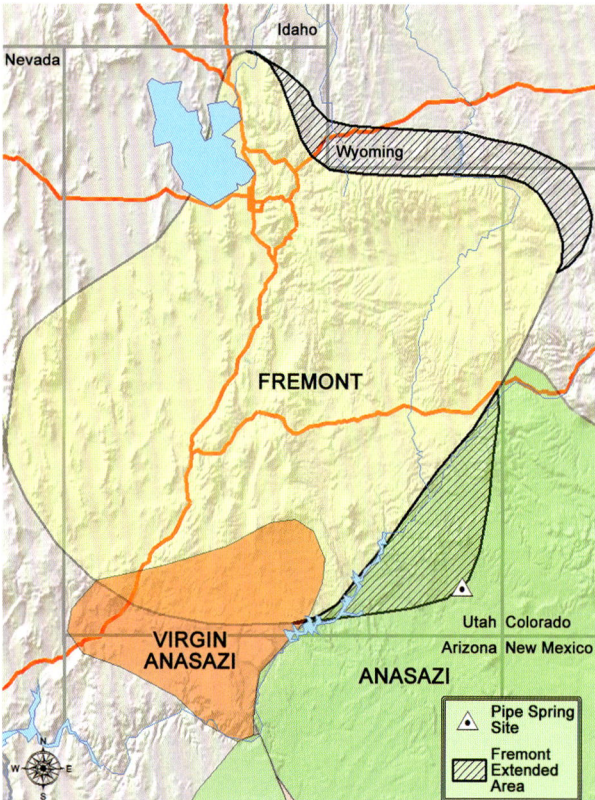

Figure 1. Traditionally accepted Fremont cultural area shown in yellow, with expansions shown by cross-hatched areas. Note Pipe Spring site on southeastern boundary.

Figure 2. Overview of Pipe Spring site. Panel 1 located at circle, Panels 2–4 are at arrow. Note small Pueblo structure in center of photograph.

rimmed pool located immediately behind the small pueblo structure in the alcove's approximate center.

This small 7 x 2 m four-room pueblo (Figure 3) is oriented on a NE/SW alignment. Walls of this small farmstead are constructed of single-course tabular sandstone blocks. Between the blocks are small chinking stones, an architectural feature found throughout the region. The block work is covered by adobe tempered with ceramic sherds and small pebbles. Also present is a T-shaped doorway—another distinctive characteristic of Mesa Verdean architecture. The pueblo's still largely intact roof is constructed of juniper vigas that support

Figure 3. Small Pueblo structure in alcove. Opening at far left is T-shaped door.

the waterfall, between rock art Panels 1 and 2 is a permanent spring seep, where an eastern exposure ensures that water flows beneath the ice throughout the winter. Additionally, there is a second spring that fills a grass-

smaller overlying willow latillas. Laid over the latillas is a thick adobe layer. Near the pueblo are two metates; one a large boulder metate exhibiting numerous grinding slicks indicating an agricultural economy. All the grinding slicks are the result of one-handed manos; a Basketmaker trait (Matson et al. 1988).

Although the site has been heavily scavenged and is thus almost devoid of artifacts, architectural style and the few remaining ceramics allow us to date the site. Mancos Corrugated (A.D. 900–1100) and Mancos Black on White (A.D. 975–1175) wares suggest a primary occupation during Pueblo II times, probably extending into the early Pueblo III. Located within a smaller alcove to the south of Panel 4 is a buried cultural component whose artifacts indicate that it is the result of Basketmaker II period occupation. It attests to the site's long use history.

Four rock art panels are at the site. The three main panels, numbered 2 through 4 are located just south of the spring on the alcove's west side, and contain most of the petroglyphs and pictographs. Panel 1 (Figure 4) consists of a single painted handprint and anthropomorph located all the way across the alcove more than 75 m north of the main rock art concentration. Panel 2 is a palimpsest of petroglyphs and pictographs from Basketmaker, Fremont, and Pueblo cultural traditions and shows a complex series of superimpositions involving anthropomorphs, animals, and handprints. Panels 3 and 4 have an animal trackway, anthropomorphs with birds on their heads, birds, mountain sheep, and other pecked Basketmaker imagery.

Figure 4. Pictographs at Panel 1 include a small, trapezoidal body, Basketmaker human and a handprint. DStretch enhancement LDS+AC.

Research Approach

Our primary research goal was to do a full-scale recording of the incised "Fremont-like" anthropomorphs on Panel 2. The senior author obtained permission from the Monticello BLM to do this recording and to set up scaffolding for a few days in order to access the anthropomorphs on Panel 2. Superimpositioning, erosion, extensive mud flows on this panel, and ghost pigment presented unique recording challenges. Once we could access these figures close-up with the use of scaffolding, however, it became apparent that we could not fully interpret these figures without understanding the complex superimposition sequence on the panel. Thus, our goal changed slightly to recording the panel with sufficient detail and accuracy that we could determine the order in which the various "episodes" of rock art had been applied. The various episodes included combinations of prepared surface areas, painted handprints, painted and pecked bicolor birds, large pecked and incised Fremont anthropomorphs, a pecked mountain sheep, red pigment spatter, white ghost pigment, and miscellaneous incised petroglyphs.

Our field methods used direct tracing on two-mil vinyl sheets combined with close-up and distance photography. Photographing in various lighting conditions was essential, and Conti made several additional trips to the site in addition to our two visits to obtain particular photographs that we needed. Tracing was necessary to obtain details that would have gone unnoticed with photography; but likewise, photographic enhancement was required in several instances to fully understand the panel as a whole and place the tracing into the sequence of rock art episodes.

Laboratory methods involved using both DStretch and color brightness/contrast enhancements to render our final recording of individual figures and the entire panel. In several instances during laboratory work we discovered our tracings were incomplete without additional information from various photographic enhancements, but even during field tracing we had realized that the traced image would not be complete without adding information from photographs. This was especially true for the white ghost pigment used for the large Fremont anthropomorphs, but it also proved to be the case with understanding the sequence of red paint spatter. Laboratory research also included a literature review of federal archives, focusing on sites that contained either "Faces Motif" imagery or unusual mixtures of Anasazi and Fremont material culture.

Following publication of this report we provided all of our records (tracings, photocopy reductions, sketches, and a suite of photographs that we used in our analysis) and a copy of this publication to the Monticello BLM for their files and communication to the Utah SHPO as they deem appropriate.

The Rock Art

Painted and carved on the four identified rock art panels at Pipe Spring are more than 150 images representing seven classes of representational motifs and a few non-representational figures (Table 1). The most common images are human handprints, with at least

40 painted at the site. Other common images are boat-form birds—often polychrome images whose second and/or third colors are sometimes fugitive and no longer visible. Some of these birds have pecked or abraded outlines and/or legs, and all the birds on one extensive surface on Panel 3 (more than half of the total on the panel) are pecked. Trapezoidal body anthropomorphs are also quite common, occurring as both painted and pecked examples. The largest of these approaches a meter tall, while the smallest measure less than 15 cm high. Other less numerous forms include feline paw prints, human footprints, plant forms, four Fremont anthropomorphs, and a long trackway of 26 pecked cloven hoofprints.

Table 1. Pipe Spring Element Distribution

Elements/Motifs	Panel 1	Panel 2	Panel 3	Panel 4
HUMANS				
Basketmaker	1	5	8	3
Bird-headed				4
Fremont		4		
Pueblo		1		
Handprints	1	35	3	
Patterned		2		
Footprints		3	1#	
ERODED ELEMENTS			10+	1
PLANT FORMS			1	2
ANIMALS				
Bird		7	15	3**
Duck		1		1**
Crane			1	
Bighorn Sheep		1	1	
Snake		1	1	
Unidentified			3	2
Ungulate trackway*			26	
Feline Track		4		
GEOMETRIC FORMS				1
Miscellaneous		10+	3	
SPATTER "CLOUD"		1++		
Worked Pebble			13+	7+
TOTALS	2	75	86	20

- *   Trackway is 26 hoofprints
- ** Shown as human head, not counted separately
- \#   Petroglyph
- \+   Approximate number
- ++ 200+ droplets compose this spatter "cloud"

Panel 1

In the extreme northeast part of the alcove a badly spalled cliff face contains Panel 1. Situated slightly over two meters above the current ground surface here (Figure 4), is a small, red-painted trapezoidal body anthropomorph and what appears to be the right handprint of a small child. The handprint is stamped in a brighter red pigment than the finger-painted human. Other red staining is evident around these elements, but the surface is so eroded here that no other figures are recognizable.

Panel 2

Panel 2 (Figures 5 and 6) contains both pictographs and petroglyphs. The imagery includes painted and incised anthropomorphs, a large pecked bighorn sheep, painted cat tracks and human hand- and footprints, and numerous boat-bodied birds made by a combination of painting and incising. The birds are painted in two or three colors and shown in a stylized "flying" posture indicated by legs trailing backward from the body at an angle. These are part of the Chinle Representational style, which Grant (1978) describes as "Modified Basketmaker-developmental Pueblo." Grant believed the style terminated around A.D. 1000 in Canyon De Chelly.

Using our recording and a 2008 site form sketch (Larmore 2008), combined with photographic enhancement techniques, we can positively identify ten anthropomorphs on this panel. They are numbered from left to right.

On the panel's far lower left (Figure 6F/1, G/1) is a pair of small painted anthropomorphs (numbered 1 and 2) that appear to be "floating up" from a noticeable natural hole just below the broken edge of the panel. Although Anthropomorph 1 is situated so that its lower body and legs appear to be broken off with the missing edge, close examination shows that it was painted after the edge was broken to make it appear to rise up from the hole directly underneath it.

Anthropomorph 3 (Figure 5 at top) is painted on the upper part of the panel, above a break that resulted from the collapse of a thick slab that fell away sometime long before any rock art was done. Standing approximately 70 cm tall and painted in a dark red pigment used for most of the handprints (but not most of the birds) on this panel, the figure has straight legs extending straight down, a round head, and a headdress consisting of two short vertical lines emanating from its top (Larmore 2008). Recent rock fall at the top of the cliff, which has altered drainage down the face, has resulted

Figure 5. Overview of Panel 2. Fremont anthropomorphs on lower, lighter-colored part of surface.

sociated with Basketmaker art. The left hand[1] terminates just above a second red feline paw print. The upper body and head of this figure is surrounded by a "halo" of handprints, some done in similar colored red pigment, others stamped in a lighter red. One darker red partial handprint shows only three fingers, but what relationship this might have to the three-fingered hand of the anthropomorph is unknown.

Anthropomorph 4 (Figure 6B/2) is a deeply and precisely pecked Puebloan image with a small round head sitting atop a very slightly tapered rectangular body. The figure is superimposed over the largest

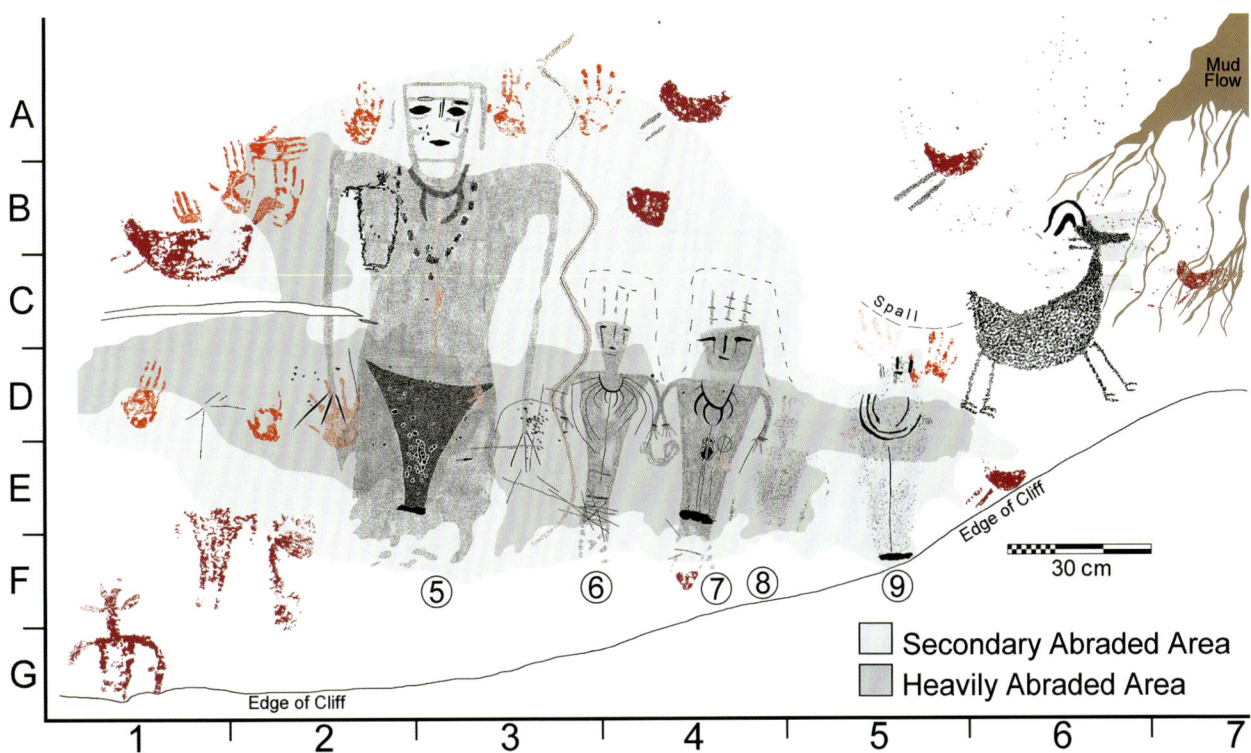

Figure 6. Tracing of Panel. 2 showing Basketmaker, Fremont, and Pueblo imagery with superimpositioning. Fugitive white pigment indicated on Fremont anthropomorphs as extremely fine stippling. Circled numbers 5–9 indicate fugitive pigment anthropomorphs visible with optimal lighting conditions.

in a mud flow that once ran parallel to the figure now flowing down its center. This has somewhat obscured the head and headdress but DStretch enhancement shows its shape and reveals a faded red feline paw print just to the right and slightly above it (Figure 7). The triangular body has the hunched shoulders typically as-

Fremont image, Anthropomorph 5, and has an attenuated arm coming off its left shoulder.

Five large anthropomorphs painted in a fugitive[2] white pigment are unique at the site (Figure 6D/2-5). These are numbered 5 through 9 from left to right. Four of these (numbers 5 to 7 and 9) have incised or

Figure 7. Anthropomorph 3 on upper surface of Panel 2, enhanced to show head shape and feline paw print (in circle) to right and slightly above head. Second paw print positioned just below left hand. Note typical Basketmaker style hunched shoulders posture. DStretch enhancement CRGB.

pecked elements on their bodies and heads, and (in two cases) headdresses that identify them as Fremont images. The fifth anthropomorph (number 8) is painted without any incised elements. It was recognized only after photographic image enhancements that revealed a ghostly, white-painted, trapezoidal body with round head and faint headdress elements. All five of these anthropomorphs are partly or entirely carved/painted on a previously abraded surface that has been modified at least twice. Initially this surface was heavily abraded in a 10 to 40 cm high band that stretches nearly 2 meters across the panel. Later the same area was expanded by lighter abrasion for as much as 60 cm above the original abraded surface and 10 to 20 cm below it. The result is an oval-shaped abraded band that is nearly a meter high in its center and 30 to 40 cm high at its ends stretching across 2 meters of the cliff face. Four of these five anthropomorphs were the original focus of our recording at Pipe Spring. During our fieldwork we discovered their ghost-like appearance that results from the fugitive pigment (see Keyser et al. 2018). Then, during our literature review for this article we later learned that some of these images had been previously described in the literature in preliminary fashion by Manning (2004) who noted the fugitive pigment but did not record the figures in detail. Manning also apparently thought that some of these figures had parts that were added later, a suggestion that was disproven by our detailed recording (Keyser et al. 2018). We describe each of these five anthropomorphs in turn.

Anthropomorph 5, located in the panel's approximate center, is the largest Fremont image. It is clearly superimposed by Anthropomorph 4 and clusters of large impact dints on and around its breechcloth and right hand, but the deeply incised fingers of the left hand are superimposed over an earlier Basketmaker handprint. Double necklaces adorn its upper chest and a thin painted red line bisects the body from the upper necklace to the top of the breechcloth. The face has tear streaks below the eyes, with the one below the left eye formed of four dots in a crude zigzag arrangement and that below the right eye a vertical line (Figure 8). Fugitive white pigment forms a wasp-waisted body that begins to flare out just above the breechcloth and then continues straight down past the well-defined breechcloth bottom. Long thin arms extend down

Figure 8. Head and upper body of Anthropomorph 5, largest Fremont figure. Fine stippling represents fugitive white pigment. Note different tear streaks, long braid-like hair bobs, white pigment extending through incised left eyebrow, and face paint design with arcs below eyes and on cheeks. Dashed line at right shoulder shows area where white pigment has apparently eroded away. White outline on left chest is "ghost" of superimposed P III pecked anthropomorph.

from hunched shoulders to incised trident hands, one of which was noted earlier as being superimposed on a red stamped handprint. The face is outlined with a thin white line forming a trapezoidal mask-like configuration that is decorated with a horizontal line across the forehead through the incised eyebrows and four small lunate lines positioned two on each side of the face, one under each eye and one where each cheekbone would be.

Anthropomorphs 6 and 7 are nearly twin figures. Both are incised and have bodies, arms, and heads painted with fugitive white pigment. Faces have eyes with carved tear streaks, and both figures wear a bear claw necklace (although it appears that the necklace of Anthropomorph 6 was later modified by someone either adding long very thin-line claws or extending claws that did exist far past the body outline). These extensions are particularly evident for the outer three claws on the left side and the outer four on the right side of the necklace. Without these very extended "claws" the necklace much more closely resembles those worn by Anthropomorphs 5 and 7. Several very shallow impact dints occur across the upper body of Anthropomorph 6, near the necklace, one of which directly superimposes one extended claw. The necklace of Anthropomorph 7 is very precisely drawn with a matching set of three claws on each side of the midline, drawn from smaller, shorter, and more gracile to longer and bulkier in descending order.

Both anthropomorphs have long ghost-like, white-painted arms ending in three and four fingers. Both also wear very shallowly abraded arm bands just above each wrist. The right arm of Anthropomorph 6 is linked with the left arm of Anthropomorph 7, but we cannot determine with certainty whether the two anthropomorphs' arms are crossed or just touch at the elbows.[3] The two anthropomorphs carry some sort of U-shaped object in their hands, but this was only painted, and fugitive white pigment was used, so too little of it remains for it to be identified with current technology.

Both Anthropomorphs 6 and 7 (Figure 6C/3–4) wear headdresses consisting of three tall, thin, fugitive white-painted spires, each crossed by perpendicular "breaks." For Anthropomorph 6 these breaks are simply narrow unpainted areas in which we could find no evidence of surface modification (despite close examination) except at the top of the middle and right spires where they terminate roughly at perpendicular incisions. For Anthropomorph 7 the spires are crossed by perpendicular incisions, with only one missing on the left spire (again with no evidence despite close examination). The similar pattern for both headdresses is unlikely to be coincidental. Anthropomorph 7 has a long white-painted braid or hairbob extending down from the right side of the head.

Both Anthropomorphs 6 and 7 have a belt to delineate the waist and have a long, incised line that bisects the body extending from at or near the necklace to the belt. Both are superimposed by apparently random shallow incised lines and a few pecked impact dints. Trapezoidal heads are perched directly on straight shoulders that define the tops of trapezoidal bodies, all painted in very faint fugitive white pigment. Bodies taper severely to the belt and then extend more or less straight down for a short distance but once the pigment continues out past the abraded surface onto the natural-textured surface it becomes impossible to define its shape with any accuracy. There are hints of legs, but these cannot be verified with current technology.

The depiction of Anthropomorphs 6 and 7 with linked arms and carrying something together, and each wearing a nearly identical headdress clearly indicates the artist intended to show some type of relationship between them, but what that was remains a mystery. Possibly they were intended to represent dancers or participants in a ceremony of some sort that involved standardized regalia and postures.

Anthropomorph 8 (Figure 6 E/4–5) is a faint, ghost-like, white-painted image visible only in enhanced photographs. In the field we did not recognize any part of this image, but during laboratory analysis we noted an odd "empty" space in the rank of what we thought were four Fremont anthropomorphs and wondered if there had once been a figure painted there. When we enhanced photographs of these four incised and painted images (using both DStretch and color contrast techniques) to emphasize the fugitive white pigment used to paint them, the body and very faint head of a fifth painted figure were visible in the space between Anthropomorphs 7 and 9. Using color-replacement techniques with these enhanced photographs we could tease out much of the trapezoidal body form and identify a round head sitting atop a short neck. Even some elements of a headdress, similar to those on Anthropomorphs 6 and 7, were recognized. Some additional pigment appears to represent arms hanging down from the shoulders, but these features are even more ephemeral than the body and head. Because the pigment is so incredibly faint for this anthropomorph, some of the "white color" that we note could actually be abrasion from pigment being "chalked" onto this figure, much like that documented for a shorthand Fremont anthropomorph at a Wyoming site (Keyser 2015:209).

Other than a strongly trapezoidal body, this anthropomorph lacks any specific attributes (e.g., necklace, belt, earbobs) that would allow us to classify it as to type and assign it to a cultural style. Its form is similar to images carved and painted by artists from Basketmaker, Fremont, and Pueblo groups. The use of fugitive white pigment is similar to the Fremont figures, but the image itself is smaller than the other Fremont figures and not carefully aligned with them. Likewise, the occurrence of an abraded "bar" pattern elsewhere on the panel suggests that there may have been earlier Basketmaker anthropomorphs painted here. Currently, we cannot be certain of this figure's cultural affiliation.

Anthropomorph 9 (Figure 6 D/5) is the sketchiest of the four incised and painted Fremont figures consisting of little more than three U-shaped necklaces, a belt and incised line centrally bisecting the torso, and some incised lines in what would be the face area that might originally have been facial features or tear streaks. One of these lines in the face area appears to form a typical mouth. Very faint fugitive white pigment is visible for the trapezoidal body of this anthropomorph and occurs in the area of what is likely to have been a head whose shape cannot now be determined. No arms could be discerned for this figure. Given that the pigment is so faint here, these incised parts ("facial" features, necklaces, torso line, and belt) more closely resemble what has been termed an archetypal shorthand Fremont anthropomorph (Keyser and Poetschat 2017; Noxon and Marcus 1982:86–92). In fact, as is the case with Anthropomorph 8, some of the "white" discoloration visible here could be abrasion from fugitive pigment being "chalked" onto the surface to create this figure.

Anthropomorph 10 (Figure 6 B/6) is a pattern of six abraded horizontal "bars" placed at the bottom of a four-episode superimposition sequence involving a pecked Bighorn sheep, a painted bird, and a cloud of spatter droplets in that area of the panel. The center of this pattern shows a vertically aligned group of three fairly wide bars, arranged in order of decreasing size from widest to narrowest (Figure 9). Just above this group is a small abraded patch. Additionally, just to each side of the empty space between the lowest two central bars is a much smaller abraded bar. The pattern here is strikingly reminiscent of painted bodies of Basketmaker anthropomorphs at several nearby sites, whose bodies are structured with pigment bands

Figure 9. Superimposition sequence of the spatter cloud pattern. Note droplets around, but not within, the Bighorn sheep's head and front quarters; and droplets superimposed on the abraded pattern of bars (lightest grey) and legs of the bird above the sheep. Brown tendrils are mud flow.

stacked in arrangements like the central group at Pipe Spring. At present, we know of no similar figures with the smaller side bars, but in the pattern at Pipe Spring they are placed in a position that would be well suited to represent some sort of bracelet or hand decoration. The uppermost small bar would be somehow associated with the figure's head.

Identification of this as an anthropomorph is based in part on the assumption that it once was completed with pigment that has since disappeared—so this image is, in fact, the only figure with completely fugitive pigment on this panel. We believe that the pigment did not survive in this area because it is out from under the protective overhang that served to preserve what little of the white pigments remain for Anthropomorphs 5 to 9. This suggestion is given credence by the presence of the large mudflow that runs through this area of the panel. We plan future work to more fully understand this figure and compare it to others in the local area.

A few other figures on Panel 2 deserve mention. At the apex of the superimposition sequence involving Anthropomorph 10 at the far lower right of Panel 2 is a large, deeply and carefully pecked Bighorn sheep (Figure 6C/6). This animal shows a strongly boat-form body with ears, horns, and cloven hooves, but no defined tail. Because of the cloud of small red paint spatter droplets clustered quite densely about the head and front quarters of this animal we know that the pecking postdates this bespattering, since no droplets are found within the animal's pecked head, neck, or horns (Figures 9 and 10). The color of these spatter droplets is the same as the paint used for several flying birds right in that area, strongly suggesting that it was part of some ritual reuse of these images. This is supported by the fact that spatter droplets superimpose the abraded legs of one bird.

Figure 10. Head and horns of Bighorn sheep showing paint spatter on all sides but not within pecked figure. Spatter droplets (in circle) have edges sheared off by pecking. Abraded areas composing earliest figure visible above and below head and to the left of neck. Note that all abraded areas are superimposed with spatter droplets.

There are three stamped human footprints—two side-by-side right feet and one left foot impression—elsewhere on Panel 2. The most heavily pigmented footprint is paired with another right footprint at the panel's far left (Figure 11), just above the break that marks where the large slab fell away below the panel's upper part. The second footprint of this pair is largely obscured by mudflow. A fainter footprint is at the bottom center of the lower part of the panel, just to the right of Anthropomorph 2 (Figure 6F/2). Clearly, these were made by someone pressing the paint-covered sole of their foot flat against the cliff surface, either while accessing the panel by a ladder or while lying on their back on some sort of scaffold or the roof of a building built against the cliff.

Two ovoid patterns of chevron shapes stamped, one just above the other, in red pigment on the smooth cliff surface, appear very much like the tread on a tennis shoe (Figure 12d). After much discussion and consultation with colleagues, we identify these as patterned handprints where only the palm of the hand was painted and then had pigment carefully removed to

Figure 11. Vertical arrangement of different motifs at the left side of Panel 2. At the top a large polychrome duck superimposes one of two handprints. At the bottom are two footprints (the one at left nearly obscured by mudflow). Above the right footprint is an upside-down W form that may represent Bears Ears Buttes, a landmark visible from near the site. DStretch enhancement LABI+AC.

form a pattern resembling plaited basketry before the palm was stamped on the cliff. There is no indication of digits, even with DStretch enhancement, indicating that fingers were left unpainted. But both patterns have a small, roughly centrally located, approximately circular void that would correspond to the hollow often left when a handprint is not thickly pigmented and only loosely pressed against the rock surface (Figure 12). Such patterned handprints are quite common in late Basketmaker and early Pueblo rock art (Grant 1978:158), although more typical patterns are curvilinear swirls and spirals.

Finally, there is a small geometric figure, shaped something like an upside-down block-letter W (Figures 11 and 13) that we believe to be a depiction of the Bears Ears formation—a distinctive pair of buttes that rise to an elevation of 9500 feet and are visible for miles when one is high enough on the plateau surrounding this site. Although the depiction of landscape features is rare

Pipe Spring: Fremont-Anasazi Interaction in Southeastern Utah

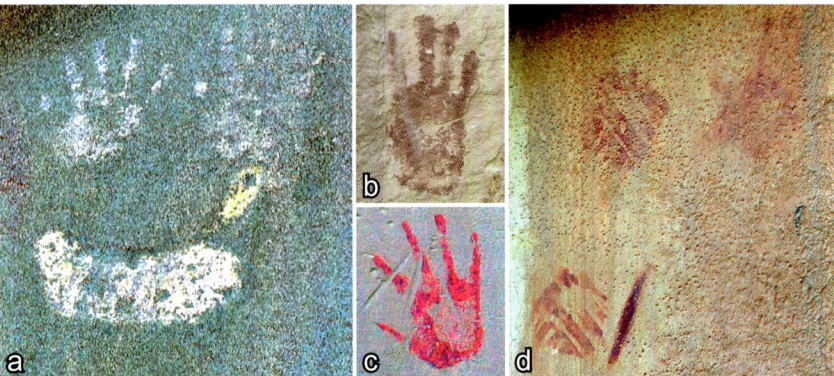

Figure 12. Various handprints from Panel 2 all show the unpainted flexor-surface hollow in the center of each palm. Note two patterned palm prints, at left, in d, also have unpainted flexor-surface hollows). (a) DStretch enhancement LABI+AC; (b) no enhancement; (c) DStretch enhancement LAB; (d) DStretch enhancement LRD+AC.

in rock art, this particular symbol has been identified in rock art at two other locations (Conti 2015; Conti and Walker 2018). At one nearby site (42SA23075) a very similar image (Figure 13b) is carved as a petroglyph, where it interacts with a sun-dagger "bear" at certain times of the year. Given the prominence of the bear claw regalia on Fremont Anthropomorphs 5 to 7 and the possible bears ears headdress on the largest Basketmaker human (Anthropomorph 3), we suggest that Pipe Spring may also have had some as yet undiscovered connection to bear symbolism that is further manifested by this small image of a landscape feature. Unfortunately, mud flow just to the right of this Bears Ears image obscures any other motifs that may or may not be associated with it.

Panels 3 and 4

Panels 3 and 4 (Figure 14) consist primarily of petroglyphs, although a few red pictographs are found on the right margin of Panel 3 that is nearest Panel 2. The two panels are adjacent, and separating them is more a factor of the original recording than any cultural division. Some petroglyphs and pictographs are pecked and painted extremely high on the cliff in this area—between three and four meters above the present ground surface. Since there is no place for a building to have been placed against the cliff here, and most of the imagery predates the large pueblos characteristic of other sites in the region, it seems most likely to us that some sort of scaffolding or leaning trees were used to access these upper cliff faces. The number of representational images on these two panels (Table 1) is about equal to the number of images on Panel 2—if you consider the trackway to be a single "motif" rather than 26 separate tracks. However, the images on Panels 3 and 4 show much less variation, both in temporal span and subject matter than those on Panel 2.

Petroglyphs account for 75 percent of the figures on combined Panels 3 and 4 (Figures 15 and 16). These are deeply pecked Basketmaker images showing strongly trapezoidal-body anthropomorphs (three of which are aligned in a row, posed with flying birds for heads), bighorn sheep and other quadrupeds, several different species of birds, a cloven-hoof trackway, a stylized human footprint, and three tall botanical forms, which probably represent flowering yucca (or, less likely, maize). In addition, we noted at least 18 places where small spherical, marble- to golf-ball-sized "concretions" (quite possibly river-rolled pebbles), which are commonly seen naturally projecting slightly from the cliff surface in this area, had been carefully pecked around so that each modified pebble/concretion appears to sit in a shallow dimple (Figure 17). One such worked pebble/concretion is positioned

Figure 13. Examples of the Bears Ears motif. (a) Panel 2, Pipe Spring (42SA27325); (b) Den of the Spirit Bear (42SA23075).

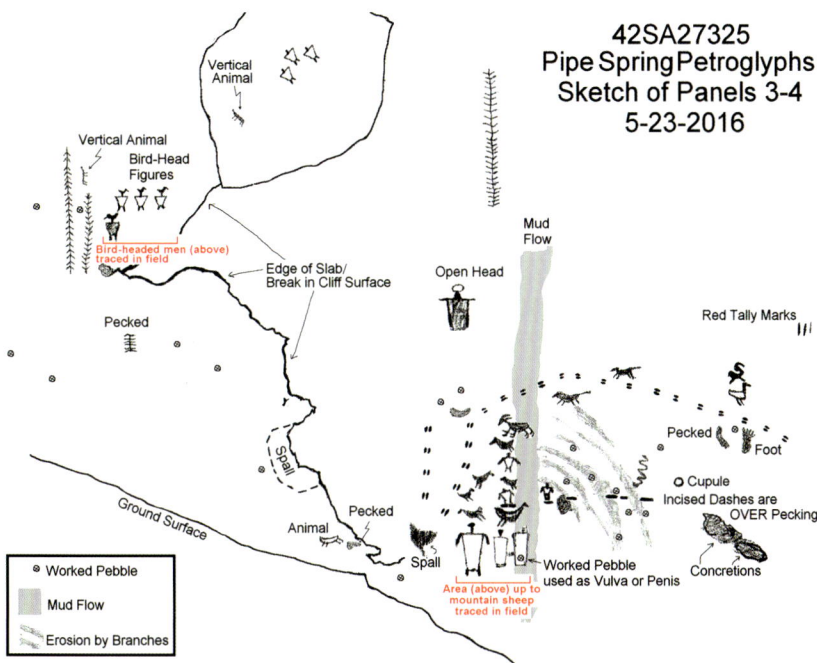

in the extreme lower torso of a very simple anthropomorph represented by only the trapezoidal body and a vestigial neck (that seems likely to be partially obscured by mud flow). We suspect that this represents a primary sexual organ, but whether it was intended to be a vulva or a penis is debatable. We also found one cupule that was probably just a concretion/pebble that had been completely removed. In addition, there is a long series of horizontal "dashes" that are superimposed on several pecked areas.

One unique motif is a cloven hoof trackway (Figure 14) comprising at least 26 small hoofprints that begin near the leftmost petroglyphs and extend across the panel and downward nearly to the bottom before turning up again where the trackway stops. These hoofprints are very small with each toe only about two cm long and one cm wide.

The dozen pictographs include five multicolored flying birds whose legs and lines surrounding the body are abraded; a group of three tall, somewhat robust tally marks; a rectangular body style human; three hand-

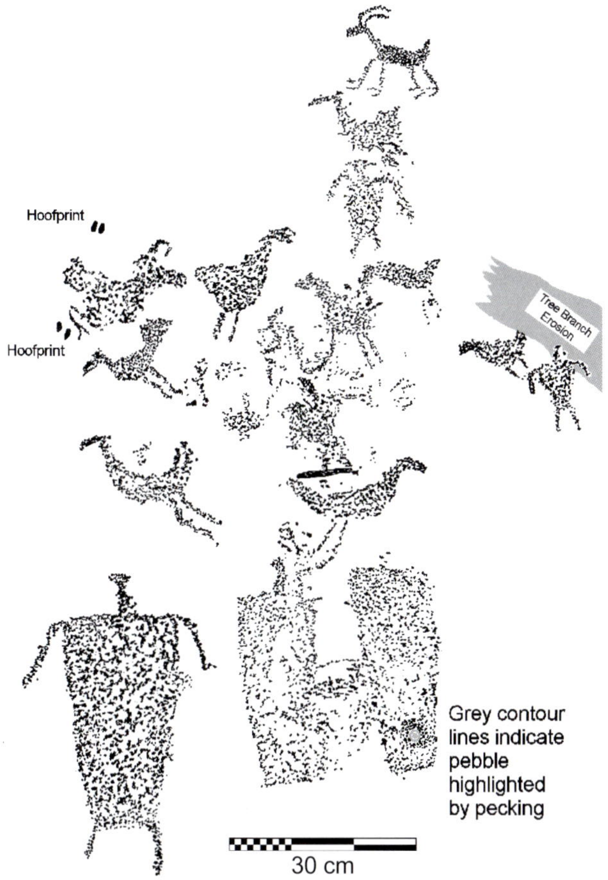

Figure 14. Field sketch of Panels 3 and 4. No Scale. Note two areas that were traced in field.

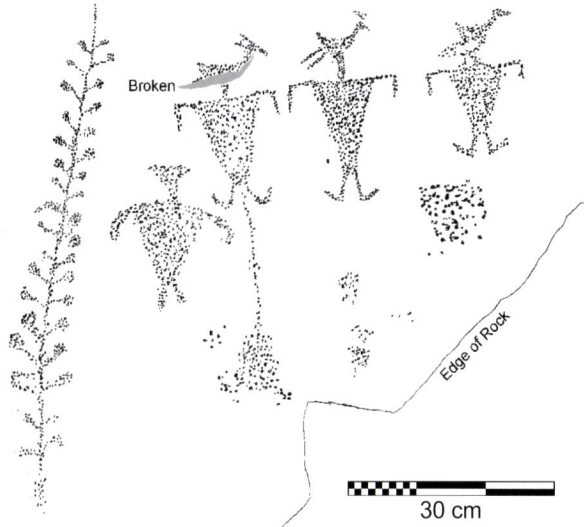

Figure 15. Tracing of central portion of Panel 3. Compare with Figure 14 to locate exact placement. Note pebble/concretion in lower body of human at lower right. Hoofprints at upper left are part of trackway that crosses almost entire panel.

Figure 16. Tracing of upper left portion of Panel 4 showing row of bird-headed humans and plant form (at left). Human at lower left may also have a bird head, although this is not as well drawn as others. Note topknots for birds on middle two humans. Connection of human to amorphous blob below is unexplained.

Figure 17. Row of three pecked humans on Panel 3. Note pebble/concretion in lower torso of third human (indicated by arrow) that is emphasized by heavy pecking. Compare with Figure 15.

prints; and two geometric forms that are partly obscured by mud flows. These are actually more similar to the paintings on Panel 2 than they are to the petroglyphs on the remainder of Panels 3 and 4, even though the primary subject matter—flying birds and a human—also occur in the petroglyphs.

Finally, a significant part of the center of Panel 3 has been badly damaged by tree branches brushing against it and partially or completely erasing at least ten pecked images in that area. In addition, one wide mud flow ranging from 10 to 20 cm across and several smaller flows run down across the center of the panel, also serving to obscure several images and soften the details of others.

Interpretations

Chronology and Cultural Attribution

Large broad-shouldered anthropomorphs with trapezoidal to triangular bodies, and round, rectangular, or helmet-like heads that sit directly atop the shoulders or on necks of varying length are typical of late Basketmaker (BM II–BM III) art (Cole 1994:289–311). Anthropomorphs fitting this description are the most common type at Pipe Spring and in the overall Harris diagram constructed for Panel 2 they are clearly among the earliest images drawn there. In the absence of any other obviously earlier anthropomorphs, these strongly suggest that Basketmaker artists were the first to paint and peck rock art at the site (Figure 18). One of these is a ghost-like figure (almost completely eroded away) that was painted entirely with fugitive white pigment. It has no incised attributes. Although it is situated in a rank of four identifiable Fremont figures, it lacks any Fremont indicator except the strongly trapezoidal body. For this reason, we suspect that it is an early Basketmaker image. Another is a truly fugitive pigment anthropomorph now represented only by six abraded bars arranged in a distinctive pattern that apparently represents a torso, partial head, and bracelets or partial hands. The ghost-like, white-pigmented, Anthropomorph 8 is painted entirely on the earliest abraded surface on the panel, and does not extend onto the later, lighter abrasion, suggesting that it is very early in the use sequence of the panel. Likewise, the fugitive pigment anthropomorph

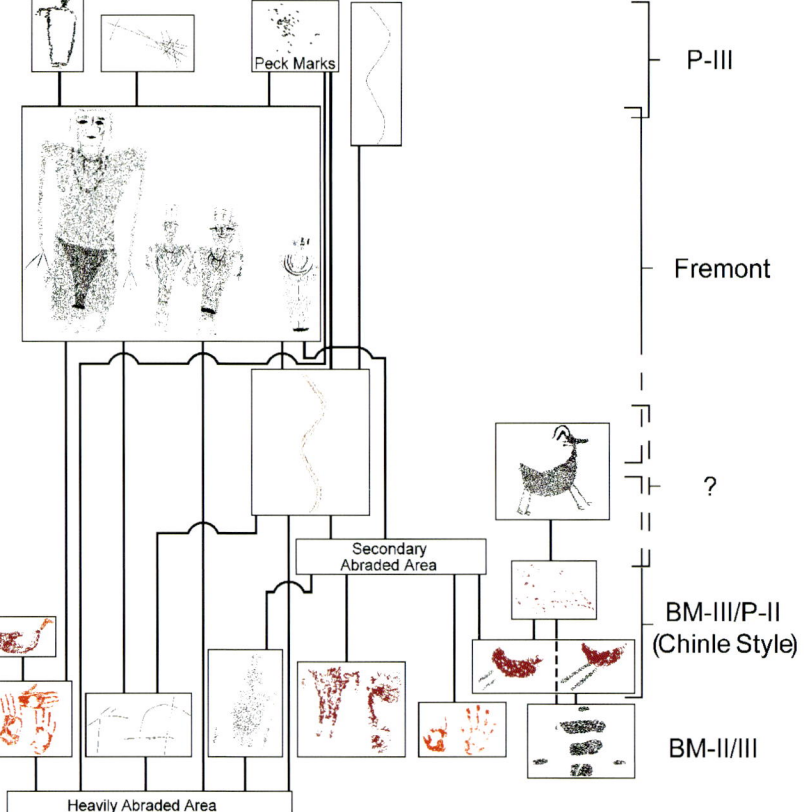

Figure 18. This Harris Diagram graphically illustrates the superimpositions on Panel 2. Dashed line at lower right indicates that spatter droplets are superimposed on both Chinle style birds and underlying pattern of abraded bars.

represented by the abraded bars is at the bottom of a four-episode superimposition sequence, underneath Chinle representational style imagery. This indicates that it, too, is very early in the panel's use history.

Likewise, Pipe Spring Basketmaker art also contains at least two dozen birds, including examples that can be identified as a duck, a crane (Figure 19), and possible quail and roadrunner. The other birds show a variety of body types, postures, topknots, and tail configurations, but most of them are shown with legs trailing backward in the conventionalized flight posture typical of Chinle Representational style art. Although no turkeys can be positively identified, given the popularity of turkey representations in Basketmaker art, some of the unidentified birds are almost certainly that species. Because most of the painted birds have no heads—presumably because they were painted with fugitive pigment—we suspect that other ducks and turkeys were originally identifiable. Four pecked birds (one obvious duck, two others with topknots, and one very rudimentary example) are part of the bird-headed anthropomorph motif. Three of these are pecked in a row of three distinctly triangular-body humans on Panel 4, the other is located directly below. Birds—including this bird-headed human motif—are common Basketmaker imagery, especially in the Chinle Representational style (Cole 1990:114; Grant 1978:171–174; Schaafsma 1979:194).

The large Bighorn sheep on Panel 2 is stylistically quite similar to others that have been classified as Basketmaker, but it also resembles animals pecked by Fremont and Pueblo artists. Based on the absence of paint spatter droplets inside the pecked form of this animal, we know that it superimposes the paint spatter episode in this area of Panel 2. And we know that the paint spatter itself superimposes at least one (and possibly two) of the Chinle Representational style painted birds in the same area. Finally, we know that the Bighorn sheep also superimposes the pattern of abraded bars that represents a Basketmaker anthropomorph whose fugitive pigment is completely gone. Furthermore, these abrasions are also superimposed by both the paint spatter and one Chinle Representational style bird. Thus, we know that the Bighorn was pecked after one episode of carving and two episodes of painting, but we cannot tell how much time elapsed between any of these four rock art events (Figure 18). Finally, a smaller Bighorn sheep, directly associated with the Basketmaker style birds and trapezoidal body humans on Panel 3, is similar in general form to this larger one. This lends some limited credence to the idea that this larger Bighorn is also a Basketmaker image, and thus, all four rock art events on this part of the panel were done in BM II–III and Pueblo II times.

The apparent ritual reuse of Panel 2, as evidenced by the paint bespattered around and on top of at least two of the painted birds is corroborated by the superimposition of the two largest birds (one a duck and the other possibly a turkey) on previously painted handprints in two other areas of the panel. Handprints also seem to be clustered around the largest painted anthropomorph at the uppermost part of Panel 2. All these actions strongly imply that Basketmaker artists routinely interacted with their own art, and also with other images that were previously painted at the site.

Superimposed on several of the Basketmaker handprints and the large sinuous vertical painted line "snake" on Panel 2 are four pecked/incised, and/or painted anthropomorphs larger than all but one Basketmaker anthropomorph at the site. Identification of these as Fremont art hinges on both general and specific attributes. Initially, at a general level, all four figures are aligned in

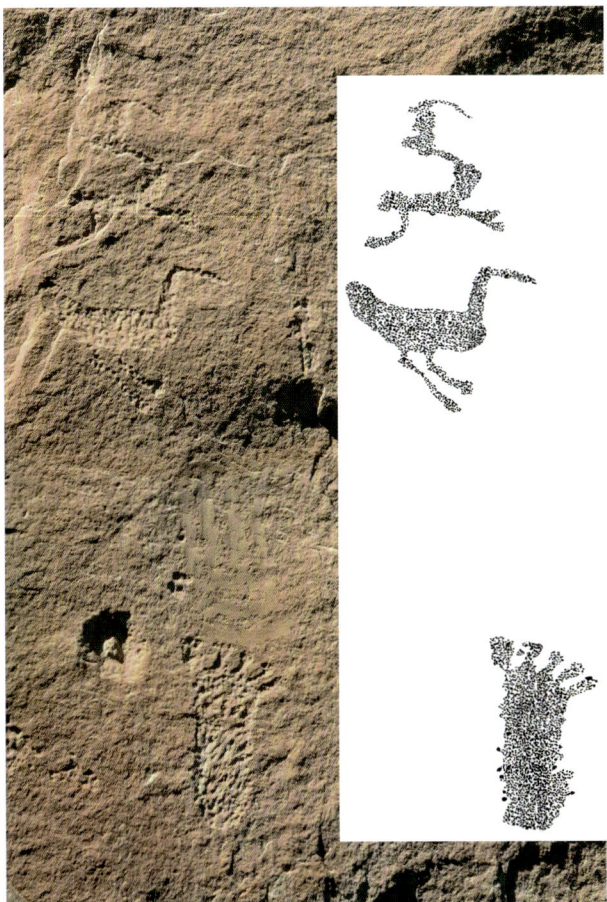

Figure 19. Two birds (at top) and a footprint are pecked at the right side of Panel 3. Also note pebble/concretion exposed by deep pecking just to left of footprint in photograph.

a row of closely spaced, front-facing personages, each with a trapezoidal body, necklace, belt/breechcloth, torso centerline, and facial features. For all figures the head and torso was originally painted with a fugitive white pigment that has now all but disappeared. All of these attributes, from overall organization to specific small details, can be duplicated in Fremont anthropomorphs in both the Uinta and southern San Rafael style zones (Morss 1931; Noxon and Marcus 1985; Schaafsma 1971:43–49, 1980:166–171).

More specifically, Anthropomorphs 6 and 7 hold an object jointly in their hands, and they either have their arms crossed or are standing so closely together (in a nearly arms akimbo position) that their elbows merge. Three of them wear distinctive upright headdresses, and the larger figure's necklace of individual sub-rectangular elements is like many of those typical of Classic Vernal style anthropomorphs found far to the north and a few found in the Fremont River area to the west. Likewise, the multiple necklaces motif worn by Anthropomorphs 5 and 9 is found on many Classic Vernal style figures. Tear streaks are prominent on Anthropomorphs 5 to 7, although Anthropomorph 5 has the unusual configuration of different forms of tear streak under each eye. Tear streaks of various forms and in many different configurations are characteristic of Fremont anthropomorphs (Schaafsma 1971), in fact more so than for anthropomorphs of any other style or time period in Southwestern rock art. Finally, Fremont Anthropomorph 5 has pronounced hunched or shrugged shoulders, visible only when photographic enhancement reveals the white pigment forming his body. While such shoulders are characteristic of some Basketmaker figures (Grant 1978:167–177; Schaafsma 1980:124), they also occur occasionally on Fremont anthropomorphs (Castleton 1984:54; Cole 2009:253; Keyser and Poetschat 2017; Schaafsma 1971:45–46).

But to what Fremont style do these anthropomorphs most closely relate? Comparison of individual elements and their combinations (Figures 20 to 22) shows that they are, in fact, slightly more similar

ELEMENTS OF CLASSIC VERNAL STYLE FREMONT ANTHROPOMORPHS

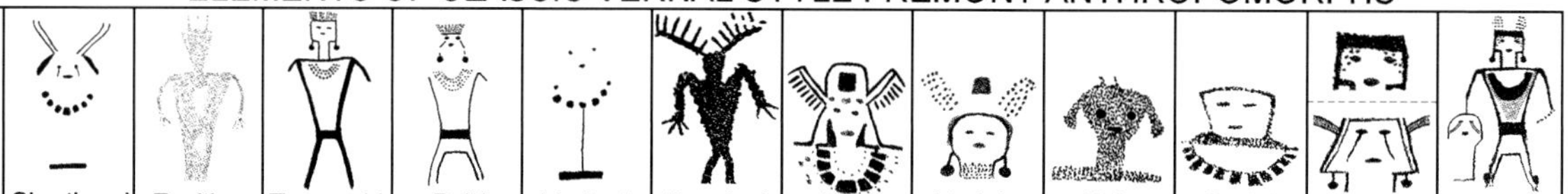

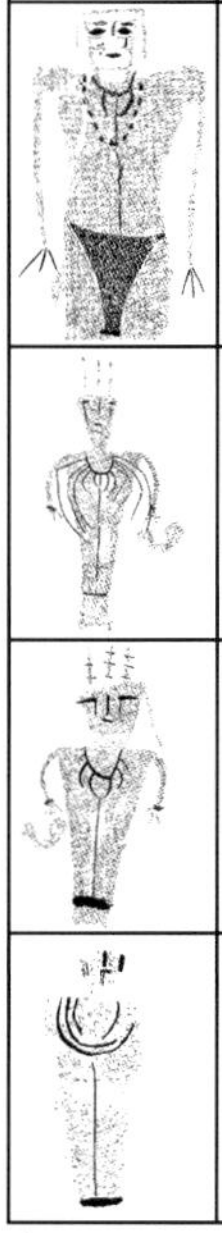

PIPE SPRING IMAGE	Shorthand Figure	Fugitive Pigment	Trapezoid Body	Belt/ Breechcloth	Vertical Torso Line	Hunched Shoulders	Necklace	Upright Headdress	Hair Bobs	Facial Features	Tear Streaks	Holding Object
(figure 1)	✓	✓	✓	✓	✓*	✓	✓		✓+	✓	✓#	
(figure 2)	✓	✓	✓	✓	✓		✓	✓		✓	✓	✓
(figure 3)	✓	✓	✓	✓	✓		✓	✓	✓+	✓	✓	✓
(figure 4)	✓	✓	✓	✓	✓		✓	✓		?	?	

* Vertical torso line is painted # Different tear streak under each eye + Hair "bob" is long braid

Figure 20. Comparison of Pipe Springs Fremont anthropomorphs to Classic Vernal style. Smaller, grey checkmark indicates relative rarity of trait in Classic Vernal style (hunched shoulders) or slight difference in form for Pipe Spring figures (longer braids rather than more typical, shorter hair bobs).

to Classic Vernal style anthropomorphs from the Uinta Fremont area than they are to Southern San Rafael style anthropomorphs found along the Fremont River in Canyonlands National Park (cf. Morss 1931:34–42; Schaafsma 1971:43–49). Furthermore, they share only very general similarities with the much nearer Faces Motif style, some examples of which were first described in detail by Schaafsma (1971) but which were much later named as a complex by Noxon and Marcus (1985) and then slightly later given a style designation (Tipps and Hewitt 1989).

Faces Motif style images, many of which have a striking resemblance to Fremont figurines, are primarily found at sites in the Canyonlands area just to the west of Pipe Spring. But—like the Fremont imagery at Pipe Spring—they are routinely found associated with Pueblo II–III cultural materials and not Fremont occupation debris (Sharrock 1966). What this means in terms of social interaction has not been fully elucidated, and probably cannot be from this one site, but we offer some thoughts below. What it does suggest is that by about A.D. 1000–1100 one or more Fremont artists visited this site and drew what are, for all indications, a phalanx of four Classic Vernal style images, with only minimal attributes that can be assumed to be related to local cultural aspects. That has strong implications for cultural dynamics in this area of the Colorado Plateau.

The final artists to use this site were most likely affiliated with Pueblo III groups. They did not carve or paint many images, but they did superimpose a small, pecked, rectangular body human figure (Anthropomorph 4) over the largest Fremont human (Anthropomorph 5) and they did a lot of apparently random pecking and incising that superimposes Fremont Anthropomorphs 5 to 7. If these later artists were not responsible for the large Bighorn sheep on this panel, why they made only this single representational human figure while making numerous scratches and random peck marks over the Fremont anthropomorphs cannot be readily explained.

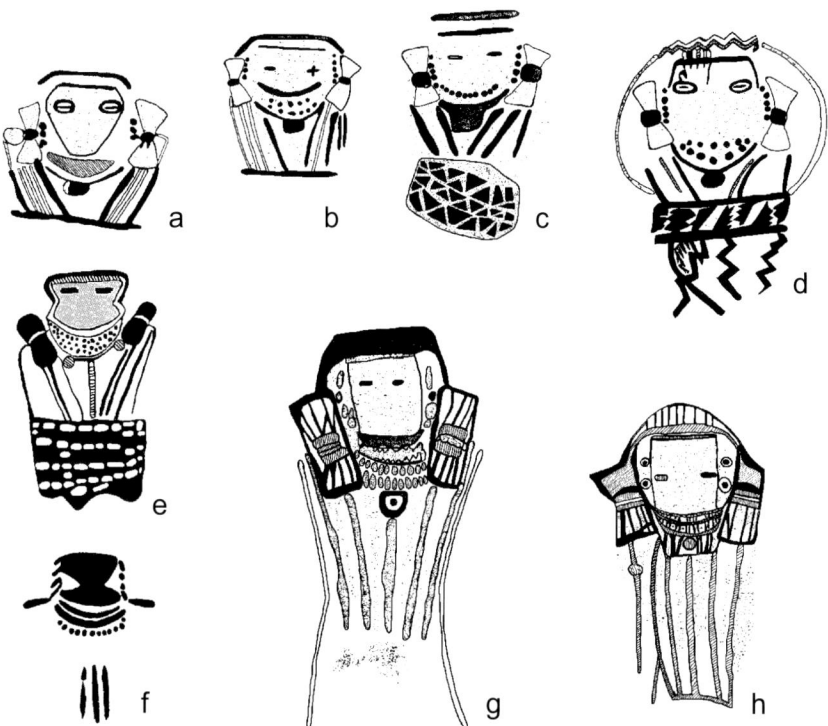

Figure 21. Faces Motif style images from Canyonlands sites show attributes very different from the Pipe Spring Fremont anthropomorphs. (a–d) Four Faces site (42SA1629) natural grouping; (e) Eleven Faces site (42SA16826); (f) Nine Faces site (42SA1486); (g–h) Five Faces site (42SA7736). Illustrations adapted from Noxon and Marcus 1985 (different patterns indicate multiple different pigment colors).

Function and Meaning

Three aspects of this site are worthy of further discussion, since they can add to the already abundant literature on Southwestern/Colorado Plateau rock art. One is the presence of fugitive white pigment and what this indicates about other shorthand Fremont figures found throughout the eastern Fremont style zones. A detailed discussion of this can be found in the companion piece to this paper in this volume (Keyser et al. 2018). The other two aspects are the use of small concretions/pebbles embedded in the cliff surface as focal points for pecking during the Basketmaker period, and the affiliation of the Fremont anthropomorphs at the site and their relationship to the Anasazi occupants who built the pueblo structure and left all the occupational debris known from the contemporaneous use of this large alcove.

Focus on Concretions

Scattered across Panels 3 and 4 in no apparent meaningful distribution (except for one associated with an anthropomorph—discussed below) are approximately

PIPE SPRING IMAGE	 Shorthand Figure	 Trapezoid Body	 Necklace	 Belt/ Breechcloth	 Vertical Torso Line	 Bandolier Torso Line	 Hunched Shoulders	 Long Arms Hands	 Horned Headdress	 One Feather Headdress	 Hair Bob "Braids"	 Facial Features	 Tear Streaks
ELEMENTS OF SOUTHERN SAN RAFAEL STYLE FREMONT ANTHROPOMORPHS													
(figure 1)	✓	✓	✓	✓	✓*		✓	✓			✓	✓	✓ #
(figure 2)	✓	✓	✓	✓	✓		✓					✓	✓
(figure 3)	✓	✓	✓	✓	✓		✓				✓	✓	✓
(figure 4)	✓	✓	✓	✓	✓		✓					?	?

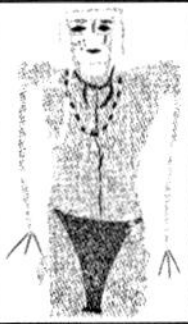

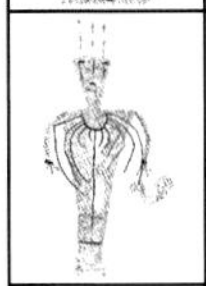

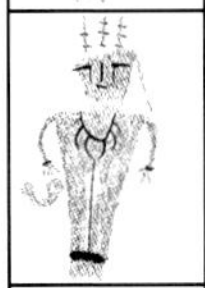

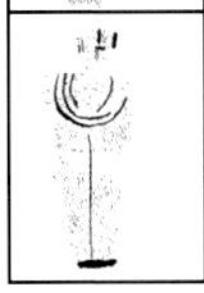

* Vertical torso line is painted   # Different tear streak under each eye

Figure 22. Comparison of Pipe Springs Fremont anthropomorphs to Southern San Rafael style. Smaller, grey checkmark indicates relative rarity of trait for Southern San Rafael style (vertical torso line, hair bob "braids," tear streaks) and difference in characteristic Southern San Rafael style form of tear streaks compared to other Fremont anthropomorphs.

20 small, naturally spherical concretions (quite probably river-rolled pebbles) that were the focus of pecking by Basketmaker artists (Figure 23). Their obvious modification enhances these small spheres (of which there are many other unmodified examples found on both panels) by pecking away the soft sandstone around the natural little "bump" in the cliff surface. This creates a small, protruding, marble- to golf-ball-sized, pimple-like bump or knob in the center of a circular, shallowly pecked dimple. In a few cases, where the pebble/concretion already protruded significantly, the rock artist simply used very light pecking to make a narrow, pecked margin around its base. One of these pebble/concretions is situated in a fairly significant dimple placed in the lower torso of the trapezoidal body of a sketchy human figure, suggesting that it represents genitalia or an umbilicus. Our first thought was that this example indicated a vulva or navel, but the slightly protruding concretion might just as well represent an erect, albeit short, penis. The fact that one occurs in the body of a human figure positioned as genitalia suggests that the others may also have represented genital or navel imagery. If so, whether penis, vulva, or navel they apparently encoded some sort of symbolism; possibly fertility or some sort of emergence from the spirit world.

Defying Definition: The Fremont Problem

Defining the Fremont—especially in this area of southern Utah—has long been problematic for researchers. Morss (1931) was one of the first to describe this as a distinctive entity by recognizing Fremont traits unique from the Anasazi. Other early Fremont researchers used similar trait lists, with artifacts present or absent as the basis of definition (Burgh and Scoggin 1948:81). In some cases, Fremont occupation is relatively easily recognized by these unique material culture items, including Utah style metates, deer hock moccasins, elaborately appliquéd unfired clay figurines, and "one rod and bundle" basketry.

But while there are several types of apparently diagnostic Fremont artifacts, the material culture assemblage from all Fremont sites is neither homogeneous nor uniform (Madsen 1989), and further confusion results because many artifacts—and especially certain rock art motifs—appear in cultural contexts and areas that have traditionally been thought

Figure 23. Pebble/concretions were the focus of pecking on panels 3 and 4 at Pipe Spring. These three examples have also been eroded by a tree branch sweeping back and forth across the cliff face, resulting in the lighter surface of the eroded areas.

of as Anasazi (Sharrock 1966). So similar are some parts of the material culture assemblages that accompany what would otherwise be Fremont rock art motifs—particularly in the border areas—that some researchers have proposed the terms Freazi or Anamont (Madsen 1982; Madsen and Simms 1998; O'Connell et al. 1982) to designate melded groups presumably incorporating both Fremont and Anasazi individuals.

More recently, archaeologists have attempted to define Fremont not solely by artifact assemblages, but by subsistence strategies (Madsen 1979; Madsen and Simms 1998; Simms 1986, 1990). Some see the Fremont as the result of a long process with its roots seated deep in the archaic (Jennings 1966, 1978) with an in-situ population eventually transitioning to sedentary agriculture when influenced by Anasazi farmers migrating northward (Simms and Gohier 2010). Others argue that any particular Fremont group may have operated as both foragers and agriculturalists depending either on the seasonal availability of resources or more broad-scale changes in climate over greater time spans (Madsen and Simms 1998; Wilde and Talbot 1996). And many Fremont agriculturalists were clearly opportunists, joining with (or becoming) nomadic hunting groups when crop yields were insufficient (Metcalf et al. 1993; Upham 1994:139). In other peripheral areas not typically thought of as good agricultural land, Fremont farmers routinely relied on hunting but maintained a low-level food production economy, apparently because it enhanced their opportunities to hunt and kill larger numbers of high value big game animals and increase their general foraging output (Nash 2012).

In short, Fremont folk were highly adaptive (Madsen and Kirkman 1988; Reed and Metcalf 1999; Spangler 2006), and more than one of these strategies may have been practiced by a single group within one individual's lifetime (Madsen and Simms 1998). In addition to this highly variable economic base, Fremont trade was far-reaching and goods and ideas were exchanged with surrounding areas in a network that apparently reached from the Great Plains to the Pacific Ocean and south into Mexico (Janetski 2001; Upham et al. 1987). However, despite this variation in adaptation, the long-distance contacts, and the relatively intimate contacts evidenced with neighboring groups; a Fremont religious entity appears to be united across its territory by a common rock art tradition. Given this strong allegiance to a distinctive rock art tradition, we feel that even in frontier areas where Fremont populations were constantly in contact with foreign groups and ideas, we should expect to see the presence of a relatively pure artistic expression overlaid onto "foreign" territory, just as we do in the rock art at Pipe Spring. The challenge is to determine why the art is located here.

These Pipe Spring Fremont anthropomorphs do not show a hybridization of attributes between what is thought of as distinctively Fremont and either Basketmaker (Chinle Representational style) or later Pueblo. Except for the shrugged shoulders motif, and the trapezoidal to triangular body form, there is no great similarity between Fremont and Basketmaker/Pueblo anthropomorphs. While the shrugged shoulders are sufficiently unique that they might indicate some exchange of ideology, the fact that this motif extends throughout the eastern Fremont area as far as southwestern Wyoming (Keyser and Poetschat 2017) argues against it representing specific contact limited to people occupying the southern frontier between Fremont and Basketmaker/Pueblo artists responsible for the Chinle Representational style. Instead, this seems likely to represent a much broader exchange of ideology that may have its roots much further back in prehistory. Correspondingly, the trapezoidal body shape seems to be a generic form common to several styles in this region that have a long history rather than indicative of any specific contact.

Likewise, the difficulty of assigning the Bighorn sheep to any particular style says more about the generic nature of boat-form style mountain sheep than a hybridization of ideologies between neighboring groups.

Conclusion: Explaining the Multicultural Signatures at Pipe Spring

The rock art at Pipe Spring clearly evinces a multicultural "signature," with the great majority of earlier art representing Basketmaker and Basketmaker/Modified Pueblo artists. It is difficult to differentiate what are almost certainly earlier Basketmaker (BM II) pictographs from the archetypal Chinle Representational Style painted imagery representing BM III/P II artists. Likewise, petroglyphs of very similar birds, mountain sheep, trapezoidal body humans, and bird-headed humans could have been carved by either BM II or Chinle Style artists.

Nevertheless, we know that one or more later artists added four unmistakable Fremont anthropomorphs that show strong relationships to both Classic Vernal and Southern San Rafael style figures further north and west in Utah (Figures 20 and 22), but little similarity to the more local Faces Motif style of Fremont representation found in this area of the southeast Utah Canyonlands (Figure 21). The only seemingly local attribute to these figures is the presence of dramatic bear claw necklaces worn by three of them, which may be related to the prominence of the nearby Bears Ears Buttes natural feature, and bear-related imagery commonly found in other rock art of this area (Conti 2015). Finally, later Pueblo people carved a few images at the site after the Fremont artists had left their mark. This multicultural rock art signature contrasts directly to the material culture assemblage from the large alcove, which points exclusively to Basketmaker-Pueblo occupation.

Based on a broad-scale survey of Canyonlands National Park that found numerous instances of Fremont pictographs and petroglyphs in shallow alcoves that otherwise showed "complete Mesa Verde affiliation," Sharrock (1966:61–62) argued forcefully that "Fremont design motifs were borrowed by the Mesa Verdeans without significant (distinguishable) population interchange" (Sharrock 1966:62). Twenty years later, Noxon and Marcus (1985:65–66) question the identification of the Faces Motif style as Fremont, and suggest instead that the Canyonlands Anasazi originated it independently as a product of "a similar ideology as [represented by Fremont] figurines." Obviously, full investigation of the question of Fremont association for the Faces Motif style is beyond the scope of this paper, and—in any case—the Pipe Spring anthropomorphs are not closely related to the Faces Motif style. However, we point out that most current rock art specialists still classify the Faces Motif style as Fremont, and the formal similarities of the style with Fremont figurines are extremely striking.

In either case, however, neither of these models fits the data for the Pipe Spring anthropomorphs, since they show detailed similarities to Fremont forms located a great distance away, rather than nearer Faces Motif imagery. Finding such detailed similarities between these anthropomorphs and other Fremont images is exactly the same argument (but in reverse) as that posited by Sharrock to exclude Fremont as makers of the material culture represented by the occupational debris at Canyonlands sites, and it should be no less powerful in excluding the Anasazi as carvers of the petroglyphs. What is needed is a model that can explain both data sets: undeniable Fremont images in sites with an equally undeniable Anasazi architecture and material culture assemblage. In other words, why would Fremont artists have carved at Anasazi living sites?

Leticia Neal (2010), has also studied Anasazi/Fremont interaction in this area of southeast Utah, just to the north of the Pipe Spring site. And she believes that people, pots, and petroglyphs moved across a fluid frontier. For her, the stylistic expressions found in rock art are the result of preferential adoption. Neal sees two plausible explanations for having both cultural signatures at one site. Over time, on a fluid frontier, sites are abandoned and reoccupied, and sometimes sites would be shared by both groups simultaneously. Her area of interest did show some sites with small quantities of Fremont ceramics and other diagnostics, which would suggest some co-occupation (either sequential or simultaneous) of sites, but that seems unlikely at Pipe Spring, given the uniform Basketmaker-Pueblo cultural assemblage represented by the occupation debris. Her second possibility involves borrowing of motifs, but not in the grossly oversimplified way proposed by Sharrock (1966) and Noxon and Marcus (1985).

Instead, Neal (2010) suggests that Mesa Verde Anasazi people migrating into the Canyonlands region at about A.D. 1100 (a time of significant cultural upheaval and conflict across the area) were using Fremont imagery to indicate social ties (in the form of trade networks) with Fremont people to the north. She says:

> This [borrowing] is…a result of individuals established widening alliances and networks and consciously making choices about how to represent their social identity. In this scenario, San Rafael Style [Fremont] anthropomorphs are symbolic markers of group membership that signaled alliances on a social landscape. The alliances that these images signaled would have been recognizable indicators of in- versus out-groups.
>
> Thus, rock art could be an effective form of communication that conveyed social roles and group membership. The stylized anthropomorphic figures may point to a particular manner in which these identities were expressed, despite or because of boundaries among groups…the images found in rock art may be an indicator of commemorated acts that defined group identity and expressed this identity to others—a social landscape. I propose that the stylistic expressions found in rock art are a result of cultural transmission where some cultural variants were preferentially adopted over others and in turn symbolically displayed in rock art [Neal 2010:234–235].

So what Neal seems to be arguing is that Canyonlands Anasazi adopted Fremont rock art to identify themselves as somehow allied with people otherwise identified as Fremont who would see this art and recognize the site occupants as trading partners with whom they were allied rather than viewing them as strangers or even enemies. This fits reasonably well with the size and visibility of the Pipe Spring Fremont anthropomorphs—which are obviously public art meant to be seen from a significant distance (e.g., the canyon rim across from the site). But, interestingly, it also fits well with how the Pipe Spring Fremont anthropomorphs combine elements of both Classic Vernal and San Rafael styles, and yet still integrate more localized bear-related regalia, giving the images a distinctly local "flavor" that would nevertheless be recognizable to a broad spectrum of Fremont visitors.

But we do not believe that the Anasazi occupants of this site simply copied (e.g., borrowed) these images from Fremont sites seen elsewhere, as Neal seems to imply. The specific, fine-scale detail, down to such things as tear streaks, torso center lines, headdress elements, and belts/breechcloth are so carefully executed that they cannot be anything but Fremont. Coupled with the measured firmness of stroke, the careful pecking/abrading for several parts of these figures, and the varying depth of line that is characteristic of finely made Fremont figures elsewhere (and not characteristic of any other petroglyphs at this site), this combination of details leads us to believe that the anthropomorphs were carved and painted by an artist steeped in the Fremont cultural/artistic milieu.

The only means by which we can imagine this happening is some sort of exchange of artists between Anasazi and Fremont groups. Perhaps Anasazi villages sent young, talented scribes off with Fremont traders to absorb Fremont religion and become proficient in creating "Fremont" art when they returned home, but it seems more likely to us that they simply asked Fremont traders to post these large "billboard advertisements" at known sites where trading would take place on some regular schedule. Such a system would do all the things Neal (2010) suggests while still maintaining the specific "Fremont" character of these images.

If this model has any validity, it should be testable against other Fremont imagery in the Canyonlands region—those images identified as "borrowed" by Sharrock (1966) and Neal (2010), and the Faces Motif style discussed by several authors (e.g., Cole 2009; Noxon and Marcus 1985; Schaafsma 1971). Careful and detailed recording of images, classification and analysis of their minor details and elements, and comparison of these to Fremont imagery in other areas should show the same sorts of detailed similarities we have noted here if our model has any explanatory value. And with such detailed research (and comparison of the Faces Motif style paintings to Fremont figurines) it might be possible to develop a better understanding of how the Faces Motif style relates to the broader Fremont tradition. We look forward to someone taking on such a study.

Acknowledgments. We would like to thank those who enhanced the quality of this project by generously contributing their time and resources. Thanks to Don Simonis and Cameron Cox at the Monticello BLM who provided both access and research reports. Winston Hurst offered technical advice and theoretical perspectives. Maria Ortiz helped with editing. The Oregon

Archaeological Society provided funds to rent scaffolding. We are grateful to the folks at the National Park Service Southwestern Group who provided necessary field reports. Thanks to NPS archaeologist, Todd Scarborough, who illustrated our map.

Notes

1. All references to right and left are from the viewer's perspective when seeing figures on the panels.

2. Fugitive pigments or colors are termed as such because they are impermanent and lighten over time (even to the point of disappearing) when exposed to ambient environmental conditions. A fuller discussion of such pigments and their use for the Fremont anthropomorphs at this site is found in the article by Keyser, Conti, and Kaiser elsewhere in this volume (Keyser et al. 2018).

3. Additional DStretch analysis after this article was submitted for publication strongly suggests that the arms of the figures do not cross, but instead simply touch at the elbows. A more detailed DStretch image (Figure 24) shows the shortest digit of each hand (representing the thumb) on the side of the arm closest to the torso for each figure. That is, the thumb points toward the body, as it would if the arm was held in a modified "arms akimbo" posture with hands held just away from the body rather than on the hips. Support for this interpretation is provided by the fact that this would create a symmetrical arm position for both figures, something that is consistent with the great majority of Fremont anthropomorphs.

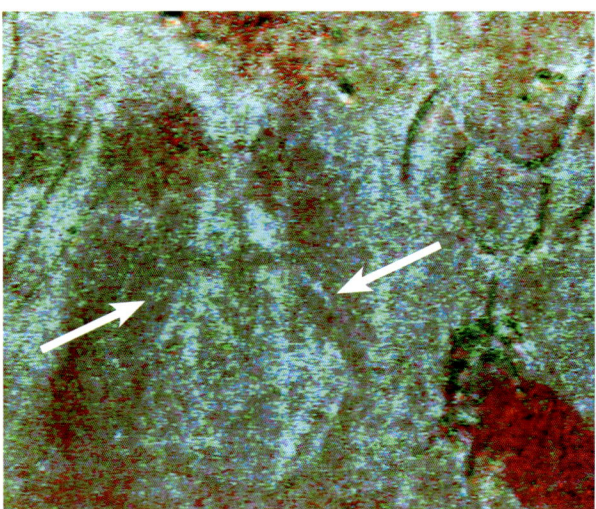

Figure 24. DStretch enhancement YWE of arms for Anthropomorphs 6 and 7 show shorter "thumb" on the side of the hand nearest the body. Arrows point to thumbs, which are markedly shorter than other fingers.

References Cited

Burgh, Robert F., and Charles R. Scoggin
 1948 *The Archaeology of Castle Park, Dinosaur National Monument.* University of Colorado Studies, Series in Anthropology, No. 2, Boulder, Colorado.

Castleton, Kenneth B.
 1984 *Petroglyphs and Pictographs of Utah. Volume One: The East and Northeast.* Utah Museum of Natural History, Salt Lake City.

Cole, Sally J.
 1994 Roots of Anasazi and Pueblo Imagery in Basketmaker II Rock Art and Material Culture. *Kiva* 60(2): 289–311.
 1990 *Legacy on Stone: Rock Art of the Colorado Plateau and Four Corners Region.* Johnson Books, Boulder, Colorado.
 2009 *Legacy on Stone: Rock Art of the Colorado Plateau and Four Corners Region.* Revised and Updated Edition. Johnson Books, Boulder, Colorado.

Conti, Kevin M.
 2015 In the Den of the Spirit Bear. In *American Indian Rock Art, Volume 41,* edited by James D. Keyser and David A. Kaiser, pp. 87–97. American Rock Art Research Association, San Jose, California.

Conti, Kevin M., and William H. Walker
 2018 Animate Shadows of Bear and Giants. In *The Archaeology of Light,* edited by Konstantinos Papadopoulos. Oxford Handbooks. Oxford, England. (In press.)

Grant, Campbell
 1978 *Canyon de Chelly: The People and Rock Art.* University of Arizona Press, Tucson.

Horn, J. C., A. D. Reed, and S. M. Chandler
 1994 *Grand Resource Area Class I Cultural Resource inventory.* Alpine Archaeological Consultants, Inc. Document on file, Moab Utah Field Office, Bureau of Land Management.

Janetski, Joel C.
 2001 Trade in Fremont Society: Contexts and Contrasts. *Journal of Anthropological Archaeology* 21:344–470

Jennings, Jesse D.
 1966 *Glen Canyon: A Summary.* University of Utah Anthropological Papers, No. 81, Glen Canyon Series, No. 31. University of Utah Press, Salt Lake City.
 1978 *Prehistory of Utah and the Eastern Great Basin.* University of Utah Anthropological Papers No.98. University of Utah Press, Salt Lake City.

Keyser, James D.
 2015 Preliminary Recording of Images at the Henry's Fork Petroglyphs (48SW88). In *Seeking Bear: The Petroglyphs of Lucerne, Wyoming,* edited by James D. Keyser and George Poetschat, Appendix II, pp. 205–220. Oregon Archaeological Society Press, Publication 23, Portland.

Keyser, James D., Kevin Conti, and David A. Kaiser
 2018 Finding Faded Fremont: Shorthand Anthropomorphs and Fugitive Pigment at Pipe Spring, Utah. In *American Indian Rock Art, Volume 44,* edited by David A. Kaiser sand James D. Keyser, pp. 145–158. American Rock Art Research Association, San Jose, Calfornia.

Keyser James D., and George Poetschat
 2017 Uinta Fremont Rock Art in Southwestern Wyoming: Marking the Fremont Northern Periphery. *Plains Anthropologist* 62:157–178.

Larmore, S.
　2008 IMACS site form for site 42Sa27325. BLM Monticello field office. Document on file at Edge of the Cedars Museum, Blanding, Utah.

Madsen David B.
　1979 The Fremont and the Sevier: Defining Prehistoric Agriculturalists North of the Anasazi. *American Antiquity* 44:711–722.

　1982 Salvage Excavations at Ticaboo Town Ruin (42Ga2295). In *Archaeological Investigations in Utah at Fish Springs, Clay Basin, Northern San Rafael Swell, Southern Henry Mountains*, edited by David B. Madsen and Richard E. Fike, pp. 1–41. Utah Bureau of Land Management Cultural Resources Series 12, Salt Lake City.

　1989 *Exploring the Fremont.* University of Utah Occasional Paper No. 8. The Utah Museum of Natural History. Salt Lake City.

Madsen, David B., and James E. Kirkman
　1988 Hunting Hoppers. *American Antiquity* 53:593–604.

Madsen, David B., and Steven R. Simms
　1998 The Fremont Complex: A Behavioral Perspective. *Journal of World Prehistory* 12:255–336.

Manning, Steven J.
　2004 The Fugitive-Pigment Anthropomorphs of Eastern Utah: A Shared Cultural Trait Indicating a Temporal Relationship. In *Utah Rock Art, Volume 23*, edited by Steven J. Manning, pp. 61–177. Utah Rock Art Research Association, Salt Lake City.

Matson, R. G., William D. Lipe, and Williams R. Haase IV.
　1988 Adaptational Continuities and Occupational Discontinuities: The Cedar Mesa Anasazi. *Journal of Field Archaeology* 15:245–263.

Metcalf, M. D., K. J. Pool, K. McDonald, and A. McKibbin
　1993 *The Round Spring Site, Vol. III. Hogan Pass: Final Report on Archaeological Investigations along Forest Highway 10 (State Highway 72), Sevier County, Utah.* Metcalf Archaeological Consultants, Eagle, Colorado.

Morss, Noel M.
　1931 The Ancient Culture of the Fremont River in Utah: Report on the Explorations under the Claflin-Emerson Fund, 1928–1929. *Papers of the Peabody Museum of American Archaeology and Ethnology* 12(3). Cambridge, Massachusetts.

Nash, Robert Bruce
　2012 *The Role of Maize in Low-Level Food Production among Northern Peripheral Fremont Groups in the Northeastern Uinta Mountains of Utah.* Ph.D. dissertation, University of California, Davis. ProQuest LLC, Ann Arbor, Michigan

Neal, Leticia A.
　2010 *Moving Beyond Boundaries: Fremont and Anasazi Archaeology and Rock Art in Southeastern Utah.* Master of Arts Thesis University of Nevada, Reno. ProQuest LLC, Ann Arbor, Michigan

Noxon, John, and Deborah Marcus
　1982 Significant Rock Art Sites in Arches and Canyonlands National Parks and in Natural Bridges National Monument, Southeastern Utah. Document on file with Canyonlands National Park, Moab, Utah.

　1985 Significant Rock Art Sites in the Canyonlands National Park, Southeastern Utah. Document on file with Canyonlands National Park, Moab, Utah.

O'Connell, James F., K. T. Jones, and S. R. Simms
　1982 Some Thoughts on Prehistoric Archaeology in the Great Basin. In *Man and the Environment in the Great Basin*, edited by David B. Madsen and James F. O'Connell, pp. 227–240. Society for American Archaeology Papers 2, Washington, D.C.

Reed, Alan D., and Michael D. Metcalf
　1999 *Colorado Prehistory: A Context for the Northern Colorado River Basin.* Colorado Council of Professional Archaeologists, Denver, Colorado.

Richards, Kristina Katie
　2014 *Fremont Ceramic Designs and Their Implications.* Master of Arts Thesis, Brigham Young University, Provo, Utah. BYU Scholars' Archive

Schaafsma, Polly
　1971 *The Rock Art of Utah.* University of Utah Press, Salt Lake City.

　1979 Rock Art of the San Juan Drainage: From Pre-Horticultural Hunter-Gatherers Through the Anasazi. In *CRARA '77: Papers from the Fourth Biennial Conference of the Canadian Rock Art Research Associates*, edited by Doris Lundy, pp. 185–202. Heritage Record No. 8, British Columbia Provincial Museum, Victoria, B. C., Canada

　1980 *Indian Rock art of the Southwest.* University of New Mexico Press, Albuquerque.

　2008 Shamans, Shields, and Stories on Stone. In *The Great Basin: People and Place in Ancient Times*, edited by Catherine S. Fowler and Don D. Fowler, pp. 145–152. School of Advanced Research Press, Santa Fe, New Mexico

Sharrock, Floyd W.
　1966 *An Archaeological Survey of Canyonlands National Park.* University of Utah Anthropological Papers, No. 83. University of Utah Press, Salt Lake City.

Simms, Steven R.,
　1986 New Evidence for Fremont Adaptive Diversity. *Journal of California and Great Basin Anthropology* 8(2):204–216.

　1990 Fremont Transition. *Utah Archaeology* 3(1):1–18.

Simms, Steven R., and François Gohier
　2010 *Traces of Fremont: Society and Rock Art in Ancient Utah.* University of Utah Press, Salt Lake City.

Spangler, Jerry D.
　2006 *Paradigms and Perspectives Revisited: A Class I Overview of Cultural Resources in the Uinta Basin and Tavaputs Plateau.* Uinta Research, Salt Lake City.

Tipps, B. L., and N. J. Hewitt
　1989 *Cultural Resource Inventory and Testing in the Salt Creek Pocket and Devils Lane Areas, Needles District, Canyonlands National Park, Utah.* Selections from the Division of Cultural Resources 1, Rock Mountain Region, National Park Service, Denver.

Upham, Steadman
　1994 Nomads of the Desert West: A Shifting Continuum in Prehistory. *Journal of World Prehistory* 8(2):113–167.

Upham, Steadman, Richard S. MacNeish, Walton C. Galinat, and Christopher M. Stevenson
　1987 Evidence concerning the Origin of Maiz de Ocho. *American Anthropologist* 89(2):410–419.

Wilde, James D., and Richard K. Talbot
　1996 Research Context. In *Steinaker Gap: An Early Fremont Farmstead*, edited by Richard K. Talbot and Lane D. Richens, pp. 11–22. Brigham Young University Museum of Peoples and Cultures, Occasional Paper 2, Provo, Utah.

Finding Faded Fremont: Shorthand Anthropomorphs and Fugitive Pigment at Pipe Spring, Utah

James D. Keyser, Kevin Conti, and David A. Kaiser

Shorthand anthropomorphs are a hallmark of Fremont rock art in both the Uinta and Southern San Rafael style zones. Such anthropomorphs show pecked or abraded facial features and/or headdress elements accompanied by items of attire such as a necklace or a belt, but they lack a textured body or body outline. Since they lack an obvious body, experts have assumed these anthropomorphs were originally painted with fugitive pigment long since eroded away. Four such shorthand Fremont anthropomorphs were recorded at 42SA27325, and during that project we discovered they still had faint white pigment remaining, even though this was not readily evident on initial observation. Our recording proves unequivocally that at least some such shorthand figures originally were filled out with pigment.

Shorthand (or non-outline) anthropomorphs (Figures 1 and 2), defined as having pecked or abraded facial features and/or headdress elements accompanied by items of attire such as a necklace or a belt, but lacking a textured body or body outline (Schaafsma 1980:166), are one of three primary variants of Fremont anthropomorphic figures (Schaafsma 1971:8, 15, 1980:166, 171). Such shorthand figures are common at Fremont sites only in the Uinta and Southern San Rafael style zones (Figure 3, see also Schaafsma 1971:7), and are one stylistic attribute used by Schaafsma to propose an as yet unexplained link between the art from the two areas (Schaafsma 1971:43–45).

Nearly all Fremont rock art scholars (Cole 2009:245; Schaafsma 1971:8; Simms and Gohier 2010:115; Wellmann 1979:105) propose that these shorthand figures originally had some or all other body parts drawn with some sort of pigment that has long since disappeared because it did not bond to the rock surface in the same way that is typical for paints used to make still-visible pictographs. Such pigments or colors are termed "fugitive" because they are impermanent and lighten over time (even to the point of disappearing) when exposed to ambient environmental conditions. Fugitive pigments could have been pastel colors derived from mineral pigments applied to the rock surface with no binding agent—much as one might draw on a blackboard with white or colored chalk—or they could have been vegetable-based liquid paints that color brightly in the short term but simply do not bond well to an open-air rock face. We know that Fremont artists used such pastel pigments of several colors on other types of artifacts (Simms and Gohier 2010:66, 98–99) and there are even a few apparently well-protected rock art sites (e.g., Simms and Gohier 2010:50–51) where very faded red, white, and green pigments have survived.

James D. Keyser
Oregon Archaeological Society
Portland, Oregon

Kevin Conti
Independent Researcher
Monticello Utah

David A. Kaiser
Oregon Archaeological Society
Portland, Oregon

Figure 1. Shorthand Fremont anthropomorph formed of drilled holes at 5MF88 in Echo Park in the Colorado portion of Dinosaur National Monument. This classic form for a shorthand anthropomorph shows head with facial features and headdress elements, necklace, and belt. Photograph courtesy of Peter Faris.

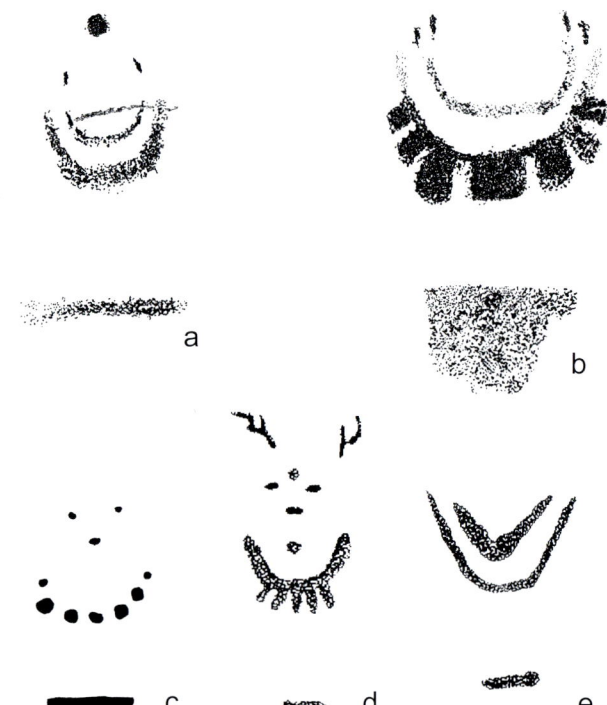

Figure 2. Shorthand Fremont anthropomorphs are common only in the Uinta (a–c) and Southern San Rafael style zones (d–e). (a, b) 48SW61, Minnies Gap, Wyoming (natural grouping); (c) 48SW88, Henry's Fork, Wyoming; (d) Capitol Reef (Capitol Gorge site); (e) Capitol Reef (Pleasant Creek site). Images d and e adapted from Castleton 1984:145–147.

Until now however, the only direct evidence that pigments were used specifically to fill out the forms of shorthand anthropomorphs are a few incompletely reported occurrences at sites scattered throughout the Fremont area. The earliest of these are observations by Albert Reagan at the well-known sites in the Ashley/Dry Fork Creek valleys northwest of Vernal, Utah. On four separate panels at different sites (including the McConkie Ranch site) Reagan (1931:169, 174, 179, 195) noted "blotches" or "patches" of pigment associated with shorthand anthropomorphs and in one case he went so far as to indicate shorthand figures' "missing parts by [dashed] lines as far as he could make them out" (Reagan 1931:195). These dashed-line reconstructions are shown in one of his photographs and a drawing made from it (Schaafsma 1971:9, 1980:Figure 127).[1] More recently, Manning (2004) reports pigment associated with a few of his "Fugitive Pigment" type anthropomorphs,[2] but it is often difficult to determine which of these are actually shorthand figures with remnant fugitive pigment and which are simply figures with both painted and pecked or incised parts. These latter figures do not involve fugitive pigment,

and tell us nothing about whether shorthand figures were ever painted.

Pipe Spring (42SA27325)

The Pipe Spring Site sits on the south flank of the Abajo Mountains at an elevation of 5,900 feet. Located in the West Central Mesa Verde Cultural Region, about 10 miles west of Blanding, Utah, the immediate site area is a transition zone where pinyon/juniper slopes of the Abajo Mountains give way to slick rock drainages filled with lush cottonwood stands. Pipe Spring sits in a large alcove at the head of one such canyon (Figure 4) in the San Juan River drainage, directly below a slick rock cascade, which features a substantial waterfall after episodes of significant precipitation and snow melt. Located at the base of the waterfall is a permanent spring seep and for several hundred meters down the slick rock canyon below the cascade there are large natural tanks (tinajas) that retain excess water after every large precipitation event. A second spring fills a grass-rimmed pool located immediately behind the small, four-room pueblo structure constructed in the alcove.

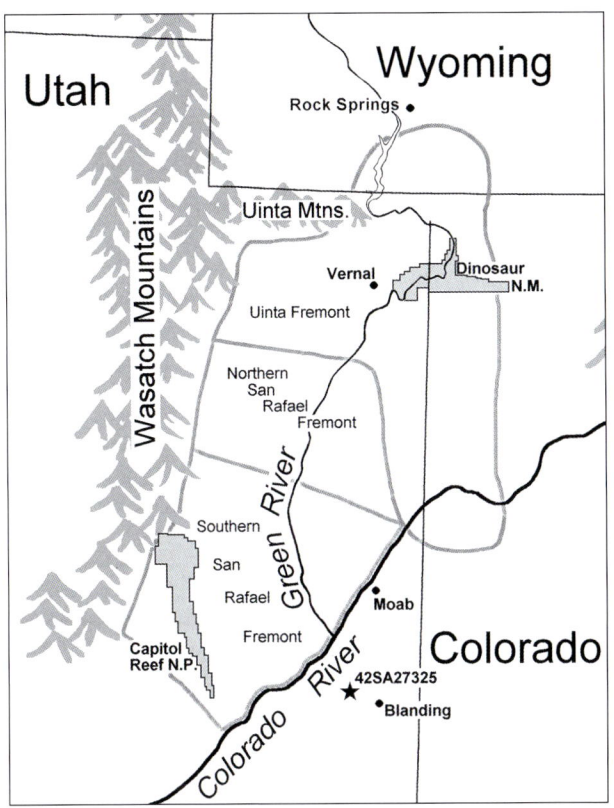

Figure 3. The eastern Fremont area extends from about Rock Springs, Wyoming, to south of Capitol Reef National Park in Utah. Uinta Style zone at north, Southern San Rafael just west of Colorado River. Pipe Spring (42SA27325) indicated by star located just west of Blanding, Utah.

Although the site area has been heavily scavenged, and is thus almost devoid of artifacts, the structure's architectural style—showing single course tabular sandstone blocks chinked with mud and small stones and a T-shaped doorway—is typical of Mesa Verdean and Chacoan construction. Combined with the few remaining ceramic sherds, which represent Indented Corrugated, Undifferentiated Black on Red, and Mancos Corrugated wares along with Undifferentiated Graywares and Whitewares, this suggests a primarily Pueblo II occupation dating from about A.D. 900 to 1100. A few Mancos Black on White sherds appear to be transitional Pueblo II to early Pueblo III artifacts, dating from approximately A.D. 975 to 1175. Also within the alcove are two metates; one of which is a large boulder metate covered with numerous grinding slicks produced by one-handed manos; a trait associated with Basketmaker sites (Matson et al. 1988). These Basketmaker grinding slicks and plentiful Basketmaker rock art images attest to a significant earlier occupation of the site.

Within the alcove are four rock art panels (three face northeast and one faces south) at the base of the steep cliffs forming the alcove. Due to the height of the cliffs and their slight overhang, the rock art at their base is shaded from the sun. Of the four panels, Panel 2 is of interest here. It is a palimpsest of pictographs and petroglyphs illustrating small and large anthropomorphs, flying birds, handprints, a footprint, feline paw prints, and a large bighorn sheep. Cultural traditions evident in these images include Basketmaker, Fremont, and Pueblo.

The Pipe Spring site is on land administered by the Monticello District of the Bureau of Land Management (BLM). Kevin Conti obtained permission to do the recording work at the site. All records generated during this project (tracings, sketches, and a suite of photographs used in our analysis) and a copy of this report will be submitted to the BLM, Monticello District, following its publication.

The Pipe Spring Project

In 2013, the three of us visited the Pipe Spring site prior to the IFRAO meeting in Albuquerque. The reason for our visit was because Conti knew that Keyser was studying Fremont imagery on the extreme northern periphery of Fremont territory, and wanted to show Keyser what he thought were Fremont anthropomorphs at the extreme southern periphery, super-

Figure 4. The Pipe Spring site alcove. Note Pueblo structure in center of photograph. Rock art Panel 2 with Fremont figures is at arrow.

imposed on Basketmaker and Pueblo imagery in the large Pipe Spring alcove. During our initial visit, we photographed the site and identified what appeared to be four shorthand Fremont anthropomorphs,[3] three of whom each wore a distinctive bear claw necklace. A year later, at the annual ARARA meeting in Rock Springs, Wyoming, the three of us discussed a project wherein we would use a scaffold to record these figures so we could closely examine them and evaluate exactly how they related to the other panel imagery.

Thus, on May 22–23, 2016 we visited the site together for a second time to do this recording. David Minick, a third Oregon Archaeological Society Rock Art Research Group member, also was part of the 2016 field crew. Conti had installed the scaffolding the previous week, so we could immediately begin recording the major panel once we arrived at the site. Close-up examination facilitated by use of the scaffolding (Figure 5) quickly revealed the presence of fugitive white pigment in several areas of these figures. It was particularly noticeable around the face of Anthropomorph 5 (hereafter FA 1 [Fremont Anthropomorph 1]) and as headdress elements of Anthropomorphs 6 and 7 (FA 2 and FA 3), but faint traces could also be seen on the arms and along the right[4] side of the body of FA 1. We were aided in recognizing these traces—especially for the arms—by the fact that the three-fingered hands for FA 1 are incised and one of them is clearly superimposed over an earlier red handprint. These incised hands provided us an orientation and ultimate termination point for arms that might have been painted. We recorded these pigment traces on the first day of fieldwork and left the site for the evening, believing that we had found some very faint trace evidence of fugitive white pigment—an interesting occurrence, but little more than that.

The following day we returned to the site and recorded parts of a second extensive panel of petroglyphs that were threatened by a combination of mud deposits washing in from above the alcove and erosion caused by tree branches swaying back and forth across the rock face as they were moved by the wind. As part of this effort we made an extensive scale sketch of the entire remaining area of petroglyphs (Panels 3 and 4) at the site (Conti et al. 2018). Sometime in the late afternoon, as we integrated the petroglyphs on Panels 3 and 4 with the more centrally positioned Panel 2, which contains both petroglyphs and pictographs, we again looked with some intensity at Panel 2. Probably because the afternoon had a somewhat higher ambient humidity than the day before, we were astonished to see entire ghost-like, greyish-white-painted bodies, complete with arms for FA 1, FA 2, and FA 3 (Figure 6). We could even recognize painted hands for FA 2 and FA 3.

Figure 6. Photograph of Fremont Anthropomorphs 2 and 3 with ambient light.

Figure 5. Tracing the Fremont anthropomorphs at Pipe Spring required the use of a scaffold, but this enabled us to closely examine and evaluate superimpositions.

Using our DStretch-enabled cameras we re-photographed the four Fremont anthropomorphs and could ascertain almost the complete configuration of those three (Figure 7a). And interestingly, once we had recognized them and knew what we were "supposed" to see, it was even possible to see the white pigment parts of the figures in earlier, unenhanced photographs. Such an initial failure to see these fugitive-color bodies and limbs coupled with subsequent success at doing so once they are finally recognized is typical of the human brain when it is tasked with searching for and identifying small details (e.g., facial features, necklace, and belt) in one medium (deeply engraved petroglyphs) and then integrating those to make an identifiable figure while the other medium (pictographs) is so faint as to be nearly invisible. In addition, it was obvious to us that lighting conditions and ambient humidity greatly increase or decrease one's ability to see the fugitive pigments that complete these figures.

Returning to laboratory with the extensive photograph collection that we made at the site, we conducted several different analytical experiments. Various DStretch algorithms gave different results, but all showed clearly that there was fugitive pigment completing FA 1, FA 2, and FA 3, and algorithm LWE even hinted at a body configuration for FA 4 (Anthropomorph 9). But it was only when we began enhancing contrast and reducing brightness in the Paintshop Pro© program (Figure 7b–d), to emphasize the fugitive white pigment used to paint these anthropomorphs, that we could clearly recognize FA 2 and FA 3 are holding something in their adjacent hands. These enhancements also showed that originally FA 4 unquestionably had a white-painted trapezoidal body and probably a white-painted head.

We were also intrigued that there was an apparent "empty" space between FA 3 and FA 4. Our first DStretch enhancements (especially algorithm lwe) provided tantalizing hints that a fifth, just slightly smaller-sized, trapezoidal-body anthropomorph was painted (with no incised elements) in that space. Then, working with greatly enhanced color brightness/contrast images (e.g., Figure 7d), we were able to discern much of the form of a fifth anthropomorph in this row, positioned between FA 3 and FA 4. This figure has a trapezoidal body form and a round head sitting atop a short neck. We were even able to recognize faded headdress elements, somewhat similar to those on FA 2 and FA 3, and hints at arms hanging down from the shoulders.

Are These Figures Fremont?

Traditionally, Fremont and Anasazi cultural areas have been separated by the Colorado River in southeastern Utah, with Fremont north and west of the River and Anasazi to the south and east (Figure 3). While many contemporary Fremont scholars still use these traditional borders as originally defined (e.g., Richards 2014), recent research (e. g., Horn et al. 1994; Keyser 2016; Keyser and Poetschat 2015, 2017; Neal 2010)

Figure 7. Fugitive pigment for the Fremont anthropomorphs can be clearly seen in both DStretch enhancement LWE (a) and contrast-enhanced images (b–d). Close observation of (b) and (d) shows object being carried by middle two anthropomorphs, and (d) also shows very faint pigment for newly recognized Basketmaker anthropomorph.

has identified sites in the "Anasazi area" that show a strong Fremont signature. Pipe Spring is one of these sites that sit "out of bounds" of these traditional frontiers.

Compounding this boundary issue is the fact that defining exactly what Fremont is in these various areas has long been problematic for researchers. Local populations identified by different experts as Fremont apparently practiced a variety of substance strategies at different times and in different places. Sometimes they were hunter-gatherers, while at other times or other places they were sedentary agriculturalists, and yet at still other times and places they show an adaptation somewhere between these two extremes; characterized by a mixture of horticulture and hunting (Keyser and Poetschat 2017; Madsen and Simms 1998). Further confusion results along the southern frontier because many artifacts and rock art styles appear in both Anasazi and Fremont sites, and so similar are rock art motifs and material culture items along these border areas that some researchers have proposed the terms Freazi or Anamont to designate the apparent mixing of traits (Madsen 1982; Madsen and Simms 1998; O'Connell et al. 1982).

In the southeastern corner of Utah, several researchers have noted the apparent mixing of Fremont and Anasazi material culture, and explained it in various ways. The earliest was that Fremont pictographs and petroglyphs at Anasazi sites simply represented wholesale borrowing of rock art motifs by resident Anasazi populations (Sharrock 1966); an idea that was later espoused by Noxon and Marcus (1985:65–66) to account for the "Faces" motif at Anasazi sites in Canyonlands. Later authors speculated that this mixing of art styles resulted from a fluid frontier in which sites—over time—are abandoned and reoccupied by different groups, and sometimes even shared by both groups simultaneously (Marwitt 1970).

Leticia Neal 2010 has most recently addressed this issue, noting a mixed signature of Fremont and Anasazi rock art motifs at numerous sites east of the Colorado River in an area extending from Moab in the north to Indian Creek and Verdure Canyon on the north flank of the Abajo Mountains. She feels that San Rafael style Fremont anthropomorphs painted and carved at Anasazi sites north of the Abajo Mountains reflect Mesa Verde peoples' attempts to indicate their social ties with Fremont neighbors to the west (Neal 2010:234). She sees this resulting from the establishment of wide-ranging trading alliances across the landscape, and the subsequent creation of a "social landscape" whose purpose was to convey membership in a broadly based group of trading partners and to preserve this group identity through time by representing particular acts performed to commemorate these alliances.

The Pipe Spring anthropomorphs extend the area of Fremont/Anasazi interaction significantly further to the south, so it seems likely that other sites with a Fremont signature await discovery. Adopting Neal's basic idea for our own research, however, we have hypothesized (Conti et al. 2018) that the occupants of Pipe Spring actually had Fremont artists versed in the Classic Vernal style carve these images to create this site as a part of the proposed "social landscape" envisioned by Neal.

What is the Pipe Spring Evidence?

Several diagnostic attributes of the Pipe Spring anthropomorphs FA 1, FA 2, FA 3, and FA 4 strongly indicate a Fremont origin (Figure 8). Their shorthand form, especially since we now know all four were originally augmented by pigment, is a characteristic Fremont trait (Schaafsma 1971, 1980), as is the "hunched" or "shrugged" shoulders posture of FA 1 (Keyser and Poetschat 2017:167). The lower necklace form of FA 1—composed of separate sub-rectangular "plaquettes" arrayed in a characteristic U-shape—is a typical Fremont form throughout its range. Likewise, the vertical central line bisecting the torso that ties together the necklace element and belt (painted for FA 1 and incised for the other three) is characteristic of many Fremont anthropomorphs in the Uinta style zone (Figure 9), but also occurs on at least one Southern San Rafael style anthropomorph (Castleton 1984:17–25, 37, 144; Morss 1931:Plate 16; Schaafsma 1971:11, 16; Simms and Gohier 2010:95). Additionally, tear streaks (Figure 10) utilizing both single straight lines and series of dots, like those found on three of the Pipe Spring anthropomorphs, are very common on Fremont examples in the Uinta style zone (Castleton 1984:20–21; Schaafsma 1971:10–11; Simms and Gohier 2010:97). While the same "tear streak" concept occurs on a few anthropomorphs in the Southern San Rafael style zone (Schaafsma 1980:167), the predominant configuration has a significantly different form.

While the bear claw necklaces worn by three anthropomorphs are unique to this site, their basic configuration resembles the more common plaquette necklaces that are so commonly worn by other Fremont anthropomorphs (including FA 1 at this site). In addition, the fact that FA 2 and FA 3 carry something

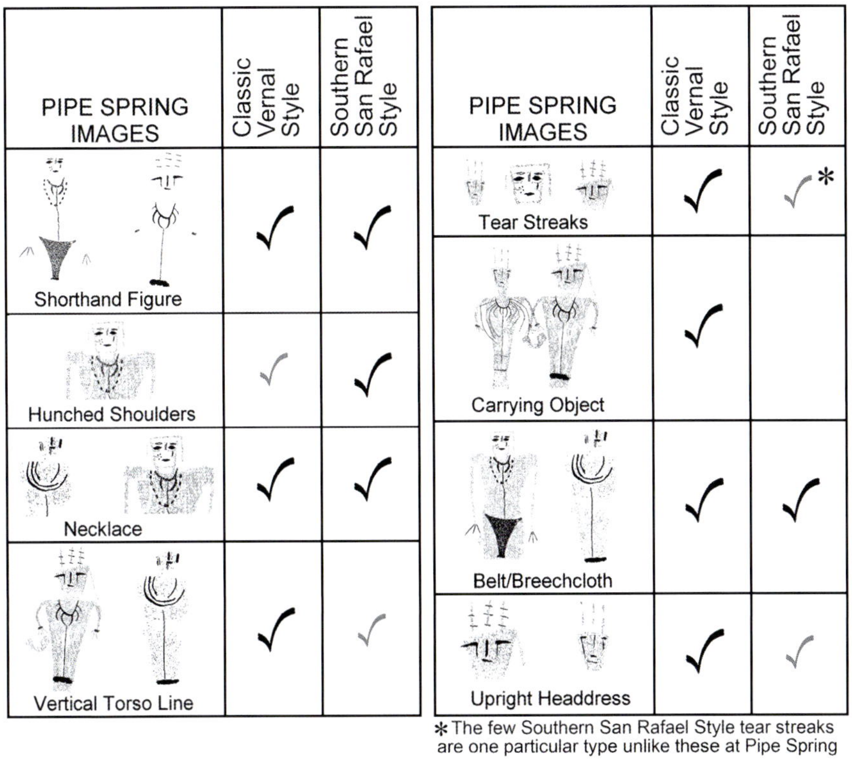

PIPE SPRING IMAGES	Classic Vernal Style	Southern San Rafael Style	PIPE SPRING IMAGES	Classic Vernal Style	Southern San Rafael Style
Shorthand Figure	✓	✓	Tear Streaks	✓	✓*
Hunched Shoulders	✓	✓	Carrying Object	✓	
Necklace	✓	✓	Belt/Breechcloth	✓	✓
Vertical Torso Line	✓	✓	Upright Headdress	✓	✓

*The few Southern San Rafael Style tear streaks are one particular type unlike these at Pipe Spring

Figure 8. Pipe Spring Fremont anthropomorph attributes compared to typical anthropomorph attributes in Classic Vernal (Uinta style zone) and Southern San Rafael styles. Note that attributes correspond slightly more closely to the Classic Vernal style. Smaller gray checkmark indicates trait is present but rare.

Figure 9. The torso midline on Fremont anthropomorphs is more common in the Classic Vernal style.

in their adjacent hands mimics the carrying of trophy heads by other Fremont anthropomorphs in the Uinta style zone. Finally, the vertical headdresses worn by FA 2 and FA 3 are like some found in the Uinta style zone, but similar headgear is not typical of the Southern San Rafael style zone. Taken together as a suite of attributes, all these features serve to identify these four anthropomorphs as Fremont, and none of them would be out of place at any major Fremont rock art site in the Uinta style zone, nor would they be seen as anything more than slightly anomalous at sites in the Southern San Rafael style zone.

Unfortunately, no amount of enhancement that we could perform enabled us to identify what object was being held by FA 2 and FA 3. Suspended just at their fingertips, between their two bodies, the best image we can determine is an amorphous, shallowly U-shaped object with a larger knob at each end. Small unpigmented ovoids are apparent in the larger knob at the right end, and although it is tempting to want these to be "eyes," they do not have a convincing eye-like orientation or placement. Until more powerful enhancement techniques are available (if sufficient pigment even remains) the identity of this carried object remains a mystery.

Anthropomorph 8, situated between FA 3 and FA 4, does not appear to be of Fremont origin. Initially, we thought it might be, because it is painted in a fugitive white pigment and has a trapezoidal body. But it has

Figure 10. Tear streaks like those used at Pipe Spring are most like those portrayed in the Classic Vernal style. (a, c, d) McConkie Ranch, Utah; (b) 48SW88, Henry's Fork, Wyoming.

no other diagnostic Fremont attribute. It lacks the belt, necklace, facial features, and central torso line that occur on all four identifiable Fremont figures. In addition, it is smaller than all the Fremont anthropomorphs and does not "fit" comfortably in the phalanx formed by the four of them. Finally, it appears to be entirely painted on the earlier, more heavily abraded area, and does not extend outward on the area of lighter abrasion (as do all four Fremont anthropomorphs). In fact, its upper right shoulder area appears to be damaged by the lighter abrasion that was apparently done to prepare a broader surface for the Fremont anthropomorphs. These clues, plus the discovery of a pattern of abraded "bars" in front of the pecked bighorn sheep that appears to represent another Basketmaker period fugitive pigment anthropomorph with no pigment remaining, suggest that Anthropomorph 9 is an earlier Basketmaker (BM-II) painting (see Conti et al. 2018).

Reconciliation of Manning's Earlier Observations and Our Recording

As we began our Pipe Spring literature research, we discovered that we were not the first to notice the faded pigment at this site. Larmore (2008) mentions a white pigment "outline" for some of the abraded anthropomorphs, but photographs in the IMACS site form are not of sufficient detail to show this. Additionally, Steve Manning (2004:138–139) recognized the fugitive pigment augmenting three of these anthropomorphs more than ten years ago; but not in the field. He states: "when standing in front of the panel, the images appear to have been constructed entirely by abrasion and incising; no trace of pigment is visible" (Manning 2004:138). Instead, he noted this faded pigment only after digitally enhancing the contrast for photographs of FA 1, FA 2, and FA 3, which he then published. We were not aware of either of these observations at the time of our project, however, because none of us had read Manning's article. Additionally, Manning apparently did not examine the figures as closely as we did, and he published no recording like the one we have made and publish here.

Finally, even before we were aware of Manning's discovery of fugitive pigment at this site, we made close observations as to the various superimpositions between images on Panel 2, and by combining these with additional use of the DStretch program and careful observation of what images are impacted by various episodes of abrasion, we can construct a Harris Diagram (Figure 11) that permits us to establish a chronology for the site. This enables us to reconcile our close-up observations with Manning's claims as to this panel's use-history.

Initially, we need to quote Manning's (2004:138–139) comments about this panel, substituting our designations for the three anthropomorphs he recognized:

> …three fugitive-pigment anthropomorphs were…constructed by first painting the images and then adding various features by abrading away the pigment. Some incised features were also added. When standing in front of the panel, the images appear to have been constructed entirely by abrasion and incising; no trace of pigment is visible, how-

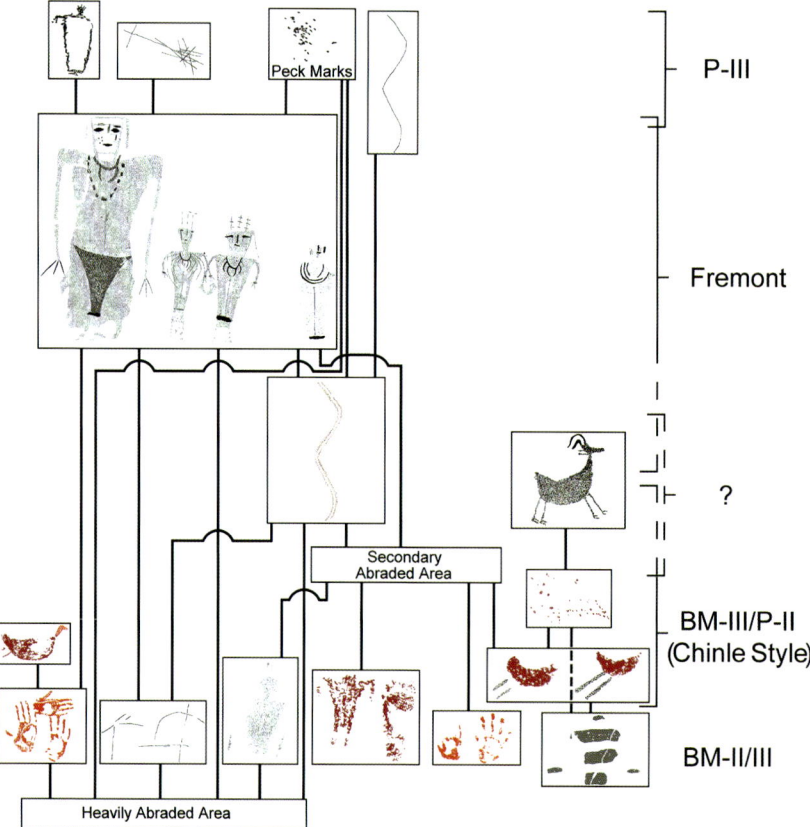

Figure 11. Harris Diagram showing superimpositions on traced (lower) area of Panel 2 at Pipe Spring.

ever, when photographs of the images are digitally enhanced...evidence of...[fugitive] pigment becomes visible [and] bodies, arms and facial features can be seen...The [pigment is] preserved here more than at other locations because the panel's orientation and the overhanging cliff above protected the panel. It [is] also apparent that other images existed here before these were created.

The square and upraised shoulders and long narrow arms of [FA 1] are visible, but the hands are not easily seen. This is because the hands are superimposed by three radiating incised lines. These lines, and the others described below are inconsistent with this type of image and thus appear to have been added later. Further evidence of this conclusion is that the incised lines are superimposed over red handprints, which are clearly superimposed over the images. Traces of white pigment outline the head; thus its trapezoidal form can be easily seen. The image also has pecked out eyebrows over the eyes and the typical U shape necklace, here consisting of 12 dots. There are also two crudely incised U-shaped lines. The triangular feature below the waistline is especially visible because it is deeply abraded. Notice that the body goes to a narrow waist, and then flares out...

[FA 2]'s body and arms are also visible, and it becomes apparent that its necklace, or at least the wildly radiating lines, was added after the image was created, as are the incised lines at the bottom of the figure. The body of this figure is markedly different from [that of FA 1]; it is long and tapering. Just above [the] wrist on both arms, there is a faint pecked-out area that appears to have represented bracelets, since they are just above the hands. To the right of the figure is [FA 3]'s arm...It also has a bracelet and the arms are crossed. [FA 2] appears to be carrying something in its hands that is round, but this feature is indistinct.

[FA 3] also has a long tapering body, however it is not as visible because it is near the edge of the protecting overhang and has been eroded. This image also has pecked facial features and a crude necklace that was likely not part of the original creation. It is obvious that the lower to middle section of this panel has been extensively abraded before the figures described here were placed upon it...There is a very faint abraded triangular feature just visible below the crossed arms of [FA 2 and FA 3], which suggests that other images once present on this surface were similar to those visible today.

Manning makes 18 observations—both general and specific—about these figures, and he is correct for 11 of them. Four of his five general observations are accurate. Initially, he correctly notes that in the field the images appear to be shorthand anthropomorphs with no pigment visible, but digitally enhanced photographs do reveal faint pigment. This is consistent with our observations, although we note that once the eye is trained to see the very faint pigment, it can be discerned at the site in ambient light, under favorable atmospheric conditions. He is also correct in noting that this fugitive pigment is better preserved here than is typical because of the protected location and orientation of the panel, and that FA 3 is less well preserved because it is nearer the less protected area of the panel.[5] Additionally, he accurately identifies the extensive abrasion that has been used to modify the middle section of the entire panel, and he notes that other images were painted on the panel before the Fremont anthropomorphs were drawn.

However, the one general observation that is in error, at least in part, is his blanket assertion that the anthropomorphs were first painted and only then were the incised and abraded features cut through the pigment. We know that at least one incised feature—the left eyebrow of FA 1—was carved before the head was outlined with white pigment since the pigment extends completely into and through that carved eyebrow. We found no other obvious place where pigment superimposed incised or abraded features, but many of the lines composing some of these elements (e.g., necklace claws, tear streaks, central torso line) are so fine, and the pigment is so faint that it seems all but impossible to determine which one was done first. It is true, however, that major features such as the breechcloth of FA 1 and the bracelets of FA 2 and FA 3 do appear to have been abraded through the pigment. Finally, the headdress spires of FA 2 and FA 3 show gaps in the pigment, some of which were not filled by incisions, and others that do have incisions. But in several of these gaps the incisions do not appear to have been the cause of the pigment discontinuity. In short, it appears that the artist(s) who painted and carved these images did not do so in a rigid way with all painted features done before any incised/abraded features or vice versa.

Manning is accurate for half of his image-specific observations. He correctly determines the general body shapes and presence of arms on the three anthropomorphs he recognized. He also notes the outlined head, abraded loincloth, and lower necklace for FA 1; the presence of hands and bracelets on FA 2 and FA 3, and the addition of very elongated lines to the bear claws in the necklace worn by FA 2. Additionally, he correctly identifies the superimposition of seemingly random lines on the bodies of FA 2 and FA 3, and an indistinct "round" painted object carried by FA 2 and FA 3.

Unfortunately, these accurate and well considered observations are paired with seven errors that we must address individually. Three of these erroneous observations concern the trident hands of FA 1 and their position in the superimposition sequence for Panel 2. Manning claims to see painted hands for FA 1, which he argues are indistinct because they are superimposed by trident radiating lines forming superimposed hands. He further suggests that the incised trident hands are inconsistent with Fremont anthropomorphs and appear to be added later because they are superimposed over red handprints that are themselves superimposed over the body of FA 1. Initially, Manning is incorrect in asserting that these tridents are not part of the shorthand anthropomorph because they are inconsistent with Fremont style. Anthropomorphs throughout Fremont territory have pecked or incised hands in this position, and a significant minority of these are shown as three to five long lines like this.

Additionally, although Manning is correct that these incised trident hands are superimposed over one actual red-paint-stamped handprint (not handprints), he is incorrect in asserting both that this red handprint is superimposed on either white hands for FA 1 (which we found no evidence of) or on the white-painted body of FA 1. Close observation while tracing the image gave no indication of any white painted hands on either arm, and no such painted hands were revealed by either DStretch or color contrast enhancements. Additionally, there was no evidence of superimposition of the red handprint on any white pigment. Although examination of DStretch was inconclusive, color-contrast-enhanced, close-up photographs of this area show small "islands" of white pigment (which forms the lower body of the figure) superimposed on the red pigment of the handprint and occurring in the relatively unpainted hollow in the palm's flexor surface.

However, the heel of the red handprint shows no white pigment.[6] This is consistent with Loubser's observations that fugitive pigment disappears more quickly and easily from a heavily painted surface than a sparsely painted or unpainted one (cf. Loubser 2010:155). This occurrence is so prevalent that it sometimes fools the casual observer into thinking that the earlier painted image (in this case the handprint) was superimposed over the later pigment (in this case the white) that failed to adhere well to the previously painted surface (cf. Loubser 1997:18–20, 2010:155). Additionally, this confusion would have been much more likely to have occurred over a decade ago before the advent of highly detailed digital photographs that we had the fortune of enhancing and using.

Certainly, the incised, three-fingered hand is superimposed on the actual stamped handprint but that does not preclude it from being a part of the original FA 1. This is especially true since there are so many apparently free-floating incised and abraded parts to this figure that are tied together only by the white pigment.

Finally, Manning's claim that FA 1 has indistinct painted hands is simply wrong—no such hand was visible at the end of either arm during our close observation, nor is it evident in either DStretch or in high-contrast enhancements. Apparently Manning was convinced that there must be painted hands because he was first convinced that the incised hands were a stylistic anomaly that were later superimposed on the figure.

Although Manning failed to identify the necklaces of FA 1, FA 2, and FA 3 as representing bear claw necklaces, his errors regarding these were in assuming that the upper necklace of FA 1 was two crudely incised U shapes and that the necklace of FA 3 was likely "not part of the original creation." Admittedly, the bear claw necklace worn by FA 1 is somewhat simplistic, and its shallow depth does make it difficult to accurately identify from the ground below, but there is no reason to assume that the bear claw necklaces worn by either FA 2 or FA 3 are not their own original regalia, especially since all three anthropomorphs wear essentially the same item.

Finally, Manning reports "a faint abraded triangular feature just visible below the crossed arms of [Figures FA 2 and FA 3]" and suggests that this is some sort of remnant of an earlier figure drawn in this area. Here, it is unclear as to what he actually saw. If he is referring to the irregular lower margin of the heavily abraded area that spans the middle of Panel 2, there is a vaguely triangular area just below the Fremont anthropomorphs' hands holding the object. However, the entire heavily abraded area has many marginal irregularities, and in these do not appear to make figures of any sort. Conversely, to the right of FA 3 we found a very faded white-painted figure that appears to predate the Fremont anthropomorphs. Could this figure be what Manning is referencing, and he simply misstated where it was located? Certainly it appears that there was at least one older figure on this heavily abraded area, so it is possible that there were others—maybe ones that are now completely eroded away more than ten years later.

Chronology of These Shorthand Anthropomorphs

With the discrepancies between Manning's earlier observations and our own recording addressed and clarified, we can now construct a chronology for Panel 2 using Harris Analysis techniques (Loubser 1997) based on superimpositions that we observed during our tracing of the images from the scaffold we erected on-site. Combined with approximate dates for the various cultural entities that were apparently responsible for the imagery, we can construct a relatively secure chronology for the area of Panel 2 that we traced (Figure 12).

The earliest modification of the surface of Panel 2 was heavy abrasion of a wide band across the lower middle of the area that was later marked with pictographs and petroglyphs (Figure 11). Whether this was done to prepare the surface for some of these images or for some other purpose cannot now be determined. On that heavily abraded surface, Basketmaker artists then stamped handprints, incised a few lines, and painted at least one white, trapezoidal body anthropomorph (Figure 11). We do not know whether these few images were contemporaneous or not, since there are no superimpositions involving them, but the handprints and white "ghost" figure probably indicate Basketmaker II or early Basketmaker III artists. Apparently somewhat later Basketmaker artists began to paint polychrome birds and stamp other red handprints on the panel outside the heavily abraded area, since a duck and another bird are both superimposed on handprints. These slightly later Basketmaker artists also painted a large vertically oriented, snake-like, curvilinear zigzag down the approximate middle of the panel with a brownish-red pigment. The number of birds at the site (both as pictographs on this panel and as petroglyphs of birds and bird-headed humans on Panels 3 and 4) strongly suggest artists of the Basketmaker III–Pueblo II period.

These images fit comfortably in the Chinle Representational style as defined by Schaafsma (1979:192–

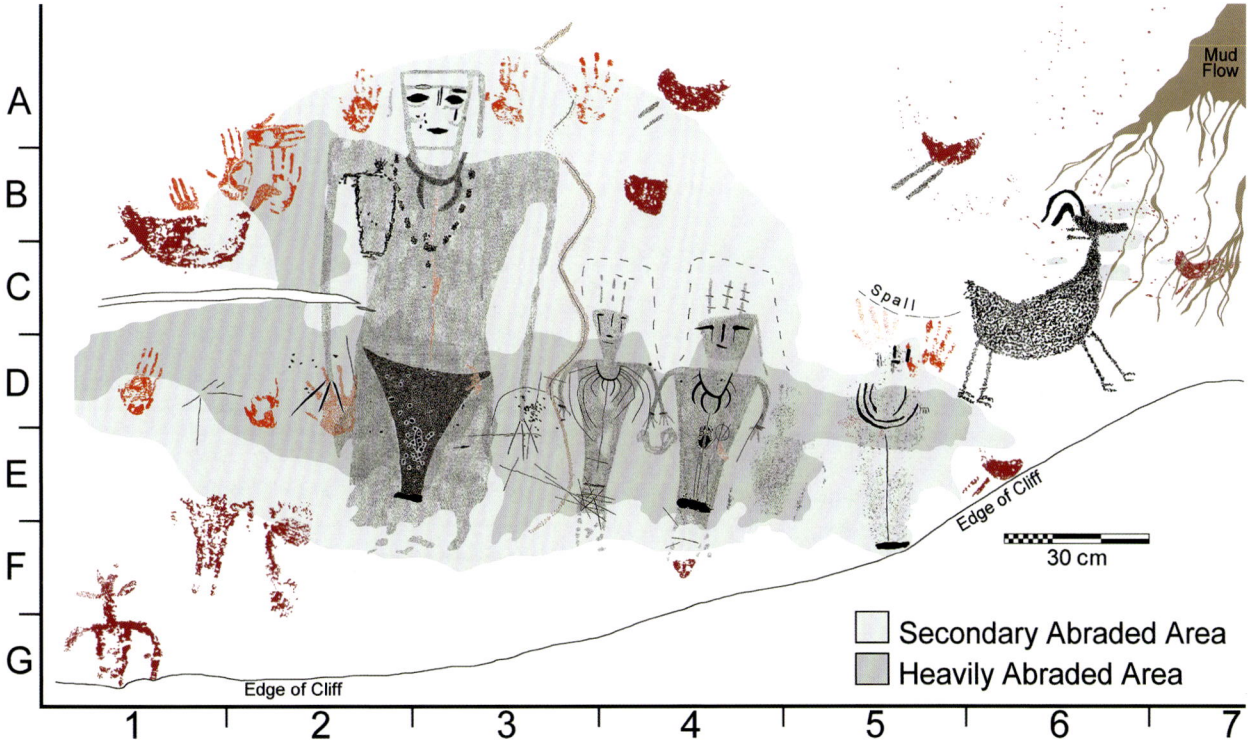

Figure 12. Tracing of Panel 2 showing Basketmaker, Fremont, and Pueblo imagery with superimpositioning. Fugitive white pigment indicated on Fremont anthropomorphs as extremely fine stippling. Dashed line outlining heads of middle two anthropomorphs indicates area of slightly heavier abrasion, apparently done as surface preparation by Fremont artist.

198, 1980:122–127). At least three different shades of red and one brownish-red pigment used for various images suggest several different painters working in the Chinle Representational style, but superimposition of one duck over two different handprints in a cluster at the panel's upper left and the vertical zigzag over the earlier incised arced line proves that there were at minimum two temporally separated episodes when artists painted and carved during this Chinle Representational style period. Also during Chinle Representational times an artist flicked liquid red paint (of the same shade as that used for several of the birds' bodies) across the far-right part of the panel, leaving small red spatter marks on a pattern of abraded "bars" (that probably represents an early BM-II fugitive pigment anthropomorph that we have not yet fully identified) and the unmodified cliff surface (Figure 12B/6). Some of these small spatter marks also superimpose the legs of one flying Chinle Representational style bird (Figures 11–13).

Figure 13. Superimposition sequence of the spatter cloud pattern. Note droplets around, but not within, the Bighorn sheep's head and front quarters; and droplets superimposed on the abraded legs of the bird above the sheep. Brown tendrils are mud flow.

Following the relatively heavy use of this panel by artists painting in the Chinle Representational style, both Fremont and Pueblo artists carved and painted images on Panel 2. Initially, Fremont artists appear to have lightly abraded a much larger area surrounding the heavily abraded band spanning the lower middle of the panel. This abrasion, neither as heavy nor as deep as the earlier abrasion, is particularly evident where it has lightly "erased" parts of earlier painted figures including birds (Figure 12B/1, A/4), handprints and the toes of a footprint (Figure 12D/2, E/2), smudges, the vertical zigzag, and probably the head of Anthropomorph 2 in the lower left corner of the panel. Each of these partially "erased" images shows distinctive erosion of its "high" spots so that the underlying rock surface shows through the pigment. This secondary abrasion is somewhat heavier around the heads of FA 2 and FA 3 and the upper body of FA 1, suggesting that it was done specifically to prepare a surface on which these images could be easily painted and carved.

The Fremont Anthropomorphs (Figure 12C/2-D/5) were painted, abraded, and incised as a single artistic event, and the initial abrading to prepare the surface impacted several different Chinle Representational style images. The figures themselves superimpose two handprints (the incised left hand of FA 1 superimposes a stamped-red handprint and one of the lines in the head of FA 4 superimposes the thumb of a different stamped-red handprint), the necklace of FA 4 is carved over a red smudge, and the white-painted arms of FA 1 and FA 2 are superimposed on an incised arced line.

Also, after most, if not all, of the Chinle Representational style images were painted, an artist pecked the large Bighorn sheep near the right side of Panel 2 (Figure 12C/6). We know this animal postdates at least two Chinle style painting episodes and an earlier pattern of abraded "bars" because it is pecked through the "cloud" of red spatter marks in this area and it removed the very ends of the three central, vertically aligned bars. Furthermore, the spatter marks themselves superimpose at least one flying Chinle Representational style bird and five of the six abraded bars (Figure 13). But whether this sheep image predates or postdates the Fremont anthropomorphs is unknown, so we do not know if it was drawn by a Pueblo II, a Fremont, or a Pueblo III artist. We do know, however, that a trapezoidal-body anthropomorph pecked on the upper left torso of FA 1 (Figure 12B/2) superimposes both the fugitive white pigment and one small plaquette element of the lower necklace, indicating that it postdates the Fremont period and is therefore a Pueblo III image. Also postdating the Fremont anthropomorphs are clusters of closely spaced, random peck marks superimposed on the right wrist and hand and the loincloth of FA 1 as well as the center torso of FA 3 (Figure 12D/3, E/4). Other peck marks of similar size and depth are scattered across the panel and were probably done at the same time, but since they superimpose only the Chinle Representational style handprints, we do not know if they were done before or after the Fremont anthropomorphs.

Finally, small, randomly oriented scratches and a small circle were carved on the bodies of FA 2 and FA 3, and some fine lines were probably carved at this time to greatly extend the length of the bear claws in the necklace worn by Figure 2. These lines extend far outside the figure's body, and often bend at an extreme angle inconsistent with the general claw shape of the primary line. Although we think it likely that these latest peck marks and minor incised lines were done by Pueblo period artists, it is possible that they were made much later by Ute or Navajo people visiting this site after Pueblo III abandonment at approximately A.D. 1300.

In summary, on this panel we have an initial period of Anasazi art that may have begun as early as Basketmaker II in the first centuries A.D. and reached its zenith during the Chinle Representational style period in Basketmaker III/Pueblo II times between A.D. 400–1100. Then we see a short-term episode of Fremont art, likely dating to about A.D. 1100 and then limited Pueblo III art dating between A.D. 1100 and 1300. Possibly some of the latest peck marks and small random incisions date even later after Pueblo abandonment, but this cannot be demonstrated.

The images left by each of these phases of activity remain clear for us to appreciate and interpret after hundreds of years. However, some of the pigment used in composing the Fremont anthropomorphs has faded near to invisibility, leaving (at first glance) shorthand anthropomorphs like many other Fremont images around the Southwest. Likewise, one earlier Basketmaker anthropomorph can be recognized only by the faded ghostly white pigment visible in enhanced photographs. But we are lucky that these Pipe Spring anthropomorphs have been somewhat protected by a natural overhang, allowing us to tease out their faded details through close inspection and image manipulation. Other Fremont and Basketmaker sites with fugitive pigment, particularly ones protected from the elements, may likewise benefit from closer inspection for such details that are often hidden from view.

Finally, this project illustrates the importance of revisiting sites that have previously been "recorded" and even "published," since changes in technology and enhanced documentation techniques may well lead to the discovery of additional information. As this site demonstrates, such information not only expands our knowledge about specific sites, but it can yield new and different avenues of interpretation. Such interpretations can greatly expand our understanding of the past.

Acknowledgments. We thank Don Simonis and Cameron Cox at the Monticello BLM who provided both access and research reports. David L. Minick provided photographs of the site for this paper and did some of the DStretch analysis for the project. Thanks to Winston Hurst who offered technical advice and theoretical perspectives. The Oregon Archaeological Society provided funds to support the Pipe Spring project, including scaffold rental. The National Park Service Southwestern Group provided necessary field reports.

Notes

1. Note that Schaafsma's 1971 drawing of this panel is reversed from the correct orientation seen in the 1981 photograph.

2. In this article, Manning (2004) includes non-outline Fremont anthropomorphs like these we report from Pipe Spring in a much broader category that he named "Fugitive Pigment Anthropomorphs." Despite his claim that these fugitive pigment anthropomorphs represent a "shared cultural and temporal relationship" his sample is actually a broad range of figures that includes all sorts of different Fremont anthropomorphs (fully outlined and possibly never painted, fully painted, outline-painted, and bas-relief) along with Late Archaic period—pre-Fremont—pecked outline figures, and some random Basketmaker-type images that are probably not anthropomorphs. He did, however, note fugitive pigment on a few anthropomorphs scattered throughout eastern Utah, some of which are true non-outline/shorthand Fremont images. Among those are three of the five anthropomorphs we recorded at Pipe Spring.

3. Of the 10 anthropomorphs on Panel 2 the four Fremont figures we originally noted are numbered 5–7 and 9 (see Conti et al. 2018).

4. Right and left are indicated from the perspective of the viewer.

5. The fact that FA 4 and the fugitive pigment Basketmaker figure (Anthropomorph 8) are almost completely unprotected by the overhanging cliff face is certainly the reason why they have the least obvious pigment, and probably also why FA 4 has slightly less obvious incised elements. The erosion that these figures have suffered may well be why Manning did not report them.

6. These small islands of pigment are impossible to see from the ground, so it does appear from a distance that the handprint is superimposed on the white pigment.

References Cited

Castleton, Kenneth B.
1984 *Petroglyphs and Pictographs of Utah. Volume One: The East and Northeast.* Utah Museum of Natural History, Salt Lake City.

Cole, Sally J.
2009 *Legacy on Stone: Rock Art of the Colorado Plateau and Four Corners Region.* Revised and Updated Edition. Johnson Books, Boulder, Colorado.

Conti, Kevin, James D. Keyser, David A. Kaiser, and David L. Minick
2018 Pipe Spring: Fremont-Anasazi Interaction in Southeastern Utah. In *American Indian Rock Art, Volume 44,* edited by David A. Kaiser and James D. Keyser, pp. 123–143. American Rock Art Research Association, San Jose, California.

Horn, J. C., A. D. Reed, and S. M. Chandler
1994 *Grand Resource Area Class I Cultural Resource Inventory.* Alpine Archaeological Consultants, Inc. Document on file, Moab Field Office, Bureau of Land Management.

Keyser, James D.
2016 Vermillion Alcove: Iconography on the Uinta Fremont Frontier. *Southwestern Lore* 82(1):21–46

Keyser, James D., and George Poetschat
2015 *Seeking Bear: The Petroglyphs of Lucerne Valley, Wyoming.* Oregon Archaeological Society Press Publication 23, Portland.

2017 Uinta Fremont Rock Art in Southwestern Wyoming: Marking the Fremont Northern Periphery. *Plains Anthropologist* 62:157–178

Larmore, S.
2008 IMACS site form for site 42SA27325. BLM Monticello field office. Document on file at Edge of the Cedars Museum, Blanding, Utah.

Loubser, Johannes H. N.
1997 The Use of Harris Diagrams in Recording, Conserving, and Interpreting Rock Paintings. *INORA (International Newsletter On Rock Art)* 18:14–21.

2010 Layer by Layer: Precision and Accuracy in Rock Art Recording and Dating. In *Seeing and Knowing—Rock Art With and Without Ethnography,* edited by G. Blundell, C. Chippindale, and B. Smith, pp. 149–167. Wits University Press, Gauteng, South Africa.

Madsen, David B.
1982 Salvage Excavations at Ticaboo Town Ruin (42Ga2295). In *Archaeological Investigations in Utah at Fish Springs, Clay Basin, Northern San Rafael Swell, Southern Henry Mountains,* edited by David B. Madsen and Richard E. Fike, pp. 1–41. Utah Bureau of Land Management Cultural Resources Series 12, Salt Lake City.

Madsen, David B., and Steven R. Simms
1998 The Fremont Complex: A Behavioral Perspective. *Journal of World Prehistory* 12(3):255-336. Salt Lake City, Utah.

Manning, Steven J.
2004 The Fugitive-Pigment Anthropomorphs of Eastern Utah: A Shared Cultural Trait Indicating a Temporal Relationship. In *Utah Rock Art, Volume 23,* edited by Steven J. Manning, pp. 61–177. Utah Rock Art Research Association, Salt Lake City.

Marwitt, J. P.
1970 *Median Village Fremont Culture Regional Variation.* University of Utah Anthropological Papers, No. 95. University of Utah Press, Salt Lake City.

Matson, R. G., William D. Lipe, and Williams R. Haase IV.
1988 Adaptational Continuities and Occupational Discontinuities: The Cedar Mesa Anasazi. *Journal of Field Archaeology* 15(3):245–264.

Morss, Noel M.
1931 *The Ancient Culture of the Fremont River in Utah.* Report on the Explorations under the Claflin-Emerson Fund, 1928–1929. Papers of the Peabody Museum of American Archaeology and Ethnology 12(3). Cambridge, Massachusetts.

Neal, Leticia A.
2010 *Moving Beyond Boundaries: Fremont and Anasazi Archaeology and Rock Art in Southeastern Utah.* Master of Arts Thesis, University of Nevada, Reno.

Noxon, John, and Deborah Marcus
1985 Significant Rock Art Sites in the Canyonlands National Park, Southeastern Utah. Document on file with Canyonlands National Park, Moab, Utah.

O'Connell, J. F., K. T. Jones, and S. R. Simms
1982 Some Thoughts on Prehistoric Archaeology in the Great Basin. In *Man and the Environment in the Great Basin,* edited by D. B. Madsen and J. F. O'Connell, pp. 227–240. Society for American Archaeology Papers 2, Washington, D.C.

Reagan, Albert B.
1931 The Pictographs of Ashley and Dry Fork Valleys in Northeastern Utah. *Transactions of the Kansas Academy of Science* 34:168–216

Richards, Kristina Katie
2014 *Fremont Ceramic Designs and Their Implications.* Master of Arts Thesis, Brigham Young University, Provo, Utah.

Schaafsma Polly
1971 *The Rock Art of Utah.* University of Utah Press, Salt Lake City.

1979 Rock Art of the San Juan Drainage: From Pre-Horticultural Hunter-Gatherers Through the Anasazi. In *CRARA '77: Papers from the Fourth Biennial Conference of the Canadian Rock Art Research Associates,* edited by Doris Lundy, pp. 185–202. Heritage Record No. 8, British Columbia Provincial Museum, Victoria, British Columbia, Canada

1980 *Indian Rock art of the Southwest.* School of American Research, Santa Fe, and University of New Mexico Press, Albuquerque.

Sharrock, Floyd W.
1966 *An Archaeological Survey of Canyonlands National Park.* University of Utah Anthropological Papers 83. University of Utah Press, Salt Lake City.

Simms, Steven R., and François Gohier
2010 *Traces of Fremont: Society and Rock Art in Ancient Utah.* University of Utah Press, Salt Lake City.

Wellmann, Klaus
1979 *A Survey of North American Indian Rock Art.* Akademische Druck- und Verlagsanstalt. Graz, Austria.

Tobacco-related Rock Art and Vertical Series Rock Art in Montana and Wyoming

Lawrence Loendorf and David A. Kaiser

Images of tobacco seeds, plants, gardens, and other tobacco paraphernalia have been identified at about a dozen rock art sites in Montana and Wyoming. Recently researchers have recognized that the rock art tradition known as Vertical Series has an association with tobacco rock art. Vertical Series motifs on tubular pipes used for smoking tobacco are an important clue to an association, but equally important is the finding of Vertical Series arrangements at the Tensleep Alcove site (48WA2285) and the Comanche Creek site (24ST403), that also contain tobacco-related imagery. Newly discovered Vertical Series at the Comanche Creek site are superimposed on a large Foothills Abstract bison, which offers support for a post-Archaic age.

Images of tobacco seeds, plants, gardens and other tobacco paraphernalia have been identified at about a dozen rock art sites in Montana and Wyoming. These images were first noted at Montana sites thought to be associated with Crow Indian sacred tobacco ceremonialism (Francis and Loendorf 2002; Loendorf 1994; Loendorf and Porsche 1985). Understanding these tobacco-related images as part of Crow tobacco ceremonialism is an important contribution to regional Plains Indian rock art research (Loendorf 2016a).

A possible connection between tobacco related rock art and the rock art tradition known as "vertical series" has been proposed to account for vertical series motifs found on tubular pipes used for smoking tobacco (Loendorf 2016a). Equally important is the finding of Vertical Series arrangements at the Tensleep Alcove site (48WA2285) and the Comanche Creek site (24ST403), sites that also contain tobacco-related imagery.

Published reports for the Tensleep Alcove[1] show the Vertical Series (Mack 1971; Sundstrom 1987; 2004) and the tobacco imagery (Francis and Loendorf 2002; Loendorf 2016a). The Comanche Creek site is less well known, although a Vertical Series motif at the site has been used in discussions about the genre (Conner and Conner 1971; Greer and Greer 2003; Keyser et al. 2012; Sundstrom 1987, 2004). Tobacco imagery at Comanche Creek has not been widely reported.

In this paper, we explore the interrelationship between tobacco rock art and Vertical Series rock art at the Tensleep Alcove and Comanche Creek sites. Before that discussion, however, we present brief overviews of tobacco-related motifs and Vertical Series rock art.

Tobacco-related Rock Art in Montana and Wyoming

Tobacco plants are a recognized rock art image at Montana and Wyoming sites. They may also be found in other states and possibly Alberta but have not yet been positively identified. They are variable in form (Figure 1) with some

Lawrence Loendorf
Sacred Sites Research, Inc.
Albuquerque, New Medxico

David A. Kaiser
Oregon Archaeological Society
Portland, Oregon

that are bushy and others that look more like the native tobacco plant (*Nicotiana multivalvis*). Most of the recorded examples are painted in red, yellow or shades of those colors. There are recognized incised examples but no pecked forms have been documented.

Rock art images of tobacco plants are readily identified because they are found on Crow Tobacco Society bags, moccasins, and other artifacts (Figure 2). No examples are known in ledger art or robe art but they are extremely common on tobacco bags (Nabokov 1988). The Crow did not smoke their ceremonial tobacco so these are not pipe bags, rather they held tobacco seeds, stems, and leaves from dried tobacco plants.

Depictions of tobacco seeds are also common in rock art and on Tobacco Society regalia. They are as variable as the plants with some that resemble *Nicotiana multivalvis* seed pods and others that are less rep-

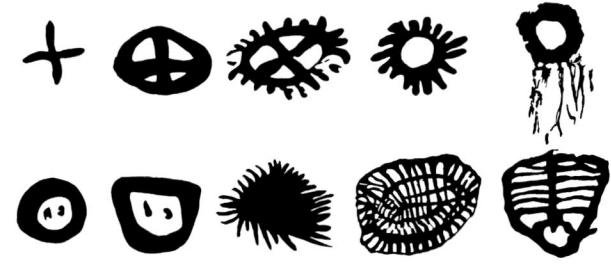

Figure 3. Possible tobacco seeds. The equilateral cross is the most recognized symbol for a tobacco seed. The encircled cross is another common tobacco seed motif. The remaining examples are found at the Tensleep Alcove site where the fringed figures are possibly the hairy calix associated with the tobacco seed pod. Other examples with chambers suggest the complicated interior of a tobacco seed pod. Illustrations by Terry Moody.

resentational. They usually have a circular form (Figure 3). One common type has an equilateral cross or plus-sign inside the circle which is much like the *multivalvis* seed pod. One variety is filled with dots or seeds, another has interior grid-like patterns. Some images have lines radiating away from the circle or on some occasions they converge inward. These are possible representations of the hairs on the calix and leaves associated with the seed pod. One type has lines radiating from the lower portion of the circular seed form. These may represent rootlets for a growing seed.

Representations of gardens are also found in rock art and on Crow Tobacco Society regalia (Nabokov 1988:198). These are usually rectangular forms with interior parallel lines representing rows. Rows of seeds, or sometimes a single seed, are shown in the rows. A different variety of a garden shows the garden fence with plants inside.

An image of a Tobacco Society lodge with an altar is known from the Tensleep Alcove site. The altar is recognized by comparison to historical photographs of Crow Tobacco Society altars with a wicket-like frame along its sides.

Images of flat headdresses with tobacco leaves incorporated into

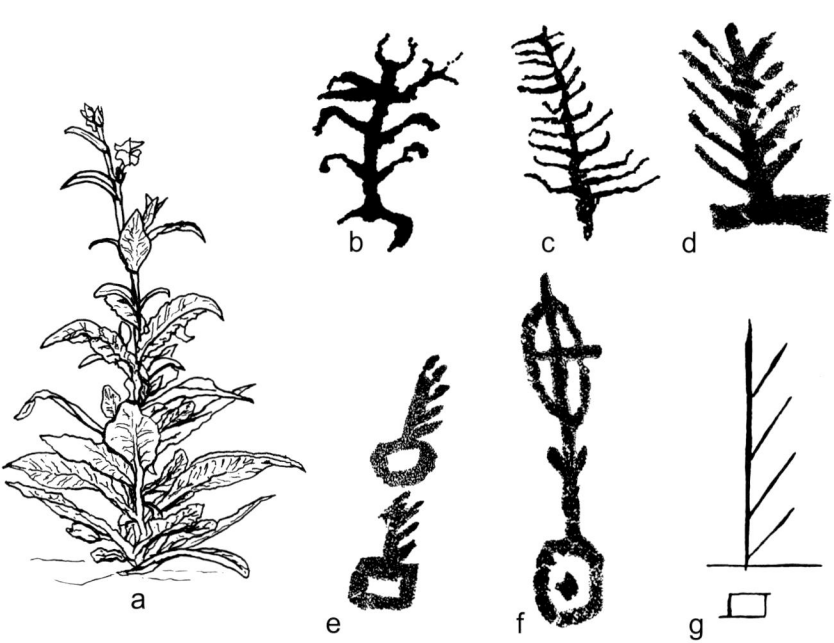

Figure 1. Depictions of tobacco plants. (a) Nicotiana multivalvis plant, (b) and (c) Frozen Leg Cave, (d) and (e) Tensleep Alcove, (f) Comanche Creek, and (g) 24CB1160.

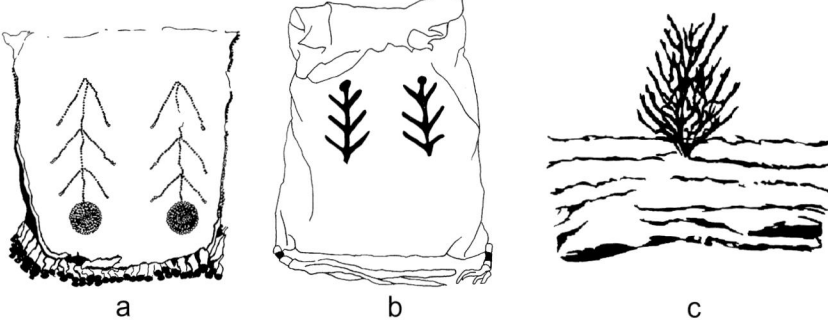

Figure 2. Tobacco depicted on Crow Tobacco Society bags (a and b) and bundle (c).

them (Figure 4) are found at several rock art sites (Francis and Loendorf 2002:168-169; Loendorf 2016b). Historical photographs show Crow women wearing these headdresses to Tobacco Society functions (Francis and Loendorf 2002:172). Some of the rock art headdresses include the tobacco seed motif.

A final form that is not well recognized in connection with tobacco is a bison head design. It is found at the Tensleep Alcove site and the Comanche Creek site where it apparently designates the importance of bison. Several of the main tobacco rock art sites have depictions of bison or bison-human combination figures as important parts of the rock art (Loendorf 2016b)

made during the Protohistoric and Historic periods (Sundstrom 2004:180). Other researchers think the series they have studied are much older, perhaps dating well into the Archaic period (Greer and Greer 2003). An important observation is that researchers have relied upon photographs to make their observations and when they visit or record a site, they change their mind about age. This is the case with the Atherton Canyon Vertical Series where the figures were found to be older than originally reported (Keyser et al. 2012:213).

It is also apparent that some Vertical Series arrangements are more recent with examples that may date to the Historic Period. Linea Sundstrom (1987) supports

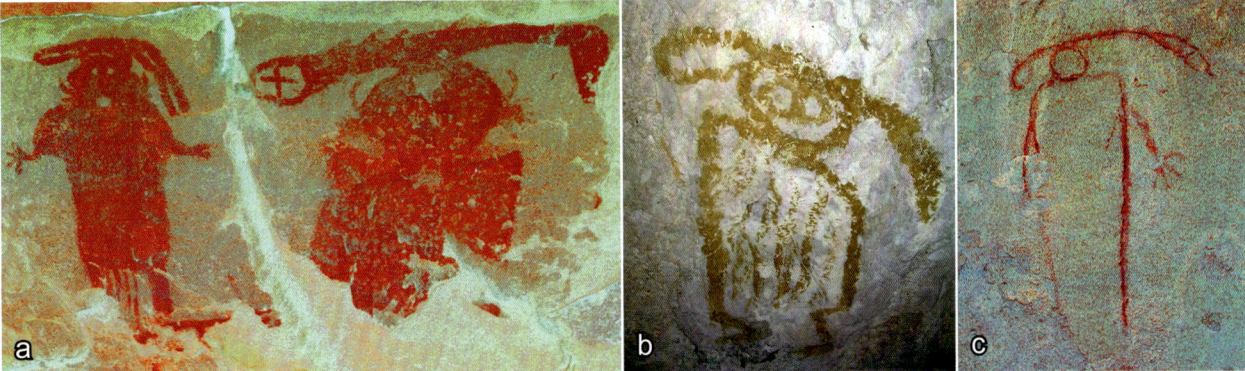

Figure 4. Flat headdresses with tobacco leaves. Circles on one end represent tobacco seed pods, sometimes containing the cross shape. (a) Tyrell site, DStretch LRE; (b) Frozen Leg Cave; (c) Red Buffalo, DStretch LRE. Photographs by David Kaiser.

Vertical Series Rock Art

Stuart Conner was the first researcher to recognize Vertical Series rock art, when he described it as "a series of identical or nearly identical designs arranged in a vertical series which sometimes bends to the right at the top" (Conner and Conner 1971:27). Vertical Series rock art has been studied and reported by other researchers (Greer 1995; Greer and Greer 2003; Keyser and Klassen 2001; Sundstrom 1987, 2004). A recent and comprehensive review of vertical series rock art is found in the Bear Gulch and Atherton Canyon report (Keyser et al. 2012:212–214).

Individual Vertical Series motifs are highly variable although several of them superficially resemble English alphabet letters like E, H, I, T or V. Embellishments of these designs are also common, like an I with a side arm or an inverted V with a dot in it. Other figures do not resemble letters but they are recognizable forms like a segmented rectangle or the plus sign, a common Vertical Series motif.

A debate regarding Vertical Series rock art revolves around its age. Some authors think it is recent and

this recent age for sites in the South Dakota Black Hills. She also originally believed that Siouan-speaking tribes were the makers of Vertical Series rock art but as more sites were found she realized it is too widespread to represent a single language group (Sundstrom 2004:179). In other words, Vertical Series rock art was made for a long period of time on the Northwestern Plains, possibly from the Archaic to the Historic Period and it was likely made by more than one cultural group.

Vertical Series Rock Art and Tobacco-related Imagery

Two sites exhibit a clear relationship between tobacco-related rock art motifs and Vertical Series arrangements: Tensleep Alcove and Comanche Creek. The Tensleep Alcove site contains numerous depictions of tobacco plants, seeds, gardens, and other figures that symbolize tobacco (Figure 5). Further, the high concentrations of tobacco pollen in the floor of the Alcove strongly suggest that there was once a tobacco garden at the site (Loendorf 2015). Unlike the pollen of many plants, tobacco pollen does not drift far from the parent plant.

Figure 5. Vertical series at Tensleep Alcove. The four rectangles containing two dots are interpreted as tobacco seeds, above which two additional rectangles are topped with forms resembling tobacco plants. Photograph by Jon Harman.

Figure 6. Vertical series geometric at Tensleep Alcove topped with plant images. Red painted image, DStretch CB+LDS. Photograph by Jon Harman.

There are several vertical series at the site as well (Mack 1971; Sundstrom 1987; 2004). One is an arrangement of four rectangles containing two dots, interpreted as tobacco seeds. This column continues upward to include two additional rectangles each topped with a line sprouting a series of upward pointing lines along one side, resembling tobacco plants (Figure 5). The inclusion of tobacco imagery in the Vertical Series makes it clear that a relationship exists between the two rock art motifs. Another geometric shape occurs at the site, resembling a capitol letter F. Similar images have been recognized as part of the Vertical Series tradition at other sites (Sundstrom 1987:13; 2004:179), with an almost exact copy found at Atherton Canyon (Keyser et al. 2012:74). However, at Tensleep Alcove this shape is augmented with two plant forms rising from the top, which we also identify as tobacco (Figure 6). Other Vertical Series arrangements at the Tensleep Alcove may also represent tobacco but they are not as evident as the seeds and plants.

Tubular smoking pipes with Vertical Series motifs arranged on them also support an association between tobacco and Vertical Series motifs (Loendorf 2016b). A pipe from Killarney, Manitoba, and the Mehling pipe from the southwestern corner of North Dakota have the designs in vertical arrangements on them (Loendorf 2016a). The Mehling pipe had high levels of nitrogen on its inside lip which suggests it was a smoking pipe rather than a sucking tube. This is important as it indicates the Vertical Series motifs on the pipes are associated with tobacco.

The Vertical Series motif, known as the "Lazy E", using livestock branding terminology for an inverted image, is found on the Killarney and Mehling pipes and at the Comanche Creek site in south-central Montana. Because the Comanche Creek site has never been fully recorded, Sacred Sites Research, Inc. (SSR) selected it for additional investigation. It is another site with obvious tobacco related images and vertical series.

Comanche Creek Site (24ST403)

Stuart W. Conner reported the Comanche Creek site in 1963 when he completed a site inventory form and assigned it a number. In addition to photographing the pictographs, Conner and members of the Billings Archaeological Society illustrated some of the figures. Conner subsequently discussed the vertical series rock art figures at the site and compared a Comanche Creek anthropomorph with an anthropomorph at Frozen Leg Cave (24BH411), another site with tobacco imagery (Conner and Conner 1971:27–28; Figure 36).

Tim Urbaniak, as far as we are aware, is the only other person to visit the site in a professional capacity.

About two decades ago, Urbaniak took a series of photographs of the rock art at the site and in recent discussion he recognized they might be important to the discussion about tobacco-related rock art imagery. In 2014, he sent SSR six photographs of the site. On September 1, 2016, Jon Harman, Cobe Chatwood, David Kaiser, and Lawrence Loendorf completed some basic recording at the site.

The Rock Art

The site is in a small valley along South Comanche Creek in Stillwater County, Montana. The surrounding terrain is flat rolling grasslands almost exclusively planted in crops but with some occasional relief like that at the site. The creek has exposed Upper Cretaceous age sandstones that are intermixed with Claggett shale. The rock paintings are on a south-facing low rimrock of what appears to be poorly consolidated Eagle formation sandstone.

Three locations with rock art are found at the site. The rock art at each location is dominated by paintings in several shades of red indicating multiple painting episodes. Superimposition confirms that the site was used over a period of time although there is no current method to determine how many years separate the initial and later paintings. Unfortunately, the rock is in very poor condition so the panel surfaces have suffered considerable exfoliation. This can make it difficult to examine the details of the paintings in places where they overlap one another.

The westernmost location is in a rock shelter that faces south and measures about 15 m across its opening by 3 m high and 2 to 3 m deep. Chokecherry bushes are thick in front of the paintings. The figures form a single panel of highly spalled abstract shapes, horned head figures, possible plant forms, and many small figures too badly eroded to be identified (Figure 7). The right side of the panel has abstract forms including rows of upright parallel lines and a segmented rectangular form both in a dark purple color of paint. These are superimposed by much redder painted images that include vertical lines and a large smudged area.

Three rows of H-like images are stacked over one another. While these images have suffered natural erosion, many of the remaining series appear to have had some of their pigment scraped away some time after they were painted in an apparent ritual reuse of the site. The Vertical Series occurs next to three plant-like forms, each showing a stalk emerging from a ground line with various leaves protruding. While each of these plants is different in design, two of them have large triangular heads likely depicting the flower in bloom. The bushy example is very like some tobacco plants depicted on Crow Indian tobacco bags.

Two horned head figures, prominent in the panel, are forms often found at sites with tobacco related images. There are also some seed-like figures, but the severe exfoliation of the panel surface makes it difficult to study their detail.

Several figures appear to be more recent than others in the panel. Because the surface is so eroded, superimposition is difficult to study but the variety of pigment hues indicates separate episodes. An elongated stick-figure human drawn with an ocher crayon is superimposed on the three plant images. Its limbs are spread, and it has two long toes on each foot.

Another Comanche Creek location with rock paintings is about 100 m east or downstream from the first group. It is also in a rock shelter that measures about 4 m across by 2.5 m high and 1.3 m deep. A large sandstone slab that blocks the opening of the rock shelter offers some protection to the small interior area. Standing on this sandstone slab allows access to the upper canyon wall above the sheltered area.

Panel one of two at this location is on the canyon wall above the rock shelter (Figure 8). A series of six or seven "lazy E" motifs in a vertical arrangement are reported in several publications about Vertical Series rock art (Conner and Conner 1971:27; Greer and Greer 2003; Sundstrom 1987:6). These figures are described by Conner (1971:27) with "the back of each E on top." At another regional site, Robison Rock Shelter, the "lazy E" motif is reversed with the back of each figure on the bottom. This motif is found at other Vertical Series rock art sites (Sundstrom 1987) as well as carved

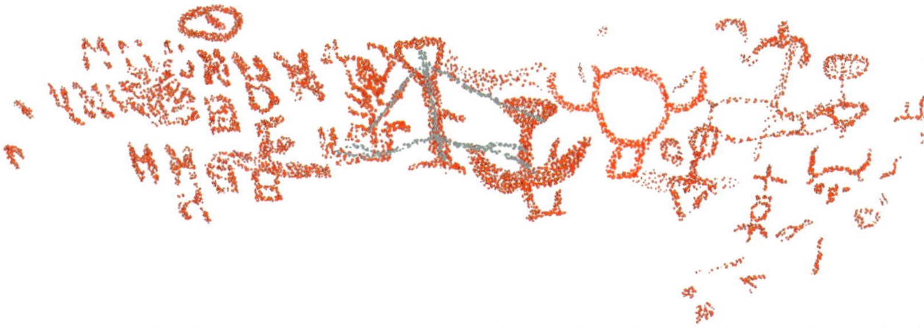

Figure 7. Left half of Panel 1, Locus 1, Comanche Creek. Red crayon human figure, depicted in grey, superimposes plant forms.

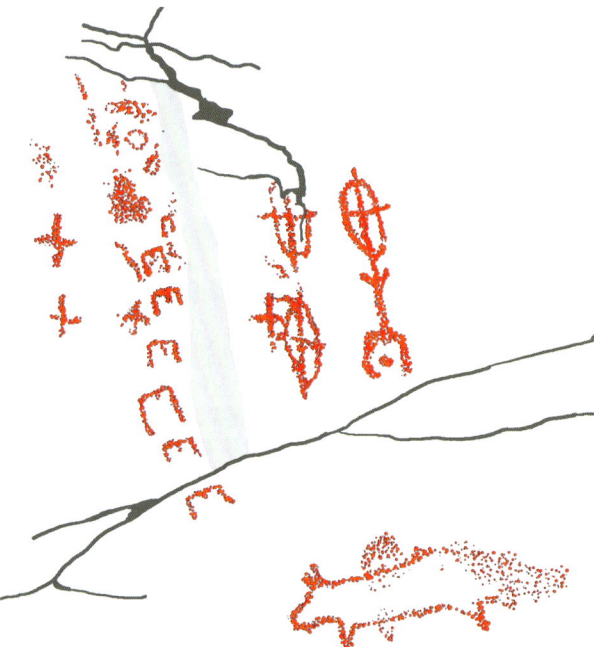

Figure 8. Vertical Series at Panel 1, Locus 2, at Comanche Creek. Grey streak is precipitate wash, likely eroding some of the figures.

on two steatite pipes with other Vertical Series imagery (Carmichael 1982; Loendorf 2016a).

A plant form on this panel is depicted with a nucleated circle on the base, paired upward angled lines on the stem, and topped with a large oval with a cross inside. This is identified as a tobacco plant. Similar plants have been recognized in rock art at five other sites in Montana and Wyoming, either as freestanding plants or incorporated into a horizontal headdress worn by women during Crow tobacco ceremonies (Loendorf 2016b:22–24). The encircled cross likely depicts the tobacco seed pod.

Two additional encircled crosses, or seed pods, are stacked next to the plant image at Comanche Creek. From these images a series of crosses moves to the viewer's left and then turns upwards (the wide space between the leftmost crosses is likely due to a precipitous wash eroding the image). Despite its name, Vertical Series images are not only found in vertical columns. They are sometimes arranged horizontally, and it is not unusual for them to change direction. The plus designs, at the far left of the panel, emphasize the tobacco theme, again connecting it with the Vertical Series art tradition.

Immediately below this group is one of the few animal figures at the site. This might represent a weasel skin or perhaps otter skin medicine bag of the sort that was common among Plains Indians (Figure 9). The figure has a linear body with a snout and ears, short pointed legs and a pointed rear that terminates in an obscure painted area that might represent a tail or it could be the opening of a medicine bag. A branching line attached to the back of the figure might represent a tie used to suspend the bag in ceremonies.

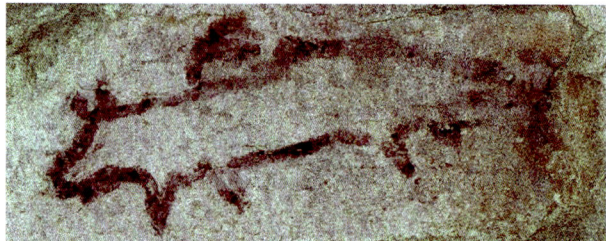

Figure 9. Possible weasel or otter skin medicine bag at Comanche Creek, DStretch YRE. Photograph by Jon Harman.

A second panel is found on the back wall of the rock shelter (Figure 10). It contains several dozen figures that are especially important because they are in layers of superimposition. The paintings which are found in an area about 3 m across are so faded on the west end that they cannot be studied in detail, even with DStretch. The eastern portion of the panel is in much better condition and it contains valuable information.

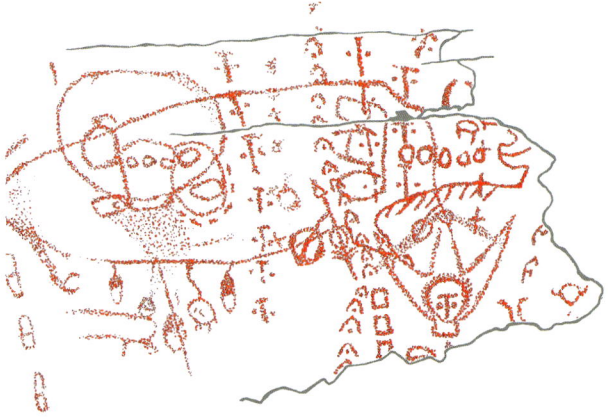

Figure 10. Panel 2, Locus 2, Comanche Creek.

Foothills Abstract

Based upon superimposition, the oldest image on the panel is a red bison that is 1.7 m from head to tail (see Harris Diagram, Figure 11). It is painted in outline form, with a long, hump-back body, a tail that bends back over the body, and two legs ending in cloven hoofs shown in plan view (Figure 12). The figure has horns, long neck hairs, head, and an open mouth with a protruding tongue. A large oval-shaped eye appears to be weeping. A series of circles and other shapes depict interior organs, including what appears to be its heart and lungs.

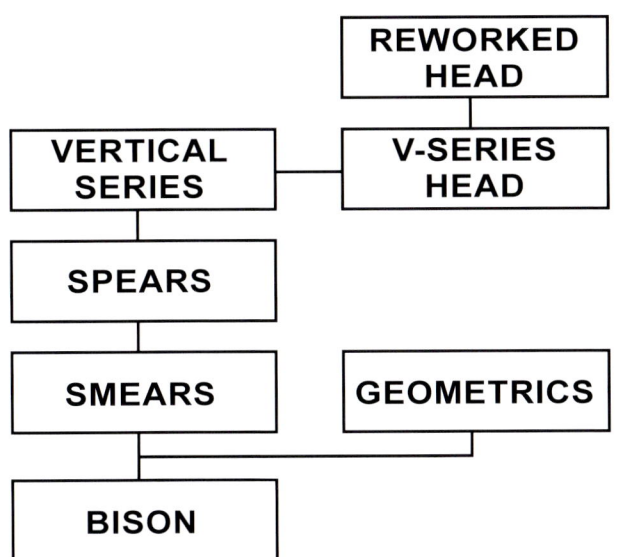

Figure 11. Harris Diagram showing superimpositions on Panel 2 at Comanche Creek.

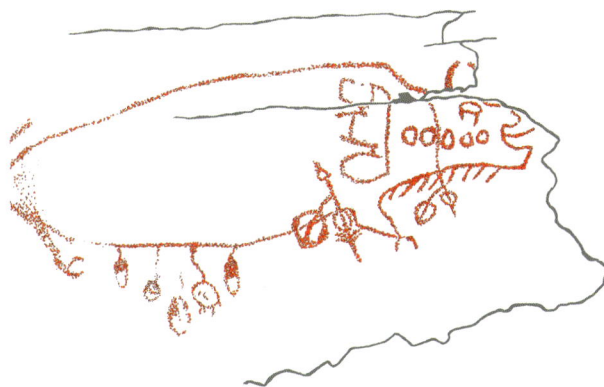

Figure 12. Foothills Abstract bison at Comanche Creek, 1.7 m from head to tail.

Two spears penetrate the body of the bison from its underside. One of these has a spear point and feathers, while the other has feathers but it ends without the point. An oval is attached by a line to the sides of these spears. One wonders if they are a convention for the atlatl that was used with the spear or dart. These spears appear to have been added in separate episodes, as the pigment and level of detail varies considerably. There are also pendant feathers and perhaps other objects hanging from the bison's belly.

A series of connected circles and circles inside circles interact with the bison figure. These shapes may represent additional abstracted internal organs of the bison, as seen in other Foothills abstract figures, but some of the circles protrude outside of the bison image and were likely added at a different time and are not part of the larger image. Red paint smears are also found on the rock surface at several places around the bison figure. These likely were painted around the same time as the bison.

The bison, the abstract circle forms, and the red smears represent Foothills Abstract rock art that is found across central Montana (Greer 1995; Keyser and Klassen 2001; Keyser et al. 2012). Outline bison are not common Foothills Abstract figures but large bears, made in much the same manner with interior details that appear to include organs, are found at several Foothills Abstract sites (Greer 1995:109; Keyser 1977, 2004:53; Keyser and Klassen 2001:157). The bison at Comanche Creek adds to the repertoire of Foothills Abstract large outline animals.

Foothills Abstract sites often contain numerous positive handprints that are stamped on the animal figures. The fact that they are not found at Comanche Creek is unusual and especially so because in their place there are vertical series figures superimposed on the large bison.

Vertical Series Figures

Nine columns of Vertical Series occur on Panel 2 (Figure 13), superimposing the Foothills Abstract bison. These nine Vertical Series columns occur in various lengths, many of which have been truncated by erosion. Shorter columns include squares, bisected elongate ovals, and curved F-shapes with the arms terminating in serifs. An arc or inverted V over a single dot forms the longest column at the site. Repeated 17 times, this column snakes between existing images on the panel. Two columns of plus signs or crosses occur, as well as three columns of a T-shape flanked with two dots and with an angled top.

In addition to the columns of T-shapes flanked by dots, the motif occurs separately elsewhere on the panel,

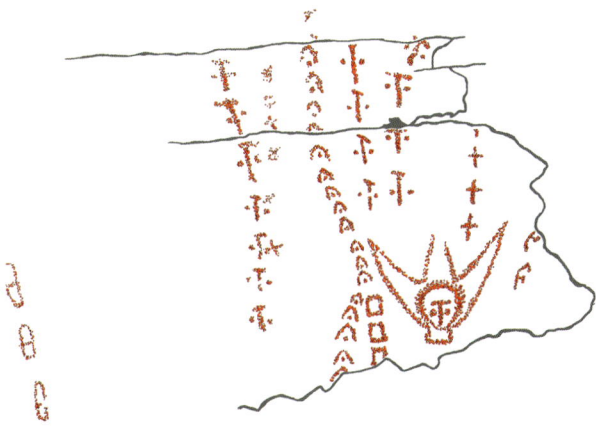

Figure 13. The Nine columns of Vertical Series which occur on Panel 2, Locus 2, at Comanche Creek.

converted into a human face: the dots forming eyes and the T forming a brow and nose. An oval head encircles this image replete with a head of hair (Figure 14). The outline of this image was formed in two different episodes, or partially refreshed, based on varying pigment colors and fading. This is not the only human image associated with Vertical Series (Keyser et al. 2012:214, Sundstrom 1987), others being identified at Atherton Canyon, Robison Rockshelter also in Montana, Tensleep Alcove in Wyoming, and Okotoks Erratic in Alberta, but this is the only such figure that appears to incorporate one of the repeated geometric shapes.

A third location at Comanche Creek exhibits two anthropomorphs, which are not just face-like forms and have no vertical series associated with them.

Figure 14. Vertical Series image converted into a human face at Comanche Creek. Note the differing color of pigments indicating the repainting of the image. DStretch LRE.

Establishing an Age for the Comanche Creek Rock Art

Foothills Abstract rock art has been dated using several methods. An important one of these was by Mavis Greer (1995) who used examples of superimposed painted figures that were executed in assorted colors and application techniques to establish a relative chronology. After establishing the paint types and colors, Greer used a seriation to suggest the oldest orange liquid and medium light red liquid paints may date to the Middle Archaic or more than 2000 years before the present. She was confident that Foothills Abstract figures, at the very least, dated to the Late Archaic or 1500 years of age.

Radiocarbon dates for Foothills Abstract figures were obtained at sites near Helena, Montana, and at a site near Hyatteville, Wyoming. At the Helena sites, dates of 1225± 50 B.P. and 1280± 50 B.P. were assigned to two red painted walls or red paint smears (Scott et al 2005:67). These dates, as well as one for a stick-like anthropomorph of 1170±45 B.P., were established by ^{14}C dating through the Rowe Plasma Oxidation Method (see Rowe 2001 for an overview of the method). In addition, an oxalate date of 1440±45 B. P. was obtained for the mineral accretion covering a red paint smear (Scott et al. 2005:67).

A vertical line with crossing horizontal lines, painted in red, was dated at 800 ±55 B.P. at the Medicine Lodge Creek site in northcentral Wyoming (Loendorf et al. in press). This date suggests a range of 600 to 700 years for Foothill Abstract rock paintings or an age between A.D. 500 and A.D. 1200. It seems reasonable to suggest the Comanche Creek Foothills Abstract figures date circa 1000 years before the present.

As noted above, there is debate regarding the age of Vertical Series rock art with suggested dates in the Archaic (Greer and Greer 2003; Keyser et al. 2012) and the Protohistoric to Historic periods (Sundstrom 2004). The Comanche Creek Vertical Series are superimposed on the Foothills Abstract figures so they are more recent than 1000 years of age. It seems likely that the Comanche Creek figures are associated with Crow tobacco ceremonialism and if so they date to the past 500 years or an age that is more in line with Sundstrom's assessment for Vertical Series in the Black Hills of South Dakota. It should be noted that in the Greer's seriation, used for the Vertical Series age estimates, the Comanche Creek site was identified as the most recent (Greer and Greer 2003:9).

Reflections

Comanche Creek is an important addition to the suite of sites where vertical series figures are associated with tobacco images. The Tensleep Alcove site is another site with vertical series associated with tobacco rock art, but other sites will likely be discovered with the same association. One candidate is the Okotoks Erratic in the foothills southwest of Calgary, Alberta, where a possible image of a tobacco plant appears to top a vertical series (Keyser and Klassen 2001:283).

The Robison Rockshelter site, to the west of Comanche Creek in Gallatin County, Montana, is also a site where Vertical Series figures, similar to those at Comanche Creek have been found. Tobacco plants are not identified at the site, but it has not been studied with DStretch. With the findings at Comanche Creek, not known before the present study, it seems possible that tobacco figures will be found at Robison Rockshelter. Other Vertical Series sites will also need to be studied to learn if they might also have heretofore unrecognized tobacco related figures.

At present the Crow Indian association between vertical series images with tobacco plant figures is the most apparent. The Crow association is recognized in the images they created on their Tobacco society regalia. It also occurred as face paint on women participating in Tobacco society ceremonies. Lowie describes their cheeks painted with designs consisting of "a stem with two pairs of branches symmetrically arranged, forming the beginning of a herringbone pattern" (1919:144). He was told that these designs represented tobacco, as seen in the vision of someone who slept near the tobacco garden (Lowie 1919:149). Other tribes may have had similar tobacco imagery that has not been recognized. It also seems likely that more artifacts will be found that indicate vertically arranged designs are found among other tribes.

The cross is the most commonly duplicated symbol in Vertical Series rock art (Sundstrom 1987). This may reflect the association of the cross design with stars, stars with tobacco, and the cross pattern on the seed pod of Nicotiana multivalis, the Crow sacred tobacco, but a tobacco also used by other Plains tribes. To the Crow the cross design is often associated with the Morning Star. As part of the Crow tobacco society ritual, Grey Bull described, "Tobacco seeds on which the figure of a star—taken to be the morningstar—is visible" (Lowie 1919:151). It was the stars that gave tobacco to the Crow and taught them the proper rituals for its cultivation and use. Thus, "Tobacco is universally identified with the stars" (Lowie 1919:177).

Vertical Series rock art is complicated. It was made as early as the Archaic Period through the Protohistoric, and possibly into the Historic Period on the northern Plains. It was made at sites across a wide area from the Black Hills of South Dakota to western Montana and southern Alberta. This distribution in time and space indicates it was made by multiple cultural groups.

The often abstract figures are purposeful and they were meaningful to those who made them. Their meaning was shared across generations of individuals with diverse backgrounds. It seems possible that tobacco symbolism, perhaps shared by those with the right to know, may be an explanation for some Vertical Series rock art.

Note

1. Also referred to as Bighorn Site 2 (Sundstrom 1987), Powwow Cavern, the amphitheater, or the Alcove (Francis and Loendorf 2002)

References Cited

Carmichael, Patrick
    1982 Unusual Artifact from the Northern Plains Periphery, *Plains Anthropologist* 27(98):327–328.

Conner, Stuart, and Betty Lu Conner
    1971 *Rock Art of the Montana High Plains*. The Art Galleries, University of California, Santa Barbara.

Francis, Julie, and Lawrence Loendorf
    2002 *Ancient Visions: Petroglyphs and Pictographs of the Wind River and Bighorn Country, Wyoming and Montana*. University of Utah Press, Salt Lake City.

Greer, Mavis
    1995 *Archaeological Analysis of Rock Art Sites in the Smith River Drainage of Central Montana*. Ph.D. dissertation, Department of Anthropology, University of Missouri, Columbia.

Greer, Mavis, and John Greer
    2003 Seriation and Vertical Series Rock Art. Paper presented at the 68th Annual Meeting of the Society for American Archaeology, Milwaukee, Wisconsin.

Keyser, James D.
    1977 Audrey's Overhang: A Pictographic Maze in Central Montana. *Plains Anthropologist* 22(77):183–187.

    2004 *Art of the Warriors: Rock Art of the American Plains*. University of Utah Press, Salt Lake City.

Keyser, James D, David A. Kaiser, George Poetschat, and Michael W. Taylor
    2012 *Fraternity of War*. Oregon Archaeological Society Press, Publication 21, Portland.

Keyser, James D., and Michael A. Klassen
    2001 *Plains Indian Rock Art*. University of Washington Press, Seattle.

Loendorf, Lawrence
    1994 Traditional Archaeological Methods and their Applications at Rock Art Sites. In *New Light on Old Art: Recent Advances in Hunter-Gatherer Rock Art Research*, edited by David Whitley and Lawrence Loendorf, pp. 95–103. University of California Press, Los Angeles.

    2015 *Tensleep Alcove Report*. Report submitted to the Tensleep Nature Conservancy. Sacred Sites Research, Albuquerque, New Mexico. Electronic copies on file with the Conservancy and Sacred Sites Research, Inc.

    2016a Vertical Series Rock Art and the Mehling Steatite Pipe. *Archaeology in Montana* 57(1):53–59.

    2016b *Frozen Leg Cave Montana 24BH425, Report*. Sacred Sites Research, Albuquerque, New Mexico. Electronic copy on file with Sacred Sites Research, Inc.

Loendorf, Lawrence L., and Audrey Porsche
    1985 *The Rock Art Sites in Carbon County, Montana*. Contribution No. 224. Department of Anthropology, University of North Dakota, Grand Forks.

Loendorf, Lawrence, Lukas Wacker, and Marvin W. Rowe
 2017 Radiocarbon Dating a Pictograph at Medicine Lodge Creek, Wyoming. *Plains Anthropologist* (online). Electronic document, https://www.tandfonline.com/doi/full/10.1080/00320447.2017.1394035, accessed March 15, 2018.

Lowie, Robert H.
 1919 *The Tobacco Society of the Crow Indians.* Anthropological Papers of the American Museum of Natural History 21(2).

Mack, Joanne
 1971 Archaeological Investigations in the Bighorn Basin, Wyoming. *Wyoming Archaeologist* 12(2–4):17–115.

Nabokov, Peter
 1988 *Cultivating Themselves: The Inter-play of Crow Indian Religion and History.* Ph.D. Dissertation, Department of Anthropology, University of California, Berkeley.

Rowe, Marvin
 2001 Dating by AMS Radiocarbon Analysis. In *Handbook of Rock Art Research*, edited by David S. Whitley, pp. 139–166. Altamira Press, Walnut Creek, California.

Scott, Sara, Carl Davis, Karen Steelman, Marvin Rowe, and Tom Guilderson
 2005 AMS Dates from Four Late Prehistoric Period Rock Art Sites in West Central Montana. *Plains Anthropologist* 50 (193):57–71.

Sundstrom, Linea
 1987 Vertical Series Rock Art and its Relationship to Protohistoric Plains Indian Symbolism. *Archaeology in Montana* 28(2):3–17.

 2004 *Storied Stone: Indian Rock Art of the Black Hills Country.* University of Oklahoma Press, Norman.

Another Look at the Rock Art of Southeastern New England

Peter Anick

This paper presents a recent survey of petroglyph sites in southeastern New England which lie along a water route from Narragansett Bay, on the southern coast of Rhode Island, to Assawompset Pond, the largest inland body of fresh water in Massachusetts. I review the known history of these sites, assess their current condition, and offer possible interpretations based on ethnographic and historic considerations.

New England's forested landscape, with its tough bedrock and rough glacial moraine, provides a poor canvas for the production of rock art. Nevertheless, small isolated petroglyph sites throughout the region confirm that rock art was produced in the northeast. In the centuries following the arrival of European settlers, interest in stone carvings waxed and waned. As early as 1680, Massachusetts scholars were debating the meaning of images found on a boulder in Taunton (Delabarre 1928). In the 1760s, the Reverend Ezra Stiles sought out and documented inscribed rocks, convinced that they were the work of Phoenician navigators (Dexter 1916). In the 19th century, Viking enthusiasts cited "rune-shaped" inscriptions to bolster their contention that Leif Eriksson had made landfall in New England (Rafn 1837). Brown University psychology professor Edmund Delabarre photographed all the sites he could locate around Narragansett Bay in the 1920s. Convinced he had found evidence of early Portuguese explorers among the engravings, he surmised that Indians had taken up carving in stone only after seeing Europeans do it (Delabarre 1919). In 2002, after several decades of tracking down sites, archaeologist Edward Lenik published the most comprehensive survey of rock art throughout the northeast (Lenik 2002). Drawing on archaeological evidence, Algonkian Indian ethnography and a growing body of American rock art research elsewhere, he concluded that most of these engravings, both prehistoric and historic, were best explained as the handiwork of Indian shamans.

Despite these occasional bursts of interest, New England's rock art remains relatively unknown and unprotected today, vulnerable to the destructive forces of nature, vandalism, and expanded land use. Although a long-time Massachusetts resident and rock art enthusiast myself, I was unaware of any local rock art until 2006 when I joined the New England Antiquities Research Association (NEARA), a volunteer organization studying New England's enigmatic lithic sites (www.neara.org). Like the handful of curious researchers before me, I began the process of tracking down leads, looking into ethnographic and historic records, visiting and recording sites, and speculating about their origin

Peter Anick
*Brandeis University
and
New England Antiquities
Research Association
(Massachusetts State Coordinator)*

and function. This paper will focus on a collection of petroglyph sites in southeastern New England that lie along a water route from Narragansett Bay, on the southern coast of Rhode Island, to Assawompset Pond, the largest inland body of fresh water in Massachusetts (Figure 1). For Native Americans, this was a major thoroughfare and a bountiful ecosystem from the end of the Ice Age through the European Contact period. As I attempted to track down petroglyphs described by previous researchers, I discovered that some had disappeared or suffered degradation since they were last documented. In some cases, repeated visits to a site under varying lighting conditions revealed additional context not previously reported. And on occasion, a new find turned up, augmenting the relatively meager local inventory. This paper presents a summary of my findings and impressions. It is intended to (1) provide an introduction to sites in the region, with pointers to previous research; (2) report on the current state of the sites, wherever possible comparing their current states with former conditions; and (3) explore plausible interpretations and dates based on historic, ethnographic, and geological considerations.

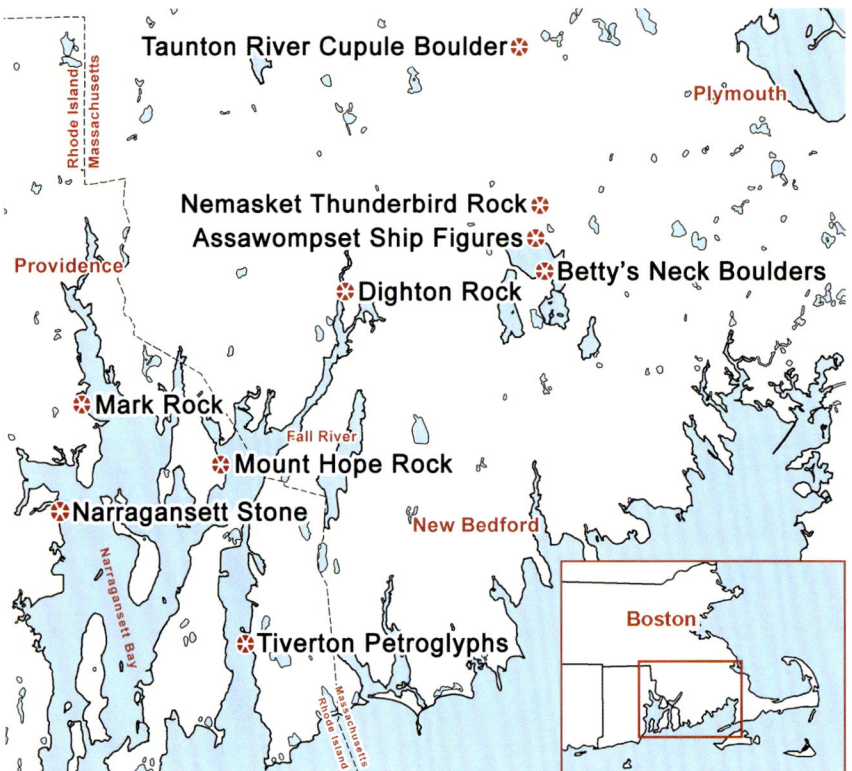

Figure 1. Map showing the approximate locations of petroglyph sites described in this paper in eastern Rhode Island and southeastern Massachusetts.

Dating and Interpretation of New England Rock Art

Before launching into our survey of sites, a few comments regarding dating and interpretation of petroglyphs in the northeast are in order. Archaeologists divide Native American prehistory into three broad periods based on changes in tool technology (Lenik 2002). The *PaleoIndians* (ca. 12,500–10,000 B.P.) were nomadic hunter gatherers who moved into the area after glaciers receded at the end of the last Ice Age. As the climate warmed and open grassland was replaced by forest, the *Archaic* period (ca. 10,000–3,000 B.P.) saw the development of more diverse lifestyles, along with larger settlements and more elaborate ceremonialism. The *Woodland* period (ca. 3,000–400 B.P.) was characterized by the adoption of horticulture and ceramics. The arrival of Europeans ushered in the *Historic Contact* period (ca. A.D. 1500–1800).

Because rock art is usually found above ground rather than within a definitive archaeological context, it is notoriously difficult to date. Evidence of metal tool use or depictions of European artifacts (e.g., clothing, ships, or houses) can help identify a carving as Post-Contact. For earlier imagery, comparing rock art figures with designs on portable art found within known archaeological contexts can be suggestive. If a site is located along a coast, it is sometimes possible to bracket a petroglyph's age based on sea level change over time. As glaciers receded, ground which had been compressed below the weight of the ice sheet underwent "isostatic rebound", increasing in altitude. At the same time, the melting ice caused sea level rise. Depending on the rate of these two competing processes, the coastline fluctuated over time, either exposing fresh stone or covering it.

At some Scandinavian petroglyph sites, such as Alta in northern Norway, stylistic differences have been observed that correlate with the images' height above the current shoreline (Tansem 2014). This suggests that rock art was created close to the shoreline where the sea spray suppressed vegetation and lichen growth, exposing new smooth surfaces for carving. As the land rose higher due to isostatic rebound (which outpaced sea level rise in Norway), vegetation spread over the former coastal carvings while newly exposed shoreline became available as a fresh canvas. Mark Hedden (2004) applied a similar logic to dating rock art sites in Machias Bay, Maine. There, unlike in Norway, sea level rise has exceeded the rate of isostatic rebound for millennia. As the seas rise, wave action removes the thick glacial till overlying the coastal bedrock, while the tide differential (up to fourteen feet) keeps a wide swath of shoreline free of vegetation. Hedden observed that freshly exposed bedrock is more suitable for carving, since the rock becomes more brittle with longer exposure. Using height above sea level along with other evidence, he has been able to establish a chronology of styles of anthropomorphs, which he interprets as illustrating an evolution of shamanic practices from 3,000 years ago into the Post-Contact period.

In southern New England, post-glacial isostatic rebound resulted in some thirty meters of land rise between 16,000 and 10,000 years ago (Oakley and Boothroyd 2012). After that time, the shoreline was determined primarily by sea level rise. Between 10,000 and 5,000 years ago, waters rose sharply by about 25 meters. The last 5,000 years contributed an additional rise of about 4 meters, with the rate slowing over time. Assuming that land even a short distance from the shore would soon be covered in vegetation, the extent of exposed rock available for coastal rock art for much of the Holocene would have been a relatively narrow strip along the ever-rising intertidal zone. Merwin et al. (2003) note that all the known rock art sites along Narragansett Bay are currently within the intertidal zone. They reason that the choice of the interface of land, sea, and sky may have been culturally intentional, not simply a matter of availability of carvable stone. Therefore, they date coastal sites to the Historic or Proto-Historic (Late Woodland) periods and speculate that underwater archaeology along shorelines might yield earlier examples of rock art. However, a storm surge could certainly expose rock above the intertidal zone, which widens the window of possible dates for New England's coastal rock art sites.

As with dating, the interpretation of rock art in the absence of direct ethnographic knowledge is problematic and, at best, a matter of informed speculation. At the time of European contact, most New England tribes spoke a dialect of the Algonkian language family, also widely spoken in Canada and around the Great Lakes. Algonkian ethnography, as recorded from the Great Lakes to Maine, reveals a world view which places great value on knowledge obtained from dreaming and visions (Lenik 2009). Spiritual beings known as *manitous* were thought to inhabit special places in the landscape. Individuals who could communicate with these beings could derive power and medicine from them. Among the Contact period Ojibway, medicine men (shamans) often memorialized their encounters with spirit beings using pictures drawn on birch bark scrolls. Grace Rajnovich (1994) argued that red ochre pictographs found painted on cliff walls along lakes and rivers throughout the Canadian Shield could be deciphered in a similar way. Shamans had the ability to take on the forms of the animal and human-like *manitous* which they encountered while in trance. Thus, the zoomorphic and anthropomorphic beings painted on the rock walls may have portrayed both the spirits who dwelt there and the transformed shamans themselves. We will consider southeastern New England petroglyphs in a similar light.

Mark Rock

We begin our survey at Mark Rock, which lies on the shore of Warwick, Rhode Island, below the mouth of the Providence River in the northwest corner of Narragansett Bay. Ironically, while the Reverend Ezra Stiles is known to have visited the Greene family who owned the property in the late 1700s, he was apparently unaware of the inscriptions nearby (Delabarre 1928:240). Thomas H. Webb, Secretary of the Rhode Island Historical Society, inspected the site in the 1830s but dismissed it as containing only modern graffiti. A century later, Edmund Delabarre recognized Indian carvings among the European names and dates. He described the site as an outcropping of fine grained sandstone ("graywacke") composed of a number of fractured sections with smoothly worn surfaces. A photograph (Figure 2) shows it lying mostly within the intertidal zone, stretching some seventy-five feet along the water's edge, and some fifty feet up a slight incline to a ledge crowned by houses and vegetation. Delabarre identified fourteen pecked figures he felt could be Native American in origin, including several geometric designs and oddly shaped anthropomorphs (Figure 3). His diagram of the site (Figure 4) shows that the carvings were dispersed throughout the site, with each of his four anthropomorphs appearing on a different rock surface. He believed that these images were the product of 17th century Indians who were inspired to carve on stone after having observed the European settlers doing it. As to their meaning, he interpreted some as Post-Contact Indian "signatures." He

Figure 2. Photograph of Mark Rock ledge as it appeared in 1928 (Delabarre 1928:Figure 69).

Figure 3. Delabarre's sketches of four anthropomorphs carved into different slabs, in areas labeled b, f2, i, and j (Delabarre 1928:Figure 84).

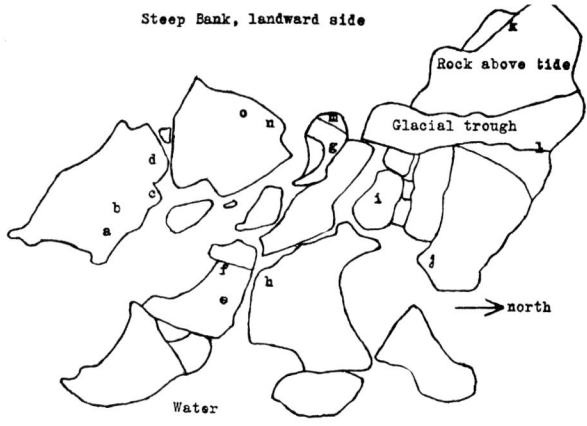

Figure 4. Delabarre's diagram of Mark Rock panels with alphabetically labeled image locations (Delabarre 1928:Figure 70).

felt, for example, that a simple boat-like image and a bow and arrow matched Indian signatures found on 17th century deeds. But, noting that the other figures were "scattered, individual, unrelated, like the modern initials," he dismissed their significance. "There is no story told," he wrote, "no historical event indicated, no information conveyed." (Delabarre 1928:253–254)

In 1978, Ed Lenik visited the site and interested a Warwick resident, Charles Devine, in continuing the search for any surviving glyphs. Devine felt that some 60 percent of the ledge was by then buried in sand, perhaps as a result of major hurricanes in 1938 and 1954 (Lenik 2002). But he managed to locate and photograph two of Delabarre's anthropomorphs (Figures 5, 6), several geometric designs (Figures 6, 7), and one further anthropomorph that Delabarre appeared to have missed (Figure 8).

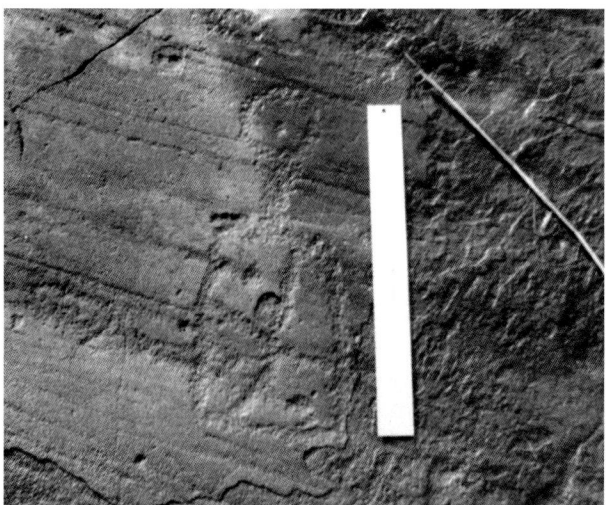

Figure 5. Charles Devine's 1979 photo of Delabarre's anthropomorph in area j, with one-foot rule alongside.

Figure 6. Charles Devine's 1979 photograph of anthropomorph and geometric design in Delabarre's area i, both chalked, with one-foot rule alongside.

When I visited the same spot thirty years later in 2008, I was dismayed to find that sand and sea grass had enveloped most of the ledge pictured in Delabarre's photo. Only a few graywacke slabs remained exposed on the beach (Figure 9). A comparison of the images to of the complete figure (Figure 5), the outline consists of a series of densely pecked dints. I could also barely discern the anthropomorph shown chalked in Devine's photo in Figure 8 (shown unchalked in Figure 10). Although marred by substantial spalling of the rock's thin crust, the outline, composed of many tiny indentations, appears to depict a head or mask with two feathers or horns, a triangular neck and two arms bent upwards at the elbows, consistent with the interpretation rendered in Devine's chalked photo. Some natural pitting on the boulder adds to the obfuscation of the figure.

On a second slab just up the slope to the west, above the intertidal zone and surrounded by vegetation, I located part of a floral design previously recorded by both Delabarre (Figure 11a) and Devine (Figure 11b). In 2008, two of its deeply pecked petals were still clearly visible but the remainder of the stone containing the image had severely deteriorated (Figure 11c). Comparing my photo to Delabarre's 1928 and Devine's 1978 photos reveals the progression of deterioration. Delabarre's image (Figure 11a), chalked for better visibility, shows an intact "flower" with a pitted, possibly drilled, center and five broad petals, each containing a large pecked dot. In Devine's photo (Figure 11b), unchalked,

Figure 7. Charles Devine's 1979 photograph of two zig-zag lines, with one-foot rule alongside.

Figure 8. Charles Devine's 1979 photo of a chalked anthropomorph not mentioned in Delabarre (1928), with one-foot rule alongside. Note the deeply carved initials above.

Figure 9. Exposed rock surfaces at Mark Rock site in 2008. Photo by Peter Anick.

visible on these slabs with those labeled in Delabarre's diagram revealed that the surviving outcrops were remnants of the very northwestern section of the original ledge. Brushing away some sand at the edge of one boulder, I was able to locate the top of the anthropomorph in Delabarre's area j. As shown in Devine's pho-

Figure 10. Unchalked close-up of Charles Devine's anthropomorph, showing lines made up of many small dints. Photo by Peter Anick, 2008.

original center of the image, which had begun spalling. Given the rapid decay of this exposed image, the burial of most of the other boulders over the past century may actually have served to preserve them better than continued exposure, although root action by the vegetation now growing over them may also pose a threat. In 2017, I returned to the site. Sand and vegetation had further covered the few remaining boulders and some previously identified images were harder or impossible to find. Sand continually washing over the boulders in the tidal zone was abrading the already faint engravings. More spalling was apparent as well.

Concerned about the rate of disappearance of the site, I contacted Charles Devine to learn how he had managed to take photographs of many images which I could no longer locate at all. To my surprise, he told me he had used Delabarre's map to dig nearly a foot down through mud and vegetation in order to expose carvings which had been buried, he believed, since the earlier hurricanes. Figure 12 shows the depth of carvings in Delabarre's Area f before high tide returned to

Figure 11. (a) Chalked floral motif on Mark Rock, as photographed by Delabarre (1928:Figure 86, image rotated to match orientation of later photos). (b) Unchalked floral motif, photographed by Charles Devine in 1979, showing the presence of a large fissure running through the lower petal. (c) Photograph taken in 2008 showing further damage to the boulder containing the floral motif. The entire bottom of the slab has broken off and disappeared. A new fracture now runs through the center of the design. Photo by Peter Anick.

the outline remains clear but a large natural fissure has appeared, probably due to freezing/thawing of water in a fine crack over the intervening half century. By 2008, the entire lower section of the boulder had gone missing, a victim of either natural processes or the opportunistic prying of a vandal. The disappearance of the fractured section had further weakened the remaining stone such that a new crack now ran through the

Figure 12. Charles Devine's 1979 photo of chalked carvings in Delabarre's area f, now located more than a foot below the current ground level. Note the ripples in the Bay water at the top of the photo.

refill the hole with sand (Devine 1981). He had found that, even though spalling of the thin crust had nearly eradicated some images, the camera was able to pick up traces of pecked lines that were barely visible to the naked eye. Devine was unable to excavate all the figures documented by Delabarre, but his photos increase our confidence in the accuracy of both Delabarre's map and his hand-drawn renditions.

Delabarre's dating and interpretations, however, can be called into question. To be sure, the many names, dates, and initials carved into the rocks demonstrate the use of Mark Rock well into historic times. There is even a large pecked profile of a man's head in a hat smoking a pipe (Figure 13). Looking very much like a comic caricature, it is accompanied by the initials "R F P." The "flower" motif, located above the high tide mark, is also likely a Post-Contact petroglyph, albeit older and probably Indian. Prior to European contact, Indians used stiff porcupine quills in their sewn decorations on clothing and therefore favored straight, geometric designs. But once the French taught the Indians how to embroider using silk thread and beadwork, naturalistic curved designs such as floral representations became very popular (American Indian Publishers 1981:545–548). Figure 14 shows many examples of late 19th century floral designs on clothing.

As for the anthropomorphic carvings, Delabarre speculated that the crossed lines on the torsos of his figures in Areas j and f2 represented the uniforms of Colonial soldiers. However, the lines could also be interpreted as sashes worn by a chief or shaman. Sashes and belts (e.g., wampum) were known to have been used in civil and religious ceremonies, a practice that contin-

Figure 13. Head, neck, and shoulders of pipe smoking caricature on Mark Rock, with the initials "R F P" to the right. Photo by Peter Anick, 2008.

Figure 14. One-Called-From-A-Distance (Midwewinind), a Chippewa from White Earth Reservation, Minnesota, 1894, wearing sash and floral designs. (National Archive, American Indian Select List number 14.)

ued into historic times. Early photos of Ojibway often showed them wearing one or more sashes (as in Figure 14). Tales of the legendary warrior hero Glooscap describe him receiving power from a magic belt (Leland 1884). Other features of Delabarre's anthropomorphs may also reflect shamanistic practice. The missing arms and/or legs and the "one-eyed" and zoomorphic faces could be intended to signal a trance state in which the shaman was transformed into a spirit being. The raised arms of Delabarre's figures in Areas f2 and i (Figure 3) may indicate the giving or receiving of medicine, similar to the "arms up" motif depicted on Ojibway song scrolls (Rajnovich 1994:75).

Lenik's dating of the figures deviates from Delabarre's Post-Contact assessment, instead ascribing many of them to the pre-contact Woodland period (Lenik 2002). Given the rate of sea level rise, the lower portions of the ledge could have been stripped of glacial till and vegetation by storm action as early as 3,000 years ago. The pecking styles used to produce the various petroglyphs on Mark Rock also fit a rough chronology. Of the two anthropomorphs that I was able to photograph in 2008, the outlines consist of many small, shallow dints, as if produced by direct percussion with a stone tool. These images appear very worn and are extremely difficult to see. Sections have gone missing due to spalling of the thin crust. In contrast, the flower design is pecked using much deeper and broader overlapping dints, resulting in a bolder and more readily detectable outline. Located on higher ground, this boulder may have been exposed later as sea level continued to rise. There is less spalling of the crust at this level, although degradation due to splitting along deep fissures is progressing rapidly. Finally, the pipe-smoking caricature, not likely of Native American origin, is produced with longer and, in some places, more widely spaced dints, as if made by indirect percussion with a metal chisel-like tool. The many initials and dates are also either very deeply pecked or abraded with a metal tool.

Tiverton Petroglyphs

In 1768, Ezra Stiles made detailed drawings of anthropomorphic petroglyphs he found on two graywacke boulders located at the water's edge in Tiverton, Rhode Island, on the east side of Narragansett Bay (Delabarre 1928). Both of these boulders were documented again by Rhode Island antiquarians Thomas H. Webb and John R. Bartlett in 1835 (Delabarre 1928). When Delabarre went searching for them in the 1920s, he could locate only one of them (Delabarre 1928). Lenik also reported finding only one when he visited in 1978 (Lenik 2002). Thirty years later, when I scoured the beach at low tide, taking advantage of the low morning sun to cast shadows in even the most shallow of grooves, I spotted the missing slab. It was jutting out of the intertidal zone in a cluster of boulders, partially covered in gravel, its smooth flat top sloping up slightly towards the water. It is possible that previous searchers had passed by when the sun was too high or when gravel concealed the stone, although I learned later that archaeologist Daniel Lynch had also rediscovered the boulder a few years earlier (Lynch 2005). The second of the two stones recorded by Stiles was in the same cluster of boulders, located slightly further into the bay. I had arrived close to low tide and at that point its base was gently lapped by water. A photo by Lenik from 1978 shows it resting in a completely dry gravel bed (Lenik 2002:148).

Following Delabarre's numbering scheme, I will refer to these boulders as "Stiles 1" and "Stiles 2." Stiles's 1768 drawings are reproduced in Figures 15 and 16, while the Webb and Bartlett drawings are shown in Figure 17. Figure 18 shows the relative locations of the

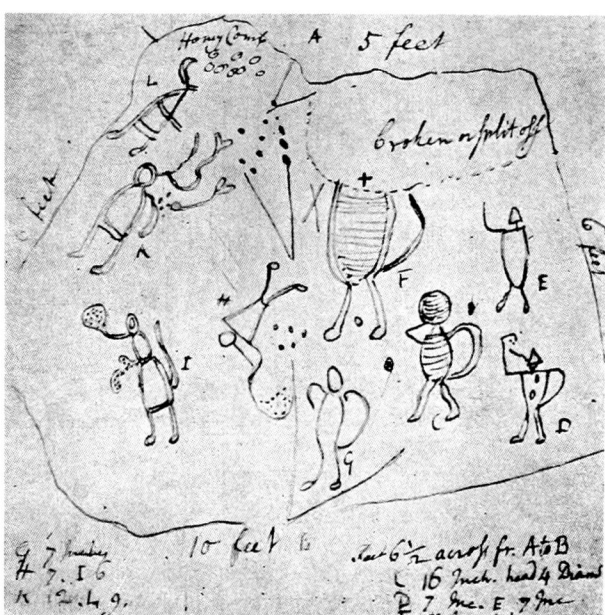

Figure 15. Ezra Stiles' 1768 drawing of the first of two carved boulders at Tiverton, Rhode Island (Delabarre 1928:Figure 62).

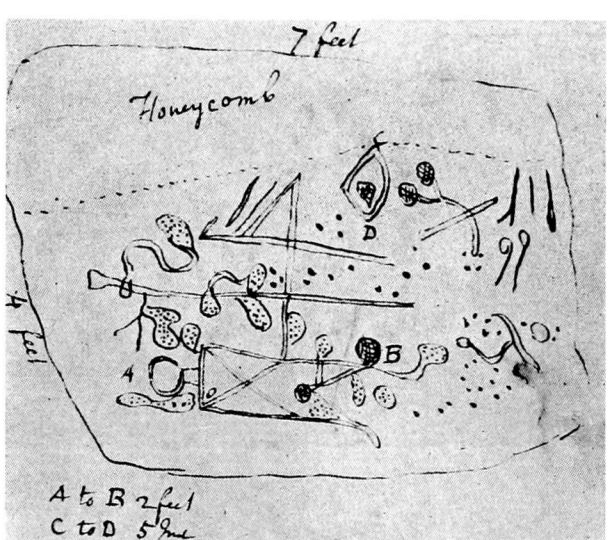

Figure 16. Ezra Stiles' 1768 drawing of the second of two carved boulders at Tiverton, Rhode Island (Delabarre 1928:Figure 63).

two boulders. At high tide, the water level may rise two to four feet higher, enough to submerge the images on both stones. The surface of the Stiles 2 boulder (in the foreground) is much rougher, partially honeycombed. Its pecked images are carved deeper and thicker. The images on Stiles 1 are smaller, more elegantly executed, and worn smooth, likely due to years of abrasion by salt water and gravel.

Comparing my 2008 photo of the Stiles 1 boulder (Figure 19) to Stiles' drawing, it is straightforward to match up the four figures with triangular torsos. The

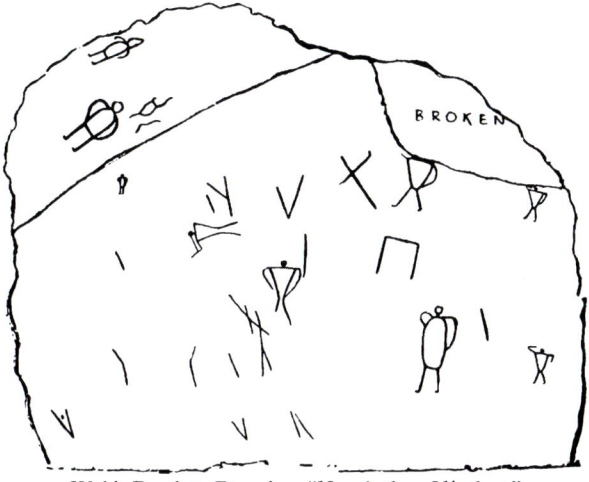

Webb-Bartlett Drawing "No. 4. 6 x 8½ feet."

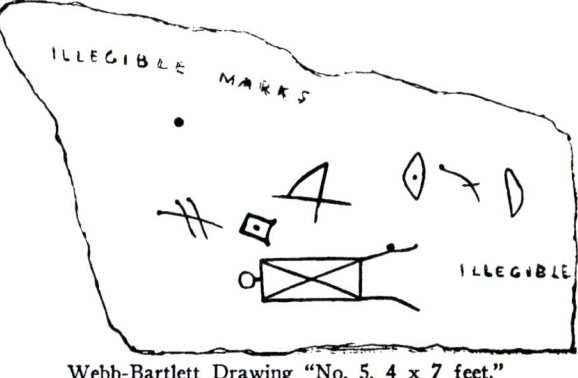

Webb-Bartlett Drawing "No. 5. 4 x 7 feet."

Figure 17. Webb and Bartlett's 1835 drawings of the two Tiverton petroglyph boulders (Delabarre 1928:Figure 230.)

Figure 18. 2008 photo showing Tiverton, Rhode Island, petroglyph boulders. "Stiles 2" is in the foreground. "Stiles 1" is the smooth, flat slab on the shore. Photo by Peter Anick.

Figure 19. Tiverton "Stiles 1" petroglyph boulder in 2008. Photo by Peter Anick.

upper left portion of the boulder has broken off since Stiles visited the site, leaving behind only a pair of legs where Stiles had indicated two full figures once existed. Stiles' drawing includes three additional figures on the foreground panel which are not apparent in my photo. While they may have been partially obscured by gravel covering the bottom of the slab, my impression at the time was that Stiles may have interpreted natural grooves and pockmarks as elements of the engraving. The Webb-Bartlett drawing also excludes one of Stiles' figures.

While scratching my head over these contradictory impressions, I discovered a set of photographs in the New England Antiquities Research Association (NEARA) Archives taken by Malcolm Pearson in 1942. A professional photographer and amateur antiquarian, Pearson is best known for his photographs of stone ruins at Mystery Hill in New Hampshire and Upton Chamber in Massachusetts (Goodwin 1946). His Tiverton photos include close-ups, both chalked and unchalked, of several of the figures. Chalking (now discouraged as harmful to petroglyphs) allows the accentuation of features that don't show well in photographs, but it also conceals details and can make it difficult for later reviewers to make an independent assessment of the images. At the time Pearson took his photos, much more of the boulder was exposed than when I visited in 2008. The upper left section, containing two large figures when Stiles first recorded it, had not yet fractured off! Several of his photos appear to have been taken after further removal of up to a foot of gravel around the base of the stone, no doubt to check for more engravings (Figure 20). No further carvings were evident. In fact, considered together, the figures appear to form a ring around the upper portion of the boulder, suggesting that this upper section was the full extent of the exposed surface when the carving was done. Poses and stylistic similarities shared among some of the figures raise the possibility that they were intended to portray

Figure 20. Malcolm Pearson's 1942 photo of the Tiverton "Stiles 1" boulder after excavating around the base and chalking the figures. Photo courtesy of NEARA Archives.

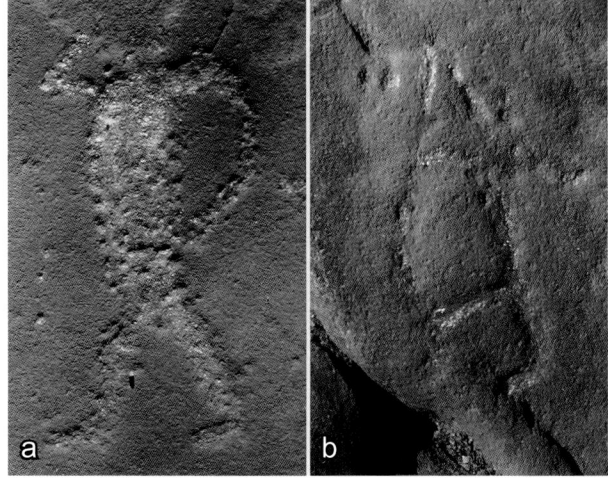

Figure 21. (a) Malcolm Pearson's 1942 close-up of the fully pecked figure on "Stiles 1" Tiverton boulder, bottom row, second from the right. The head area has spalled off and was not included in his photo. (b) Malcolm Pearson's 1942 close-up of the outlined figure on "Stiles 1" Tiverton boulder, upper left corner. Photos courtesy of NEARA Archives.

a single scene. Feet pointing consistently to the left imply motion in that direction. One of the nine figures, in the center of the lower line, is upside down relative to the tilt of the stone and to all the other figures. Assuming that the lower line of figures ringed the bottom of the exposed stone at the time of carving, the single upside-down figure is suggestive of a scene commemorating the death of an important person. Or, to give it a shamanic reading, the configuration could portray a shaman descending into the earth (or into the sea at high tide) while surrounded by dancers, some raising their right arms, not unlike the motion made by Delabarre's figure i on Mark Rock (Figure 3). Vastokas and Vastokas (1973:70-71) cite ethnographic descriptions of Ojibwa shamans' birch bark records to assert that rock art depictions of raised hands, such as those found at the Peterborough Petroglyph Site in Ontario, denote "gestures of reverence, supplication, or communication with the sky, and more specifically to the Great Spirit, Kitchi-Manitou."

Stylistic differences among some of the figures appear to weaken the case for a single-scene interpretation. Two of the figures on the right have fully pecked bodies (e.g., Figure 21a), while two on the far left have large rotund outlines and unusually shaped, hood-like "heads" (e.g., Figure 21b). The remaining five figures with triangular torsos are slightly smaller and more elegantly pecked and abraded. Treating these distinctions as significant, the ensemble could be seen as four *pairs* of figures surrounding the central upside-down figure. The two (vertically associated) pairs on the right side of the boulder appear to have one arm raised and one akimbo, while the two triangular figures on either side of the upside-down figure have both arms akimbo and share similar, leftward tilting orientations. While some features of the two figures on the upper left section are now missing, the Webb-Bartlett diagram (Figure 17) shows them both oriented in the same direction, with their arms aimed down.

Pearson's chalked photo (Figure 20) helps to visualize the arrangement in terms of paired figures. These differences may reflect temporally distinct carving episodes by different "artists." However, they could also have been intended to represent persons of different status or participants playing different roles within a single activity. Several similar figures can be found some three hundred miles to the north on a narrow ledge of shale projecting into the Kennebec River in Embden, Maine. Among dozens of pecked designs are three anthropomorphs with hollow triangular torsos, portrayed with one arm bent down and the other bent up at the elbow (Lenik 2002:Figures 36–38). Hedden (1996) identifies these figures as belonging to "Style 6" in his chronological classification, dating them to the Late Woodland/Early Contact period. He writes, "Style 6 anthropomorphs representing entities with spiritual potency are distinguished by triangular torsos, either outlined or solidly dinted, with angular corners… These angular figures are frequently represented in active postures with unidirectional linear feet and/or legs bent at the knee to suggest running"(Hedden 1996:17). He further observes that "a number of anthropomorphs associated with Style 6 figures lack the triangular torso, a distinction that may indicate supplicants or participants in shamanistic performances who have not yet gained spiritual power" (Hedden 1996:18).

In my 2008 photos, the upside-down figure (Figure 22) appears to be without arms and with a long, extended head, suggestive of a mask. However, Pearson's 1942 photo, while partially chalked, reveals details that have since eroded (Figure 23). In his image, we can see what appears to be an upraised arm bent at the elbow

Figure 22. 2008 close-up of the upside-down figure (photo inverted). Photo by Peter Anick.

Figure 23. Malcolm Pearson's 1942 lightly chalked image of upside-down figure, showing more detail. Photo courtesy of NEARA Archives.

holding a long thin object that might be a pipe. This conforms with the line drawings made by Stiles (Figure 15) and Webb-Bartlett (Figure 17). For most North American Indians, the pipe is considered a sacred possession with living power (Rajnovich 1994:122).

The second boulder ("Stiles 2") also shows signs of erosion, presenting a number of ambiguities between natural and artificial features (Figure 24). Stylistically distinct from its neighbor, it is dominated by a single deeply pecked rectangular anthropomorph with interior crossed lines. Both Stiles and Webb-Bartlett saw a long neck and circular head emanating from the torso. However, these are not very deep and may be natural features of the rock. Lenik interpreted a deeper cupule within the purported "neck" as the figure's head (Lenik 2002:148). Several other deeply cut angular lines also stand out in the oblique sunlight, along with a shallower diamond shaped outline with a central inscribed dot. Another large cupule, possibly a natural pit which has been manually enhanced, can be seen to the right, along with a straight groove. A photo taken by Malcolm Pearson in 1942 (Figure 25) shows that the boulder has remained relatively unchanged since then. His lighting angle offers another look at the relative depth of the lines associated with possible artificial features.

The rectangular anthropomorph, with its interior crossed lines, is reminiscent of several figures we have encountered on Mark Rock, especially Delabarre's figure j, with its long neck and circular head (Figure 3). There are several lines adjacent to the torso which could be interpreted as an arm and legs, although they

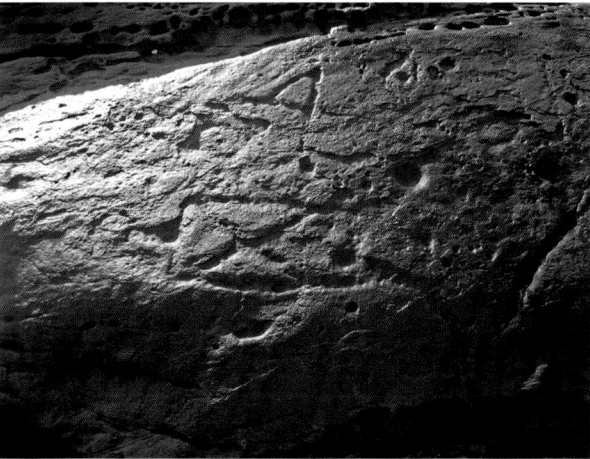

Figure 24. Close-up of figures on Tiverton "Stiles 2" boulder. Rectangular "anthropomorph" is in the foreground. Its shallower round head and thick neck (containing a cupule) may be natural features. Other features, such as legs on the "torso" and a diamond shape with central dot above the torso are ambiguous as well. Photo by Peter Anick, 2008.

Figure 25. Malcolm Pearson's 1942 photo of Tiverton "Stiles 2" boulder. Photo courtesy of NEARA Archives.

seem oddly placed relative to the torso. Again, the choice of a boulder in the intertidal zone may have been significant, especially as this particular boulder, riddled with honeycomb and natural ridges, might seem an unlikely choice for carving when smoother surfaces were available on nearby boulders strewn along the shore. Perhaps the round head and neck were already natural features of the rock, drawing attention to the boulder as the abode of a spirit or a place of power. In Native American folk tales, shamans are described as sorcerers with a wide range of special talents, including the ability to travel underwater (Speck 1919). Thus, carving an image on a rock that would be underwater part of the day may have served to assert or enhance that particular power. As noted earlier, if we assume a one-meter rise in sea level over the past 1000–2000 years, both of the Tiverton boulders (like much of the Mark Rock ledge) would have been within the intertidal zone from the Middle Woodland period on. Hedden's observation that freshly exposed surfaces were preferred for carving would also lend credence to a Middle Woodland date for these sites. On the other hand, the pace of natural degradation we have observed over the last fifty to hundred years might be evidence for a shorter effective lifespan and hence a more recent (i.e., Late Woodland or Proto-Historic) creation date.

Mount Hope ("Northmen's") Rock

Mount Hope is a natural hill on the eastern shore of Bristol, Rhode Island, a peninsula situated between Narragansett Bay and Mount Hope Bay near the mouth of the Taunton River. The area was a spiritual high ground for the Pokanokets. It was the birthplace of the powerful Wampanoag sachem (chief) Massasoit who befriended the Pilgrims, as well as the site of his son Metacomet's capture in the waning days of King Philip's War, the Indians' ill-fated uprising against Colonial encroachment. In the 1830s, an exchange of letters between Thomas Webb, then Secretary of the Rhode Island Historical Society, and the Danish antiquarian Carl Christian Rafn put Mount Hope on the map for a totally different reason. Rafn had been studying the Norse sagas to determine where Viking explorers had made landfall in the Americas. Webb's accounts of inscription rocks around Narragansett Bay, including one mentioned by Ezra Stiles at Mount Hope, fit right into Rafn's theory. With the publication of Rafn's *Antiquitates Americanae* in 1837 (Rafn 1837), local Norse enthusiasts got caught up in the search for anything even vaguely resembling Viking remains. And it wasn't long before "Northmen's Rock" was reported found on the beach just north of Mount Hope. On one corner of the large graywacke slab was a small but distinct outline of a boat and, below it, a cryptic inscription. Edmund Delabarre located and photographed the carvings but he strongly objected to the popular Norse explanation. Regarding the boat image, he concurred with another recent skeptic who found that its form reminded him "not of a Norse bark, or Indian's canoe, but of a modern white man's boat with its bow uplifted and its stern set low in the water" (Delabarre 1920). He likewise dismissed any resemblance between the purported inscription and Norse runes.

In 2017, I located the boulder on the beach to the east of "Viking Drive" and "Erickson Lane" in Bristol (Figure 26). It took a while to make out the boat image and inscription, as the rock was now littered with carved names and dates. The boat outline, thin and shallow, lay directly underneath the more boldly carved date "1920", which is oriented in the opposite di-

Figure 26. Mount Hope Rock, Bristol, Rhode Island. Photo by Peter Anick, 2017.

rection (Figure 27). The name "E. King" accompanies the date, occupying the space between the boat and the supposed Viking inscription. As best I could determine, the so-called Viking inscription was composed primarily, if not entirely, of natural ridges and fissures in the rock, which would explain why it matched no known alphabet!

Figure 27. Close up of boat carving and "Viking inscription" on Mount Hope Rock (2017). Both are now partially overwritten with the name "E. King" and the date "1920" (upside down in the photo). The date is carved right over the shallow boat image, indicated by the arrow. The supposed inscription lies just under the upside-down "E. King" below it and extends to the right. Photo by Peter Anick.

Because of the significance of the area to the Wampanoags during the contact period, it is tempting to interpret the boat outline as an Indian creation. Lenik (2002) argues that it is similar to Indian marks found on deeds at that time, as well as to a glyph on Mark Rock. The style of the boat, as noted earlier, does not resemble an Indian canoe, although a similar outline is said to appear on an inscribed sandstone tablet found on a shell heap in Long Island in the late 19th century (Delabarre 1928:259)

Rafn's theory of a Viking presence in Narragansett Bay continues to resonate with some antiquarians. In the 1960s, a boulder known as the Narragansett Stone which contained two lines of clearly identifiable runes (Figure 28) was discovered in the tidal zone off Pojac Point. However, its antiquity has proved difficult to ascertain and the fact that it had never been reported earlier, in spite of great local interest in Viking inscriptions in the 19th century, has lent to suspicion that it is a recent forgery. In 2015, following a controversial disappearance, it was recovered and moved to the Old Library Park in Wickford, Rhode Island.

Figure 28. The Narragansett Runestone at low tide in its original location off Pojac Point in Narragansett Bay (2008). Runic characters can be seen in the foreground, just under the water. Photo by Peter Anick.

Dighton Rock

Twelve miles up the Taunton River from Mount Hope lies what is arguably the most written about petroglyph in the Americas. Here, where the salt water of the bay meets the fresh water of the Taunton watershed, Dighton Rock rested for millennia on a gravelly bank within the intertidal zone. Its five-foot-high, eleven-foot-long face would have served as a natural billboard for anyone navigating up the river (Figure 29). The glacial erratic was described by Delabarre (1928:21) as "a gray, medium to coarse grained feldspathic sandstone boulder, presenting toward the river a nearly plane and smooth natural face, inclined at an angle of 39° to the vertical." Just upstream from it lay "Grassy Island," a thin strip of land that was host to Indian settlements dating as far back as the Archaic period but deserted six hundred years ago due to rising tides (Johnson and Raup 1947). Across the river at a higher elevation ideal for viewing game, the "Boats" archaeological site saw ac-

Figure 29. Dighton Rock, in its original location in the intertidal zone along the Taunton River (Delabarre 1928:Frontispiece).

tivity from the PaleoIndian through Contact periods, with heavy occupation and ceremonialism evident during the Late and Transitional Archaic (6,000–2,700 B.P.) (Bello 2015). The boulder's location below the head of tide of a major waterway within a biologically rich and diverse zone would have made Dighton Rock a very attractive place for ceremony.

The rock became an object of fascination for Colonial scholars just a few years after the Wampanoags were driven out of the area in the wake of King Philip's War. It was illustrated as early as 1680 by the Reverend John Danforth (Mallery 1898:Plate LIV; Schoolcraft 1854, Vol 4:119). Although the local Indians likely had oral history relating to such a prominent landmark, the settlers at that time were more interested in eradicating Indian religion than studying it. By the time the Reverend Ezra Stiles began recording petroglyphs a century later, the thought of indigenous origins was already being dismissed in favor of the more Biblically relevant Hebrews and Phoenicians (Dexter 1916). In the mid-19th century, Carl Christian Rafn's adherents championed its inscriptions as compelling evidence of the Vikings' discovery of New England (Delabarre 1928), even though the Scandinavian interpretation was rejected by ethnologist Henry Rowe Schoolcraft in 1854. Edmund Delabarre himself, while judiciously disparaging such earlier conjectures, ended up developing his own theory of foreign origins. Teasing a name and date out of the maze of lines carved into the rock, he convinced himself that the Portuguese navigator Miguel Corte-Real had left his marks on the stone in 1511 (Delabarre 1928).

Twenty years after the publication of Delabarre's book, his theory caught the attention of Portuguese-American Manuel Luciano da Silva, a Rhode Island doctor who examined the markings and managed to identify even more Portuguese symbols (Da Silva 1971). Da Silva was aghast that the rock had been left in the river where tides submerged it in polluted water twice a day. In 1962 he successfully lobbied to have it lifted onto a nearby coffer dam and ten years later secured further protection in the form of an enclosed pavilion to house it. With the addition of maritime displays and signage detailing the wide range of theories, he turned it into a museum and became its first volunteer curator. As a result of his tireless advocacy we can now visit Dighton Rock by appointment rather than by wading into the Taunton River at low tide.

When Dr. da Silva unlocked the museum door for my first visit in 2008, I found the forty-ton boulder lurking behind a glass wall, lit from below by a row of yellow lights (Figure 30). It did not take long to understand why no two diagrams or chalked photos from 300 years of scrutiny were ever identical. Its rough rock face contains many engraved lines that are difficult to follow or make sense of. They cross each other and blend into indentations in the rock that may or may not be man-made. Horizontal fractures, some quite wide, run across the stone like lines in a notebook. In a few places, modern graffiti obscures the carvings underneath. After my initial disorientation, I found myself focusing on the major discernable figures that most published diagrams (such as the early illustrations assembled in Mallery 1898:Plate LIV) and photos portray. From left to right, these are (1) a face with deeply pecked, human-like eyes and mouth above a large triangular torso (Figure 31); (2) a small quadruped with a vertically partitioned body and two long, straight horns (Figure 32); and (3) a pair of round faces perched on oddly shaped torsos (Figure 33). Geometric designs and unidentifiable figures fill the remaining space. It is helpful to compare the current state of the rock with a daguerreotype from 1853 on which figures were chalked (Figure 34). Published by Schoolcraft (1854, v.4:Plate 14), this daguerreotype was the basis of widely circulated later illustrations (e.g., Mallery 1898:Figure 49). We can see that the long horizontal fractures were much thinner then. Deep zig-zags have been incised above the eyes of the large face on the left, giving the impression of a king's crown. Loss of stone around a horizontal fissure on the right side of the boulder has left a large gap in the long, curvy torso belonging to the rightmost face. It is clear that the freeze-thaw cycle would have continued to wreak damage had the stone been left in the river exposed to the elements.

Figure 30. Dighton Rock on display at the Dighton Rock Museum in 2008. Photo by Peter Anick.

Figure 31. Figure with human-like head, deeply pecked eyes, and triangular torso on left side of Dighton Rock. Photo by Peter Anick, 2008.

Figure 32. Quadruped with horns, vertical lines and dots in torso, located in lower center portion of Dighton Rock. Photo by Peter Anick, 2008.

Figure 33. Right section of Dighton Rock, showing a pair of round faces attached to curving torsos without arms. The eyes of the rightmost face lie just below the zig-zag line in the upper right corner. Much of its torso is now missing. To their left are enigmatic superimposed designs and modern graffiti. Photo by Peter Anick, 2008.

Figure 34. Daguerreotype of Seth Eastman on Dighton Rock, with chalked inscriptions, 1853. Attributed to Horatio B. King. Image has been reversed from original daguerreotype. Digital image courtesy of the Getty Open Content Program, image No. 84.XT.182.

On the whole, the designs on Dighton Rock bear little resemblance to other known rock art around the Bay. But, as with the anthropomorphs at Mark Rock and Tiverton, it is possible to interpret the figures within the context of Algonkian shamanism. Frank Speck, who collected stories of Penobscot shamanism in Maine, wrote that "Every magician had his helper which seems to have been an animal's body into which he could transfer his state of being at will…It could be sent on any mission whatsoever according to the shaman's will" (Speck 1919:249–251). Thus, the human faces attached to non-human bodies may represent spirit beings or shamans who are transforming into animals while in trance. On the far right, a pair of faces peer out from irregularly shaped and apparently limbless bodies (Figure 33). A wavy line emanates from the head of the rightmost figure, reminiscent of the "radiating power lines" emanating from a shaman's head at a pictograph site in northwestern Ontario (Rajnovich 1994:Figure 113). The hourglass body shape of the large figure on the left most resembles Algonkian hourglass and X-shaped representations of eagles and thunderbirds (e.g., Rajnovich 1994:Figures 34, 35, 66, 98), although it lacks the wings typically attached to such a torso. The thunderbird is one of the most important creatures in Algonkian mythology, a powerful bird-like spirit with the ability to change into a man (Lenik 2012). If the shape of the torso was indeed intended to resemble a bird, its missing wings may have conveyed the same information as the missing arms on the oddly shaped beings on the far right. Medicine men are commonly depicted without arms on Algonkian birch bark song scrolls (e.g., Rajnovich 1994:Figures 48, 74, 102, 132). Several of the anthropomorphs on Mark Rock are also missing arms (Figure 3).

Speck writes that one of the roles of the Penobscot shaman was to protect the family's hunting territories against trespassers: "A shaman could detect when other hunters were intruding upon his family tract. He could then take measures to thwart and punish the infringement. From this situation arise numerous tales in which we hear how intruders are discovered in animal guise, in which traps are sprung, hunting trips spoiled by bad luck and the like. The malefactors are then spiritually persecuted by the shaman of the group, who may himself be the proprietor of the territory" (Speck 1919:244). Seen in this light, the large anthropomorphs with their human-like faces and deep, forward-peering eyes may have been carved into this public billboard as part of a prehistoric security system, intended to warn intruders that this territory was under shamanic surveillance.

Another fascinating figure on the panel is the quadruped. It is smaller than the human-faced figures on the far sides and located in a central position on the rock. Its long, straight "horns" look less like the short ears or elaborate antlers typically associated with naturalistic Algonkian deer images and more like the horns or feathers found on some anthropomorphs (e.g., Susquehanna River glyph in Nevin 2004:251) or "mythic creatures" (Lenik 2010). The torso is divided by vertical lines into four sections, each containing a pecked dot. Rajnovich (1994:98) relates that a line or lines through the body of an animal is a common device on bark scrolls and pictographs of the Canadian Shield to indicate spirituality, in which case the quadruped here may represent a spirit animal or animal "master." The dots within each partition, however, are an unusual addition. Lenik (2002) offers the suggestion that the lines and dots are ribs and internal organs of a deer or elk drawn in x-ray style. I am reminded of the anthropomorphs documented by Delabarre on Mark Rock, some of which also show partitioned torsos containing dots (Figure 3). Perhaps the lines and dots on this animal were intended to portray the garments of a shaman, in which case the quadruped, with its long "horns," extended legs and wide hooves, may be a depiction of a shaman in flight in animal form. In any case, this figure would have spent much of its existence journeying between the worlds above and below water.

Ed Lenik may have been the first researcher to seek out a local Native American interpretation when he corresponded with Manitonquat, an elder of the Assonet Band of the Wampanoag, in 1998 (Lenik 2002:133). Manitonquat ("Medicine Story") ascribed the carvings to Weetucks, a traditional culture hero and medicine man. According to his account, passed down from his grandfather, Weetucks had received a vision about people of greed and violence who would one day reach New England from across the eastern sea. Weetucks carved the panel on Dighton Rock as a warning to "continue to follow in a sacred path, the way of the Creator" in order to "survive to help heal the earth and restore the balance of life" (Lenik 2002:133–134). For Manitonquat, then, the rock is a teaching device within which each design element plays a role. The two figures on the right are a pair of humans, one who looks back upon the imposing figure of the Creator and the "marvelous figures of the Creation" and one who looks east across the sea. A lightning bolt above the head of the east-gazing figure warns of the destruction that would come from following the new ways. This interpretation shows that the rock continues to have modern relevance for Native peoples, while differing from academic conjectures about shamanism.

Estimating the antiquity of the Dighton Rock carvings is difficult since there are few definitive constraints. Delabarre (1928:186) dated them to the Contact period, in part because he felt the Indian-made images should post-date the initial use of the rock face by Portuguese navigators. If the images were related to shamanism, they may have been carved within the intertidal zone for symbolic or magical reasons, thereby dating their creation to Woodland times when sea levels had risen sufficiently to bring tides high enough to submerge the images. However, unlike the low lying graywacke slabs at Mark Rock and Tiverton, the Dighton boulder stands as a five-foot-tall glacial erratic. It could have been a prominent feature of the river bank even before the tides of the bay rose high enough to lap at its base. As a supernatural territorial marker, it could have been exploited as far back as the Archaic period, when local populations were growing and ceremonial activity was on the rise at the neighboring Boats occupation site.

Taunton River Cupule Stone

Continuing upstream along the Taunton River, its path takes a sharp turn to the east at the city of Taunton, then winds to the northeast and into the town of Bridgewater. A number of major archaeological sites lie along this stretch. Dr. Curtiss Hoffman, a Bridgewater State University anthropology professor, offered occasional canoe trips along selected sections of the river to introduce paddlers to the region's prehistory. In 2012, he was scouting out a route for one canoe trip when he chanced upon a cupule boulder in the river just downstream from one of the Taunton watershed's most significant early Archaic (8000–9000 B.P.) occupation sites.

Cupules, small hemispheric cup-shaped hollows, may be the most widespread form of "rock art" throughout the world. Yet very few examples are known in New England. In New Hampshire, there is a flat slab known as the Endicott Rock with dozens of small, tightly packed cupules (Lenik 2009:44). It once rested at the outlet of Lake Winnipesaukee, close to Indian fish weirs built to catch anadromous fish returning to spawn each spring. A second cupule stone, containing four smooth tennis-ball sized depressions, sits high atop a rocky seaside cliff in Niantic, Connecticut (Lenik 2002:159). As a participant in Dr. Hoffman's 2012 Taunton River trip, I was fortunate to inspect and photograph the freshly discovered cupule boulder, possibly the first found in Massachusetts. As shown in Figure 35, it sits close to the western bank, surrounded by water. Eighteen cupules appear in two rows along the upper sloped ridge of the northern side of the boulder. No carvings were observed on the southern side. The water level was relatively low at the time of the trip and detritus still lodged on the boulder indicated that the river level had until recently been higher, closer to the lower edge of the two rows of cupules. This may explain why all cupules were carved along the top: any lower surfaces were likely below water at the time the work was done.

Interpretation of cupules, like rock art in general, is highly speculative, although ethnography elsewhere in the Americas associates some cupule sites with fertility and rainmaking (Gillette and Greer 2014). The appearance of the Taunton boulder bears little similarity to the two aforementioned New England cupule stones. The Endicott Rock's location near a fish weir, along with its random distribution of many small cupules resembling fish eggs, hints at shamanic magic related to the annual fish run. By contrast, the Niantic stone's orderly arrangement of four large, evenly smoothed cupules reminds me of a palette suitable for the preparation of paints or plants. As for the Taunton River boulder, Dr. Hoffman noted that it was located at the last convenient canoe pull-out before reaching a section of rapids further downstream. Thus, it may have served as a kind of fluvial road sign. The fact that all cupules were located on the upstream face of the rock lends some support to this hypothesis. Another possibility is that, perhaps like the Endicott slab, it was somehow related to the annual anadromous fish run. Although we saw no evidence of a stone weir here, the boulder, located so close to a major prehistoric settlement, may have served as a convenient staging area for netting fish, especially fish coming up the narrow channel on the boulder's western flank.

It is tempting to date the cupules to the Early Archaic, the period when the nearby occupation site saw its greatest use. However, the site continued to be occupied sporadically up through the Early Woodland period (2,000 B.P.) and the Taunton River would have been used as a major transportation route throughout prehistory.

Assawompset Pond Petroglyphs

Following the Taunton River back downstream from Bridgewater brings us to the junction with its tributary, the Nemasket River. The name is Wampanoag for "place where the fish are" and if we were to navigate up the Nemasket, as the Wampanoags did each summer, we would be tracing the route of the largest herring run

Figure 35. Taunton River Cupule Stone in 2012. Note the detritus and lighter coloration on the lower portions of the rock, which provide an indication of the typical water level for the river. Photo by Peter Anick.

on the eastern seaboard. Eventually we would reach the north shore of Assawompset Pond, the Wampanoags' "place of the white stone" and the largest body of fresh water in Massachusetts. When the glaciers receded at the end of the last ice age, they left a glacial lake here, and when it drained, winds created dunes out of the silt left behind. By 9,000 years ago, the northwest shore of the remaining pond formed an ideal ecological niche for human occupation and the area remained seasonally utilized well into the Historic period (Robbins 1980).

What lured me to the area in 2007 was not an abundance of fish but rather an odd assortment of petroglyphs described in Lenik's Picture Rocks book. These included foot and hand prints, a flying thunderbird, and a "carved figure of a ship on a boulder off the north shore of Assawompsett Lake" (Lenik 2002:128). The ship image, with what appeared to be a raised mast, was sometimes cited (Boland 1961) as evidence that the Indians had recorded seeing a Phoenician vessel here 2,000 years ago! Lenik felt that shamans had carved these images on particular rocks and ledges to derive power and leave permanent messages on spiritually charged features of the landscape. This practice could have continued into the Contact period, at which point shamans would have availed themselves of metal tools. Lenik thought this could have been the case with the ship glyph, which appeared cut with a metal tool.

As with most New England petroglyphs, locating this one took some effort. A local informant remembered seeing it as a youth carved into a boulder just off the north shore of Assawompset Pond, not far from the site of the Wapanucket archaeological excavations of the 1970s (Robbins 1980). It was located within a marshy area usually inundated, but the water level was unusually low in the winter of 2007, exposing a number of boulders along the shoreline. Surveying each in turn, I eventually spotted it on the south vertical edge of a large flat-topped stone, facing into the lake (Figure 36). The carving was quite small, about six centimeters long, and very easy to miss. As the photo in Figure 37 shows, the indentations are v-shaped, as if made by blows with a chisel-like metal tool. The wide "hull" at the bottom has slight indentations curving up on both ends. If this were indeed a sign produced by a shaman, its positioning on the vertical side of the stone rather than the top might be consistent with either a desire to keep it inconspicuous or to allow it to descend beneath the water when lake levels are high.

Lenik (2002) reports a thunderbird pecked into a boulder nearby as well. After scouring the shoreline

Figure 36. Boulder at the shore of Assawompset Pond containing a small ship-like figure (arrow). The ship glyph appears as a dark shadow located slightly above the smaller stone in the foreground. Photo by Peter Anick, 2007.

Figure 37. Close up of the Assawompset Pond ship figure. The fin-like "rudder" at the bottom is a shadow effect, not an intentionally carved feature. Photo by Peter Anick, 2007.

with my local informant who, again, had seen it years ago, we determined that the boulder in question now lay almost completely buried in sand and thick vegetation. We left this bird in its nest.

Across the lake, a small plot of land known as Betty's Neck had long remained an enclave for Wampanoag families who had survived the devastation of the tribe in the aftermath of King Philip's War. A pair of long boulders still lounge on the narrow beach, their smooth faces gleaming in the afternoon sunlight (Figure 38). Exquisitely carved initials, names, and dates ranging from 1712 to 1955 adorn their vertical faces like a giant visitors' log. At opposite ends of one of the stones, along its lower edge, a pecked footprint and pecked handprint look oddly out of place (Figures 39, 40). Local lore has it that the footprint is that of Betty (Assowetoh), daughter of John Sassamon, a Christianized Indian who, suspected of treason by the Wampanoags, was murdered and dumped under the ice of this very lake shortly before the commencement of King Philip's War. Lenik (2002:122), noting their stylized designs with splayed fingers and toes, finds it more likely that both footprint and handprint were the work of Indian shamans. If so, these two imprints may have been the first items carved on the rock. Given all the available surface area to choose from, the selection of spots along the bottom edge is interesting. The lower right corner is not a particularly easy place to work, nor the most eye-catching. Perhaps being close to the ground and the water was of significance to the maker.

Figure 39. Pecked footprint on lower left side of boulder at Betty's Neck. Photo by Peter Anick, 2012.

Figure 38. Pair of boulders containing historic engravings on the south side of Assawompset Pond at Betty's Neck. The oval indicates where a footprint is pecked just above the sand line on the left boulder, along with the boldly carved date "1749." A pecked handprint in the lower righthand corner of the same boulder is blocked by the boulder in the foreground. Photo by Peter Anick, 2007.

As NEARA Massachusetts state coordinator, I would occasionally organize field trips to the area, and on one of these trips I was told of a second ship glyph carved somewhere along the northern shore, again visible only when the water level was low. A few years later,

Figure 40. Pecked handprint on lower right corner of boulder at Betty's Neck. Photo by Peter Anick, 2007.

during a drought, we kayaked up the unusually shallow Nemasket River to the dam that separated the river from the lake and searched in vain for the rumored petroglyph. Disappointed, we stopped to inspect the simple gatehouse before heading back to our kayaks. It was no more than a cement platform designed to support long wooden planks that could be slipped in and out to control the amount of water draining from the lake. A subsequent web search revealed that it had been constructed in 1894 after the City of Taunton was authorized to use the lake as their water supply. Damming the lake had raised the water level by some five feet.

About a year later during another dry spell, I got word that the second boat glyph had been located. Its position was somewhat unexpected, on the side of an unexceptional low stone among a string of small boulders that lined the shore just west of the outflow of water into the Nemasket. As seen in Figure 41, the glyph is very similar to the first ship figure in shape and manner of production, with sharp v-shaped incisions and upward curls on both ends of its "hull." It is also nearly identical in its dimensions, with a 6 cm. hull length, 4.5 cm. height and 2.8 cm. "sail" length. But I was most curious to compare the heights of the two glyphs relative to the water level of the lake. Using string, poles, and plumb bob, we managed to compute the heights of both glyphs, confirming my hunch that they would be identical. The similarity in shape, size, and height strongly suggest they were made at the same time by the same person(s) for the same reason. To be at the same height relative to the water level implies either that (1) they were both carved when the water level was up to the hull, or (2) the carver made an effort to measure the height of each glyph relative to the water level. If the water level of the lake before the dam was put in place was truly five feet lower, option 1 seems less likely. This suggests a creation date *after* the dam was built and a function somehow related to the water level, such as a high or low water marker.

While researching this possibility, I ran across a reference to a drill hole made in a boulder in the Nemasket River in 1897. It had been utilized by local businesses to record the high water mark of the river after the dam was installed (Romaine 1969). This brought to mind a shallow conical drill hole I had noticed on the boulder containing the first ship glyph. It can be seen in Figure 42 as the small dark hole to the right of the glyph at roughly the same height. Taken together, these observations provide circumstantial evidence that the two "ship" glyphs are actually 19th century survey symbols designed to mark a desired water level of the lake, perhaps utilized during the construction of the dam/gatehouse to determine its proper height.

Figure 42. Close-up of boulder containing the first Assawompset Pond "ship" figure, showing a conical drill hole to its right at roughly the same height. Photo by Peter Anick, 2016.

Nemasket Thunderbird Rock

We will conclude our survey with another relatively recent find, located a short distance back down the Nemasket River from Assawompset Pond. The *Bulletin of the Massachusetts Archaeological Society* reported a thunderbird and a cross-in-circle design discovered by a hiker in 2007 (Taylor 2008). A few years later, responding to an inquiry by Ed Lenik, I decided to include the site in a field trip I was organizing with a local researcher familiar with the area. The petroglyphs, it turned out, were carved into adjacent sides of a large granite boulder that rested atop a wooded hill overlooking the river (Figure 43). Encroaching office park development nearby may have aided in the discovery. As shown in Figure 44, the 21 cm wide x 23 cm tall cross-in-circle design is deeply chipped into the center of the flat, vertical side of the boulder. Ed Lenik, who joined us on the trip, commented that the cross within a circle is a common Indian motif with a number of symbolic interpretations.

Walking around the boulder to the left brought us face to face with a second carving, a stick figure rendition of a thunderbird (Figure 45). Unlike the deeply

Figure 41. Second "ship" figure on the north shore of Assawompset Pond, just west of the outlet into the Nemasket River. Photo by Peter Anick, 2016.

Figure 43. Nemasket Thunderbird Boulder. The thunderbird figure is near the top of the shadowed portion of the rock face, just above the head in the foreground. The star figure is on the lower left side, to the right of the man's wrist. The cross-in-circle motif is on the face to the right, in front of the woman with the white hat. Ed Lenik is standing behind the boulder, in the white jacket. Photo by Peter Anick, 2011.

Figure 45. Close-up of thunderbird figure on Nemasket Thunderbird Boulder. Photo by Peter Anick, 2011.

Figure 44. Close-up of cross-in-circle motif on Nemasket Thunderbird Boulder, showing lichen and moss covering it in November, 2011. Photo by Peter Anick.

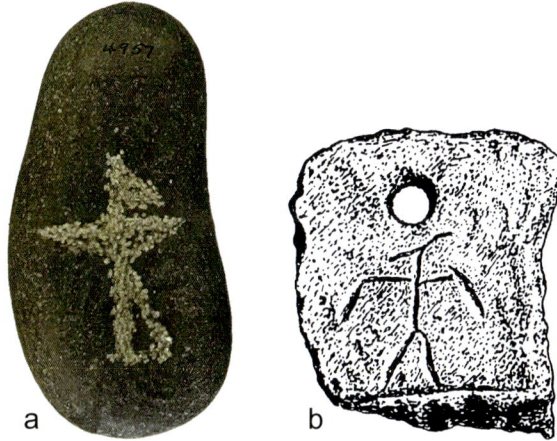

Figure 46. (a) Thunderbird image carved onto a pebble, found in Late Archaic layer (4,300 B.P.) of Wapanucket excavation. On display at Robbins Museum, Middleborough, Massachusetts. Photo by Peter Anick, 2017. (b) Late Woodland pendant from Duxbury, Massachusetts, containing incised thunderbird image. Drawing by William Fowler, courtesy of Robbins Museum.

chiseled motif hacked into the adjacent rock face, this 11 cm. tall image was more delicately incised into the smooth surface. The stick figure design is one of several different renderings believed to represent the thunderbird in prehistoric New England iconography (Lenik 2012). It appears, for example, on incised pebbles excavated in a Late Archaic context (4,300 B.P.) at the Wapanucket site, barely two miles away (Figure 46a), and on a pendant dated to the Late Woodland period in Duxbury (Figure 46b). After admiring the thunderbird, I carefully scanned the rest of the rock and detected a third image below it to its left, camouflaged against the lichen speckled wall. It was a small "star" in the shape of an asterisk (Figure 47).

The star and thunderbird were likely made at the same time, by abrading with either a fine metal tool or sharp stone. The stylistic similarity with the Duxbury pendant figure (Figure 46b) would suggest a Late Woodland date. The cross-in-circle motif on the adjacent rock face, however, appears to have been made by hacking at the surface with a heavy metal tool, perhaps an axe. Inspecting the lines comprising the center cross, we can see that in some sections the stone fractured cleanly, leaving a long, straight, v-shaped line, while in other areas the hacked lines are awkwardly executed, with several blows not even angled correctly. While it is

Figure 47. Close-up of star figure on Nemasket Thunderbird Boulder. Photo by Peter Anick, 2011.

reasonable to assume that a boulder perched atop a hill overlooking the important Nemasket River would be considered a place of *manitou* or spiritual power for a shaman, several features of the carvings make me suspicious of an early provenience. The age of the trees surrounding the stone (as seen in Figure 43) suggest that the area had been relatively clear of trees until quite recently. Given the size and depth of the circle, it seems unlikely that it would have gone unnoticed for so long, even if partly camouflaged by lichen and moss. When I revisited the site in 2017, I found that all the lichen and moss had been stripped away, presumably by someone seeking to take unobstructed photographs. As shown in Figure 48, the exposed lines now look freshly cut, showing no repatination. Since we have photos taken before the lichen was removed, an analysis of the rate of repatination and lichen/moss growth for this boulder might provide a window of possible dates.

Figure 48. Close-up of cross-in-circle figure after removal of moss and lichen. Photo by Peter Anick, 2017.

As for the thunderbird, the horizontal line drawn below it feels anachronistic. Representing a ground line is common in modern drawings but very rare in Indian petroglyphs. One exception is the Duxbury thunderbird pendant (Figure 46b), which appears to include a horizontal line below the figure. As a result of NAGPRA (Native American Graves Protection and Repatriation Act) repatriation, the pendant is no longer on display at the Robbins Museum. However, a close examination of the drawing suggests that the apparent ground line may actually be a natural ridge in the stone itself. Given the uncanny similarity of the image on the boulder to the image on the pendant, it is possible that the boulder thunderbird is a recent copy of the pendant figure, including the apparent ground line. On the other hand, if a report of the carving can be found which predates the Duxbury find, the close resemblance between the two would be good evidence for a contemporaneous (Late Woodland) provenience.

Conclusions

This survey of sites in southeastern New England demonstrates that the region's indigenous inhabitants were not immune to the urge to leave their marks in stone. Whether these examples represent the tip of an iceberg, i.e., a continuous tradition of rock art over millennia, or the sporadic ventures of a few inspired individuals remains unclear. Until relatively recently, any carvings that could not be ascribed to trans-Atlantic seafarers were typically dismissed as inconsequential, as "nothing but the scratches of some idle Indians, without any meaning" (John Bartlett, quoted in Delabarre 1919:297). Thanks in large part to the efforts of archaeologists like Grace Rajnovich, Mark Hedden, and Edward Lenik, researchers now have access to a growing body of data from which to explore plausible contexts in which these scratches do have meaning. Sadly, our study shows that nature and neglect are taking a toll on sites through spalling, fragmentation, abrasion, sea level rise, and the encroachment of soil and vegetation. Petroglyphs at the water's edge are particularly vulnerable, highlighting a need to apply modern recording techniques such as photogrammetry and laser scanning before sites deteriorate further or disappear altogether.

As new data comes in, we may find that some petroglyphs are not necessarily ancient, or not Native American. But there is a good chance that many more prehistoric sites await discovery and documentation. A North Carolina recording project begun in 1997 using public outreach and collaborative partnerships has increased the number of documented rock art sites in their state from seven to fifty (USDA Forest Service 2017). A similar effort is overdue in New England.

Acknowledgments. I would like to thank many colleagues, most met through the New England Antiquities Research Association, for their assistance in locating and interpreting the sites referenced in this article. These include Ellen Berkland, Charles Devine, Jim Egan, Joe Freitas, Linda Grubb, Curtiss Hoffman, Dan Kelly, Edward Lenik, Kenneth Leonard, Bruce McAleer, Manuel Luciano da Silva, Donn and Sandi Stangohr, Donna Thompson, and Walter van Roggen.

References Cited

American Indian Publishers
  1981 *Dictionary of Daily Life of Indians of the Americas, Volume One.* American Indian Publishers, Newport Beach, California.

Bello, Grace
  2015 *A Walk Through Time at the Boats Archaeological Site in Dighton, Massachusetts.* BSU Honors Program Theses and Projects, Item 86. Electronic Document, http://vc.bridgew.edu/honors_proj/86, accessed May 2017.

Boland, Charles Michael
  1961 *They All Discovered America.* Doubleday, Garden City, New York.

Da Silva, Manuel Luciano
  1971 *Portuguese Pilgrims and Dighton Rock.* Self published, Bristol, Rhode Island.

Delabarre, Edmund Burke
  1919 *Recent History of Dighton Rock.* John Wilson and Son, Cambridge, Massachusetts.
  1920 The Inscribed Rocks of Narragansett Bay. *Rhode Island Historical Society Collections* 13(1).
  1928 *Dighton Rock: A Study of the Written Rocks of New England.* Walter Neale, New York.

Devine, Charles
  1981 An Historical Sketch of "Mark Rock" on Narragansett Bay, R. I. *NEARA Journal* 15(4):86–94.

Dexter, Franklin Bowditch, editor
  1916 *Extracts from the Itineraries and Other Miscellanies of Ezra Stiles, D.D., LL.D. 1755-1794 with a Selection from his Correspondence,* edited by Franklin Bowditch Dexter. Yale University Press, New Haven, Connecticut.

Gillette, Donna L., and Mavis Greer
  2014 Spirituality in Rock Art Yesterday and Today: Reflections from the Northern Plains and Far Western United States. In *Rock Art and Sacred Landscapes,* edited by Donna L. Gillette, Mavis Greer, Michele-Helene Hayward, and William Breen Murray, pp. 252–273. Springer, New York.

Goodwin, William B.
  1946 *The Ruins of Great Ireland in New England.* Meador Publishing Company, Boston.

Hedden, Mark
  1996 3,500 Years of Shamanism in Maine Rock Art. In *Rock Art of the Eastern Woodlands: Proceedings from the Eastern States Rock Art Conference,* edited by Charles H. Faulkner, pp. 7–24. Occasional Paper 2. American Rock Art Research Association, San Miguel, California.
  2004 Passamaquoddy Shamanism and Rock-Art in Machias Bay, Maine. In *The Rock-Art of Eastern North America,* edited by Carol Diaz-Granados and James R. Duncan, pp. 319–343. University of Alabama Press, Tuscaloosa, Alabama.

Johnson, Frederick, and Hugh M. Raup
  1947 *Grassy Island: Archaeological and Botanical Investigations of an Indian Site in the Taunton River, Massachusetts.* Phillips Academy, Andover, Massachusetts.

Leland, Charles G.
  1884 *The Algonquin Legends of New England.* Sampson Low, Marston, Searle & Rivington, London.

Lenik, Edward J.
  2002 *Picture Rocks: American Indian Rock Art in the Northeast Woodlands.* University Press of New England, Hanover and London.
  2009 *Making Pictures in Stone: American Indian Rock Art of the Northeast.* University of Alabama Press, Tuscaloosa.
  2010 Mythic Creatures: Serpents, Dragons and Sea Monsters in Northeastern Rock Art. *Archaeology of Eastern North America* 38:17-37. Eastern States Archaeological Federation.
  2012 The Thunderbird Motif in Northeastern Indian Art. *Archaeology of Eastern North America* 40:163–185. Eastern States Archaeological Federation.

Lynch, Daniel
  2005 Tiverton Petroglyph Site in Rhode Island "Rediscovered." *Eastern States Rock Art Research Association Newsletter* 10(1):3–5. Eastern States Rock Art Research Association, St. Louis, Missouri.

Mallery, Garrick
  1898 *Picture-Writing of the American Indians.* Tenth Annual Report of the Bureau of Ethnology, 1888–'89. Facsimile reprint edition 1972, Dover Publications, New York.

Merwin, Daria E., Daniel P. Lynch, and David S. Robinson
  2003 Submerged Prehistoric Sites in Southern New England: Past Research and Future Directions. *Bulletin of the Archaeological Society of Connecticut* 65:41–56.

Nevin, Paul
  2004 Rock Art Sites on the Susquehanna River. In *The Rock-Art of Eastern North America,* edited by Carol Diaz-Granados and James R. Duncan, pp. 239-257. University of Alabama Press, Tuscaloosa, Alabama.

Oakley, Bryan A., and Jon C. Boothroyd
  2012 Reconstructed Topography of Southern New England Prior to Isostatic Rebound, with Implications of Total Isostatic Depression and Relative Sea Level. *Quaternary Research* 78(1):110–118.

Rafn, Charles Christian
  1837 *Antiquitates Americanae Sive Scriptores Septentrionales Rerum Ante-Columbianarum in America.* Typis Officinae Schultzianae, Copenhagen.

Rajnovich, Grace
  1994 *Reading Rock Art: Interpreting the Indian Rock Paintings of the Canadian Shield.* Natural Heritage/Natural History Inc., Toronto, Ontario.

Robbins, Maurice
   1980 *Wapanucket: An Archaeological Report*. Trustees of The Massachusetts Archaeological Society, Attleboro, Massachusetts.

Romaine, Mertie E.
   1969 *History of the Town of Middleboro, Massachusetts, Volume 2*. Reynolds-DeWalt Printing, New Bedford, Massachusetts.

Schoolcraft, Henry R.
   1854 *Information Respecting the History, Condition and Prospects of the Indian Tribes of the United States*. Lippincott, Grambo & Company, Philadelphia.

Speck, Frank G.
   1919 Penobscot Shamanism. *Memoirs of the American Anthropological Association* 6:238–288. Lancaster, Pennsylvania.

Tansem, Karin
   2014 Rock Art of Alta. In *Cuadernos de Arte Rupestre, Volume 7*, pp. 59–75. Electronic document, http://www.cuadernos-dearterupestre.es/arterupestre/7/Articulo5.pdf, accessed May 2017.

Taylor, William B.
   2008 Thunderbirds in Southeast Massachusetts. *Bulletin of the Massachusetts Archaeological Society* 69(2):64–67.

USDA Forest Service
   2017 *The North Carolina Rock Art Project*. Electronic document, https://www.fs.usda.gov/detail/nfsnc/learning/history-culture/?cid=stelprdb5209551, accessed May 2017.

Vastokas, Joan M., and Romas K. Vastokas
   1973 *Sacred Art of the Algonkians: A Study of the Peterborough Petroglyphs*. Mansard Press, Peterborough, Ontario.

Rock Art in "The Land of Fire" (Azerbaijan): Discovering the Gobustan Rock Art Cultural Landscape (UNESCO World Heritage List)

Angelo Eugenio Fossati

In 2003 I was requested by the UNESCO World Heritage Centre to lead a mission in the Republic of Azerbaijan with the aim of preparing a management plan for the Gobustan rock art area that the state of Azerbaijan wished to nominate to the World Heritage List. This project enabled me to learn about the beautiful and important rock art of Gobustan, today recognized with the name Gobustan Rock Art Cultural Landscape, one of the few rock art areas on the World Heritage List. The rock art spans from the Upper Paleolithic period to the end of Middle Ages with even a few engravings belonging to the Modern Era.

The Gobustan Rock Art Cultural Landscape is situated in a key position, in central Azerbaijan west of Baku, its capital (Figure 1). This location, between the slope of the Greater Caucasus Mountains and the Caspian Sea (Figure 2), forms a geographic "bridge" between Europe and Asia. The name Gobustan, apparently derives from the many deep ravines (*gobu* in Azerbaijani) that etch the plain in this area at the foot of the Greater Caucasus Range (Figure 3). The cultural landscape shows an outstanding collection of more than 6,000 petroglyphs engraved on thousands of rock surfaces. These span a long period of time, and tentatively date from the Paleolithic age until Modern times. The petroglyphs, carved on the vertical limestone faces of the Absheron formation by percussion and deep scratching, are mainly found on

Figure 1. Map of Azerbaijan and the Middle East area.

Angelo Eugenio Fossati
Catholic University of the Sacred Heart
Milan, Italy
and
Footsteps of Man Archaeological Cooperative Society
Valcamonica, Italy

Figure 2. The Caspian Sea (background) and Kichikdash Mountain (at right) seen from the top of Boyukdash hill. All photographs are by the author unless otherwise noted.

Figure 3. This ravine on Boyukdash hill is typical of Gobustan.

big boulders in three mountains: Boyukdash, Kichikdash, and Jingirdagh (Rustamov and Muradova 2008).

Today this is a semi-desert area (Figure 4) whose vegetation regime of short grasses, bushes, and sparse trees is similar to that common for semiarid desert areas throughout the Mideast. In the past Gobustan was greener, a sort of savanna, populated with wild animals that today are either extinct, or no longer found in this

Figure 4. A wadi (deep arroyo) in the northern territory of the Reserve.

area. The primary extinct species is the aurochs *(Bos primigenius)*; and the main species that have since disappeared from this area include wild horses and gazelles.

The initial discovery of Gobustani rock art was by quarry workers who accidentally found the first carvings as recently as the 1930s. After the earliest archaeological investigations, the principal scholar interested in the petroglyphs was I. M. Jafarzadeh, who conducted regular fieldwork in the area from 1947 to 1965 (Jafarzadeh 1973). He discovered more than 750 rocks and studied approximately 3,500 petroglyphs (Figure 5). From 1966 onward, J. N. Rustamov and F. M. Muradova, scholars of the National Academy of Science, conducted further archaeological research in the area (Figure 6). They discovered additional petroglyphs, and increased the number of known rocks with carvings to 1,000, and the number of petroglyphs to 6,000. They also discovered and studied settlements

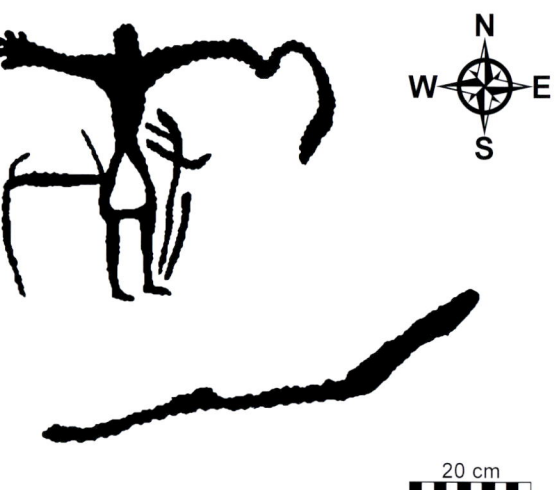

Figure 5. Tracing of the rock 32 of Jingirdağ–Yazilitepe hill (from Jafarzadeh 1973).

Figure 6. Firuza Muradova and Jafargulu Rustamov at work on a rock in the Gobustan Reserve (photo Rustamov 2000).

and burials, including 40 kurgans (cemeteries). The importance of these discoveries attained national fame during the period when Azerbaijan was part of the USSR; and in 1966 Gobustan was declared a National Historical-Artistic Reserve. In this reserve are petroglyph sites on other hills including Dashgyshlag, Gayaalty, Shongardag, and Shikhgaya.

Following Azerbaijani independence in 1991, the Historical-Artistic Reserve was maintained, and new research was conducted by the Reserve director, Malahat Farajova, and her team. This research program resulted in the inclusion of Gobustan onto the World Heritage List (WHL) in 2007. The WHL site is called the Gobustan Rock Art Cultural Landscape, since it includes not only rock art, but also burials, settlements, cultural traditions tied to traditional sites and places, and natural resources (Fossati 2004). Figures 7 through 11 illustrate some of the various resource types found within this landscape. The Reserve today extends 100 km north to south and 80 km east to west. In 2011 a new Museum was constructed at the base of Boykdash Mountain, replacing the old building in the same location. This Museum contains more than 100,000 archaeological objects, and in 2013 was among the winners of the Best European Museums of the Year (Figure 12). During the last 70 years—since systematic research began to be undertaken—many famous adventurers such as Thor Heyerdahl, and rock art scholars like Emmanuel Anati (Anati et al. 2001) have visited the Gobustan area.

A research team, composed of Abdullayev Rahman, Şirinli Sevinc, Abbasov Kamran, Musayeva Saida, and Aliyeva Leyla, and supervised by the newly appointed director, Rüfat Nuriyev, is now working on documenting and digitizing the petroglyphs of the Gobustan Reserve. In addition, they are systematizing and digitizing research materials and written information such as archeological reports contained in the archives of the Reserve (Gobustan National Historical-Artistic Reserve 2016).

Figure 7. Ancient graves at the foot of Boyukdash hill.

Figure 9. Tomb of the Black Rider. Note the red paintings on the wall of the tomb.

Figure 8. Cold mud volcano in Gobustan territory.

Figure 10. The Yalli dance—a traditional dance—is still performed during their wedding ceremonies in front of rock 31 on Boyukdash hill by people living in the Gobustan settlement.

Six different styles are recognizable in the petroglyphs of Gobustan according to the studies of major scholars (Farajova 2011; Rustamov 1994, 2000). The oldest styles are associated with Paleolithic and Mesolithic cultures of this area and represent large land animals, human figures (men and women), and symbols. Women are sometimes depicted with breasts and exaggerated adipose hips, probably to show and symbolize fertility (Figure 13). This has led some to hypothesize that they may relate to the same basic ideas as the famous statuettes called Paleolithic Venuses. Animals represented are aurochs (Figure 14), wild horses (Figure 15), and wild goat-like animals (Figure 16), all large fauna that really existed during those eras. Felines (Figure 17) and deer (Figure 18) are also known, but these may date to a slightly younger age. Among the oldest figures, the carved boats (Figure 19) are notable (Sigari 2017). Sometimes these images are very similar to those known in rock art elsewhere.

Other, later rock art styles are associated with cultures whose economy was based on herding and the domestication of animals. Hunting scenes (Figure 20) and figures of horsemen (Figure 21) and camels (Fig-

Figure 11. Rock 31 on Boyukdash hill shows petroglyphs of humans. It is believed that the humans engraved there are performing the traditional Yalli dance.

Figure 12. An exhibit of tools in the Gobustan National Museum (photo by Dario Sigari).

Figure 13. A woman figure engraved on a rock on Boyukdash hill.

Figure 14. Several aurochs and one horse engraved on a boulder on Boyukdash hill.

Figure 15. A nice composition of wild horses has been etched into rock 45 on Boyukdash hill.

Figure 16. Wild goats engraved on rock 35 in Jingirdağ–Yazilitepe hill.

Figure 17. Two felines in a typical attacking position at Jingirdağ–Yazilitepe hill.

Figure 18. A stag engraved on a boulder on Kichikdash hill.

ure 22) relate to cultures occupying this area near the end of the prehistoric period. Still other images relate to the art of the Scythians, revealing similarities that can be explained only by direct cultural influences coming into this area.

The end of the Gobustani rock art tradition is marked by the presence of inscriptions: the most famous being a Latin inscription in the foothills of Boyukdash mountain (Figure 23), but there are also writings in Greek, Persian, and Arabic. Tribal signs of historic times, probably related to traders traveling through with camel caravans, are also found (Figure 24).

Gobustan has attracted many visitors and scholars, in both past and recent times. Although much has been learned about the region's rock art, some questions remain unsolved, especially those pertaining to the most

Figure 19. Boats engraved on rocks 29 (left) and 8 (right) at Boyukdash.

Figure 20. A dog shown hunting a wild boar. Boyukdash hill.

Figure 21. Boulder 47 in Jingirdağ–Yazilitepe shows a group of wild goat-like animals on one side and a rider on horseback on the other.

to paleolithic Venus figurines (Figure 25). Like the silhouette-style humans, another style depicting figures of bulls shows outstanding similarities with paleolithic animals carved at open-air sites on the other side of Europe in Spain and Portugal. Exploring these issues of interpretation and chronology awaits more complete study of the Paleolithic open air rock art elsewhere in Europe and the continuation of archaeological rock art fieldwork undertaken by the Gobustan Reserve research team.

But not all problems involve paleolithic art. Images of some boats in the Gobustan Reserve show uncanny similarities to carvings found in the rock art of Norway and Sweden. But while these likenesses are intriguing, the proximity of the Caspian Sea and its importance for fishing and trading probably better ex-

Figure 22. Group of dromedary camels, drawn in a very angular style. The animals each show the typical (triangular) hump on their back. Kichikdash hill.

Figure 23. This Latin inscription on the foothill of Boyukdash Mountain is the farthest from Rome so far found. It is reads: IMP DOMITIANO CAESARE AVG GERMANICO LVCIVS IVLIVS MAXIMVS LEG XII FVL, which translates: Under imperator Domitian, Caesar, Augustus Germanicus, (this script was made by) Lucius Julius Maximus, (soldier of the) 12th Fulminata Legion.

ancient phases. Some of the most enduring mysteries include the origin and relationships of the beautiful stylized human figures, represented in silhouette, that are typical of early Gobustani art and may relate

Figure 24. Tribal signs on a boulder in Jingirdağ–Yazilitepe hill.

plains most of the boats in Gobustan rock art. Later carvings of ships on the walls of the Shirvanshah Palace in Baku attest to the importance of such images to local people (Figure 26).

The resolution of these and other problems of interpretation and chronology in Gobustan rock art is linked to additional study by the team of the Gobustan Reserve. Gobustan is one of most interesting areas for future rock art research in the Mideast, because it shows distinct similarities to the art of Western Europe, but also expresses its own unique characteristics. In this sense the study of the Gobustan rock art is a point of great significance for reconstructing the prehistoric origins of both prehistoric European and Asian cultures.

Acknowledgments. I would like to thank the following people for providing help during my UNESCO mission:

• Rizvan Bayramov, former Head of the Department for Protection, Restoration and Utilization of Historical and Cultural Monuments in the Ministry of Culture of the Azerbaijan Republic;

• Malahat Farajova, former Director of the Gobustan State Historical-Artistic Reservation;

• Jafargulu Rustamov and Firuza Muradova, Institute of Archaeology and Ethnography of the National Academy of Sciences, Azerbaijan.

I also thank Dario Sigari for providing photographs of the Gobustan National Museum.

My deep gratitude also goes to Dr. James D. Keyser and Mike Taylor for inviting me to present the Gobustan rock art to the U.S. academic public, for providing transportation to Oregon for the ARARA conference, and for help in editing this report.

References Cited

Anati, Emmanuel, Giafargulu Rustamov, Firuza Muradova, and Malahat Farajova
   2001 Gobustan Azerbaijan. *Archivi* 13. Capo di Ponte, Italy.

Figure 25. Human figures holding some sort of an object (a weapon?) engraved on a wall of a cave on Boyukdash hill.

Figure 26. Ships engraved on one of the outside walls of the Shirvanshah Palace in Baku, Azerbaijan.

Farajova, Malahat
   2011 Gobustan Rock Art Cultural Landscape. *Adoranten* 2011:41–66. Goteborg, Sweden.

Fossati, Angelo
   2004 Gobustan Rock Art Cultural Landscape. Management Plan. Manuscript on file with UNESCO World heritage Centre, Paris.

Gobustan National Historical-Artistic Reserve (editor)
   2016 *Gobustan New Analisys, Jingirdağ-Yazilitepe, 2016—Researches in the Desert*. Baku, Azerbaijan.

Jafarzadeh, Ishak M.
   1973 *Gobustan, Rock Engravings*. Edition Elm, Baku, Azerbaijan.

Rustamov, Jafargulu
   1994 *Qobustan Dünyasi*. Azerneshr, Baku.

   2000 *Gobustan-Očag Drevneĭ Kulturj Azer*, Azerbaijan*baidžana*. Nurlan, Baku, Azerbaijan.

Rustamov, Jafargulu, and Firuza Muradova
   2008 *Gobustan, Kichikdash abideleri*. Edition E.L., Baku, Azerbaijan.

Sigari, Dario
   2017 Portrayal of a sea in a semiarid environment: Boat engravings in Böyük Daş, Gobustan. *Journal of Arid Environments* 143:57–63.